A FLAME IN SUNLIGHT

Emily De Quincey, youngest daughter
Thomas De Quincey Margaret, eldest daughter, with baby Eva

From a crayon drawing by J. Archer, 1853
By courtesy of the Misses Bairdsmith

A FLAME IN SUNLIGHT

THE LIFE AND WORK OF

THOMAS DE QUINCEY

Edward Sackville West

NEW EDITION WITH PREFACE AND NOTES BY

JOHN E. JORDAN

THE BODLEY HEAD

LONDON SYDNEY

TORONTO

ISBN 0 370 10494 3
Printed and bound in Great Britain for
The Bodley Head Ltd
9 Bow Street, London WC2E 7AL
by William Clowes & Sons Ltd, Beccles
First published 1936
This edition 1974

To

RAYMOND MORTIMER

CONTENTS

LIST OF ILLUSTRATIONS

Even as the rain shows up, in transparent quivering threads, the flower of heaven, which is invisible in sunlight.
JEAN PAUL, Titan.

A chacun son infini.
VILLIERS DE L'ISLE-ADAM.

EDITORIAL PREFACE

SOME justification may seem necessary for the republication now of a biography of Thomas De Quincey that first appeared in 1936. When Edward Sackville West began work on the study to be called *A Flame in Sunlight*, De Quincey had, as Sackville West notes in his Preface, apparently been long neglected : there had been no full-scale biography of the Opium-Eater since Alexander H. Japp's two-volume life published in 1877 and revised in one volume in 1890. Others, however, were at work in the thirties, and even before Sackville West's book came out, Malcolm Elwin published his vivid short life, while Horace Eaton's magisterial biography appeared in the same year as Sackville West's work. Since then the harvest has continued, producing several more lives of De Quincey, most recently Françoise Moreaux's *Thomas De Quincey; La Vie—L'Homme—L'Œuvre* (1964) and Judson Lyon's short life in the Twayne's English Author Series (1969). Why then reprint Sackville West's work?

Shortly after De Quincey's death, Mary Gordon, who had known the Opium-Eater as a guest in the house of her father, John Wilson, declared, " If this singular man's life were written truthfully, no one would believe it, so strange the tale would seem." That very singularity led him to an evasiveness and reclusiveness that made a truthful account all the more difficult. What has survived about De Quincey, besides a few dull financial records, is mostly a sketchy array of sensational anecdotes. The " strange tale " tends to obscure the man. This was a life that could be " written truthfully" only by someone of great sensitivity, sympathy and imagination. Those qualities Sackville West possessed. His study remains uniquely valuable, perhaps the most perceptive and essentially truthful of the lives—because one can " believe it ", or most of it.

Other studies of De Quincey are valuable of their kind. Eaton's is the most authoritative on biographical facts ; it is a solid monument. Elwin's is a vigorous and perceptive quick sketch ; John Calvin Metcalf's *De Quincey: A Portrait* (1940) is not scholarly or up-to-date, but is a charming and loving work ; Lyon's *Thomas De Quincey* is a reliable and thorough brief study, the latest summary of the known facts and established critical positions. But none supplants Sackville West, and probably no study of De Quincey will do so.

This is not to say that Sackville West's work is without faults. He paints a portrait of the De Quincey in which he is interested—which is the essential De Quincey—but he does not try very hard to run down all the facts and present them precisely. About De Quincey's legal aspirations he says, " He seems, indeed, to have kept a few terms here and there in the next few years ; but with his settlement at Grasmere in 1809, all real intention to pursue the course of his legal studies must virtually have ceased, though he continued for some time to pretend that he was still pursuing them " (p. 100). This is annoyingly vague : we want the " here and there " and the " pretending " spelled out—and we find the documentation in Eaton. Sackville West is especially unsatisfactory on the details of De Quincey's tenure as editor of the *Westmorland Gazette*, says rather contradictory things on pages 167 and 176, and does not appear to realize that De Quincey was asked to resign from the post. What he says about De Quincey's use of opium needs to be supplemented by Elisabeth Schneider's work in *Coleridge, Opium and Kubla Khan*, and his comments on De Quincey's knowledge of German thought and literature corrected by René Wellek's *Immanuel Kant in England 1798–1838* and " De Quincey's Status in the History of Ideas ", and the series of articles by Peter Michelsen (see the Supplementary Bibliography).

Sackville West depends a great deal on De Quincey's autobiographical writings, often virtually paraphrases them, and sometimes out of sheer pleasure at their richness incorporates material not very relevant to his account—as when he includes the adventures of De Quincey's brother " Pink " in the Galapagos Islands. Yet he feels free to believe or reject them at will. The rejections have the uncertain authority of Sackville West's forays into Freudian psychology. Not every reader will accept his reconstruction of the episode of the French letter with the mysterious bank draft ; I think he rather distorts the evidence to fit his interpretation. Moreaux, however, goes even further in psychologizing over De Quincey, pronouncing him a masochist. I have attempted some modification and up-dating of Sackville West's statements through editorial footnotes, which are placed together at the end of the book and identified by the number of the page to which they refer. Whenever such a note is available, the reader is alerted by an asterisk in the text.

The merits of Sackville West's work, however, more than outweigh its shortcomings. First, it is well-written; it is certainly the most readable of the full-scale lives. Surely such a master of language as De Quincey deserves to be treated by someone who has a way with words. Sackville West is not up to De Quincey's word music—who is?—but he is on the same wave-length. Take, for instance, his description of De Quincey's Grasmere wanderings, of the sharply-etched "impression of concentrated, rock-garden-like greenness in the immediate vicinity of the lake itself—the look of a specially and capriciously favoured tuft, planted with selective care and lovingly watered, in the midst of a whole field of reckless grass" (p. 121). This is precise and powerful. And there is much similar description with a touch of the poet. So too is there much pleasant, uninhibited personal comment that puts blood in this book. Sackville West's politics seems to show through in such an opinion as that Wordsworth's later conservatism "won him the thoughtless hatred of minds too unstable for useful meditation on experience, or of those who, like Byron and Hazlitt, were permanently embittered by their own inability to come to terms with society" (p. 112). We enjoy such an aside as the remark that Sara Hutchinson's charge that De Quincey was drinking heavily was probably unwarranted but was "an accusation which women, when they are annoyed with a man, frequently make on the smallest, or no, provocation" (p. 152). And we are amused at the intensity of the comment on De Quincey's habit in his later days of drinking cocoa: "no more unhealthy foodstuff can be imagined" (p. 275).

Most important, Sackville West is not content just to write De Quincey's life; he brings his literary sensitivity to a fairly complete analysis of De Quincey's writings. This is the fullest, most informative one available in English, although the "LŒuvre" section of Moreaux's book is perhaps more elaborate. And, despite the facts that Sackville West is not as much aware of De Quincey's dependence upon source materials as Goldman's study (see Supplementary Bibliography) has made us, and perhaps goes too far in claiming that De Quincey "spoiled" the *Confessions* in revising them, his judgments are on the whole sound, his taste reliable. He has built solidly to his neatly put conclusion :

> In the community of the Helpless, De Quincey will always occupy a throne of eminence ; yet too much emphasis can easily be laid on this most obvious feature of his character. For his achievement, though little appreciated to-day and perhaps never likely to reach a very wide public, was in fact considerable (p. 330).

True, but Sackville West has by his warm book increased that appreciation, widened that public.

John E. Jordan
BERKELEY, CALIFORNIA, *29 May 1973*

AUTHOR'S PREFACE TO THE ORIGINAL EDITION

It is a very singular thing that a writer of De Quincey's importance should for so long have escaped the hyena-like activities of professional biographers. During years when no famous or notorious figure, whether male or female, has avoided the tribute of at least two 'Lives', and when writers have been driven out into the highways and hedges in search of still obscurer prey, whom their colleagues might by chance have overlooked, De Quincey has, by some miracle, remained untouched. The amount of attention devoted to him in the years after his death, when he was a more actual figure in the world of letters than he is now, was sufficient unto the day: a few memorial essays (Hogg's, Findlay's, Hill Burton's), a monograph in the English Men of Letters Series (by David Masson[1]), two volumes of correspondence, and one full-length biography, by Alexander Japp ("H. A. Page").

The latter has remained, up to the present time, the only detailed source for the facts of De Quincey's life.* Contemporary sources of information are comparatively meagre: De Quincey wrote a good deal more about his friends and contemporaries than they wrote about him. A few references in the correspondence of Coleridge; a considerable body of material in the letters of the Wordsworth family; occasional references scattered up and down the Carlyle letters and reminiscences; bare mention by Hood, by Charles Knight, by Crabb Robinson: the list is short. De Quincey was odd, shy, retiring, remote, come one day and gone the next; he escaped contemporary notice in much the same way as he has escaped ours to-day; for his mysterious life had a quality of unreality, which caused him to be overlooked—I had almost said, to be invisible. And the spell continues. Yet such is the power and fascination of one of his works that there is no one to-day, among those at all instructed

[1] Since writing these lines, Mr. Malcolm Elwin's admirable short *Life* has come out, thus superseding Masson's little volume.

in English literature, who does not know at least one fact about him. If questioned, they will answer: "He ate opium and described the effects in a book of Confessions"; and they may add, if they are exceptionally well-informed: "Didn't he write an essay on Murder, or something?"

'Or something. . . .' That is the limit of most people's knowledge of De Quincey to-day; and it is in the hope of extending that limit, not only in favour of a life of exceptional interest and a character of exceptional charm, but also in the domain of his writings, that I have undertaken this book. "If the art of biography be the development of 'the ruling passion'," said Isaac D'Israeli, "it is in strong characters that one must seek for the single feature." But De Quincey was not, in that sense, a strong character; and though his life might perhaps be regarded in the light of a ruling passion for knowledge, no account of his character which attempted to force it within the frame of any "single feature", could possibly be adequate. Hence, in some sort, the length of this book, which is also in no small measure due to the fact that I have purposely been lavish with quotations, feeling that, in the case of a writer who was himself singularly free with personal revelations, it was better to allow him to explain himself, wherever possible, rather than to rely on my own qualifications as an expositor of his character. At the same time, in making these quotations, especially with reference to his literary qualities, I have tried to keep in mind his own stricture, that "it is always injudicious, in the highest degree, to cite for admiration that which is not a *representative* specimen of the author's manner."

Again, though my pretensions to scholarship are small, I have nevertheless risked teasing the reader's eye by a constant mass of references, always given where a matter of opinion is broached and on most other occasions as well; being unwilling to join the ranks of those biographers who rely mainly on 'delineative conjecture' and neglect to disclose their exact sources, thus making it impossible for the reader to check the conclusions they draw. Hence, although certain passages of De Quincey's life are sufficiently obscure to warrant some degree of interpretation, I have endeavoured, on those occasions, to base my theories on statements of fact, and to keep as close as possible to the available evidence.

A consideration of the forms into which De Quincey cast his

work at once suggests a reason for the neglect from which, as a writer, he has suffered. With the exception of the *Confessions* and *Klosterheim*, he never managed to produce a whole book, and his work consists entirely of essays which, until late in his life, remained scattered up and down the back numbers of various periodicals. Thus the public long lacked an opportunity to judge his work as a whole; and even after the publication of *Selections Grave and Gay*, the lack of homogeneity—the general effect of journalistic improvization—presented by the collection, militated against that uniformity of impression which is so necessary to the growth of a reputation. It is one of the objects of the present volume to show that a kind of unity is in fact detectable in his work—a unity in the light of which much that has hitherto been neglected receives a glow that is far from dim.

There are three extant editions of De Quincey's works, all of which differ from one another in what they include. The first is the American edition of Messrs. Ticknor and Fields, issued in the 'fifties; the second is the *Selections Grave and Gay* published, also in the 'fifties, by James Hogg, under the supervision of De Quincey himself. Lastly there is the Masson edition, published by the house of Black, in 1889–90. Of these, the first two have been long out of print and are now not easily come by (this applies particularly to the American edition). The titles of the various articles in the latter edition, as well as the arrangement of material, are substantially different from those of De Quincey's own choice. The Hogg edition is still, in the matter of print, paper and format, the most pleasant to read in, though it is of course far from complete, De Quincey having died before his work of revision was finished. The Masson edition, therefore, which is still in print, remains up to date the definitive one. The arrangement according to subject seems, in spite of Professor Saintsbury's strictures, to have much to recommend it; and the editor's notes and prefaces supply a great deal of needful information. The fourteen volumes also contain far more material than the former editions, though a certain amount of matter still remains unpublished.* The references throughout this book are to the Masson edition. The references to the first version of the *Confessions* are to the *third* edition, which differs only from the first in pagination and was used here because I happen to possess it. The references to Japp's book are to the one-volume revised edition, published in 1890. For reasons of brevity I have referred to the two volumes of letters, entitled *De Quincey Memorials*, as Letters, I and II.

My thanks are due, first and foremost, to De Quincey's granddaughters, Miss Florence and Miss Margaret Baird-Smith, for the extreme kindness they have shown in allowing me free use of their invaluable collection of MSS. and letters, and also for permission to reproduce the miniatures and the portrait in their possession. Without the constant help they have accorded me, my task would have been much more arduous than it has been. I am hardly less indebted to the late Mr. Christopher Wordsworth who, not long before his death, gave me copies of the unpublished and exceedingly important letters of De Quincey to William and Dorothy Wordsworth. Further, I must mention my friends, Mr. Maurice Bowra, of Wadham College, and Mr. Roy Harrod, of Christ Church, Oxford, for their invaluable help in 'vetting', respectively, the essays on Homer and Herodotus, and those on Political Economy—tasks for which I felt myself eminently unfitted. My thanks are likewise due to Mrs. Rawnsley, of Allan Bank, Grasmere, for leave to print the letter of Sara Coleridge, quoted on page 232, and also for her kindness in giving me access to her interesting collection of books and portraits. Lastly, I wish to express my gratitude to my cousins, Harold and Vita Nicolson, for reading the proofs and making many valuable suggestions; and to Mr. Desmond McCarthy, who has for years urged me to write this book, and to whose communicated wisdom, humour and experience I owe a debt I can never repay.

KNOLE, *October* 1935.

A FLAME IN SUNLIGHT

CHAPTER I

SENSE AND SENSIBILITY

I

THE forbears of a man of genius are a subject which never fails of a certain appeal, particularly when some notoriety, from which deductions can be drawn, has attached to any one of them. Byron is, of course, the most obvious example of this truism. But if the ancestors of De Quincey possessed qualities—apart from vague literary leanings—which marked them out sharply from their contemporaries, in such a way that he himself might have pointed with pride to any one of them as the prototype of his own talents, we are not made aware of it. De Quincey, in his autobiographical writings and recorded remarks, is reticent on the subject, and the rather bald information which he gave to George III on his accidental meeting with that monarch at Frogmore in 1800, seems to have been dictated by a desire to emphasize the Norman, at the expense of the French, origin of his family* (for "of all things, I could not endure to be supposed of French descent"[1])—an early example, this, of a prejudice which was to remain with him through life. At a later date, however, he added the following remarks:

> At some unlucky moment when the Crown commanded unusual resources, the De Quinceys met with the fate ascribed, perhaps fabulously, to some small heavenly bodies. . . . On some dark day, by mistake perhaps, they exploded, and scattered their ruins all over the central provinces of England, where chiefly had lain their territorial influence. Especially in the counties of Leicester, Lincoln and Rutland were found the fragments of the vast landed estates held by these potentates when Earls of Winchester.[2]

[1] I, 267. [2] *Posthumous Works*, I, 201.

But of these fragments few remained, at the end of the eighteenth century, to connect themselves at all nearly with the Lancashire branch which produced the Opium-Eater.

There seems no doubt that the family was of Norse origin. Migrating to Normandy in the ninth or tenth century, they established themselves there and, in return for services rendered to Duke William, obtained the village of Quincey and therewith the right to the 'de'. Thence they radiated to England and, in much later times, to America, in which country they attained to distinction in worldly and official consideration. But the history of these collaterals, though it can no doubt be traced, has little bearing on the subject of this biography, whose peculiar character and temperament are very substantially accounted for by his immediate forbears; and about these, fortunately for us, De Quincey was far less reticent.

Of his father, Thomas Quincey (he modestly omitted the 'de', which was restored after his death by his wife) we know a good deal. Born in 1753, one of twenty-two children, he found it necessary, on growing up, to take to trade as a profession. Evidently he had some talent for business. That part of the Quincey family to which he belonged had settled in the north of England, and the first we hear of Thomas the elder is that—no doubt by virtue of the £6000 which was his patrimony—he held a partnership in the firm of Quincey and Duck, linen drapers, in Manchester. After a time he sold out this partnership and became a merchant on a larger scale, and on his own account. This meant constant absences from Manchester—in Portugal, in America, in the West Indies; but did not prevent him from marrying (in 1781) and rapidly producing eight children. He did not, however, live long to enjoy the fruits of his ability. Probably his health had always been delicate; in any case, soon after the birth of his fifth child, Thomas, he developed consumption and was obliged to spend still more of his time abroad. In 1793, at the age of forty, he came home for the last time, to die.

In character he seems to have been not untypical of his century. "A plain and unpretending man," says De Quincey, at the beginning of his *Autobiographic Sketches*; and indeed modesty seems to have been the outstanding quality of his character. He was fond of books, which he read for amusement rather than instruction;

revered Cowper and Dr. Johnson; cared little (too little, says De Quincey) for music; and having been denied the advantages of a college education, had an exaggerated respect for those who had enjoyed them. De Quincey afterwards admitted that his father had always been a shadowy figure to him, come one day and gone the next, conspicuous rather by his absence, invariably gentle and indulgent, but indifferent almost, no doubt with the low vitality of an invalid; and, at the last, unreal—even ghostly.

Yet he had had an appetite for life and a fastidious appreciation of its pleasanter aspects, and some desire to make known his impressions of them into the bargain, as is shown by his publication, in 1774, in the *Gentleman's Magazine*, of "A Tour in the Midland Counties in 1772, with some account of another Tour in 1774", which was afterwards thought worthy of being reprinted in a volume. This agreeably tasteful, if tepid and unoriginal, work is a 'rural ride', written in the leisurely, cultivated style with which the recently published Torrington Diaries* have made us so pleasantly familiar, though it lacks their humour and independence of vision.

De Quincey, in another place, drops two further hints which enable us to complete our impression of his father. He says that the "expansive love" that characterized himself and his sister Elizabeth came to them from their father, not from Mrs. De Quincey; and in the *Confessions* [1] he claims that, of all the children, he was the most like his father. These remarks are particularly illuminating, for they explain both the faint atmosphere of unreality that hangs round the mild, receding features of Thomas Quincey and also his son's evident feeling that, in spite of this ghostliness, his father was a man eminently worthy of a love which his unenthusiastic temperament perhaps had not the power of eliciting to the full.

His wife, *née* Elizabeth Penson, was a very different type of person. She was the daughter of an officer and came, like her husband, from solid middle-class stock, though De Quincey indicates (it was probably her own opinion) that this stock was socially superior to her husband's. Her father is described as having been a man of varied talents. The only other member of

[1] III, 425.

her family with whom we are here concerned is her brother, the Anglo-Indian colonel whose connection with his nephew's life will hereafter be described.

If his father had but little influence on the development of De Quincey's character, his mother had what is perhaps better described as an enormous involuntary effect upon it. For she was one of those unfortunate people whose indubitable rectitude and unceasing desire to influence others for their own good arouse opposition that, at first instinctive, soon becomes conscious and obstinate. She was a deeply religious woman, whose love for her neighbour (and even for her family) was deprived of warmth by being so obviously dictated by a severe sense of duty. This lack of warmth resulted in, among other things, an insistence upon the negative side of life. "If I could presume to descry a fault in my mother," says De Quincey, "it was that she turned the chilling aspects of her high-toned character too exclusively upon those whom, in any degree, she knew or supposed to be promoters of evil."[1] Her grand-daughter, Mrs. Baird-Smith, was of opinion that she was fundamentally diffident of her own judgment, and we find confirmation of this view in the influence exercised over her by her friend Hannah More, whose brisk self-assurance was unclouded by the doubts and hesitations conferred by an alert use of the intellect.

But in spite of this fundamental diffidence, which, however, she was remarkably successful in hiding, she was a woman of vigorous intellect. "For though unpretending to the name and honours of a *literary* woman, I shall presume to call her . . . an *intellectual* woman: and I believe that if ever her letters should be collected and published, they would be thought generally to exhibit as much strong and masculine sense, delivered in as pure 'mother English', racy and fresh with idiomatic graces, as any in our language."[2] This is no overstatement: her letters are indeed admirable, full of an acid and sarcastic wit; but these are not qualities which recommend their possessor to the young, and it is abundantly clear that Mrs. De Quincey, although an attentive mother, inspired more irritation than love in her children. One feels some of this exasperated incapacity to rise to his mother's standard of behaviour in the passage in which De Quincey records

[1] III, 315. [2] *Confessions* (1823) 73.

the fact that, although twice asked in marriage as a widow, she refused to give way, out of respect for her husband's memory and her children.[1] Furthermore, we have only to recall the fact that two of her four sons rebelled against her authority to the extent of running away—the one to Wales, the other to sea—to realize the unceasing and disagreeable nature of the pressure her personality continually exerted upon them. A miniature painted after her marriage confirms this impression of her character. It is not a very pleasing face: a certain hard fixity in the eyes, a general lack of sensitiveness in the bold, handsome features, delineate a nature uncompromising and obtuse.

Two other idiosyncrasies in Mrs. De Quincey call for notice here: a passion for building—or rather rebuilding—houses, and a definite, if unobtrusive, belief in the importance of social standing. Indications of the last propensity are faint but unmistakable: the resumption, at her instance, of the 'de' in the family name, and the fact, surprising in one whose ideas on education were generally of the severest, that she wished Thomas to go to Eton. There is something, too, in her attitude to her friend Lady Carbery that suggests that, had that lady not possessed the sanction of a title, Mrs. De Quincey would have looked askance on the somewhat liberal nature of her outlook. And there is nothing—even in De Quincey's detailed account of the milieu—to suggest that she was in any way repelled by the virulent snobbishness of Hannah More.

Her restless inability to be satisfied with houses as she found them is better documented. "Seeking her chief intellectual excitement in architectural creations",[2] she moved house no less than eight times in nineteen years—an uncommon feat in those days. In the early years of their marriage she and her husband lived in Manchester itself; they then moved to a house called "The Farm" on the outskirts of the town, and later, in 1791, built a house in the same district. The name of this house—Greenhay[3]—was Mrs. De Quincey's own invention, and we are not surprised to hear that the design was hers too.[4] After her husband's death she started out on a wild search for a home that should unite the following advantages: "Good medical advice somewhere in the

[1] III, 317. [2] I, 404.
[3] Or "Greenheys": both forms of the name are found. [4] I, 404.

neighbourhood; first-rate means of education; elegant (or what most people might think aristocratic) society; agreeable scenery;" and—this last desideratum appeared to be the most difficult to attain—"a Church of England parish clergyman, who was to be strictly orthodox"[1] yet of evangelical persuasion. The search was to prove long but not, in the end, hopeless. Starting with Bath and Somerset, followed by a brief rest at The Priory, Chester, it proceeded by way of a fruitless visit to High Wycombe, back to Bath, then to Hinckley in Leicestershire, where Mrs. De Quincey's second daughter Mary was living, and eventually came to a temporary end at Westhay, near Wrington, in Somerset.

These peregrinations must have run away with a great deal of money; for Mrs. De Quincey seldom if ever contented herself with living in the various houses she rented; she must needs pull them about and build on to them. No sooner had she arrived at the Priory, for instance, than she "immediately threw out a drawing-room in suitable proportion to the dining-room, and about six little bedrooms." This alteration cost £1000, the estate of Westhay £12,500, not including the cost of the alterations (De Quincey says this was borne by his uncle, Colonel Penson); and Weston Lea, the house near Bath in which Mrs. De Quincey spent the last years of her life, cost £1000 (also not including the cost of the inevitable alterations).[2] Like all amateur architects, moreover, she always lost on the sale of her houses.

In estimating the character of this peculiar woman, whose brilliant and scornful letters alone show what a powerful force she was in De Quincey's life, it is perhaps not fanciful to see, in this passion for rebuilding houses, the efficient symbol of an obsessing desire to interfere with the work of others, to convert them to her own view of the world and—failing that—to impose it on them.

I have dwelt upon this subject because it serves to illustrate, not only Mrs. De Quincey's character, but also the otherwise mysterious state of financial tightness in which the family lived after Mr. Quincey had died, leaving them in what would then have been thought comfortable circumstances. The estate, at his death, amounted to £1600 a year, out of which each of the sons was to be allowed £150, and the daughters £100. This arrange-

[1] I, 407. [2] I, 404.

ment, in the hands of competent trustees, and in 1793, should not have meant penury; and the mismanagement of Thomas Quincey's fortune, and the miserable pittance on which his son Thomas was obliged to live during his minority, must be ascribed as much to Mrs. De Quincey's architectural extravagances as to the obstructionist policy of the children's most active guardian, the Reverend Samuel Hall.

These guardians were four in number and De Quincey has described two of them, while naming only the third and telling us nothing whatever of the fourth.[1] The first two, a merchant and a rural magistrate, seem to have been too busy to attend to their duties as guardians; but Samuel Hall, who ran a school in the Salford district of Manchester, exercised his rights to the full, as we shall later have the opportunity of observing; and, as his school was the first to which De Quincey was sent, I shall reserve a more detailed description of him until that point is reached. Meanwhile, though he could write an angry letter to a disobedient boy, there is nothing to show that he attempted to stem the tide of Mrs. De Quincey's extravagance. Perhaps, like other people, he was afraid of her.

It will be as well, before coming to the early days and impressions of Thomas himself, to finish here our descriptions of the De Quincey family. Only six of the eight children were alive at the death of their father in 1793. The eldest, Elizabeth—first of the three muses who inspired De Quincey's life—had died in 1791, of hydrocephalus, at the age of nine. A younger sister, Jane, born in 1786 (De Quincey speaks of her as also an " elder " sister, but this is a mistake), died in 1790, of what disease we are not informed.* The remaining children, in order of age, were therefore: William, Mary, Thomas, Richard (" Pink "), another Jane, and Henry. With the exception of Thomas and the second Jane, all the children died young—William at eighteen, Mary (in childbirth) at thirty-six, Richard at twenty-five (by violence), Henry at twenty-seven. This early mortality, as well as the extremely delicate health from which Thomas suffered all his life, was no doubt due to the tubercular affection inherited from Mr. Quincey. The hydrocephalus of which Elizabeth died was probably tubercular in origin, Thomas certainly suffered from incipient tuberculosis in early life, and the

[1] III, 239.

exquisite red and white complexion which made himself and his brother Richard the objects of so much admiration as boys, points in the same direction.

2

At the time of Thomas' birth (on August 15th, 1785) the De Quincey family was living at The Farm; but he distinctly states that he was actually born in Manchester itself,[1] though efforts to identify the house have proved fruitless. Japp seems to think it was The Farm itself,[2] but this is more than doubtful, as this house was in the Greenhay district and therefore well out in the country.* However this may be, Thomas' childhood was passed in a "rural seclusion", which was deepened in 1791, when Mr. Quincey built, and removed his family to, Greenhay Hall.

A contemporary painting (the house was subsequently engulfed by Manchester and pulled down in 1852) shows a fair-sized square box of a house, with a typically eighteenth century façade (five windows and a portico), fronted by a 'sweep' of drive and backed by deciduous trees and some outhouses, while two gentlemen in top-hats and morning coats stand on the drive, the one holding a bag and the other pointing at the house. No description is extant of the interior; but we may assume that it had that comfortable, open, 'schoolroom' aspect, which distinguishes the houses of that date. At the same time, it probably had no pretensions to luxury, as Mrs. De Quincey's severe principles would have been opposed to anything of the kind and her husband was too seldom at home to care to impose his own more genial taste.

Thomas was christened at St. Ann's church (the name is curiously prophetic), in Manchester, on September 23rd, by his future guardian, the Revd. Samuel Hall. The middle members of a large family do not generally receive especial attention, and Thomas seems to have been no exception to the rule. In the *Autobiographic Sketches* he thanks Providence for four things: "That I lived in a rustic solitude; that this solitude was in England; that my infant feelings were moulded by the gentlest of sisters, and not by horrid, pugilistic brothers; finally, that I and they were dutiful and loving members of a pure, holy, and magnificent church."[3]

[1] I, 34. [2] Japp, 4. [3] I, 32.

And later in the same chapter he adds a sentence which is of the highest significance as showing, with eloquent clarity, the peculiar quality of his experience—a quality that was, both early and late, the guiding principle of his perpetual waking dream. "I am struck with the truth," he says, "that far more of our deepest thoughts and feelings pass to us through perplexed combinations of *concrete* objects, pass to us as *involutes* (if I may coin that word) in compound experiences incapable of being disentangled, than ever reach us directly and in their own abstract shapes."[1] Such objects, in these days of his childhood, were mostly simple, homely and regular, consisting not only in the persons with whom his life was lived, but in the shapes and colours of his father's house, the look of the trees and of the even, sad landscape of Lancashire under the changing seasons; for his was a mind given to impressions of a painful vividness, and for which the objects of nature lived with a life not easily distinguishable from that of human beings.

His three sisters—Elizabeth, the first Jane, and Mary—were only less impressionable than Thomas himself. In the long winter evenings the four of them would sit round the guard of the nursery fire, while the nursery-maid (about whom Thomas had already had "a remarkable dream of terrific grandeur") explained the pictures in a large illustrated Bible. "The fitful gloom and sudden lambencies of the room by firelight suited our evening state of feelings; and they suited, also, the divine revelations of power and mysterious beauty which awed us. Above all, the story of a just man—man and yet *not* man, real above all things, and yet shadowy above all things—who had suffered the passion of death in Palestine, slept upon our minds like early dawn upon the waters."[2]

This peaceful, sensuous unfolding of his mind was broken by three successive shocks. The first was the death, in 1790, of Jane. Since she was not his favourite sister and he was only five years old at the time, this death produced in Thomas not so much sorrow as "a sad perplexity"; but it was attended by a circumstance that made a profound and painful impression upon him. It came to his ears that a female servant had treated the dying child with harshness, "if not brutally"; and at once an entirely moral, very

[1] I, 39. [2] I, 39.

frightening sensation arose in him—a "feeling . . . of shuddering horror, as upon a first glimpse of the truth that I was in a world of evil and strife." [1]

The second shock, which occurred only a year later, was much worse. Elizabeth had gone, one hot summer day, to have tea in the house of a labouring man—father of one of the servants. When she started to walk back, the sun had set and a mist had risen over the fields. She caught a fever, which developed into hydrocephalus, from which she died, lingeringly and in pain. The effect upon Thomas was appalling. "O! moment of darkness and delirium, when the elder nurse . . . launched God's thunderbolt at my heart in the assurance that my sister must die. . . . Blank anarchy and confusion of mind fell upon me." [2]

After she was dead he decided that he must take a last look at her face, alone. Choosing the moment when the servants were at their midday meal, he crept up the back staircase, turned the key in the door of the death-chamber and went in. At first he noticed nothing unusual, being occupied in shutting the door noiselessly. But when he turned to face the room, he stopped in astonishment. The bed had been turned round, so that the body of his sister was invisible; what met his gaze was the tall window, through which torrents of summer sunlight poured into the room and over his face. Instantly and instinctively, the contrasting force of these tremendous symbols—the sunlight and the invisible corpse—seized upon his mind and fixed it in the image of death, as before it had been fixed in the brief image of evil. Death and summer, "the antagonism between the tropical redundancy of life in summer, and the frozen sterilities of the grave": [3] the sudden and overwhelming vision made him forget the reason for which he had come into the room and kept him standing there by the door, gazing at the light-stricken window. And when at last he came round the bed and looked at the dead face, a deeper awe, that was not fear, fell upon him, and in his ears he heard the sound of a wind, "the saddest that ear ever heard. It was a wind that might have swept the fields of mortality for a thousand centuries. Many times since, upon summer days, when the sun is about the hottest, I have remarked the same wind arising and uttering the same hollow, solemn, Memnonian but saintly swell:

[1] I, 34. [2] I, 37. [3] I, 38.

it is in this world the one great audible symbol of eternity. And three times in my life have I happened to hear the same sound in the same circumstances—viz., when standing between an open window and a dead body on a summer day.

"Instantly, when my ear caught this vast Aeonian intonation, when my eye filled with the golden fulness of life, the pomps of the heavens above, or the glory of the flowers below, and turning when it settled upon the frost which overspread my sister's face, instantly a trance fell upon me. A vault seemed to open in the zenith of the far blue sky, a shaft which ran up for ever. I, in spirit, rose as if on billows that also ran up the shaft for ever; and the billows seemed to pursue the throne of God; but *that* also ran before us and fled away continually. The flight and the pursuit seemed to go on for ever and ever. Frost gathering frost, some Sarsar wind of death, seemed to repel me; some mighty relation between God and death dimly struggled to evolve itself from the dreadful antagonism between them; shadowy meanings even yet continue to exercise and torment, in dreams, the deciphering oracle within me. I slept—for how long I cannot say, slowly I recovered my self-possession; and, when I woke, found myself standing, as before, close to my sister's bed." [1]

At the time, Thomas felt this death as an irreparable and final disaster; and, as if to press the realization in upon himself, he kept repeating: "*Life is finished!*"

But the end was not yet. Two years later his father came home for the last time, to die. This event was the third and last of the shocks to which Thomas was to be subjected, as a child. It is certain that he did not feel it to anything like the same extent to which he had felt the death of Elizabeth: his father was but feebly connected with the secret progress of his life. But the passage in which he describes Mr. Quincey's return, seen as it is in that quivering, dream-like light in which all his early experiences are set, transfigures the scene for us as it was transfigured for him.

It was a still summer evening and the four children and the servants had gone out on to the lawn in front of the house, to listen for the sound of the carriage which was bringing Mr. Quincey home. Sunset came, and darkness, but still no sound of wheels. It was nearly midnight when the little party decided to walk into

[1] I, 41.

the lane, in a last hope of meeting the carriage. But when it did come, it was proceeding so slowly that they did not hear it. "The first notice of the approach was the sudden emerging of horses' heads from the deep gloom of the shady lane; the next was the mass of white pillows against which the dying patient was reclining. The hearse-like pace at which the carriage moved recalled the overwhelming spectacle of that funeral which had so lately formed part in the most memorable event of my life. But these elements of awe, that might at any rate have struck forcibly upon the mind of a child, were for me, in my condition of morbid nervousness, raised into abiding grandeur by the antecedent experiences of that particular summer night. The listening for hours to the sounds from horses' hoofs upon distant roads, rising and falling, caught and lost, upon the gentle undulation of such fitful airs as might be stirring—the peculiar solemnity of the hours succeeding to sunset—the glory of the dying day—the gorgeousness which, by description, so well I knew of sunset in those West Indian islands from which my father was returning—the knowledge that he returned only to die—the almighty pomp in which this great idea of Death apparelled itself to my young sorrowing heart—the corresponding pomp in which the antagonistic idea, not less mysterious, of life, rose, as if on wings, amidst tropic glories and floral pageantries, that seemed even *more* solemn and pathetic than the vapoury plumes and trophies of mortality—all this chorus of restless images, or of suggestive thoughts, gave to my father's return, which else had been fitted only to interpose one transitory red-letter day in the calendar of a child, the shadowy power of an ineffaceable agency among my dreams." [1]

Thomas was not present when his father died; but he was in the room on the morning of his death and heard him cry out: "Oh, Betty, Betty! Why will you never come and help me to raise this weight?" [2]

Thus, even as a nail, whose point just pierces the board, may be hammered in up to the head in three strokes, the image of death became enthroned within the child, inextricably mingled with the prestigia of all life as he knew it. This vision was never to leave him; at Oxford, during his first opium experiences, it recurred in full force, and again in 1812 and in 1845. Death, summer sunlight

[1] I, 58. [2] Letter of De Quincey to Dorothy Wordsworth, June 21, 1812.

and warmth, the nurse, the palm-trees in the story of Jesus, the chanting of the church service, and the mysterious pathos which he connected with the sight of some crocuses in early spring—these combine into a *leit-motif* which punctuated his life with its recurrent music, weaving a dream-fugue like that which formed the body of his greatest literary inspiration.

3

A new influence, of great importance, now entered Thomas' life. This was William, the elder brother at whom the dig at " horrid, pugilistic brothers "[1] was no doubt aimed. This versatile and high-spirited boy, who alone of the De Quincey children seems to have been unafflicted with a taste for reverie, had early been found so unmanageably mischievous that he was sent for a time to Louth Grammar School, in Lincolnshire. Thence he returned, quite unchastened, to become the astonishment of the schoolroom at Greenhay and the tyrant of his brother Thomas, who was some five or six years younger than himself and whose (at that time) timid and yielding character lent itself to William's adventurous spirit. Like most boys of his type, he was of an inventive turn of mind. The schoolroom sat round and admired while he attempted to walk on the ceiling—first on the principle of skates, then on that of a humming-top; while he sent up fire-balloons and brought cats down to earth in parachutes. It listened while he told ghost stories and speculated on the possibility of a confederation of spirits that should rise and conquer man. Though affecting to despise books, he wrote a number himself, which he inflicted upon his audience. His brothers and sisters bore with patience discourses on the Thirty-nine Articles of the English Church, on pyrotechnics, legerdemain, magic black and white, thaumaturgy, necromancy and " How to raise a ghost; and, when you've got him down, how to keep him down "; but their submissiveness, already weakened by some sarcastic remarks of Mary on the occasion of the ceiling affair, broke down completely when he tried to force them to listen to a series of lectures on physics. The revolt was open, and William had to retire, muttering something about " pearls " and " swinish multitude ".

[1] See p. 8.

Thereafter Thomas had alone to bear the brunt of his brother's exuberant vitality. This was made inevitable by the two boys' being sent together, in 1793, to the school at Salford kept by their guardian, the Revd. Samuel Hall. The distance of Greenhay from Salford was two miles and the boys made the transit twice a day, on foot. Their way lay past a cotton factory and one day, as they were crossing a bridge beside it, a factory boy, happening to come out of the factory and irritated by the smartness of their trousers and Hessian boots, called out derisively: "Hulloa, Bucks!" followed by "Boots! Boots!" This was the sort of occasion to which William was more than equal. Stopping, he offered the boy to "give his flesh to the fowls of the air. The boy declined to accept this liberal invitation, and conveyed his answer by a most contemptuous and plebeian gesture, upon which my brother drove him in with a shower of stones." [1]

Thus began a feud which was to last for weeks, to Thomas' unspeakable anguish. For, unlike William, he was in no way prepared to meet the world. Almost exclusively feminine surroundings, and the cosseting that a long attack of ague, from which he had suffered from his second to his fourth year, had made inevitable: these were not appropriate introductions to what he afterwards plaintively called "the world of strife". Moreover he was both exceedingly shy and reluctant to expose his feelings to view; [2] and the hostility of death, which he could be said to know, was a very different thing—more remote, less ugly—from the stupid hostility of human beings, which he did not know. Never having felt responsibility, the idea of it terrified him: "By temperament, and through natural dedication to despondency, I felt resting upon me always too deep and gloomy a sense of obscure duties attached to life, that I never should be able to fulfil: a burden which I could not carry, and which yet I did not know how to throw off." [3] But now William was there to receive the burden, and Thomas proceeded to obey him like a slave.

While the factory feud lasted, it was not an easy slavery; for, quite apart from the fact that he could not see that the boy's remarks had been particularly offensive, the diminutive child was exceedingly afraid of the crowd of big, coarse boys; and the fact of having to conceal this fear, day after day, at the intolerable risk of being

[1] I, 70. [2] I, 37. [3] I, 71.

called a coward by his brother, told severely upon his nerves. His heart sank as the fatal bridge by the factory came in sight, where he knew for certain that William would insist upon waiting to attack the factory boys. Since there was no other way of getting to and from Salford, the battles took place twice a day, though the morning ones, owing to the fact that most of the boys were at breakfast, were not serious. But in the afternoon the hostilities followed a course that was "odiously monotonous". Armed with stones, pieces of slate, and brickbats, William and Thomas waited outside the factory for the emergence of the enemy, who, in the result, invariably won, though William would afterwards sing *Te Deums* for supposititious victories. Generally, however, before either side had had time to do the other any grave injury, Thomas would be taken prisoner. William being clearly the chief offender, the victors "were not disposed to be too hard upon me. But, at the same time, they clearly did not think it right that I should escape altogether from tasting the calamities of war. And this translated the estimate of my guilt from the public jurisdiction to that of the individual, sometimes capricious and harsh, and carrying out the public award by means of legs that ranged through all gradations of weight and agility. One kick differed exceedingly from another kick in dynamic value; and, in some cases, this difference was so distressingly conspicuous, as to imply special malice, unworthy, I conceive, of all generous soldiership."[1] The comic pedantry of this passage, which was written in 1851—towards the end of De Quincey's life—was not, however, a late development; we can be sure, judging from the letters that he was soon writing to his sister Mary, and allowing for slight differences in vocabulary, that this was the way in which, even as a child, he would have described the event.

William now had further cause to despise his brother's 'effeminacy'. Taken prisoner, as usual, Thomas was one day handed over to some factory girls who, faced by the tiny boy with his yellow curls, large blue eyes and pink and white cheeks, picked him up and kissed him, afterwards protecting him from the assaults of the boys and providing him with an opportunity to escape altogether.

Parallel to these encounters with the proletariat ran one of

[1] I, 79.

William's most elaborate inventions—the history of two imaginary countries, one of which (*Gombroon*) belonged to Thomas, the other (*Tigrosylvania*) to himself. The feud between these countries, in which William was of course always victorious, seems to have been designed as a salve to wounded pride; though De Quincey states that these imaginary battles caused him even greater anxiety than the real ones, which were, however, at last brought to an end by adult interference—but not before the De Quinceys had scored at least one real victory with the aid of one O., a boy who took lessons with them.

Soon after this solution, Thomas was suddenly released from his subjection to William by the latter's departure from Greenhay. He had shown so much talent for drawing that it had been decided to apprentice him to the artist and academician, Philip de Loutherbourgh, whose charmingly romantic landscapes recall the better-known work of George Morland. William had, however, little opportunity of proving his talent, for, before he had been long in London, he caught typhus and died, at the age of eighteen.[1]

Speaking of this separation, De Quincey says that it "contributed to deepen my constitutional propensity to gloomy meditation" and had for him "the value of a revolutionary experience. A new date, a new starting-point, a redemption . . . into the golden sleep of halycon quiet, after everlasting storms, suddenly dawned upon me."[2] With a sigh of relief, he watched the door close against the harshness of active life and turned back once more to the much more satisfactory life of his dreams: "for my constitutional infirmity of mind ran but too determinately towards the sleep of endless reverie, and of dreamy abstraction from life and its realities."[3]

Yet there is no doubt that the rumbustious William supplied something in Thomas' life which the latter missed when it was removed—something that was not to be supplied again until, many years later, he acquired the friendship of John Wilson. This something was a compound of high vitality, recklessness, and the half-contemptuous, half-affectionate protection which robust, extrovert men so often extend to those who are timid and imaginative and inapt to deal with life. And there are signs, in Thomas' case,

[1] De Quincey says sixteen, but eighteen seems the likelier age, according to Japp.
[2] I, 115. [3] III, 242.

that his subjection to William, irksome as it may have been to him in some ways, yet brought him a queer, voluptuous delight. We have his own word for it that he "had a perfect craze for being despised", feeling contempt as "a sort of luxury that I was in continual fear of losing."[1] The reason he gives for this preference is that by bowing to the contempt of a stronger person he thereby got rid of the responsibility he so much dreaded; but the evident ecstasy he experienced in yielding to this desire was more deeply involved with the appetite for feeling pain, an appetite which informed his whole adult life and shows itself strikingly in the nature of his subsequent dream-fantasies.

Thus the feminine streak in his character, which was to remain very marked, here, in this early association with his elder brother, attains at once an almost symbolical vividness. But it is necessary to distinguish carefully between 'feminine' and 'effeminate'; for De Quincey was never, at any time, in any sense effeminate; and he was quite justified in protesting, at the time of the factory feud, against William's accusation to that effect. Feminine pursuits and ideas and manner of speaking and writing: these are the distinguishing marks of the effeminate man; and De Quincey never entertained any of them. His mind developed along irreproachably masculine lines, and as a youth, until illness and worry had impaired his vigour, he showed an independence and a varied enthusiasm that would certainly have led William to revise his opinion. But the more subtle feminine characteristics—of mind as well as of body—he did have, and they were very marked. At this early stage, however, he showed only two of them—a preference for the society of women, and a disposition to confide himself to the protection of a stronger boy.

Meanwhile, the world of strife was not the only one to which he had been introduced: that of books had been partially opened to him, through his father's library and by the surly and inexpert hand of Samuel Hall. But before proceeding to an account of Thomas' schooling, reference must be made to two events. The most important of these, from his point of view, took place in his seventh year. This was a post-chaise journey to some relations in Lincolnshire; and it owes its importance not only to the extraordinary radiance of De Quincey's description of it,[2] but also to

[1] I, 59. [2] I, 275 ff.

the fact that it was the first of that series of coach journeys which became for him the very symbols of beauty and adventure.

An escort had been found for him in the person of a boy of sixteen or so, son of a rich neighbour who had advertised for a coaching companion to share the expense of the journey. Thomas rose in the darkness before dawn (it was Christmas time) and went down to the dining-room to find breakfast laid for himself alone in front of a blazing fire. At this sight he was filled for the first time with the excitement of self-importance and that compact bodily sense of adventure conferred by being abroad when others are still asleep. Outside the windows the dawn announced itself wild with wind and rain. At last the post-chaise arrived and Thomas, quivering with shyness, beheld a replica of William, who greeted him with bored condescension and a great parade of manly capability. He appeared very impatient, slapping his boot with a riding-whip and " peremptorily " refusing an offer of breakfast. After Thomas had been taken upstairs to bid farewell to his mother and receive a purse of six guineas, the two boys started on their journey. During the first stage, as far as Chesterfield, the haughty young man did not deign to favour his companion with a word, except to ask him to draw up the window; and Thomas was much too shy to attempt conversation on his own account. But luncheon, and the wine which accompanied it, induced a more expansive frame of mind in " young Mephistopheles ", as De Quincey, with subsequent malice, dubs him; and a delicious fear of highwaymen drew the two together in common sympathy. The young man primed his pistols importantly, under Thomas' wondering eyes; but the wine they had drunk sent them both fast asleep, and they were woken up with a jolt to find, not highwaymen, but merely the town of Mansfield, at which the chaise had stopped to change horses.

This journey, though entirely uneventful, yet contained enough of the elements of romantic adventure to imbue Thomas with a love of the speed and movement of travel that never left him—a love into which was concentrated the essence of danger and that ecstatic, painful tension which later formed the scaffolding of his dreams.

The second event to which I have referred belongs to the same period in Thomas' life, and though it hardly concerned him at the time, it afterwards provided the material for one of the most curious and amusing chapters in his *Autobiographic Sketches.* This event was the brief visit to Greenhay of Mrs. Lee, " The Female Infidel ". This reckless and ill-advised young woman, who was the daughter of the notorious Sir Francis Dashwood (by this time Lord Le Despenser), had done Mrs. De Quincey some small good office through the medium of common friends, and the former invited her to stay at Greenhay as a return of civility. She had already distinguished herself by running away with an Oxford undergraduate, who was now her husband. Mrs. De Quincey possibly knew this, but what she certainly did not know was that Mrs. Lee was a militant atheist whose hectic temperament did not permit her to keep her views to herself in circles where they would be unwelcome. The company at the dinner-table included two clergymen, one of whom was Samuel Hall and the other a Mr. Clowes, a learned Swedenborgian of whom we shall hear again. To these Mrs. Lee let herself go on the subject of the Christian religion, to the inexpressible horror of Mrs. De Quincey, who had " an alarming nervous attack ", partly because of the " unfeminine intrepidity " of Mrs. Lee's assault, and partly " from concern on behalf of her own servants, who waited at dinner, and were inevitably liable to impressions from what they heard." But on this point De Quincey consoles his mother in retrospect with the reflection that " women of humble station less than any other class have any tendency to sympathise with boldness that manifests itself in throwing off the yoke of religion." But in spite of Mrs. De Quincey's nervous attack, Mrs. Lee—like Shelley later, as De Quincey observes—was zealous for proselytes and refused to let the subject alone. De Quincey recounts this scene with a sly seriousness which shows that the humour of it was not lost upon him.[1]

4

The description of Thomas' first master, the Revd. Samuel Hall, is distinguished by a lack of indulgence that owes much to that gentleman's pig-headed behaviour as a guardian. He is represented as belonging to a class " who sympathize with no spiritual sense

[1] I, 134 ff.

or spiritual capacities in man; who understand by religion simply a respectable code of ethics, leaning for support upon some great mysteries dimly traced in the background, and commemorated in certain great church festivals by the *elder* churches of Christendom. He had composed a body of about 330 sermons, which thus, at the rate of two every Sunday, revolved through a cycle of three years; that period being modestly assumed as sufficient for insuring their eloquence total oblivion." And De Quincey adds, maliciously: "Possibly to a cynic some shorter cycle might have seemed equal to that effect, since their topics rose but rarely above the level of prudential ethics, and the style, though scholarly, was not impressive." [1]

One detects a certain unfairness in this description. Mr. Hall was certainly a dull, unimaginative man, and no doubt his system of teaching reflected the colour of his mind; but sermons designed to appeal to an audience mostly composed of half or totally uneducated people, if they rise above the level of "prudential ethics", risk missing their mark altogether; and no doubt Mr. Hall was aware of this. But though, as De Quincey admits, he was a good and conscientious man, he was not the kind of master to stimulate the learning capacities of so tremulous and imaginative a mind as Thomas'. The latter remained in the school until early in 1797, when he was eleven and a half, and he seems to have done well, especially in Latin, in which subject Mr. Hall was stronger than in Greek. But we are left with the impression—which is not exceptional in the history of De Quincey's schooldays—that William, the factory feud, and the history of *Gombroon*, played a vastly more important part in the boy's mind than book learning.

The immediate reason of Thomas' leaving Mr. Hall's school was an upheaval caused by the sale of Greenhay, which, owing to the depletion of the family, had become unnecessarily large and expensive. Owing to the impatience of the guardians, a hasty sale was concluded, which raised only £2500, a sum which must soon have been absorbed in Mrs. De Quincey's subsequent building activities. Had the guardians only realized it, it would have been better to have left her in peace at Greenhay.

For a few months, while Mrs. De Quincey was moving into her new home at Bath—No. 6 Green Park Buildings East—Thomas

[1] III, 237.

and "one brother" (probably Richard) were boarded out in Manchester with a young married couple named Kelsall.[1] Thomas was at all times much attached to these people and refers to this month spent in their house as a "jewelly parenthesis of pathetic happiness."[2] All too soon, however, he was sent for to Bath and placed in the Grammar School there. The headmaster was an Etonian, a Mr. Morgan, whose scholarship and general attainments appear to have been vastly superior to those of Samuel Hall; and under his tuition Thomas laid the foundations of his later mastery of Greek. Even now, in 1800, at the age of fifteen, he could converse in that language, though in the 1856 edition of the *Confessions*[3] he admits that this feat was a rather superficial attainment—a virtuoso performance based, as yet, on no very firm basis of knowledge.

Nor did it bring him much present satisfaction. A talent for composing Latin verses, which he had also discovered, caused him to be continually held up to the other boys as a model, and they were not slow in showing their resentment. This made the sensitive Thomas miserable. "I detested distinctions that were connected with mortification to others,"[4] he complains, and altogether makes it clear that, in spite of the praise accorded to him, he was on the whole unhappy and lonely.

Yet, through the meshes of this perplexity, we glimpse the beginning of the crystallization of his character. He had already begun the collection of books that was later to attain such vast proportions; and to do this he had exceeded his allowance of pocket-money by three guineas—a fact which caused him much anxiety. The world of books and the worries of an inadequate income had come into his life to stay.

To this period belongs the first of Thomas' extant letters; and, as it possesses, in embryo, most of the characteristics of his later epistolary style, I propose to quote it in full. It is dated March 12th. 1799, and is addressed to his sister Mary:

MY DEAR SISTER,—Once more after a long campaign—after 'Bella, horrida bella'—I return to the arts of peace. Don't you

[1] Kelsall was Mr. Quincey's successor in the business. He afterwards fell on evil days and De Quincey tells (III, 246) how he once saw him in the street, ragged and miserable, and shrank from disclosing himself, for fear of causing shame to his old friend.

[2] III, 243. [3] III, 256. [4] I, 154.

think this a fine metaphor? Well, I suppose you would like to hear how this war first broke out? This day six weeks, as we were up saying, Mr M. was called out, and so forsooth *little*, or rather *big Mounseer* Collins must jump into the desk. It happened that little Harman Minor wanted his hat, which hung up over Collins's head. Wilbraham asked for the cane to reach it him, which Coll. refused, and at the same time to give a little strength (I suppose) to his refusal, and to enforce his authority as a *master*, endeavoured to hit him on the shoulder (as *he* says); but how shall I relate the sequel? On poor Ego did it fall. Say, Muse, what could inspire the cane with such a direful purpose? But not on my shoulder, on my *pate* it fell—unhappy pate! worthy of a better fate! Do you see that *pate* and *fate* rhyme, ay? However, I went on with my lesson when Mr M. returned. As soon as I came home my mother sent for Mr Grant; about three o'clock he came. I was then shaved on the place, and bled with six leeches; and two of the old jockies were so fond of my head that they stayed on for three hours, and would not have departed even then, had not Mr Grant (who came again at nine o'clock) flogged them off with some salt. Next morning I was bled again by the same number. For three weeks I neither read, nor wrote, nor talked, nor eat meat, nor went out of the back drawing-room, except when I went to bed. In the fourth week I read for a *quarter-of-an-hour* per day, and eat a little bit of meat; but I did not write. I now do everything as I used to do, except dancing, running, drinking wine. I am not to go to school till Easter.

My mother wishes to know if onny of the *little Innocents* are coming to Bath; because she would wish you to come with them. I should suppose old Madame Richardson or Ingleby, or some of those old jockies, will come, and then you might take a Saturday-afternoon coach and come to tea, so write as early as you can. I believe you will be in time for Mademoiselle's ball, which was put off (as I suppose) on my account.

I was introduced last Thursday to young Lord Westport (Lord Altamont's only child), and on Sunday I dined with him at his house at Lansdown. He is a very nice boy, about my size. My mother will call upon Mr and Mrs Grace (N.B. Mr Grace is his tutor), and invite them and Lord W. to our house, where I shall have the opportunity of introducing him to you. Dr Mapleton and Mr Grant have left off coming to visit me. My mother desires her love to you. Mrs Pratt continues to grow better; she has no complaint, but is still unable to walk even upstairs without help. She goes out every day in a chair. N.B. They have a gang of robbers in Manchester. Mr Kelsall's warehouse was attempted, but John C. called the watchman, who drove them off. Some of the new books are come—viz., 'Asiatic Researches' (Sir William Jones' work), Goldsmith's 'History', 'Rambler,' Hoole's 'Orlando Furioso', Hoole's 'Tasso', Venn's 'Duty of Man', Ogden's 'Sermons', etc. Believe me,

Your affectionate sister,

TABITHA QUINCEY.[1]

Quite apart from the information it gives, there are a number of important points to be noted in this letter. Bearing in mind the fact that the writer was a boy of fourteen, one is astonished at the precocious phraseology, at the Gothic elaboration of the sentences. Subject-matter apart, one would take the whole for the letter of an old man, of which it has still further characteristics—the chirpy facetiousness, the unnecessary italics, both of them strongly marked features of De Quincey's later style. Then, what ordinary boy of fourteen would refer to a contemporary as "Lord Altamont's only child"? This is the typical language of what nurses call an "old-fashioned" boy. The story of the robber gang shows that Thomas had already acquired that poring interest in crime—in 'Assize cases'—which was to remain an absorbing passion with him and to produce some of his most successful essays in the macabre. Its fascination consoled him, in some deep substratum of his being, for the vital action in which, after one brief and disastrous experiment, his life was singularly lacking.

Remains the quaint signature—"Tabitha". It would be absurd to goggle learnedly over this little quip, which obviously had its origin in some private joke. At the same time, it is worth noticing, as evidence that Thomas himself was conscious of the feminine aspect of his character, even if only of the more superficial signs of it.

After he had recovered from the unfortunate accident to his head, his mother refused to allow him to return to Bath Grammar School—not, characteristically, because of the master's culpable carelessness, but because she was afraid that the praise he received

[1] Japp, 19.

there might turn his head. As she later observed of Macaulay who, as a small boy, was sent to lodge with her by Hannah More: " This little Macaulay is a clever boy, and puts me in mind of the elder Coleridge, but he says such extraordinary things that he will be ruined by praise." [1] In Thomas' case, she certainly had no need of apprehension; his shy, timorous nature was of the kind which is all the better for praise and encouragement, and the taking him away from Bath Grammar School, where he was making real progress in study, was an act of folly.

For a short time after this he remained at home, under the tutelage of a French *émigré*, who, however, was unsuccessful in engaging the boy's attention. Thomas was for ever wandering away from his master, round the house, while the unfortunate man followed, wailing: " Oh, Master Tomma, do be p*a*rsuaded! Do be p*a*rsuaded! "

After the failure of this experiment, Thomas was sent to a school at Winkfield, in Wiltshire, whither his brother Richard had preceded him. The master, Mr. Spencer, is described as " of religious character "; [2] but the teaching was much less good than at Bath, as Thomas seems to have realized, for he spent a good deal of his time in reading and mooning about on his own. His knowledge of miscellaneous literature was growing: during his illness in Bath, his mother had read him the whole of *Orlando Furioso* aloud (in the translation mentioned in the letter to Mary), and he had also read the whole of *Paradise Lost* to himself, in Bentley's edition.

At Winkfield, in spite of his mother's caution, he scored a considerable scholastic triumph. A London periodical, called *The Juvenile Library*, set a competition for the best translation of Horace's Twenty-second Ode, and Thomas entered for it. His version won the third prize, the first being carried off by Leigh Hunt and the second by some person unknown. As this is his earliest known composition, it may be well to give a verse or two of it.

Fuscus! the man whose heart is pure,
Whose life unsullied by offence,
Needs not the jav'lines of the Moor
In his defence.

[1] Letters, II, 94. [2] Japp, 25.

Should he o'er Libya's burning sands
  Fainting pursue his breathless way,
No bow he'd seek to arm his hands
        Against dismay.

Quivers of poisoned shafts he'd scorn,
  Nor, though unarmed, would feel a dread
To pass where Caucasus forlorn
        Rears his huge head.

And so on. The diction is not undistinguished, the rhymes are adequate. It is not unjust to assume that Thomas' effort should have been accorded a higher place.

Though this was his only public literary performance at this period, he did, while at Winkfield, write a good deal, both in verse and prose, for a school magazine, called *The Observer*, which was run by the headmaster's daughter, Miss Spencer. These efforts have, however, not been preserved; but in the Diary which he kept in 1803 we read of a "poetic and pathetic ballad, reciting the wanderings of two young children (brother and sister) and their falling asleep on a frosty moonlight night among the lanes . . . and so perishing. (I projected this at Bath . . .)."[1] The precocity shown in both these literary performances and in the "Tabitha" letter was the natural accompaniment to the physical delicacy and feebleness from which Thomas had always suffered. As a form of compensation it is by no means rare.

Thomas remained at Winkfield scarcely more than a year. During this time he received a letter from his mother which deserves quotation as a specimen of that lady's style in general and of the severe tone which she invariably adopted towards her children. She begins by making the Misses Spencer's visit to Bath an excuse for sending a letter to her son, and continues thus:

The books, I hope, will be agreeable to you. I perceived in two or three places which I just looked at, without cutting the leaves open, that the Scotchman[2] uses some inelegant words: I trust I shall never hear you say, as he does, that in a difficult argument 'people find themselves gravelled'. I do not know of any new thing. Poor Lady Carbery continues very ill: I am persuaded never likely to recover. . . . Her ladyship was here on

[1] Diary, p. 181.

[2] Probably Smollett.

Wednesday evening, and is as handsome and amiable as ever; but I fear terribly surrounded with Irish people of rank who wish to make her racket about like themselves.

You will hear of the oratorio to-day from those who will have heard it, if their organs of hearing are not frozen in the church before the music begins.[1]

The moral disapproval of the first paragraph arouses amusement at the writer's expense; but in the last, we laugh with her. Mrs. De Quincey was particularly adept at this sort of pat, acid wit. On one occasion she refers to her son Henry, who is, she says: "so blind that he cannot see a horse till it is close to his elbow, and so frightened when he does see it, that he loses the power of moving";[2] and of a visit she had been paying: "We were almost as glad to part as to meet with the Drawing-room guests; the Postillion and his Horses were the best of the company."[3]

5

So far, for one to whom friendship was to mean much, Thomas had made few friends on his own account. The exceptions were the brothers Grinfield (Thomas and Edward)—pleasant, unexciting persons, the latter of whom was to turn up, after a separation of many years, just too late to say good-bye to the dying De Quincey. These two were Winkfield pupils; the other, who was about to be instrumental in introducing Thomas to a wider world than he had hitherto known, was the Lord Westport already referred to in the "Tabitha" letter.

The personality of this boy remains vague. He was three years younger than Thomas, and the indications are that he was of the ordinary open-air type, handsome,[4] sport-loving, not unintelligent (when he found it necessary to apply his mind), and otherwise living the easy, protected, rather narrow but not particularly luxurious life of the rich landed aristocracy of the day. Nevertheless, he must have taken a quite special fancy to Thomas, whose social standing was by no means the equal of his own, and at a time when his caste was a severely exclusive one; for in the spring

[1] Letters, I, 19.*
[2] *Ibid.*, II, 105.
[3] *Ibid.*, 61.
[4] I, 212.

of 1800, when he was twelve years old and Thomas fifteen, he invited the latter to accompany him to Ireland, on a visit to his father at Westport.

This expedition was one of great importance in Thomas' young life, for in the course of it he caught his first glimpse of London and, at Frogmore and in Dublin, made the one and only acquaintance of his life with the great of the land.

The first step of the journey was to Eton, from which the two boys visited Frogmore, where they accidentally met His Majesty George III strolling in the garden. After inquiring after Lord Westport's mother and grandmother, the King condescended so far as to ask Thomas some questions about himself and his family. These Thomas answered without undue shyness, adding that his family had been in England since the Conquest. Asked if he were going to Eton, he said that he thought so, but was not sure; upon which the King spoke some words in praise of that school.

The impact of London upon Thomas was tremendous. The chapter of the *Autobiographic Sketches* entitled "The Nation of London" describes, with all the rhapsodical passion and discursiveness of which De Quincey was capable, the awful and fascinating effect of the noisy and teeming city upon the sensitive plate of his mind; and, in a characteristically poetic image, he expresses his emotion as the idea of "vast droves of cattle, suppose upon the great north road, all with their heads directed to London, and expounding the size of the attracting body, together with the forces of its attractive power, by the never-ending succession of these droves, and the remoteness from the capital of the lines upon which they were moving."[1] Changing the simile and extending it, he continues: "Already at three stages distance . . . the dim presentment of some vast capital reaches you obscurely, and like a misgiving. This blind sympathy with a mighty but unseen object, some vast magnetic range of Alps, in your neighbourhood, continues to increase, you know not how. . . . Launched upon this final stage, you soon begin to feel yourself entering the stream as it were of a Norwegian *maelstrom*; and the stream at length becomes the rush of a cataract. What is meant by the Latin word *trepidatio*? Not anything peculiarly connected with panic; it belongs to the hurrying to and fro of a coming battle, as of a coming flight;

[1] I, 178.

to a marriage festival as much as to a massacre; *agitation* is the nearest English word." [1]

When actually inside the city, this agitation gave place to a less delicious emotion—one which he came to know thoroughly by and by; that of solitude in the midst of a crowd. "Faces never-ending"; "eyes innumerable, that have 'no speculation' in their orbs . . . and hurrying figures of men and women weaving to and fro, with no apparent purposes intelligible to a stranger, seeming like a mask of maniacs, or, oftentimes, like a pageant of phantoms": these, combined with the "monotonous awe and blind sense of mysterious grandeur and Babylonian confusion, which seemed to pursue and to invest the whole equipage of human life",[2] distressed and frightened him.

Having inspected St. Paul's, and mounted into the Whispering Gallery, Thomas and Lord Westport set off back to Eton, stopping on the way at the house of Lady Howe (Lord Howe had been Westport's maternal grandfather), where Thomas had the unexpected gratification of hearing his prize translation of the Horace Ode praised by Lord Morton.

Once more at Eton, the two boys attended a ball at Frogmore, a spectacle which, curiously enough, filled Thomas with "the very grandest form of passionate sadness." [3] The reason he gives for this impression reveals his mind moving again, as at the death-bed of Elizabeth, in a world of universal symbols. "The reason," he says, "is . . . that such a scene presents a sort of mask of human life, with its whole equipage of pomps and glories, its luxury of sight and sound, its hours of golden youth, and the interminable revolution of ages hurrying after ages, and one generation treading upon the flying footsteps of another; whilst all the while the overruling music attempers the mind to the spectacle, the subject to the object, the beholder to the vision." [4] Such detachment, in the midst of a scene of festivity, argues the melancholy of an irretrievable loneliness.

The Irish visit, which now followed without further dallying, was a complete success from every point of view. The sea crossing, which Thomas described to his mother in one of his elaborately articulate letters,[5] was accomplished in a style which obviously im-

[1] I, 180. [2] I, 182. [3] I, 197.
[4] I, 198. [5] Letters, I, 26.

pressed him by its grandeur. Largeaux, the French valet, and Mr. Grace, Lord Westport's tutor, prim and hortatory, saw to it that the travellers had every possible comfort. Two incidents distinguished the journey. One concerned Mr. Grace, who, inexplicably, took offence at something that was said or done by the boys, withdrew into huffy silence, and left Lord Westport's service immediately on arriving in Ireland. Nor was it ever discovered what had offended him. One can only conjecture that the two boys, who had, while in England, invented a secret language called Ziph (shades of *Gombroon*!), may have tactlessly conversed in this tongue in the presence of Mr. Grace, and that the latter, with the touchiness of his kind, had taken it as an insult.

The second incident occurred during the night on board the ship. As it was hot, Thomas and Lord Westport slept on deck, in view of a carriage in which a beautiful woman, whom they had noticed during the day, was passing the night. Suddenly, in the starlight, the boys saw a man steal across the deck and enter the carriage, the door of which was silently opened to receive him. Their first impulse was to raise the alarm, but, moved by some vague feeling, they did not do so. Half perceiving the truth, they were much shocked and decided to say nothing of what they had seen.[1] Next day they reached Westport.

John Denis Browne, third Earl of Altamont (later first Marquis of Sligo) and father of Lord Westport, was a very charming, cultivated man. He took an instant liking to Thomas, whose exquisite manners and precocious, scholarly mind appealed to him as being all that he could desire in the way of companionship for his son. Thomas describes him as a " very fat man, and so lame that he is obliged to have two servants to support him whenever he stirs ". Of his character: " He is a very sensible man, I think, and one of the most loyal persons I know. . . . He abhors the very idea of gambling. . . . He never swears, because he thinks it both a blackguard and a foolish practice." [2]

This admirable, and moreover very kind man made Thomas free of his house, his library and his horses. Thomas thought more of the first and third than of the second, which he pronounced

[1] The lady was Lady Conyngham, afterwards the mistress of George IV. De Quincey met her, a few days later, in the streets of Dublin, and received a second shock at learning of her situation as a wife and mother.

[2] Japp, 33 ff.

to be inferior in quantity to the one in his mother's house at Bath, "and as to *quality*, it is the worst I ever saw."[1] But he managed to console himself with *Rasselas*, the discouraging tone of which did not, however, prevent him from thoroughly enjoying himself from morning till night. Indeed, his day was a remarkably full one. The two boys rose between four and six, after which Thomas read the Bible, while Westport busied himself with copies and ciphers. Breakfast was taken at nine, in the company of Lord Altamont, and then the boys were left to pass the time in riding ("wild, hard-mouthed horses") and swimming till dinner-time, which was at two or three. In the afternoon Thomas read and wrote again, while Westport amused himself with games. Supper (bread and milk and fruit) was at nine, after which the boys went to bed.[2] It will be noticed that Thomas was the more studious of the two; yet his letters home, as well as the *Autobiographic Sketches*, mention other, less usual entertainments. He was present, for instance, at the installation of Six Knights of Saint Patrick, among them Lord Altamont, which took place in the Cathedral of the saint in Dublin. The magnificence of the spectacle made a profound impression upon him; yet he watched it as a detached observer, entirely free from a snobbish desire to appear as if moving of right in these circles. He took considerable interest in the Rebellion, but was sceptical of the Irish account of it. They "speak of it as we should of a Birmingham riot,"[3] he wrote to his mother, then passed on to reply to some anxious inquiry she had made about his bathing. Indeed, there are signs that he was at last beginning to chafe under the continual assaults of his mother's fussy domination. "Much as I wish to hear from you, my dear mother," he ventures to hint, "I am sorry you should spend that time in writing to me which, I am sure, your health much requires to be spent in rest."[4] Mrs. De Quincey, however, did not—at that or any other time—take the hint, and Thomas' sense of propriety was much too delicate to allow him to proffer it a second time, or in less equivocal terms.

He also made the ascent of Croagh Patrick, and it was in the course of this expedition that he fell in love, after a highly characteristic fashion. The lady was a Miss Blake, sister to the Lady Erroll of the day. She was a bright, intelligent girl, and she and

[1] Japp, 37. [2] Letters, I, 28. [3] Japp, 38. [4] Japp, 39.

Thomas discussed the English poets together. The occasion seemed to him to mark an epoch in his life: "From that moment when women cease to be regarded with carelessness, and when the ideal of womanhood, in its total pomp of loveliness and purity, dawns like some vast aurora upon the mind, boyhood has ended. . . ."[1] That sentence establishes the surprise and its intensity; but a later one in the same passage tells us the exact nature of the emotion he experienced. "Ever after throughout the period of youth, I was jealous of my own demeanour, reserved and awestruck in the presence of women; reverencing often, not so much *them*, as my own ideal of women latent in them. For I carried about with me the idea, to which often I seemed to see an approximation, of

> a perfect woman, nobly planned
> To warn, to comfort, and command."[2]*

This attitude to women, distant and adoring, with respect uppermost among the emotions felt, was the typical neo-romantic attitude of the generation to which De Quincey belonged. It was, allowing for differences of temperament, the attitude of Coleridge, Southey, Wordsworth—even of Shelley; it removed woman outside the range of realistic considerations, making her finally, with the advance of the century, a creature of almost mythical sweetness and light, and deprived her, by the same token, of the vital qualities of action and thought to which she had as much right as man. The strength of this romantic desire, on the part of the men of that period, created women in its own image—women who were passive enough to live their lives in a stifling atmosphere compounded of exaggerated adoration and insulting intellectual neglect; and in few cases was a woman found who had strength and passion enough to refuse so ambiguous a position. In this way, Thomas was, and remained, a man of his time. But in his case another cause operated to strengthen the prevailing attitude to women—his feeling for his mother. So entirely had she come to represent womanhood for him, that he was unable, both then and later, to conceive love for a woman except under the characteristics—respect, domestic authority, protective affection (in that order)—in which she herself exhibited her sex. And if

[1] I, 319. [2] I, 325.

his marriage was to begin under somewhat different auspices, it very soon settled down into the above pattern.

The attachment to Miss Blake, being of a purely romantic order, faded almost immediately; and it is noticeable that, though he mentions meeting her in a letter to his mother, he forbears to confess to any emotion concerning her.

6

On returning from Ireland, at the end of October, Thomas and Lord Westport separated at Birmingham, the former proceeding to Northamptonshire to stay for a time with his mother's friend, Lady Carbery, at her estate at Laxton. This lady, who was the daughter of a Colonel Henry Watson, and had married George Evans, fourth Baron Carbery, in 1792, had known Thomas since he was a baby, and had always taken an affectionate interest in his progress. "Her understanding," he says,[1] "was justly reputed a fine one; but, in general, it was calculated to win respect rather than love, for it was masculine and austere, with very little toleration for sentiment or romance." Yet her treatment of Thomas shows that she was considerably more warm-hearted and imaginative than this cool description implies.

Riding, and the reading and discussion of the Greek Testament, were the order of the day at Laxton, during Thomas' visit, for Lady Carbery, in her capacity of blue-stocking, made use of the young scholar's proficiency in Greek to learn something of that language from him. But, from Thomas' point of view, by far the most important event of this time was the three-cornered dispute over the future of his education, which raged between himself, his mother, and his guardians. This dispute had begun while he was still at Westport and, as its upshot was instrumental in the tragi-comedy that followed, the opinions that flew to and fro on the subject deserve quotation.

George III, Lord Altamont and his son were all, as we have seen, in favour of Thomas' going to Eton; and Mrs. De Quincey also approved of the plan, though without much fervour. Thomas, however, was oddly set against it. He gives his reasons for this,

[1] I, 329.

as well as his considered opinion of his education, in a passage which is remarkable for its lucidity and balance: "To Eton I am sure you will not send me. As for any private school, if you knew what a dislike I have to them, how miserable I feel at the thought of going to one, you would not, I think, wish me. It is not for any particular inconveniences, which are *generally* met with at private schools, that I abhor them so much—it is for a fault . . . which cannot be remedied, which is essential to the very nature of the school. I mean its *being* private. Few private schools are much superior, even in point of *learning*, to Mr Spencer's. But the thing which makes me most unhappy at a private school is there being no emulation, no ambition, nothing to contend for—no honours to excite one. This was exactly the case at Mr Spencer's. I was at the head of the school the whole time I was there. No one but myself could make verses, and all those kind of things; but then I had no one to contend with, nor anything higher to aspire to. The consequence was that my powers entirely flagged, my mind became quite dormant in comparison of what it was at the Bath Grammar School. I had no one to praise me, to spur me on, or to help me. Nobody (except the boys) knew I was at the top of the school. With them it was considered no merit to be the head-boy, and *had* it, I should have derived but little pleasure from the applause of those who, with few exceptions, were nearly approaching to idiots. I was often pestered with such questions from the ladies, etc., as 'Are you in the same class with little Emly' (a little boy of about twelve years old, *decidedly* the greatest blockhead I ever saw). In short, *it was*, and always *will* be, as impossible for me to exert myself as much at a private as in a public school, as it would be for a person running for his own amusement to go as quick as if he were running a race or flying from his pursuers. At a private school I have 'little to fear or hope from censure or from praise'. If, then, you let me go to *any* public school, what can be better than the Bath one? The plan pursued there everyone allows to be incomparable. It is a very great improvement, I think, on the Eton method. . . . Of the *learning* it is useless to speak, since you yourself say it is just as you would wish it. If it is the *morals* you object to, are they not as good as at most places? . . . Believe me, my dear mother, if you knew my mind you would see how resolutely bent I am against anything that could give you uneasiness. Any promises you wish I am ready to make. In short, everything you desire me I will do, and only ask for that one thing to go to the Grammar School."[1]

The accents of reasonable indignation, as well as those of pleading, ring loud in this letter, and a sensible mother would have listened to them. But to Mrs. De Quincey argument or opposition on the part of children was simply 'rudeness' and 'insubordination' to which she had no intention of even lending an ear, far less of giving way. Moreover, it must have seemed to her that Thomas had given no very cogent reason for his objection to Eton. This, however, was to be supplied, a few days later. Repeating what Lord Westport had told him of the manners of the school, he reveals his real preoccupation. "Anyone who should *attempt* to differ from the rest of the boys . . . would be literally tormented to death. The first thing they do in such a case as this . . . is to fling the boy into the Thames with ropes tied to him, by which they pull him out, not, however, before he is so nearly dead as to require medical assistance to recover him. You may judge of the discipline of the school when I tell you that a week ago they beat an old porter (in defiance of the masters, some of whom were standing by, and hardly trying to prevent them) with such brutality that his life, I hear, is despaired of. My situation, as a boy on the foundation, would be still more miserable."[2]

These arguments were much better designed to appeal to his mother, and the question of Eton was definitely shelved. But, unfortunately for Thomas, there remained a third possibility—Manchester Grammar School—the suggestion of his guardians, which Mrs. De Quincey now lost no time in taking up. Desperate, and feeling with the obscure but infallible instinct of the young that his whole future was involved in this decision, Thomas attempted to enlist Lady Carbery's sympathy and influence. The former she gave, but refused the latter, urging him to submit. Then, feeling that everyone had failed him and that it was useless to resist any longer, he gave in. That he did so with a heavy heart is plain from a passage in the *Autobiographic Sketches*. "Misgivingly I went forwards, feeling for ever that, through clouds of thick darkness, I was continually nearing a danger, or was myself

[1] Japp, 40. [2] Letters, I, 37.

a. De Quincey's father
b. De Quincey's mother
c. His brother Richard, known as 'Pink'
d. Thomas De Quincey, aged 16

By courtesy of the Misses Bairdsmith

perhaps wilfully provoking a trial, before which my constitutional despondency would cause me to lie down without a struggle." [1]

His sudden yielding to a decision that his soul told him was the wrong one, is to be attributed not so much to a conviction that it was wrong to oppose his mother and his guardians as to a deep-rooted, fatalistic sense that life was against him and that, whatever he might do, he could not escape from the retribution that was the inevitable outcome of his incapacity in the face of practical life. As we have had occasion to observe,[2] this feeling was among the earliest and strongest that he knew, and it developed into a depressive mania that struck him down again and again in after-life, whenever circumstances were such that he could not deal with them by the force of his intellect alone. Like another solitary dreamer, living a hundred years later but in not very different circumstances—Franz Kafka—he was bestridden by just those nightmares of hostility, and of vague, gloomy apprehension, of which it is most difficult to free the soul afflicted by them, even when outside help can be relied upon; for it is a characteristic of this kind of loneliness that it can never bring itself to believe in the sincerity of disinterested love. In Thomas' case, delicate health, shyness, and visionary sensibility were as food to this tragic obsession.

Yet there was much in his character which fought the nightmare and indeed prevented it from ever overwhelming him completely: the serious, comically sententious charm which so delighted Lord Altamont that he continued for some time to correspond with Thomas, after he had left Westport, and to take a real interest in his welfare;[3] the personal beauty whose appealing quality had won him the favour of the mill-girls and which never failed him, even in old age; the eagerness and variety of his response to experience, which, together with his astonishing intellectual grasp of all kinds of subjects, provided his mind with a perpetual outlet from introspection; his real interest in human beings. We shall have many an occasion later on to notice the development of these several faculties and the way in which they combined to save him from spiritual wreck. But already they were all present in varying degrees of power and must be borne in mind as we look upon him, when, in this his sixteenth year, unknown to himself, he was on the eve of taking his life into his own hands.

[1] I, 377. [2] See p. 14. [3] See Letters, I, 42 ff.

CHAPTER II

ADVENTURE

I

MANCHESTER Grammar School, which Thomas entered early in 1801, was founded by a bishop of Exeter in the sixteenth century. It was very well endowed and on the way to become richer still, and it held exhibition scholarships at Brasenose College, Oxford [1]—a fact which somewhat mitigated Thomas' aversion to it. This aversion, after he had become established in the school, centred itself on the headmaster. This man, whose name was Charles Lawson, was no mean scholar; but he was pompous and pedantic and seems to have been a bad judge of the capacities of the young to absorb learning. He suffered from an incurable disease, which made the accomplishment of his duties such a burden that he was obliged to perform them as far as possible all in one piece, if he were to get through them at all; thus depriving the boys of their proper hours for meals and recreations. He was hasty and choleric, in the manner of the pedagogues of his day, addressing the scholars in terms such as "Psha! Blockhead!"—a practice which offended Thomas very much. Again, as in the case of Samuel Hall, one detects a certain unfairness in De Quincey's account of this man—an echo of the nervous irritation which pervaded his life at the time, but which had many causes other than the personality of the headmaster. In any case, there is something sniggeringly birdlike and callous about the fashion in which he describes Mr. Lawson's infirmity: "He still had his dying to do: he was in arrear as to that: else all was finished." [2] This is the tone that occasionally crept into his reminiscences of Coleridge and Wordsworth, and which so much offended their relations. It is disagreeable, if understandable.

De Quincey admits that he enjoyed many privileges at Manchester

[1] III, 249 [2] III, 249.

Grammar School. He was allowed a room of his own; he joined the Manchester library; he was even given the opportunity, at his own request, of learning to play the piano. But his pretensions in this latter field were rather exorbitant, and finding that the exertion of playing destroyed his pleasure in the music, he gave it up.[1]

The private room was possibly an error of judgment: it increased his habit of solitude. He was conscious of this danger, for he says: "the specific evil that already weighed upon me with a sickening oppression was the premature expansion of my mind, and, as a foremost consequence, intolerance of boyish society."[2] This solitude and withdrawal from the common life of his fellows naturally fostered the nervous fears and the feeling of irritated boredom with the life of the school to which he was in any case subject. It also strengthened his timid preference for adult society.

That his unhappiness did not immediately result in some violent gesture was mainly due to Lady Carbery. The latter had come to Manchester to be near a great friend of hers, a Mrs. Schreiber,[3] who was dangerously ill. With her usual kindness and an acute intuition of Thomas' present needs, she enlisted the interest of the Revd. John Clowes, that gentle Swedenborgian who had been subjected, at Mrs. De Quincey's dinner-table, to the atheistic assault of the 'Female Infidel', Mrs. Lee. This amiable eccentric was a writer of tendencious sermons and tracts, one of which, *The Caterpillar and the Gooseberry Bush*, is mentioned by Japp as calculated to enforce in children the government of the passions. He did not, however, attempt to convert Thomas to Swedenborgianism, but instead discussed Greek and Roman literature with him and—what was even more welcome to the boy—gave him the free run of his library to sit and read in. It was probably this interior of muffled dignity, with its organ and stained-glass windows, its atmosphere of safety and remoteness from the world, which kept Thomas from breaking away altogether—at any rate for the time being. He also added to his growing library, for it was one of the eccentricities of the old man to give away all his books, one by one, to his friends, as a method of weaning himself from

[1] III, 270. [2] I, 381; III, 27.

[3] This lady had acted as chaperon to Lady Carbery, when the latter was a girl. (See I, 351.)

the world he thought he must soon leave. (He did not in fact leave it until 1831.)[1]

But Mr. Clowes was not Thomas' only consolation for the rigours of school life. Lady Carbery herself gave much of her time to him, having obtained leave for him to spend four or five hours every evening in her drawing-room. She taught him some Hebrew, and in return he read her *The Ancient Mariner*, but without much success.[2]

Further entertainment was provided by Dr. White, Mrs. Schreiber's physician (he had also attended Elizabeth De Quincey), who was reputed to possess a mummy of one of his patients, a lady, who had bequeathed her body to him on the condition that he should unveil her face, in the presence of two witnesses, once a year. To this end, he was said to have enclosed the mummy in the case of a grandfather clock, so that the head, concealed by a curtain, should appear where the clock face once had been. But though Thomas made many attempts to find this clock in Dr. White's house, he was never successful.[3]

There was also a singular group of people known as the Liverpool Literary Coterie, with whom Thomas came in contact while staying in that town with one Mr. Clarke, a travelled connoisseur of pictures and Greek literature. This group consisted of Dr. Currie,[4] the biographer of Burns; William Roscoe,[5] an historian and poet and miscellaneous writer on Italian subjects; and William Shepherd,[6] the Unitarian minister of Gateacre, who was also a critic of Italian literature. De Quincey afterwards[7] wrote of these good people in a waspish manner which evoked an acrimonious reply from Mr. Shepherd, containing references to Opium.[8] The article in

[1] II, 113 ff. [2] I, 394 [3] I, 388.

[4] James Currie (1756–1905), a Scottish physician, who after spending some time in Virginia, returned to England to take his degree in medicine and eventually settled in Liverpool. He wrote a report on fevers and was at one time well known for his official biography of Burns. (*Encyl. Brit.*)

[5] William Roscoe (1753–1831) was at one time an attorney and later partner in a banking business in Liverpool. His chequered career, during which he was Whig M.P. for Liverpool (1806–7), ended in bankruptcy. He wrote a *Life of Lorenzo de' Medici*, edited Pope and wrote a number of original poems. (*Dic. of Nat. Biog.*)

[6] William Shepherd (1768–1847), a philanthropic Radical. Wrote a *Life of Poggio Bra[illegible]olini* and other kindred works. (*Dic. of Nat. Biog.*)

[7] II, 122 ff.

[8] Tait's Magazine, May 1837. A letter has since come to light, from De Quincey to William Tait, in which the former expresses consternation at having learnt, after the appearance of his article, that Shepherd was still alive. He adds that he hopes to make reparation in a later article.

the *Autobiographic Sketches* which deals with this group of people dismisses them as "literary dons"[1] living in a stuffy atmosphere of mutual back-patting, accuses Shepherd (who was still alive) of coarse buffoonery, and pokes fun at Roscoe for his poem urging mothers to suckle their babies and for the conventionality of his diction. These strictures, almost certainly exaggerated (Coleridge's opinion of Roscoe was "a man of the most fascinating manners"),[2] were simply the result of the dark glasses through which De Quincey afterwards regarded the whole of this period of his life. At the time, Mr. Clarke's house was probably scarcely less of a solace to him than Mr. Clowes'.

Meanwhile Mrs. Schreiber died and Lady Carbery removed herself from Manchester, retiring "like some golden pageant amongst the clouds; thick darkness succeeded; the ancient torpor reestablished itself, and my health grew distressingly worse."[3] The severe régime of Mr. Lawson meant overwork, lack of exercise, bad air and rushed meals. Thomas' internal constitution, never of the strongest, began to give way under the strain. His nervousness became worse and worse, which in turn reacted unfavourably on his digestion. His liver became torpid and this again begot depression of spirits. Thus the vicious circle was complete. In despair he had recourse to the advice of an old apothecary, who had only one medicine which he prescribed for all complaints. This appalling draught "must have suggested itself to him when prescribing for a tiger;"[4] it only made Thomas worse, irritating his sensitive internal organs till he was nearly mad from depression and pain.

Now began a new dispute with his mother, conducted in a series of long letters, urgent but admirably level-headed on his side, monitory and unconvincing on hers. He complains that he has now no house to go to in Manchester where he can feel really at home. Of course there was the Kelsalls'; but "Mr. Kelsall and I have not one idea in common. . . . Naturally I am fond of solitude, but everyone has times when he wishes for company. . . ."[5] He goes on to complain of the sordid ubiquity of money in all conversations in Manchester—money, the one subject for which he never had, and never could have, anything but contempt. But

[1] II, 123
[2] *Unpublished Letters of S. T. C.*, I, 149.
[3] I, 398.
[4] III, 275.
[5] Japp, 53.

his most cogent arguments occur early in this letter: "I ask whether a person can be happy, or even simply *easy*, who is in a situation which deprives him of *health*, of *society*, of *amusement*, of *liberty*, of *congeniality of pursuits*, and which, to complete the precious picture, admits of no *variety*. I think you will hardly say he can. . . ."

But Mrs. De Quincey could and did say so; for she was, as De Quincey himself says, "predisposed to think ill of all causes that required many words."[1] It is, indeed, plain that she did not properly read her son's letters, since she merely replied: "You have urged your misery and you will urge it again; but cannot you tell me what it is?"[2] She dreads his coming home, to spend his time in "desultory reading" and slacking about, obedient to no discipline; and she threatens, if all else fails, to invoke his guardian, Samuel Hall, to deal with the situation.

The assumption that, left to his own resources, he must inevitably give himself up to a life of idleness, must have been peculiarly irritating to a boy of Thomas' industrious turn of mind; and it was no doubt the feeling of despair at his utter inability to make his mother realize what sort of person he really was, that precipitated his final decision to dispense with further argument and run away. However, he contained himself yet a little and wrote again patiently to his mother, repeating what he had already told her of his reasons for wishing to leave Manchester, and adding significantly: "The third and last negative advantage attached to my remaining at school—'that it will keep me from unrestrained liberty'—I suspect to have more weight with you than all the rest put together; and yet perhaps it is the one which, of all the others, is most palpably specious."[3]

This letter produced no more effect than the first, and when Mrs. De Quincey wrote again on June 2nd. 1802, it was plain that matters were approaching a crisis. "I cannot see the force of your arguments, not with a view to combat them; I might as well engage Don Quichotte's windmills."[4] And she concludes, as if obscurely aware that she is making no headway: "I cannot help it, my dear, unhappy child, if these expressions excite your hatred; I am sure nothing but agreement with you is likely to do

[1] III, 315.
[2] Letters, I, 77.
[3] Letters, I, 80.
[4] *Ibid.*, 84.

otherwise. I am equally sure they arise from the best exercise of my understanding, in a humble dependence on divine direction, which has long ago brought me to know that the human mind is as much in ruins as its will. I shall never cease to pray for you, and never cease to love you most truly, as I do at this moment when my affection is called to a very painful effort."

Then, quite suddenly, as the next letter (written four days later) shows, Mrs. De Quincey gave way. There seems to have been some question of Thomas' going to Oxford, for she mentions the subject in the letter, the whole tone of which is heavy with a sense of grievance. "As you refuse to communicate your views to me, I should have had only to consider whether, under such an extraordinary resolution on your part, I ought to be bound to a promise which was made with hopes of serving you in some just and honourable design, however visionary it might appear to me. But you seem to speak doubtfully of your own wishes to go to college. If you then think your views, whatever they are, may be better served than by going thither, why will you let me give myself the trouble of entering you there, when probably you may quit the situation with the same dissatisfaction you have manifested in every other situation, with the additional inconvenience of giving publicity to your unsteadiness. I will produce the £100 a year. . . ." [1]

From the first sentence I have quoted of this letter, it would seem as if Thomas, in despair of making himself understood by his mother, had at last taken refuge in silence; and that this method had succeeded where explanations had failed. The doubt expressed by her, as to whether he is likely to be any less restless at Oxford than at Manchester, was a shrewd thrust and may have had something to do with Thomas' failure to take up the subject again immediately.

The extent to which Mrs. De Quincey misunderstood the sort of boy her son had become may be judged from a letter he wrote to her in 1818. In it there occurs the following passage: "When I was a boy I was possessed by that kind of ambition which with most people is the highest that they ever attain. I planned and projected constantly in the ordinary spirit of ordinary minds to raise myself to high stations and honour in the State. With boy-

[1] Letters, I, 86.

hood these purposes forsook me; and I gradually substituted a different ambition . . . that by long and painful labour, combining with such faculties as God had given me, I might become the intellectual benefactor of my species."[1] That he should have exactly realized this ambition is a remarkable example of the truth that there are very few ambitions (except those connected with love) which perpetual effort will not eventually achieve. That De Quincey should, in the same letter, have become more precise, centering his ambition on education, philosophy and mathematics, to which subjects he was not, in fact, destined to make any very remarkable contribution, does not alter the general character of his aim.

Driven back upon his own resources, Thomas made his decision: whatever might happen, his seventeenth birthday should not find him still at Manchester.[2] For one more month he delayed his escape, hoping perhaps that something would turn up from the direction of his family. When nothing of the sort occurred, he began to make his plans. First, there was the question of money; and as there is some mystery which beclouds, from this point of view, the next year of his life—a mystery which has been hinted at but never cleared up—it is necessary here to describe an event which occurred at the time when Thomas was planning his escape.[3] He received a letter through the post-office at Chester (where his mother was then living) addressed to "Monsieur Monsieur [*sic*] de Quincey, Chester". The letter had been posted in Hamburg but, on opening it, Thomas found that it was dated from some place in Normandy. He was unable, so he says, to decipher the contents, but guessed at once that the real addressee must be not himself but some member of the French branch of his family who had come to Chester, probably to teach French, and who now, owing to the Treaty of Amiens, wished to return to France. The envelope, however, contained, not only the letter, but also a draught on Smith, Payne and Smith for the sum of forty guineas. For a moment Thomas tried to think that perhaps the letter was really intended for him—a lucky windfall in time of need; but found himself unable to preserve this illusion. Thereupon, one would have thought, the simplest thing to have done would have been to return the letter to the post-office with the usual explanations.

[1] Letters, II, 111. [2] III, 280. [3] III, 285 ff.

But he did not do this, for reasons which seem curiously specious. "Throughout this farewell day," he says,[1] "I was unable to carve out any opportunity for going up to the Manchester Post-office, and, without a distinct explanation in my own person, exonerating myself, on the written acknowledgement of the post-office, from all farther responsibility, I was most reluctant to give up the letter." So he decided that, when he made his escape, instead of starting for the Lake district, to which he felt attracted by the prospect of meeting Wordsworth, he would proceed to Chester and deliver up the letter there. We shall see how this affair turned out.

Having no more than £2 of his own, he wrote to Lady Carbery and asked for a loan of £5. With her usual kindness she sent £10, at the same time hinting that he might consider it a gift.[2] Out of this he confided £3 to a friend, to dole out in tips to the school servants.

And now, as the moment for irrevocable action drew near, he became filled with a mixture of sadness and fear. "I lingered; lingered as under some sense of dim perplexity, or even of relenting love for the very captivity itself which I was making so violent an effort to abjure, but more intelligibly for all the external objects, living or inanimate, by which that captivity had been surrounded and gladdened."[3] He looked for the last time at the picture of a beautiful woman which hung over the mantelpiece in his study; he attended prayers and gazed on the detested Mr. Lawson in an agony of sadness and tremulous regret, recalling as he did so, not those aspects of his past life that had made the place odious to him, but only those hours in which he had known a tranquil happiness.

Yet there was joy and excitement also in his heart. "Already I trod by anticipation the sweet pastoral hills, already I breathed gales of the everlasting mountains, that to my feelings blew from the garden of Paradise; and in that vestibule of an earthly heaven it was no more possible for me to see vividly or in any lingering detail the thorny cares which might hereafter multiply around me than amongst the roses of June. . . . I could gather depression from the glooms of the last December."[4] (This was before he had received the forty-guinea letter and was still determined on making for the Lakes.) It was a moment of real spiritual release, but also of heart-searching uncertainty. Let there be no mistake

[1] III, 288. [2] III, 280. [3] III, 289. [4] III, 279.

on this head: the decision to run away from Manchester Grammar School meant far more to Thomas than it would have meant to an ordinarily independent boy, who should have reached that decision by the road of adventurous desire. Thomas was not by nature an adventurous character, and the knowledge that he was about to take a step which would involve fending for himself entirely, must have been an agony to him who had always been surrounded by protection and care. The realization that he had escaped, not only from the oppressive régime of the school, but also out of the world of books and dreams into the real world of action and free choice, can only have come to him *afterwards*, when he had already started on his travels. There is no indication that he was conscious of it before departure.

Almost at the moment of escape, a warning vision came to him. As he sat in his study, looking round at the objects he was never to see again, he heard a voice whisper to him, just as Westport's voice had sounded to him in the Whispering Gallery of St. Paul's: "Once leave this house, and a Rubicon is placed between thee and all possibility of return. Thou wilt not say that what thou doest is altogether approved in thy secret heart. Even now thy conscience speaks against it in sullen whispers; but at the other end of thy long life-gallery that same conscience will speak to thee in volleying thunders."[1]* This visionary prophecy, like so many others in De Quincey's life, was to be fulfilled.

The actual escape was enlivened by an incident of pure farce. In addition to the bundle which he proposed to take with him on the road, Thomas had also a large heavy trunk, containing all the rest of his belongings, which he proposed to leave with a carrier, to be sent on to him later. This trunk had to be got down the stairs, and, as he was not strong enough to shoulder it himself, he prevailed on the headmaster's groom, with whom he was a favourite, to do this for him.

Rising at half-past three, he looked out with relief on to a fine, cloudless July dawn with a crimson sky. The groom arrived, hoisted the box on to his shoulder and set off down the stairs, followed by Thomas. But the trunk was extremely heavy and unwieldy, and, just at the most perilous moment of the descent, when they were nearing the headmaster's own quarters, it slipped

[1] III, 297.

from the man's back and, gathering impetus with each successive step of the stairs, fell with a resounding crash against the headmaster's bedroom door.

Thomas instantly decided that all was lost, particularly as the groom, adding insult to injury, followed up the crash with a loud burst of laughter. But, miraculously, nothing happened; not a sound came from behind the door. Mr. Lawson's disease had, for once in a way, produced a sleep so deep that not even that thunderous bang had been able to wake him.

The rest of the descent was accomplished without noise, and taking up his bundle, with Euripides in one pocket and a copy of Wordsworth's poems in the other, Thomas set off.[1]*

2

As already stated, his original intention had been to walk to the Lakes, there to make the acquaintance of the poet who by now meant more to him than any other writer of modern times. But now he had three reasons for changing his plan: (1) he was beginning to feel ashamed at the idea of appearing before Wordsworth in the character of a fugitive;[2] (2) he wished to render up the forty-guinea letter to the Chester post-office; and (3) he wanted badly to see his sister Mary again, who was living with their mother at the Priory, Chester. It is evident that he intended to carry out the second and third of these plans and then to leave Chester without the knowledge of his mother. But events did not go according to plan.

It took him two days to walk to Chester. Soon after leaving Manchester he passed through Altrincham, in the market-place of which he renewed memories of looking out of a window there with his nurse, one sunny morning fourteen years before. That night he slept at a farm-house, and reached Chester the following day. But before going to the Priory he stopped on the bank of the river Dee to watch the *Bore*—the curious tidal wave which occurs periodically in some large rivers; and here, on the dyke (called the Cop) which ran beside the river, occurred the second act in the drama of the forty-guinea letter. What he *says* happened

[1] III, 298 ff. [2] III, 284.

is as follows: While waiting for the arrival of the Bore and worrying in his mind over the question of what to do with the letter, he noticed a woman also standing waiting to see the Bore. Though she was an entire stranger to him, he went up to her, explained the matter of the letter and asked her to take it to the post-office for him. She agreed at once and took the letter, afterwards returning to tell him that she had acquitted herself successfully of the mission which he had entrusted to her. Thus, says De Quincey, he was able, on his arrival at his mother's house, to set at rest the anxieties and suspicions of his family, which had already been aroused by a messenger from the post-office.[1] My reasons for suspecting this story to be largely a fabrication* will be given later on, when the result of the whole affair enables us to view it in perspective.[2]

Thomas' attempt to see his sister Mary without the knowledge of the rest of the household was frustrated by the servants, who informed his uncle, Colonel Penson, of his presence. Mary, as it turned out, was by this time searching for him at Ambleside, whither an express, sent from Manchester to Chester to inform Mrs. De Quincey of her son's elopement, had proceeded in hopes of catching him.

The presence of Colonel Penson was most opportune. This man, whom De Quincey calls "commonplace . . . in the character of his intellect," [3] but, as a man of action, out of the common, evidently sympathized with his nephew's escapade, and did his best to persuade his sister to behave reasonably in the circumstances. It is plain from De Quincey's own account of the incident that, had it not been for his uncle's good offices, his mother would have taken her usual line of refusing to listen to anything he had to say and treating his behaviour as mere insubordination. The poor woman was, indeed, in consternation. In spite of this, however, she offered to allow him to stay at Chester, but in such a chilling manner that he promptly declined, foreseeing her silent, nagging disapproval.[4] The alternative proposal was that he should wander about in Wales for a time—an idea which did not make its appeal to him in vain. Colonel Penson persuaded his sister to give her son a guinea a week, to be paid to him as long as he

[1] III, 302 ff.
[2] See p. 48 ff.
[3] I, 402.
[4] III, 316.

kept in touch with his family; and, with this assurance, Thomas took his leave of the Priory and started out upon the second stage of his adventure.

Having paid a visit to the ladies of Llangollen,[1] he spent some time in Bangor, whence he wrote to, and received an answer from, Lord Sligo.[2] The occasion of his leaving this town was a row with his landlady, in the course of which Thomas displayed touchiness and lack of humour. The good woman had been in the service of the Bishop of Bangor and was wont to make the most of the fact. One day, during one of her long stories about her former employer, she told Thomas how the Bishop had warned her to be cautious in her choice of lodgers and how she had replied, referring to Thomas: "O my lord . . . I really don't think this young gentleman is a swindler, because——" But before she could proceed any further, Thomas had risen "in a tumult of indignation" and rushed out of the house.[3]

Thereafter he wandered indiscriminately over the wild, bleak countryside (it was by now November), forsaking the inns, which he found too expensive for his meagre purse, to camp in the open, at first in an inadequate tent, and then—finding the tent stuffy—under the sky itself, with the tent, rolled up, for a pillow. When the weather became too bad, he lodged with whomsoever would take him in, paying for their hospitality by writing business and even love letters for the illiterate peasants. In the latter he was remarkably successful. "I contrived," he says, "so to temper my expressions as to reconcile the gratification of both feelings [kindness and maidenly pride]: and they were as much pleased with the way in which I had expressed their thoughts, as (in their simplicity) they were astonished at my having so readily discovered them."[4] But when the parents of these girls found out what he had been doing, they scowled; and he thought it better to go.

From these weeks of aimless and lonely wandering only two figures emerge. The one is an astrologer, who predicted that Thomas' hair would turn red and that he would have twenty-

[1] Miss Ponsonby and Lady Eleanor Butler. These clever, eccentric women had severed all connection with their homes and gone to live together in the wilds of Wales, in defiance of public opinion. Their defiance was highly successful and won them visits from many remarkable people of the time.

[2] Letters, I, 49. [3] III, 322. [4] III, 336.

seven children, whom he would desert.[1] This extravagance did not, curiously enough, lead Thomas to conclude that astrology was rubbish, but merely that it was useless because of the impossibility of predicting dates with accuracy. The other chance acquaintance whom he made at this time was a German called De Haren, who gave him some lessons in the language and introduced him to the works of Jean Paul Richter, an author who was to have a profound influence on his literary style.

Now began the period, which lasted for about sixteen weeks,[2] of his greatest hardships. He had almost no money, having suddenly decided not to continue to apply to his guardians for the allowance of £1 a week, in case they should discover his whereabouts and attempt to force him to return.[3] So, rather than risk an eventuality which, from his own account, he had no reason whatever to fear, he proceeded to suffer sixteen weeks of hunger and privation of the severest kind, in Wales and afterwards in London, in the depths of winter, not always with a roof to his head, and a prey to solitude, illness and vague terrors of the most desolating description.

Why did he do this? Here we touch on the only definite mystery in De Quincey's life, a series of circumstances which has never been properly explained and of which his own explanation is the least plausible.

To begin with, if he has told us the whole truth, he had no grounds for thinking that his guardians would wish to interrupt his liberty. They had, so far as we know, shown no signs of doing so and had continued to send him his £1 a week regularly, until prevented from doing so by ignorance of his whereabouts. Even supposing that he had had reason to fear such a course on their part, he would, at so great a distance from them, have had ample time to disappear, the moment any hint of pursuit reached his ears. And does it seem really likely that a boy of Thomas' temperament should have been driven to such hysterical lengths by the mere prospect of being brought back to a home to which he had already gone, of his own free will, at the outset of his escapade?

It will be seen that I am trying to suggest a hidden motive for this fear of discovery and for the utter lack of proportion between his description of these weeks and the reason he gives for having

[1] See *Sortilege and Astrology*, XIII, 259.
[2] *Confessions* (1823), p. 38.
[3] I, 399.

supported them. But at the outset I wish to make it clear that the solution I propose is offered only tentatively and with all the reservations called for by an entire lack of conclusive evidence. It has merely seemed to me, after mature thought, not only to fit in with various hints and inconsistencies embedded in De Quincey's own account of the affair, but also to be, on the whole, psychologically more acceptable than the frankly unbelievable solution given by himself.

My suggestion is, succinctly, this: That Thomas, on arriving in Chester, did not give up the forty-guinea letter to that obliging woman on the Cop; that there was, in fact, no such woman present when he watched the Bore; that he either threw the letter, then and there, into the river, or that (more probably) he kept it and destroyed it later, after it had become obvious that he could no longer own to the possession of it without acknowledging a felony; and that then, realizing that the truth must have come out, he took refuge in hiding.

Deliberate theft—whether for the purpose of realizing the forty guineas or for any other reason—is, I think, most unlikely. De Quincey, whatever his pecuniary difficulties in later years, was never anything but a scrupulously honest man. His upbringing, if nothing else, would have sufficed to guard him from so crude a procedure as forging a cheque, quite apart from the fact that nothing that we know of in his character or life would warrant such a supposition. But consider the circumstances. He had been suddenly faced, at a moment of crisis, with a tiresome and wholly unexpected complication. He was badly in need of money, when a large sum had seemed to fall from the skies into his lap. True, it did not, on second reading of the letter, appear to be intended for him; yet there it was, in his hand. . . . He must give it back, of course—but how? Would 'they' not suspect that he had meant to steal it, knowing as they did how desperately he needed money? And had he not, perhaps, for a single instant . . . ?

It is by no means uncommon for very young persons, when suddenly confronted by circumstances of awkwardness and embarrassment to which their experience provides no answer, to act not only against all reason but in ways they cannot even explain to themselves. The subsequent memory of such action frightens them so much that they make every effort to forget it—and generally succeed. This is the recognized technique by which the mind defends itself against remorse; and it is, I think, what happened to Thomas. Having failed to take the obvious course (to render the letter to the Manchester post-office) *at once*, his sense of fatality, of an ultimately hostile world—the sense which had made him yield himself, first to William, then to his mother—will now have convinced him that, were he to confess to having kept the letter—even if only for a few days—it would be impossible for him to persuade the authorities that he had done so with no dishonest intent.[1] And so, in a muddle of confused emotion, in which the letter will have assumed a kind of magical, talismanic significance (such is the way with symbols, and this one did, after all, stand for something that was all-important to him at the time) which would urge him, not to give it away, but to preserve its power by keeping it attached to his own person. Then, realizing at last that he had by now committed a felony, in a desperate effort to be rid of the whole odious affair, he took the only course which seemed possible to him—that of disappearing into the blue.

The points on which I have based this theory are seven in number. (1) Why, since De Quincey admits having altered his plans on leaving Manchester with the express intention of taking the letter back to the Chester post-office, did he not do so? What possible grounds could he have had for confiding to the hands of a perfect stranger something so precious that he had not cared to trust even the Manchester post-office with it?[2] (2) If the woman really accepted the letter and did with it as he told her—as he says she did[3]—why did he have to pay £150 on account of the affair, when he came of age, four years later?[4*] (3) This incident is the only one of importance connected with this period that is not only not described, but not even mentioned, either in the early version of the *Confessions* or in the *Autobiographic Sketches*. (4) The account he eventually gave of it, in the 1856 edition of the *Confessions*, is inconsecutive, and is interrupted by digressions and elaborate protestations calculated to blur his real preoccupation and the actual course of events.[5] (5) Why, if his conscience was perfectly clear, did he fly into a passion at the Bangor landlady's harmless joke?[6] (6) The remorse he afterwards expressed for the

[1] III, 289. [2] III, 288. [3] III, 310.
[4] III, 319. [5] III, 285 ff. [6] See p. 47.

whole of this phase of his life [1] is altogether disproportionate (even taking into account the damage to his health) if he had no more real cause for regret than disobedience to his mother—behaviour grounded, as he had made clear in his letters to her, on legitimate discontent. (7) When, in middle and old age, De Quincey sat down to recall facts and events which had occurred in his youth, his memory did not always serve him well, as the friends of Coleridge and Wordsworth indignantly attested. The long habit of opium, the distance of time, and the slight, intermittent persecution-mania to which he was undoubtedly subject, will have combined to create a set of self-justifying illusions round this, the darkest and most perplexed episode in his life. In 1821, when he wrote the first version of the *Confessions*, he was still too young to be able to dwell on the subject at all—far less to explain it away: the wound in his soul had not had time to heal. But by 1856, when he re-edited that amazing document, the whole story was already so old that it had had time to acquire in his mind the colours and lineaments of a romance, and in it the legend, which his subconscious mind had been so painfully building up through the years to cover his fatal error, now slipped into place as though it had always been there. It is common enough for minds to deceive themselves into such beliefs, and the deeper the cause the firmer and more complete is the illusion.

Apart from the lack of direct evidence in support of my case, I can see only one point which seriously militates against it: If, as I believe, Thomas did not return the letter at all, but destroyed it, what became of the prosecution that must have ensued? I suggest that it was hushed up by his family and guardians, and that this process was the origin of the £150 which he had eventually to pay. To hush up the affair would not have been difficult, since Mrs. De Quincey, her brother and the guardians were people of standing, and the real addressee of the letter was in any case a distant relation of the family, who would thus the more easily have been placated by the simple payment by the guardians of the sum due to him. Moreover, Thomas himself was absent and could easily be represented as having merely mislaid the letter, since the cheque had evidently not been cashed. However this may have been, the fact of the £150 charged against him four

[1] III, 271 and *passim*.

years later in the same connection, remains as a direct testimony against the verisimilitude of his own story.

Those to whom the methods of modern psychology are essentially suspect or repugnant will no doubt reject the whole of this exegesis out of hand, as being absurdly far-fetched, as well as malicious. But before doing so they should reflect that experience shows that in circumstances where the motives of action are driven down into the dark places of the soul, the simple explanation is almost never the right one—even where it is consistent, which is here not the case. And for those who do reject it, there remains, after all, De Quincey's own version of the story, of which I have omitted no important detail and which they are at liberty to accept *in toto*—if they can manage to swallow the inconsistencies and confusions which I have shown it to contain.

3

Having decided to plunge yet deeper into his self-imposed exile, Thomas was inevitably attracted by the idea of London. Ever since his one visit to the metropolis, two years previously, his imagination had played round the sights and sounds which had enthralled him there with such a fascinating mixture of terror and delight. So, borrowing twelve guineas from two lawyers with whom he had made friends in the course of his wanderings,[1] he started off on his journey. It was a fine November day, and the soft, distant sunlight affected him with that sadness and resignation that it was so easy for him at all times to evoke. He felt—even as he had felt at Manchester, and much longer ago in the death-chamber of Elizabeth—that all-embracing atmosphere of elegiac farewell, the emotion which the Germans call *Abschiedsstimmung*; and an intensification of his loneliness came over him in the imagined roar of the London traffic.[2]

That night he reached Shrewsbury, where the people of the inn treated him with fantastic munificence, installing him in a disused ball-room, in which there were three chandeliers wrapped in paper and space for two orchestras. Thomas at once imagined the chandeliers uncovered and glittering, the orchestras thronged, and

[1] III, 339. [2] III, 344.

himself seated on a throne; and, when left alone, he pursued this dream for three hours. Then—"I rose from my chair, and with considerable interest looked out into the night. For nearly two hours I had heard fierce winds arising; and the whole atmosphere had, by this time, become one vast laboratory of hostile movements in all directions. Such a chaos, such a distracting wilderness of dim sights, and of those awful 'sounds that live in darkness' . . . never had I consciously witnessed. Rightly, and by a true instinct, had I made my farewell adieus to summer. All through the day, Wales and her grand mountain ranges . . . had divided my thoughts with London. But now rose London—sole, dark, infinite—brooding over the whole capacities of my heart. Other object, other thought, I could not admit. Long before midnight the whole household (with the exception of a solitary waiter) had retired to rest. Two hours, at least, were left to me, after twelve o'clock had struck, for heart-shaking reflections. More than ever I stood upon the brink of a precipice; and the local circumstances around me deepened and intensified these reflections, impressed upon them solemnity and terror, sometimes even horror." [1] Suicide, he reflected, is often prompted by the depressing effect of a "crazy, dilapidated room", so that it was not surprising that the strange surroundings in which he now found himself should intensify his present frame of mind. "The unusual dimensions of the room, especially their towering height, brought up continually and obstinately, through natural links of associated feelings or images, the mighty vision of London waiting me afar off. An altitude of nineteen or twenty feet showed itself unavoidably upon an exaggerated scale in some of the smaller siderooms, meant probably for cards or refreshments. This single feature of the rooms—their unusual altitude, and the echoing hollowness which become the exponent of that altitude . . . together with crowding and evanescent images of the flying feet that so often had spread gladness through these halls on the wings of youth and hope at seasons when every room rang with music: all this, rising in tumultuous vision, whilst the dead hours of night were stealing along,—all around me, household and town, sleeping, —and whilst against the windows more and more the storm outside was raving, and to all appearance endlessly growing,—threw me

[1] III, 346.

into the deadliest condition of nervous emotion under contradictory forces, high over which predominated horror recoiling from that unfathomed abyss in London into which I was now so wilfully precipitating myself. Often I looked out and examined the night. Wild it was beyond all description, and dark as 'the inside of a wolf's throat'. But at intervals, when the wind, shifting continually, swept in such a direction as to clear away the vast curtain of vapour, the stars shone out, though with a light unusually dim and distant. Still, as I turned inwards to the echoing chambers, or outwards to the wild, wild night, I saw London expanding her visionary gates to receive me, like some dreadful mouth of Acheron." [1]

I have quoted this passage at such length, not only because of its intrinsic beauty, but because it admirably expresses the veiled, dream-like character which Thomas' life begins to take on at this juncture. To some extent, of course, the whole of his childhood and youth possesses this character—at any rate as far as they are seen through the elaborate prism of his own writings. But the grey curtains of mystery—as for dusk on the scene of a theatre—descend in front of the pathetic, Dickensian nightmare of his first London adventure, not indeed obscuring it entirely, but removing it, perhaps by sheer intensity of feeling and suffering, into the realm of poetic legend.

His plan, on arriving in London, was to borrow £200 on the security of his paternal inheritance, and somehow to live on this until his majority should have freed him from the authority of his guardians. It seems that he had already, while still in Wales, discovered the name and address of a money-lender in London and had written to him, stating his requirements. But when he presented himself at the office of this man, whose name was Dell, he was told to apply to one Brunell, who acted as agent for Dell.[2] This man lived in a fairly large, ramshackle house in Greek Street, Soho.[3] He was a rather sinister individual, recalling those seedy, furtive, dishonest lawyers whom one meets in the pages of Dickens' novels. "His eye expressed wariness against surprise, and passed in a moment into irrepressible glances of suspicion and alarm. No smile that ever his face naturally assumed but was pulled short up

[1] III, 346. [2] III, 349 ff.

[3] The house is still standing, at the west corner of Greek Street and Soho Square.

by some freezing counter-action, or was chased by some close-following expression of sadness." [1] His highly equivocal existence obliged him not only to employ several pseudonyms (Dell referred to him as 'Brown') but even to sleep in a different house every night, in order to avoid the bailiffs. And when people knocked at his door, he would first examine them through a 'Judas' before letting them in.[2] Yet he seems to have been neither unkind nor uncultured. He eventually allowed Thomas to lodge in his house (if lodging it could be called) and even went so far as to open his heart to the young man on the subject of the aspirations of his own youth. These had been of a literary kind; but, his father dying penniless, he had been obliged to put his shoulder to a less attractive wheel. An embittered man, evidently; but De Quincey seems to have felt that he had done something less than justice to him in the first version of the *Confessions*, for he afterwards much expanded his earlier description of Brunell and added the admission that "towards me he was obliging, and, to the extent of his power, generous." [3]

A further element of Dickensian fantasy was present in the house in the person of Mr. Pyment, Brunell's clerk. De Quincey gives us no description of this man's personality, beyond stating that he was, like his master, big and hulking and that he was the continual butt of Brunell's vituperative vocabulary.[4] But, reading —perhaps inexcusably—between the lines of De Quincey's narrative, we get the impression of a sulky, porridge-faced individual who resented the presence of the strange young wanderer and showed him little friendship.

On first arriving in London, Thomas took lodgings on his own (he does not say where); but when his money again began to give out and the business of the loan showed no signs of coming to a head, he begged hospitality of Brunell, who gave him leave to camp in the dirty, unfurnished rooms which abounded in the house in Greek Street.

And now hunger, pain and misery set in once more, but with an added squalor and bitterness which had been in some sort absent from the kindred weeks in Wales. London, which seemed to Thomas a nightmare and a portent, was now, in the year 1802,

[1] III, 351. [2] *Confessions* (1823), p. 41.
[3] III, 350. [4] III, 352.

at a transition stage of its development. It had not yet acquired all the driving ambition and turbid hurry of the industrial age, which was beginning, nor had the dour fog of Victorian England yet settled down upon it. On the other hand, the spacious ease and dignity of the eighteenth century were fast disappearing, and in its disintegration incongruous fragments of both centuries lived side by side, all but unconscious of each other. The population was increasing rapidly, and, with it, poverty; the underworld which the genius of Cruikshank was later to make vivid for all time, was already sordidly ubiquitous. Merry England was developing the modern slum, to which the life of the upper classes, who were still living virtually in the eighteenth century, penetrated not at all; and it was exclusively in this underworld that Thomas spent the next six weeks of his life. No wonder it dismayed him!

Brunell was not, as has been said, unkind; but he was too busy keeping his own precarious life together to have thought to spare for the condition in which his lodger found himself. Sometimes, while Brunell was breakfasting, Thomas would manage to get hold of a biscuit or a piece of bread; [1] but, if he noticed the boy's hunger, the lawyer took no further steps to allay it than in merely not forbidding this pathetic pilfering.

Thomas was not alone in his extremity. The dreary, echoing house harboured a fourth ghost, less substantial and determinate than the three others. This was a little girl of ten, bewildered, frightened and hardly more than half alive from the loveless, frozen life she was compelled to lead. De Quincey surmises that she was an illegitimate daughter of Brunell's; but, even if she was, the lawyer treated her as a servant, scarcely deigning to notice her existence and never allowing her to enter his room. Like a ghost she strayed into Thomas' life, and like a ghost she left it. She did not know who she was and her hold on life was of the slenderest. She was quite uninteresting, being neither pretty nor intelligent; [2] and years of privation had given to her face a look of premature age. But Thomas loved her, as a partner of his wretchedness, and she returned his love, seeking his protection against rats and other, more ghostly, fears. Together they would wander through the empty rooms, from attic to cellar, seeking a place to sleep; and

[1] III, 356. [2] III, 355.

when they had found it, they would lie down on the floor and huddle together for warmth, covered with an old horseman's cloak and with a bundle of law papers for pillow.[1]

Their sleep was not peaceful, for Thomas was now definitely ill. Tormented by sad dreams, he would moan aloud, waking both himself and his little companion; on other occasions, hunger provoked a twitching in his stomach, which in turn produced a reflex in the form of a violent throwing out of his legs. "Too generally the very attainment of any deep repose seemed as if mechanically linked to some fatal necessity of self-interruption. It was as though a cup were gradually filled by the sleepy overflow of some natural fountain, the fullness of the cup expressing symbolically the completeness of the rest: but then, in the next stage of the process, it seemed as though the rush and torrent-like babbling of the redundant waters, when running over from every part of the cup, interrupted the slumber which in their earlier stage of silent gathering they had so naturally produced. Such and so regular in its swell and its collapse, did this endless alternation of stealthy sleep and stormy awaking travel through stages as natural as the increments of twilight, or the kindlings of dawn: no rest that was not a prologue to terror; no sweet tremulous pulses of restoration that did not suddenly explode through rolling clamours of fiery disruption." [2]

In the daytime he would wander aimlessly through the streets, resting on doorsteps and sitting for hours on benches in the parks, his brain alight with the hysterical, livid fire which is the gift of hunger and desolation. What were his thoughts throughout those long hours? What strange, obstinate dream rivetted him, day after day, to this outcast existence? We shall never know: "for I have not mentioned in the 'Opium Confessions' a thousandth part of the sufferings I underwent in London and in Wales; partly because the misery was too monotonous, and, in that respect, unfitted for description; but still more because there is a mysterious sensibility connected with real suffering, which recoils from circumstantial rehearsal or delineation, as from violation offered to something sacred, and which is, or should be, dedicated to privacy. Grief does not parade its pangs nor the anguish of despairing hunger willingly count again its groans or its humiliations." [3] Agonies

[1] III, 355. [2] III, 355. [3] II, 55.

held in reserve often result in an effect of remoteness; and, as this passage indicates, the miseries which Thomas was now encountering and which were among his first immediate experiences of reality, produced that misting-over and veiling of his personality which is so striking a characteristic of his young manhood. In middle age he became clear and homely—in focus, so to speak—by comparison.

His only friends were prostitutes who, seeing him as destitute as themselves, took pity on him and defended him against the watchmen, when the latter tried to turn him off the steps on which he happened to be sitting. He adds naïvely [1] that his relations with these women could in no case have been impure, because the state of his purse precluded it. But poverty need not necessarily be an absolute preclusion in such cases, especially when it is accompanied by youth and beauty. I think it more likely that the purity, which there is no reason to doubt, was the result of Thomas' extreme youth, patent innocence and childlike temperament.*

Among these women, moreover, was one whose motherly instincts were powerfully aroused by the spectacle of the sick and homeless boy. Her name was Ann, and it is a sign of the immediate and instinctively profound affection and sympathy which Thomas felt for this girl (she was only sixteen) that it never occurred to him to ask her her surname. They were intimate from the first moment; and gradually, as the revelation of her humanity and goodness dawned upon his heart, he received it there and made of it a romantic image. Ann thus became the second of the three muses who informed his life; the first was his sister Elizabeth and the third his wife. It is perhaps not insignificant that, in his later opium dreams, three Sorrows should have appeared to him in female form, as the tragic inspirations of his life.[2]

Ann told him her story—the usual one—of a seducer who had abandoned her to her fate. Thomas, inexperienced in these matters, urged her to get help from a magistrate against the man who had ruined her. But her knowledge of life was deeper and more bitter than his had had time to become; and although, to please him, she pretended to be about to take his advice, she never did so, realizing the insecurity of her position in face of the law.

Thenceforward, Thomas had a companion on his leaf-like

[1] III, 359. [2] See *Levana*, XIII, 362.

drifting from street to street. Indeed, it is probable that Ann saved him from death by illness and exposure; for one night, when they had been walking, as usual, in Oxford Street, Thomas was suddenly taken with faintness and asked her to help him back to Soho Square. She did so, and there he sank down unconscious,* on the steps of the house. With a cry of distress, Ann hurried back to Oxford Street and procured a glass of port, with which she managed to revive him.

After this experience, it must have become clear to Thomas that, if he did not wish to die, he must take some definite steps to procure money and thus change his mode of life. He did not seek work of any kind, because, as he says: "It had never once occurred to me to think of literary labours as a source of profit." [1] But soon after the incident of his fainting he met, in Albemarle Street, an old friend of his family, who sent him £10 and promised not to discover him to his guardians. On the receipt of this money, Thomas decided to buy some clothes (he must up till now have gone almost in rags) and then go down to Eton, in the hope of persuading his old friend, Lord Westport, to stand security for the loan which was still hanging fire.

The journey turned out a failure. Thomas was feeling ill and weak when he boarded the coach. He was also sad at having to part from Ann, with whom, however, he made an assignation to meet on his return from Eton, five days later, at six o'clock, at the corner of Great Titchfield Street. During the journey he felt so ill that he subsided against his neighbour, who received his apology rather churlishly, until Thomas explained that he was ill and could not afford a place inside the coach. Then the man's manner instantly changed, and some hours later Thomas awoke from sleep to find himself comfortably included in the arm of the stranger. Chance acquaintances were always kind to De Quincey.

Arrived at Eton, Thomas found that Lord Westport had already left that institution for Oxford. In despair, he sought out Lord Desart, whom he knew slightly, and explained his position. Lord Desart listened kindly and seemed disposed to help, but was not unnaturally reluctant to have dealings with a money-lender. However, he promised to do what he could; whereupon Thomas returned to London in considerable dejection. This arrangement

[1] III, 364.

was, in the outcome, nugatory, since Dell refused to accept Lord Desart's security, on the grounds that the latter was still a minor.[1]

But this disappointment was as nothing compared with that which awaited Thomas on his return to London. True to his promise, he was punctual at his rendezvous with Ann. He waited and waited, but she never came. Day after day he haunted the corner of Great Titchfield Street, unable to believe that she would not come and in despair as to what steps to take to find her. For he had omitted to ask her her name, and though he knew the street in which she lived, he did not know the house. When he inquired after her, he was met either with leers or with a silence born of the suspicion that he was pursuing her to recover something that she had stolen from him. In the end he was obliged to give up the search.

His unhappiness and desolation were now complete. Not, perhaps, until he lost her for ever did he realize quite how much Ann had meant to him in the weeks since he had known her. In her directness, simplicity and disinterested kindness, she had taken the place, in Thomas' heart, of his home, his sisters, his mother—of everything, in fact, which he had hitherto held dear. And so it was that for many years he refused to believe in the finality of his loss, obstinately assuming that it was due to mere mischance and that one day Ann would be restored to him again. On many a subsequent visit to London, when life and the progress of his soul had carried him along quite other paths, he would still be drawn back to Oxford Street, after nightfall, and, recalling the exaltation and the misery of those days long past when he had walked the same street in company with Ann, he would gaze into face after face, as they moved in and out of the light of the street-lamps, in the hope that the next would prove to be the one he had lost. He felt that, in spite of the lapse of time, he would know her again among a thousand, however fleeting the glimpse. "Handsome she was not; but she had a sweet expression of countenance, and a peculiarly graceful carriage of the head." But every search was fruitless: he never saw her again. In time, though her image never faded from his mind, he became resigned to the inevitable and, in the end, came not even to desire to see her again; "her cough," he adds pathetically, "which

[1] III, 374.

grieved me when I parted with her, is now my consolation." But it was long before he attained to this resignation. "If she lived, doubtless we must have been sometimes in search of each other, at the very same moment through the mighty labyrinths of London. . . ."[1]

But, devoted as she evidently was to him, circumstances could hardly in themselves have been strong enough to prevent her from meeting him that day in Great Titchfield Street. It is more likely that she deliberately kept away, feeling—in the goodness of her heart—that, now that he was at last on the way to a reunion with the life which was properly his and in which she could have no part, she preferred to let him think that she had deserted him (an idea which, incidentally, never crossed his mind) rather than be a burden to him in the decisions and actions which he would be called upon to take.

But he never forgot her. In time her image became overlaid by that of his wife; underneath, it remained intact, indelibly printed on the palimpsest of his brain; and if, by some turn of chance, Ann ever came to read his famous invocation to Oxford Street,[2] and the spirit that haunted it for him, she will have realized that, at least once in her life, she had inspired a love that was as pure as had been her own.

4

At this point mystery again supervenes. De Quincey himself says: "Suddenly, at this crisis [the failure of the negotiations with Dell], an opening was made, almost by accident, for reconciliation with my guardians."[3] This is very vague and suggests that De Quincey was anxious not to go into the precise facts. Japp, in his article in James Hogg's book of recollections,[4] states that "a gentleman—a friend of the family—whom he had met in London" effected the reconciliation, in which case it was probably the same friend who had given him the £10 with which to make the journey to Eton. The most likely explanation seems to be that Thomas, discovering through the medium of this gentleman that the affair of the forty-guinea letter had been smoothed over and that he

[1] III, 375.
[2] III, 375.
[3] III, 374.
[4] *De Quincey and his Friends*, p. 37.

could now safely reveal his whereabouts to his family, decided to return once more to Chester. This he proceeded to do, first giving his address at the Priory to an acquaintance of Ann's, in a last hope that the latter might after all reappear.

It was now March, 1803, and Thomas was seventeen and a half years old. From an outside point of view, his adventure had been a failure: his health was undermined and he had achieved, in a practical sense, nothing at all. He was slinking home, as it were, with his tail between his legs. But the spiritual experience had been paramount: his family would find him changed. . . .

Thomas' second visit to the Priory, Chester, was chiefly distinguished by his relations with his uncle, Colonel Penson—relations which were rendered comic by the conflict between the older man's sympathy for his nephew and his feeling that he ought to treat him severely. De Quincey describes at length, and with humour,[1] the enormous arguments on the subject of politics and especially of India, in which he and his uncle indulged—arguments which Thomas, out of a sense of duty, did his best to lose, by the characteristic method of deliberate false processes of logic. But Colonel Penson, though by all accounts an excellent soldier, was no match for his nephew on intellectual grounds; he failed to detect the logical fallacies and invariably lost the battle. This does not seem to have embittered him in the least; indeed, he developed an almost pathetic respect for Thomas, as a letter written to him from India, in 1808, shows. "Rest assured I shall not invade the independence you desire to maintain," he says[2] and, by preserving this attitude throughout their relationship, he earned Thomas' respect and gratitude.

Meanwhile this Chester period was varied by a long visit to his friend Mrs. Best, at Everton, near Liverpool.[3] This visit is made

[1] I, 410 ff. [2] Japp, 101.

[3] There is some doubt about the order of Thomas' movements during the months after his return from London. Japp (*Letters*, I, 92) says that he went directly to Everton and only later to Chester, basing this assertion on the letter from Samuel Hall (*Ibid.* p. 96) which was sent to Thomas in January " c/o Mrs. Best at Everton ". But De Quincey himself makes no mention of Everton at all at this time and speaks of the second Chester visit as following straight upon the London experience (I, 400). Also, the address which he left for Ann was that of Chester. He may, perhaps, on leaving London, have felt some doubt about his reception at the Priory and have therefore thought it safer to give his address as Everton, in case it should turn out that he was not welcome at Chester. The question is, however, of no great importance, since Thomas seems (from the diary) to have alternated frequently between Everton and Chester during these months.

important by its coincidence with a diary which Thomas kept at the time and which has only recently been discovered.[1] It is a document of the first importance, for it contains a mass of information on the preoccupations of Thomas' mind at this critical time and shows us, as only a diary is capable of doing, the psychological effect which his London escapade had had upon him.

The diary only occupies some forty pages of print, but it suffices to display the continual ferment of activity in which Thomas' mind now became engaged. Released from the stultifying effects of hunger, illness and anxiety, which the futile activity of his adventure had produced, his brain began to resume its normal cast and to work again on the lines which were naturally congenial to it. The colours of tragedy, which had been so prevalent in the London phase, now change entirely. An amused, ironical, inquisitive tone obtains in the diary—now light, now serious, but never either flippant or tragic. For a short time, at least, the sad dreams and melancholy visions seem seldom to have visited Thomas' mind.[2]

But what is most clear is that he had emerged from his adventure with a certain increase in self-assurance. The letters he wrote at this period—letters written to his mother and to Samuel Hall in pursuance of the dispute over his going to Oxford—are very different from those which he had written from Manchester; there is in them no note of supplication or of over-anxious humility; they are the letters of one who has at last evolved a point of view and is prepared to stand up for it. He had found himself—in sorrow, hunger and illness, in anguish of solitude, in the loss of Ann, and in knowledge of the obdurate indifference of the world to the spiritual agonies of the individual.

It is plain that his chief preoccupation at this juncture was the pulling together and integration of his personality; hence the searching introspection of two passages in the diary. After a fragmentary discourse on *Mens sana in corpore sano*, with which it opens and which includes a resolve to practise bodily exercise, we come upon a letter to his old friend, Edward Grinfield,[3] which contains the following passage: "With me, independence of

[1] The MS. of this Diary belongs to the Revd. C. H. Steel, who inherited it from his father. Through whose hands it passed after leaving those of its author is not known. It was edited, in 1927, by Professor Horace Eaton, and published (both in print and facsimile) by Messrs. Noel Douglas.

[2] Diary, p. 144.

[3] See p. 26.

actions—independence of words—independence of thoughts are the preliminaries of friendship. Surely, Grinfield, we are Englishmen: great and awful is our high prerogative . . . and our motto is—'Th' unconquerable mind and Freedom's holy flame.'"[1] And on May 1st we find him speculating again about his character. Facility of Impression he considers his leading trait. "My hopes and fears are alternately raised and quelled by the minutest—the most trivial circumstances—by the slightest words. Witness the dismay I used to feel on the approach of the holidays . . . if any person called it a long time until they would arrive or vice versa; tho', all along, I was fully sensible that the interval was not one moment lengthened by anything they could say. Witness too the *moideration* in which I leave Mrs W [right] if anything is said less flattering than on a preceding day: though, all the while, I am fully conscious that she does not regard me more or less on one day y*n* on another."

From this curiously Proustian passage it will be seen that his exaggerated sensibility had not been mitigated by his experiences, but that at least he was attempting to deal with it by analysing it away.

Most of the entries, however, deal either with literary preoccupations or with his daily life at Everton—his visits to other people, conversations, remarks upon those he met; and it is here that his newly acquired objective view of others shows itself most plainly. Romantic literature—Burns, Southey, Coleridge, Wordsworth, Schiller, Mrs. Radcliffe and the lesser lights of the Gothic school—had awoken desire of imitation. "My Arabian Drama will be an example of Pathos and Poetry united": "What shall be my character (of a novel?) . . . wild—impetuous—*splendidly* sublime? dignified—melancholy—*gloomily* sublime? or shrouded in mystery —supernatural—like the 'Ancient Mariner'—awfully sublime?"[2] The novel in question was, of course, to be of the most terrific Gothic order,[3] complete with a sallow and volcanic hero, put together from the pages of Mrs. Radcliffe and the German novelists. Thomas' aspirations were, in fact, of the exorbitant order common among those who have just realized a desire to write. On May 26th, indeed, he drew up a list of no less than twelve works which he had planned: dramas (*Ethelfried*, *Yermak the rebel*, *Paul*), stories

[1] Diary, p. 144. [2] *Ibid.*, 163. [3] *Ibid.*, 156.

(" *a pathetic tale*, of which a black man is the hero "—another, " of which an Englishman is the hero "), essays, biographies (of Caesar, of Catiline), a pathetic ballad, " a *pathetic poem*, describing the emotions (strange and wild) of a man dying on a rock in the sea . . ." ; " *an Ode* in which two angels or spirits were to meet in the middle of the Atlantic." This ambitious list shows that he was at any rate intending to fling his net widely over the field of universal history and emotions. Needless to say, none of these projects came to anything.

More important still are two separate drafts of his first letter to Wordsworth. The version which he eventually sent [1]* is so interesting that it must be quoted in full. Thomas had evidently been screwing up his courage for some time before actually sending the letter, for the draft is dated May 13th and the letter itself May 31st.

SIR,

I suppose that most men would think what I am going to say . . .[2] strange at least or rude; but I am bold enough to imagine that, as you are not yourself 'in the roll of common men', you may be willing to excuse anything uncommon in the liberty I am now taking.

My object in troubling you, Sir, is that hereafter I may have the satisfaction of recollecting that I made one effort at least for obtaining your notice . . . and that I did not, through any want of exertion on my own part, miss that without which what good can my life do me? I have no other motive for soliciting your friendship than what (I should think) every man, who has read and felt the 'Lyrical Ballads', must have in common with me. There is no need that I should express my admiration and love for those delightful poems: nor is it possible that I should do so. Besides, I am persuaded that the dignity of your moral character sets you as far above the littleness of any vanity which could be soothed by applause as feeble and insignificant as mine . . . as the transcendency of your genius makes all applause fall beneath it. But I may say in general, without the smallest exaggeration, that the whole aggregate of pleasure I have received from some eight or nine other poets that I have been able to find since the

[1] In the Wordsworth Collection. This is the letter which Japp imagined to have been lost (see Letters, I, 120).

[2] These dots are De Quincey's own and do not represent omissions on my part.

world began . . . falls infinitely short of what those two enchanting volumes have singly afforded me;—that your name is with me for ever linked to the lovely scenes of nature;—and that not yourself only but that each place and object you have mentioned . . . and all the souls in that delightful community of your's—to me

'Are dearer than the sun.'

With such opinions, it is not surprising that I should so earnestly and humbly sue for your friendship;—it is not surprising that the hope of that friendship should have sustained me through two years of a life passed partially in the world . . . and therefore not passed in happiness;—that I should have breathed forth my morning and my evening orisons for the accomplishments of that hope;—that I should now consider it as the only object worthy of my nature or capable of rewarding my pains. Sometimes, indeed, in the sad and dreary vacuity of worldly intercourse, this hope will touch those chords that have power to rouse me from the lethargy of despair; and sometimes, from many painful circumstances—many, many bitter recollections it is my only refuge.

But my reasons for seeking your regard . . . it would be endless to recount and (I am afraid) useless; for I do not forget that the motives to any intimacy must be mutual; and alas! to me . . . unknown and unhonoured as I am, why should anyone—the meanest of God's creatures—extend his friendship? What claim can I urge to a fellowship with a society such as yours . . . beaming (as it does) with genius so wild and so magnificent? I dare not say that I too have some spark of that heavenly fire that blazes there; for, if I have, it has not yet kindled and shone out in any exertion which only could entitle me to your notice. But, though I can show no positive pretensions to a gift so high, I may yet advance some few negative reasons why you may suffer me, if but at a distance, to buoy myself up with the idea that I am not wholly disregarded in your sight . . . when I say that my life has been passed chiefly in the contemplation and altogether in the worship of nature—that I am but a boy and have therefore formed no connection which could draw you one step farther from the sweet retreats of poetry to the detested haunts of men—that no one should ever dare, in confidence of any acquaintance you might have with me, to intrude on your hallowed solitude—and lastly that you would at any rate have an opportunity of offering to God the pleasant and grateful incense of a good deed by blessing the existence of a fellow creature. As to all external points, I believe that there is nothing in them which would disgrace you.

I cannot say anything more than that, though you may find many minds more congenial with your own, and therefore proportionately more worthy of your regard, you will never find any more zealously attached to you—more full of admiration for your mental excellence and of reverential love for your moral character—more ready (I speak from my heart) to sacrifice even his life . . . whenever it could have a chance of promoting your interest and happiness—than he who now bends the knee before you. And I will add that, to no man on earth except yourself and one other (a friend of yours) [1] would I thus lowly and suppliantly prostrate myself.

Dear Sir,

Yours for ever,

THOMAS DE QUINCEY.

This touchingly adolescent letter, involved and repetitive in its urgent desire to drive home its burden, must have moved the most spoilt of famous men. Wordsworth was at this time neither of these things; though extremely conceited, he was not vain, and Thomas' letter had on him, on the whole, the effect it was intended to have. Passing over the pretentiousness and slight insincerity of such a phrase as " dreary vacuity of worldly intercourse ", as pardonable in one so young, he goes, in his answer, straight to the point. A prudent man, he was obviously a little alarmed at the *schwärmerisch* tone of the letter, and being far too realistic a character ever to have wished anyone—let alone a strange young man—to die for his sake, he proceeds to warn Thomas, as gently as possible, that he must not expect too much all at once. After saying how much Thomas' letter has pleased him, he continues thus:

My friendship it is not in my power to give; this is a gift which no man can make; it is not in our own power. A sound and healthy friendship is the growth of time and circumstance; it will spring up and thrive like a wild-flower when these favour, and when they do not it is in vain to look for it.[2]

He goes on to caution Thomas against neglecting the older

[1] Coleridge, no doubt. [2] Letters, I, 120.

writers for himself (Wordsworth), and adds that he is about to set off on a Scotch tour with his sister Dorothy and Coleridge. Then, as if realizing that he may have been a little too chilly, he concludes with a warm invitation to visit him at Grasmere.

An older, less enthusiastic man than Thomas would have heard the clear warning expressed in this letter and have proceeded with more caution. Wordsworth knew that his own fund of human affection was a strictly limited one, and he had been at pains to communicate this fact to his unknown admirer, without, at the same time, closing the door on a possible ripening of friendship between them. But Thomas either could not or would not perceive this. A few days after receiving the answer to his letter (it had been delayed for nearly two months through Wordsworth's absence in London), he seized his pen again and wrote a second, much longer, letter [1] to the poet, in which he expresses the surprise and delight he has felt at receiving an answer to his first. He apologizes for the indiscreet impetuosity of his remarks about friendship and goes on to explain that, in extolling Wordsworth's poems, he had intended no disrespect to the older poets, whom he has always loved. Above all else, however, he was touched by the poet's invitation to visit him, "because, though your kindness alone might have induced you to humour me by answering my letter, nothing less than your really thinking me in some measure worthy of your notice . . . could (I think) have made you run the risk of being pestered with an hour of my company." Yet the visit must unfortunately be postponed, for he is about to take up residence at Oxford. . . . He concludes by begging Wordsworth not to bother to write to him more often than he feels disposed.

Wordsworth took advantage of this entreaty to remain silent for eight months.

To return to the diary. Embedded in a mass of unimportant details—spelling queries ("Contr*ol*—*oul* or *oll*?" Impe*l*—or impe*ll*?"), notes of tea-drinking at the Wrights', notes of books he is reading—we come suddenly upon the following statement: ". . . go to the same fat whore's as I was at the last time;—give her 1s. and a cambrick pocket handkerchief;—go home miserable." [2] This unequivocal sentence falls like a bomb into the narrative, in which it is given no special importance. The coarse downrightness

[1] Wordsworth Collection. [2] Diary, p. 194.

of the expression is foreign to everything we know of De Quincey, at this or any other time; for where sexual matters were concerned he was the most prudish of men. Were it not for this one reference, we might have been justified in considering De Quincey as an almost entirely cerebral, sexless person; for, apart from the circumstances of his marriage (which, on close inspection, do not contradict that view), and a coy reference to one "Fanny" with whom he once exchanged a few words from the top of the Bath Mail,[1] there is not, throughout his whole life, one single contemporary reference even to a flirtation, far less to any more serious entanglement on his part. He was clearly not a person who was ever thought of in this connection. The deep fund of his emotions was afterwards turned exclusively to his wife, his children, and men friends like Wilson and Charles Knight; it showed itself, as he himself says,[2] in the form of *love-liking*—a phrase which suggests a sublimation of less convenient passions. Yet, at the same time, it must be remembered that the worshipping, respectful attitude to women, which Thomas had assumed towards Miss Blake,[3] is generally accompanied—at any rate in adolescence—by a purely physical attraction to women for whom it is quite impossible to feel respect. By no stretch of imagination could Thomas identify that "fat whore" with his mother; hence what we may safely regard as his first experience of sexual relationships. It is also not insignificant of his sensitive and fastidious nature that the affair should have filled him with self-disgust. In any case, if not unique in his experience, it was probably nearly so: opium, overwork, undernourishment and ill-health—which became De Quincey's lot in life—do not conduce to an over-brimming sexuality.

Meanwhile, his present life seemed to have become stuck in the usual three-cornered dispute between himself, his mother and his guardians. For a long time he himself seems, for no very clear reason, to have disliked the idea of going to Oxford. As far back as January of this year, soon after Thomas' return from London, Samuel Hall, primed, no doubt, by Mrs. De Quincey, had written him a thundering letter, full of conventionally expressed indignation, but showing readiness to hear what the young man might have to propose.[4] Thomas did not answer this letter till June, when he wrote a reply full of dignity and good sense. He seems by now to

[1] XIII, 285. [2] I, 174. [3] See p. 30. [4] Letters, I, 91.

have made up his mind to some extent to the Oxford scheme, for he says that, if he is allowed to go to the Varsity, "short of an absolute promise" he is "ready to give an assurance" that he will do so with a view to taking up a profession—the law, presumably, since that was the profession for which he had always been intended. But he adds that college is not "an object which I have looked to with any ardour of desire."[1] The diary contains several drafts of letters to his mother on this subject, written in the course of the summer of 1803,[2] most of which express dissent. But when he had made up his mind to the plan, fate played into his hands. One day, while he was staying at Chester and arguing, as usual, with Colonel Penson, the latter, goaded by his inability to get the better of his brilliant nephew, rounded on him—in the manner of those who suddenly interrupt an argument to stare closely at their opponent's face and exclaim: "How spotty you are to-day!"—with a jibe at him for remaining "tied to his mother's apron-strings",[3] instead of getting on with the business of life. Thomas promptly jumped at this to extract from his uncle support for the Oxford scheme.

Remained the question of money. Mrs. De Quincey, supported by the guardians, announced her readiness to allow Thomas £100 a year. This was insufficient, even in 1803. Why his full patrimony of £150 was not to be paid is not clear—unless the £50 was deducted as a disciplinary measure. As De Quincey himself said in after years: "Why in a long majority of more than fourteen years this [his patrimony] was not improved, I never could learn."[4] Mismanagement and neglect on the part of the guardians, as well as Mrs. De Quincey's building extravagances, no doubt had much to do with it.

The decision made, Thomas pondered anxiously the question of which college he should enter.[5] Had he stayed out his full time at Manchester Grammar School, he might have won an exhibition at Brasenose, which he fancied he would have preferred. In the end, however, he was obliged to choose Worcester—because it was the cheapest college.

An exquisite miniature[6] shows us De Quincey as he was at this

[1] Letters, I, 94.
[2] Diary, pp. 166, 170, 210.
[3] II, 12.
[4] III, 277.
[5] II, 24.
[6] In the Baird-Smith Collection.

time. The pale, romantic profile, with its straight fine eyebrow and long, curling eyelashes, rises, Shelley-like, from an open collar. The lower half of the face protrudes remarkably, giving to the mouth a childish pout. But what strikes one most is the superb shape of the large head—the high forehead rising straight, like a wall, from above the eye; the perfect round of the skull; the softly curling mass of light brown hair which descends in a fringe over the forehead. It is a face of exquisite sensibility and charm, and the childlike appeal which never failed to move those who saw Thomas for the first time, is most skilfully suggested by the artist.

CHAPTER III

THE RETURN TO BOOKS

I

De Quincey arrived at Oxford, in December 1803, in a snowstorm. He remained there, off and on, for the next three and a half years, though his name was kept on the books of his college until 1810. At first, he made an attempt to enter Christ Church, but the Dean, Cyril Jackson, angrily told him that his guardians should have given the college notice at least a year beforehand; now, there was no room. So De Quincey retreated and eventually matriculated at Worcester.[1] But the life he led there was just as peculiar and apart as that which he led at all other times of his life. He treated his college as a more or less inconvenient hotel, where the tuition was a hindrance rather than a help, and he left the university without taking anything from it.

Oxford, at that date and for long after, preserved an atmosphere of mediaeval learning and sequestration from the world, combined with an eighteenth century mode of life. The undergraduates were divided, even more sharply than to-day, into the sons of the rich aristocracy who lived for sport and good cheer and did little or no work, and the poor scholars who did nothing else. The university curriculum, as Shelley was to discover, seven years later, was stuck fast in a narrowly classical and theological rut, which deliberately excluded the vitalizing spirit of any new idea whatsoever and existed solely as a machine for producing degrees. Education, in the sense of a system of mind-stimulation and development, did not exist at all; the young men were not encouraged to think for themselves, as this would have meant that the tutors would have been obliged to think too; and that would have interrupted the well-nourished daydream in which they lived out their long lives. Had progress been made in learning,

[1] II, 27 ff.

the perfunctory nature of the tuition would not have mattered so much; for Oxford has always been primarily a seat of learning, and only in the second place an educational establishment—a fact which is too frequently forgotten. But no such excuse can be made for dons who in general contented themselves with mumbling over the classical texts, in the manner of a lazy priest reciting Mass, and who brought no critical intelligence to the exercise of their calling.

De Quincey was not long in discovering these facts for himself, and the result was a life which had as little connection as might be with that of the community in general. Too poor and too proud to consort with the rich undergraduates, of whose habits, moreover, he strongly disapproved, he found that even the scholars were so ill-read in English literature as to be not worth cultivating.[1] Thus " for the first two years of my residence in Oxford, I compute that I did not utter one hundred words." [2] This extreme statement gives the measure of De Quincey's aloofness from the social world of the university; but there were still further reasons for it. " My eye had been couched into a secondary power of vision, by misery, by solitude, by sympathy with life in all its modes, by experience too early won, and by the sense of danger critically escaped. Suppose the case of a man suspended by some colossal arm over some unfathomed abyss—suspended, but finally and slowly withdrawn—it is probable that he would not smile for years. That was my case." [3] Adventure and hardship had given him a measure of self-reliance, but it had done nothing to give him confidence in other men or to make him into a being to whom social relations could ever mean more than a very temporary recreation. Oxford, with her genius for bringing about just those very changes in boys fresh from the semi-barbarism of school life, failed to do this in De Quincey's case, because he did not give her the chance. " I recoiled . . . from the society of most men, but not with any feelings of dislike. On the contrary, in order that I might like all men, I wished to associate with none." [4] His reminiscences of Oxford, interesting as they are in many ways, give us, in comparison with the rest of his autobiographic writings, regrettably little detail of his daily life and impressions. One cannot help feeling that, so wilful and resolute was his turning away from life into the world of books at this

[1] II, 57. [2] II, 61. [3] II, 55. [4] II, 61.

time, the university 'scene' escaped him entirely. He writes at length of various aspects of Varsity life, but fails to connect them up into a general view.

But if the society of the place had no charms for him, the passion for work caught him up like a blast of wind and whirled him away. In those first two years at Oxford he worked harder than he had ever done before, thus acquiring the habits of inexhaustible memory and concentration that afterwards proved his main assets in life. Worcester is a secluded college, far away from the main block of the university; and though De Quincey characteristically changed his rooms there three times in the course of his career,[1] in all three sets he seems to have been left in complete peace by the rest of the college, to pursue his endless reading.

The course of his studies would seem to have been largely of his own choosing, for the man who should have been his tutor played no part whatever in his life. Soon after his arrival, De Quincey met this man in the quad, and, being asked what he had been reading, answered "Paley". Whereupon the tutor replied: "Ah! an excellent author; excellent for his matter; only you must be on your guard as to his style; he is very vicious *there*." Since De Quincey's own opinion of Paley was the exact opposite of this, he forthwith concluded that the man was a fool and never again exchanged a word with him.[2] From this little incident it will be seen that De Quincey already knew the capacity of his own intellect well enough to be unwilling to waste any time in listening to those whom he recognized as being below his own standard.

The lectures he found equally unsatisfactory.[3] In this he was not peculiar to the general run of those whose intellect is above the average; for it may be said in general that university lectures are intended for the stupid—or at any rate for those who cannot find their own way in a subject. By those who have acquired a technique for rapid and intelligent reading, lectures—however brilliant the lecturer and however well-digested his discourse—proceed at far too slow a pace to be profitably assimilated. On this same subject De Quincey afterwards emitted the opinion that it is more profitable to make one's own digest of a book, at leisure, than to listen to that of another person[4]—thereby showing, once more, that he appreciated the value of his own brain.

[1] II, 29. [2] II, 62. [3] II, 11. [4] X, II.

His one friend in the Varsity appears to have been a German called Schwartzburg, who assisted him in his study of Hebrew (begun at Manchester, with Lady Carbery) and much increased his interest, originally fired by De Haren in Wales, in German literature.[1]

His self-imposed curriculum, therefore, consisted in those classical texts, Greek and Latin, a thorough knowledge of which was necessary for his degree; an even more intensive study of philosophy, both ancient and modern; and general literature, English, French and German. This vast programme seems to have caused him no dismay; he worked night and day, with quite insufficient intermission for sleep, thus precipitating another physical breakdown.

The only department of knowledge in which Oxford tuition seems to have had some little effect upon him is that of Aristotelian Logic. His later essay on *The Logic of Political Economy* [2] is deeply imbued with the methods of scholastic logic as taught by the university in those days; from which we may presume that De Quincey attended at least some lectures, apart from reading Aristotle for himself. Richard Woodhouse, who knew him well in after years, was struck by his profound knowledge of Aristotelian Logic,[3] and one cannot read De Quincey's works without noticing his fascination by this subject on every other page.

But by far the most important intellectual interest in his life at this time was that of Kant. The philosopher was relatively, if not completely, unknown in England at this date, and De Quincey and Coleridge divide between them the honour of introducing the Kantian system to the notice of their countrymen. De Quincey's enthusiasm was at first unbounded.

> "It was a banner broad unfurl'd,
> The picture of that western world.

"These, or words like these, in which Wordsworth conveys the sudden apocalypse, as by an apparition, to an ardent and sympathizing spirit, of the stupendous world of America, rising, at once, like an exhalation, with all its shadowy forests, its endless savannahs, and its pomp of solitary waters—well and truly might I have applied to my first launching upon that vast billowy ocean of the German

[1] Japp, 81. [2] IX, 118 ff. [3] Hogg, 109.

literature." [1] And Kant himself he envisaged as " the very tree of knowledge in the midst of this Eden." He even planned, if Kant's system came up to his expectations, to retire, Thoreau-like, to Canada and establish himself, alone with a library, in the neighbourhood of Quebec. This dream, however, was a strictly individualistic one and bore no likeness, as he expressly states, to Coleridge's Pantisocracy. Though romantic, it was based on facts, for what he expected from it was " the exalting presence in an underconsciousness of forests endless and silent, the everlasting sense of living amongst forms so ennobling and impressive, together with the pleasure attached to natural agencies, such as frost, more powerfully manifested than in English latitudes, and for a much longer period." [2] He adds, anxiously: " I hope there is nothing fanciful in all this." There have been wilder dreams indulged; but De Quincey was after all to find a perfectly satisfactory substitute for the backwoods of Canada in the English Lake District.

But Kant failed to convince him and the dream was abandoned. " Gloom and blight " supervened, and six weeks' reading sufficed to destroy Kant's reputation for ever in De Quincey's mind. He found that it " destroys by wholesale, and it substitutes nothing "; that it offered " nothing splendid to the human imagination " and " nothing even positive and affirmative to the human understanding." [3] This is all very uneasy, if not positively fallacious; but De Quincey adds much, both on this and other occasions, which convinces us that he had, in fact, a remarkable grasp of the Kantian system.[4] What in all probability threw him out of his stride at this early period was the discrepancy, which his acute mind must instantly have grasped, between the world-view of the German philosopher and the ethical and religious system in which he himself had been brought up and to which he was determined to cling. De Quincey had expected a philosophy which would be a " luminous guide " to his future life—a confirmation, in fact, of his religious beliefs; what he found was a purely intellectual system, occupied mainly with the question of epistemology and entirely unsuited as a ' guide ' to practical life.*

The result was " a gloom of something like misanthropy upon my views and estimates of human nature ",[5] which no doubt had

[1] II, 85 ff. [2] II, 108. [3] II, 86.
[4] II, 81 ff. [5] II, 89.

a temporary effect in reinforcing his habits of solitude and antipathy to society.

Another constant influence throughout this time—and in the same direction—was that of Wordsworth, who had at last, not long after De Quincey's arrival at Oxford, answered the latter's second letter, and in his reply proceeded to more explicit advice than he had allowed himself on the first occasion. He warns De Quincey solemnly against "being seduced into unworthy pleasures", for when he himself was at Cambridge "the manners of the young men were very frantic and dissolute . . . and Oxford was no better, or worse." Then he becomes more precise: "I need not say to you that there is no true dignity but in virtue and temperance, and, let me add, chastity; and that the best safe-guard of all these is the cultivation of pure pleasures, namely, those of the intellect and affections . . . I do not mean to preach; I speak in simplicity and tender apprehension, as one lover of nature and of virtue speaking to another. . . . Love nature and books; seek these and you will be happy; for virtuous friendship, and love, and knowledge of mankind must inevitably accompany these, all things thus ripening in their due season." [1]

The gravity and mature wisdom of these lines sank deep into a nature already prepared to receive them; confirming De Quincey's natural disposition, they became as it were the rubric under which his whole life was lived. He answered the letter at once, at great length and in an even more expansive spirit of self-revelation than he had hitherto dared to assume in writing to Wordsworth. Beginning with regrets for the illness of Coleridge and announcing his readiness to perform any service for a man whom he admires so much, he passes on to his high expectation of *The Prelude* (of the inception of which Wordsworth had spoken in his letter) and condoles with the poet on the wretched plagiarism of the *Lyrical Ballads* by one Peter Bayley,* by which, contrary to his custom of monumental indifference to such things, Wordsworth seems to have been a good deal annoyed. After this De Quincey comes to the subject of himself:

The interest—so very gratifying to me—which you are kind enough to take in my welfare, would be of itself a sufficient check

[1] Letters, I, 124.

upon me if I were unhappily disposed to licentiousness: but I have been through life so much restrained from dissolute conduct by the ever-waking love of my mother . . .[1] and of late years so purified from dissolute propensities by the new order of pleasures which I have been led to cultivate that I feel a degree of confidence (not arrogant, I hope) that, even with greater temptations, I should not by my conduct at any rate make you repent the notice you have taken of me. The college, however, which I am at, holds out no very powerful temptations; it has indeed the character of being very riotous: but I cannot see that it deserves such a character pre-eminently—though its discipline is certainly less strict than that of any other college. But it is singularly barren (as far as my short residence there will permit me to judge) of either virtue or talents or knowledge; so that the intemperance I see practised, coming unrecommended by any great qualifications, is doubly disgusting to me. And, even though I should meet with these debauched habits in the person of a man of genius, it would be difficult for me to be so much seduced as lightly to exchange the high and lasting pleasures which I have found in other paths for such as . . . bring along with them the seeds of their own destruction. And besides, from the great aversion I have to college life, I shall pass no more of my time there than is necessary; and, for that reason as well as for the little attraction I have found in the society, I have lived almost alone since my entrance; and until I see something greater or better, I shall continue to do so. . . .[2]

Connected with this correspondence, and of great importance for the understanding of De Quincey's intellectual development during these years, is an elaborate list of the 'Constituents of Human Happiness', which he worked out while staying at Coniston and with his friends the Merritts at Everton, in August 1805. They consist of the following points:

1. A capacity of thinking—*i.e.* of abstraction and reverie.

2. The cultivation of an interest in all that concerns human life and human nature.

3. A fixed, and not merely temporary, residence in some spot of eminent beauty:—I say not merely temporary because frequent change of abode is unfavourable to the growth of local attachment. . . .[3]

[1] Dots in the original.
[2] Letter of March 31, 1804. (Wordsworth Coll.)
[3] These dots represent my own omissions from the text.

4. Such an interchange of solitude and interesting society as that each may give to each an intenser glow of pleasure.

5. Books. . . .

6. Some great intellectual project, to which all intellectual pursuits may be made tributary. . . .

7. Health and vigour.

8. The consciousness of a supreme mastery over all unworthy passions (anger, contempt, and fear), and over all appetites; together with a highly cherished benevolence. . . .

9. A vast predominance of contemplation,[1] varied with only so much of action as the feelings may prompt by way of relief and invigoration to the faculty of contemplation.

10. Both as subsidiary to the last, and also for its own value, a more than ordinary emancipation from worldly cares . . . and . . . business. . . .

11. The education of a child.

12. One which, not being within the range of any man's control, I should not mention, only that experience has read me a painful lesson on its value—a personal appearance tolerably respectable . . . [Where this is not present it is to be compensated for by] (1) That temperate and unostentatious dignity of manners and general tranquillity and composure of behaviour which bespeaks a mind at peace with itself . . . (2) A high literary fame. . . .[2]

A few days later De Quincey added the important corollary that, for men whose lives consist mainly in the exercise of the intellect, the stimulus to happiness must be sought in "a deep interest in those exhaustless and most lofty subjects of human life and human nature"[3]—an interest which he had already posited but which now, with the full release from the tyranny of Kant, had come to seem all-important to him. This expansion of generalized affection was also bound up with his study of history and of a subject which was entirely new to him—Political Economy. But the pervasive influence which can be detected throughout the list is that of Wordsworth; in many ways, indeed, the essay

[1] *Not* "contempt", as erroneously printed in Japp, 76.
[2] Japp, 75 ff.
[3] *Ibid.*, 78.

is simply an expansion of the passage in the poet's letter quoted on page 77. Of the desiderata enumerated, De Quincey failed to secure Nos. 3, 6, 7, 8 (at any rate partially), 10 (in an eminent degree). But the others he did manage to encompass, and the programme by which he lived in 1855 was substantially that which he had drawn up in 1805.

2

Agreeably to his renewed interest in other people, De Quincey now began a series of flying visits to London, partly, no doubt, in the hope of finding Ann, but chiefly in order to make the acquaintance of Charles Lamb, who was at this time[1] living in a garret in Inner Temple Lane. De Quincey's original intention in getting to know Lamb was to use him as a stepping-stone to Coleridge; but in this he was at first unsuccessful, for he did not actually meet Coleridge until 1807,[2] though in 1805 he conceived the crazy idea, quickly abandoned, of pursuing him to Malta.[3]

Lamb he did not at first find very sympathetic. De Quincey was at the age when irony and light-heartedness are not readily distinguished from frivolity; and he was much shocked by what he considered Lamb's scoffing way of treating subjects which he himself considered profoundly serious, if not sacred (*e.g.* Wordsworth). And when he attempted to restore the appropriate tone to the conversation, Lamb became sly and remarked: "If we are to talk in this strain, we ought to have said grace before we began our conversation."[4] De Quincey afterwards learned to appreciate Lamb's humorous attitude to life and the deep seriousness which it concealed; but he never quite became used to his outspoken chaff and was much put out when, in 1821, Lamb saw fit to tease him about opium and Oxford Street,[5] and praised Hazlitt at the expense of Coleridge.[6]

The only other irruption into De Quincey's world at this date was that of Mrs. Lee, "The Female Infidel", the first part of whose story I have already told. This determined precursor of "Miss 1925" now caused a scandal in Oxford by arraigning

[1] 1804.
[2] III, 38.
[3] Japp, 86.
[4] Quoted by Woodhouse in Hogg, 71.
[5] *Ibid.*
[6] III, 83.

before the law two "dissolute brothers", one of whom she accused of abducting her. She seems to have eloped with both of them, for reasons which Dr. Quincey says he does not "entirely know",[1] and had been seduced by the younger. De Quincey, intrigued as usual by anything in the nature of a crime, attended the trial of this squalid affair, which was stopped by the judge, on Mrs. Lee's admitting her disbelief in God and Christianity. De Quincey was so far prompted by his curiosity as to call on Mrs. Lee after the trial was over; but he was cheated of an interview, for directly she arrived at her house, she was hooted by the crowd, put back into her carriage and hounded out of the town.[2] De Quincey seems to have thought her ill-used in the whole matter, for his mother, to whom he had written an account of the trial, replied, with her usual astringency: ". . . I cannot see her case as you do. I think she is no more mad than any person may be said to be who outrages conscience. She always panted for celebrity, and was, when I knew her, full of rage at the world that it had taken no notice of her talents, which she thought of a high order; and she told me she should take the first opportunity of uniting herself to a man who had the wisdom to be above vulgar prejudices; and, seeing there are, in her sense, plenty of such men . . . I suppose she has been so united long before this; but still, finding the place too common to bestow distinction, she has tried to gain it by ringing a few changes on the manner of displaying her contempt of established things. What this will do for her she perhaps knows by this time." [3]

Yet, in spite of these diversions, De Quincey was far from happy. His health had never recovered from the rigours to which he had subjected himself in Wales and London—treatment which had permanently weakened his internal organs and favoured his lurking tendency to consumption. He now began to suffer acutely from gnawing pains in the region of the stomach—probably a form of colitis, or duodenal trouble. The sedentary, overworked existence which he led at Oxford was the penultimate straw; the last was an act which, one would have thought, no sane person could possibly have held to be salutary. This consisted in washing his head every day in cold water, and then, when toothache ensued, attributing this to an "accidental intermission" of the practice.

[1] I, 143. [2] I, 144 ff. [3] Letters, I, 108.

With a view to easing the toothache, therefore, he got out of bed, plunged his head into cold water and then went to sleep with his hair still wet. The result, of course, was an excruciating attack of neuralgia, which lasted with practically no intermission for three weeks.[1] No doubt the exposure to damp during the long nights when he had slept out of doors in Wales, had prepared the way for rheumatic affections of a general kind; and in this connection it is to be remembered that Coleridge, who suffered from the same ills and took the same steps to be free of them, once, when a boy, ran away from his home in a pet and spent the whole night in a field.[2]

At the end of three weeks De Quincey, almost out of his mind with pain, happened to meet an Oxford student who recommended opium. At this point the blue veils of fantasy again descend, conferring on the scene the dim, slow outlines of an uneasy dream, between ecstasy and terror; and the sad, heavy-lidded music of the long opium-trance begins to sound, for the first time, in De Quincey's life. The Hoffmann-like figure of the demon student and the "immortal" druggist seemed to rise out of the ground in obedience to his invocation, and though he afterwards sought the druggist's shop again, he could never find it.[3]

Possessed of the drug, he returned to his lodgings and took a dose. "In an hour, oh! heavens! what a revulsion! what a resurrection from its lowest depths, of the inner spirit! what an apocalypse of the world within me! That my pains had vanished, was now a trifle in my eyes; this negative effect was swallowed up in the immensity of those positive effects which had opened before me—in the abyss of divine enjoyment thus suddenly revealed."[4] The overwhelming relief from grinding pain, unattended as yet by any obvious disadvantages, and combined with a new and entirely delicious sensation of physical well-being, which acted, not as a soporific,[5] but as a definite intellectual stimulus; was quite enough at first to prevent De Quincey from realizing any danger in connection with these "portable ecstasies", which he could procure at any moment for a few pence.[6] The plunge

[1] III, 379. [2] H. I'A. Fausset: *Coleridge*, p. 18. [3] III, 380.
[4] III, 381. [5] III, 388.
[6] Laudanum (tincture of opium) was in those days the commonest remedy for all kinds of pain—as common as aspirin is to-day. It was obtainable everywhere, without a certificate, and was quite cheap. De Quincey says that East India opium,

was the more reckless in that he was unaware that it was a plunge at all. He was, in fact, to feel no ill effects from the use of opium for nearly nine years, *i.e.*, until after 1812. This may be partly attributed to the enormous amount of physical exercise which he took during those years; but also partly to moderation in the use of the drug, for even at moments of crisis he never took more than doctors have sometimes prescribed.[1]

The temporary relief from pain must greatly have assisted him in his work, clarifying his brain for the immense stores of knowledge which he was now pouring into it, from all the sources at his command. At the same time, another effect of the drug was to remove his spirit still further into regions of abstract preoccupations and indifference to the outside world, so that he lived in ever more complete solitude in the college, lining each philosophic argument, each historical fact, with the thin but delicious silk of some dream woven by the slow poison of laudanum.

3

At the end of some eighteen months of this régime, we find De Quincey again at Mrs. Best's, at Everton. Evidence for this visit is a letter to Wordsworth, dated April 6th. 1806.[2] Still faithful to his consuming desire, which illness and opium had not dimmed, of coming face to face with the man he admired so passionately, De Quincey had got as far as Liverpool on what was his first definite attempt to reach the poet's home at Grasmere. Now, however, shyness overcame him and he decided to find out, before going any further, whether he would really be welcome at Dove Cottage or not. Having made this plain, De Quincey goes into a description of his sufferings—his incipient consumption, his fevers—and proceeds to a new source of sorrow:

But my great affliction was the loss of my brother [3]—a boy of great promise who, in disdain of the tyranny exercised over him

in the dry state, cost three guineas per lb., and Turkish eight. (*Confessions*, 1823, p. 93.) The tincture was apt to vary in strength; but a pound of raw opium would produce a large quantity of tincture, hence the fact that the poorer classes were able to buy as much as they required for " some coppers ". As a form of dram-drinking, laudanum was almost as common among the poor as alcohol.

[1] See Dr. Eatwell's remarks, in Japp, 491.

[2] Wordsworth Collection.

[3] Richard (" Pink "). As we shall see in the next chapter, the truant turned up again, before very long, in De Quincey's life.

at school, went to sea at a time when I was incapable of giving him any assistance or advice: this has grown heavier and heavier as the chance of my hearing any tidings of him has diminished. In losing him I lost a future friend; for, besides what we had of alliance in our minds, we had passed so much of our childhood together . . . that we had between us common remembrance of early life. It has never happened to me before or after to meet anyone among the many young men I have slightly known with whom I had such a community of thought and feeling . . . this indeed has been my primal affliction through life and especially through my college life that *I have lived under a perpetual sense of desertion* [1] and have felt, on any demand which my situation made for a service higher than mere youthful generosity could prompt, that I was walking alone in the world: in sickness I felt this severely; for then, from the exhaustion and wasting that waits upon the hectic fever, my mind lost its energy so much that it was passive to whatever noxious influence I fell under for the time; and so by turns it was half palsied by total solitude or disentranced from its native mood by heartless society.

These things have shed a blight upon my mind and have made the two last years of my life so complete a blank in the account of happiness that I know not whether there be one hour in that whole time which I would willingly recall;—I have had intervals of bodily health but never any respite from sickness of the mind. . . .

The letter concludes by begging Wordsworth to let him know whether he shall proceed further or not.

No answer to this letter is extant,* but it is probable that one was written, for De Quincey has told us, in an unforgettable passage, of the expedition which, in fear and trembling, he now undertook to the very mouth of the lion's den:

Twice . . . did I advance as far as the lake of Coniston . . . and once I absolutely went forward from Coniston to the very gorge of Hammerscar, from which the whole vale of Grasmere suddenly breaks upon the view in a style of almost theatrical surprise, with its lovely valley stretching before the eye in the distance, the lake lying immediately below, with its solemn ark-like island of four and a half acres in size seemingly floating on its surface, and its exquisite outline on the opposite shore, revealing

[1] My italics. Depression of spirit, through illness, had brought on another attack of De Quincey's particular brand of melancholia.

all its little bays and wild sylvan margin, feathered to the edge with wild flowers and ferns. In one quarter, a little wood, stretching for about half a mile towards the outlet of the lake; more directly in opposition to the spectator, a few green fields; and beyond them just two bowshots from the water, a little white cottage gleaming from the midst of trees, with a vast and seemingly never-ending series of ascents rising above it to the height of more than three thousand feet.[1]

After thirty-three years (that passage was written in 1839) the emotion he had felt as he stood there, gazing at last on the object of his most romantic admiration and hope, was—in spite of disappointment and disillusion—still so intense, that De Quincey could describe, with the eye of an impressionist painter, the whole content of his first vision of the landscape that he was afterwards to know and love so well. " Ark-like island "—" feathered to the edge with wild flowers "—" gleaming from the midst of trees ": the images are as exact as they are exquisite; they convey to the reader all the lyrical wonder of the experience which aroused them.

But at the last moment, within sight of the " little white cottage " itself, De Quincey's courage failed him. " Catching one hasty glimpse of this loveliest of landscapes, I retreated like a guilty thing, for fear I might be surprised by Wordsworth, and then returned faint-heartedly to Coniston, and so to Oxford, *re infecta*." [2] Disheartened by his own shyness, he allowed some time to elapse before he made any further attempts to meet the objects of his admiration; and it was not till August of the following year that, while on a visit to a relation at Bristol, he called on Thomas Poole, the friend of Coleridge, at Nether Stowey, in hopes that the poet might also be in the neighbourhood. Poole received him kindly and took him to see Alfoxden, where Coleridge had lived with William and Dorothy Wordsworth, in 1797–98; but Coleridge was away at Bridgewater, and thither De Quincey had eventually to go to find him.

Riding down the main street of the town, he saw a man standing under an archway and knew instantly that it must be Coleridge. It was the " peculiar appearance of haze or dreaminess " [3] in the eyes—that look which Hazlitt described as a " dim, gleaming,

[1] II, 231. [2] *Ibid.* [3] II, 150.

uncertain intelligence" [1]—which told De Quincey that he could not be mistaken. So he dismounted from his horse and remained gazing at the poet. But Coleridge, whose natural abstractedness was at this moment intensified by an opium crisis, did not notice the young man who was staring at him and continued to pursue his private dream. De Quincey then addressed him, upon which he "started, and for a moment seemed at a loss to understand my purpose or his own situation; for he repeated rapidly a number of words which had no relation to either of us." [2] This slowness of reaction to outward stimulus, so common in victims of the drug habit, may have warned De Quincey of the presence of a fellow-sufferer, if he was ignorant of Coleridge's addiction to opium. In any case, the latter lost little time in confessing his bondage to the drug and the horror which it caused him. This was probably De Quincey's first inkling of the fate which awaited himself.

Like others, before and after him, he found Coleridge's friendship easily come by.* The poet was at this time thirty-seven, De Quincey twenty-two; both placed a particularly high value on friendship and its intimacies; and the older man, upon whom discouragement and the bitterness of self-knowledge had already made their mark, was touched into new life by the admiration and sympathy of the intelligent undergraduate. Coleridge immediately invited De Quincey to accompany him to a large dinner-party which was to take place that very evening, at the house of a Mr. Chubb, and, on De Quincey's accepting, returned without more ado to the flooded stream of his famous eloquence: "like some great river, the Orellana, or the St Lawrence, that, having been checked and fretted by rocks or thwarting islands, suddenly recovers its volume of waters and its mighty music, [he] swept at once, as if returning to his natural business, into a continuous stream of eloquent dissertation, certainly the most novel, the most finely illustrated, and traversing the most spacious fields of thought by transitions the most just and logical, that it was possible to conceive." [3]

After the dinner-party, at which Coleridge seemed tired and talked little, De Quincey felt so wrought up by the excitements of the day that he decided to walk back to Bristol through the

[1] *Spirit of the Age*, p. 62. [2] II, 150. [3] II, 152.

night. This must have been one of the first of those nocturnal walks which afterwards became so dear to him, at Grasmere and in London; and with his imaginative ability to turn quite an ordinary event into an adventure, every feature of the night was vivid to his consciousness, as he walked along the silent roads. " Once only I passed through the expiring fires of a village fair or wake: that interruption excepted . . . I saw no living creature but a surly dog, who followed me for a mile along a park wall, and a man, who was moving about in the half-way town of Cross. The turnpike gates were all opened by a mechanical contrivance from a bedroom window; I seemed to myself in solitary possession of the whole sleeping country." [1]

In December De Quincey met Coleridge again at the Bristol Hot Wells, and a lucky accident gave him an opportunity to make another attempt to raid Wordsworth's retreat, this time in company which would considerably facilitate the project. For Mrs. Coleridge, together with her children, Hartley, Derwent and Sara, were on the point of travelling north to visit Wordsworth and eventually to take up their abode with Southey, at Keswick. But Coleridge, who would naturally have accompanied them,* had contracted to deliver a series of lectures at the Royal Institution, in London, and so was unable to escort his family. Hearing of their difficulty, De Quincey at once offered himself as escort, and was gratefully accepted. His passion for children had already declared itself and the three little Coleridges were devoted to him; their mother, with her conventional amiability, liked him very much and was pleased to be travelling " under the protecting wing of kind Mr. de Quincey ", as she put it in a letter to Poole.[2]

The party took three days to reach Liverpool, where they stayed a week, in the course of which De Quincey met Madame Catalani, the famous singer, and was much inpressed by the brilliance of her personality.[3]

When they reached Grasmere, De Quincey was again seized with fright, as the party stood waiting for Wordsworth to appear. " Had Charlemagne and all his peerage been behind me, Cæsar and his equipage, or Death on his pale horse, I should have forgotten them at that moment of intense expectation. . . ." [4] So that,

[1] II, 162.
[2] *Minnow among Tritons*, p. 8.
[3] II, 233.
[4] II, 235.

when Wordsworth did arrive, De Quincey was at first too much stunned to take stock of him. Mrs. Wordsworth, however, at once came forward and welcomed him with a simple kindness that set him at his ease. He noted that her figure was "tolerably good" and that her squint, which he politely describes as a "considerable obliquity of vision,"[1] was not, curiously enough, repulsive.

But it is plain, from De Quincey's narrative of this momentous meeting, that it was neither Wordsworth nor his wife, but Dorothy, who made the profoundest impression upon him at first. His description of her is well known; but I shall not forbear to quote it, for it is as well to fix in our minds De Quincey's own image of the delicious being for whom he was to feel so tender an affection:

Immediately behind her [Mrs. Wordsworth] moved a lady, shorter, slighter, and perhaps, in all other respects, as different from her in personal characteristics as could have been wished for the most effective contrast. 'Her face was of Egyptian brown'; rarely, in a woman of English birth, had I seen a more determinate gypsy tan. Her eyes were not soft, as Mrs. Wordsworth's, nor were they fierce or bold; but they were wild and startling, and hurried in their motion. Her manner was warm and even ardent; her sensibility seemed constitutionally deep; and some subtle fire of impassioned intellect apparently burned within her, which, being alternately pushed forward into a conspicuous expression by the irrepressible instincts of her temperament, and then immediately checked, in obedience to the decorum of her sex and age, and her maidenly condition, gave to her whole demeanour, and to her conversation, an air of embarrassment, and even of self-conflict, that was almost distressing to witness. Even her very utterance and enunciation often suffered, in point of clearness and steadiness, from the agitation of her excessive organic sensibility. At times, the self-counteraction and self-baffling of her feelings caused her even to stammer, and so determinately to stammer that a stranger who should have seen her and quitted her in that state of feeling would have certainly set her down for one plagued with that infirmity of speech as distressingly as Charles Lamb himself.[2]

He noticed that her movements, like those of her brother, were curiously clumsy and ungraceful; but adds, with his usual beautiful

[1] II, 237. [2] II, 238.

exactitude: "The pulses of light are not more quick or more inevitable in their flow and undulation, than were the answering and echoing movements of her sympathizing attention."[1] It is worth while to note here the extraordinary uniformity of impression which Dorothy produced upon the most diverse people, so that we find Coleridge anticipating De Quincey thus: "Her manners are simple, ardent, impressive. In every motion, her most innocent soul outbeams so brightly." Such concurrence is a signal proof of her strong personal genius.

Coming at last to Wordsworth himself, we find De Quincey's impressions confused by the fact that from the first he compares the man as he then was with his appearance at the time of writing.[2] There emerges, however, from the first sight, the long, indigenous face of the Border country, together with a "fine, sombre complexion . . . resembling that of a Venetian senator or a Spanish monk."[3] Combined with these were clumsily shaped legs and bust, and "a narrowness and droop about the shoulders which became striking, and had the effect of meanness."[4] The eyes were large and lustrous—especially so, De Quincey tells us, after their owner had been taking exercise. But it was the mouth, and perhaps the general rather sheep-like shape of the face, which reminded De Quincey so strongly of portraits of Milton—a likeness which has, however, been disputed by others who knew Wordsworth personally. He noticed, too, that both Dorothy and William looked older than they were.[5]

As for the Wordsworths, the impression De Quincey made upon them is indicated by Dorothy in a letter to Lady Beaumont.[6] "He is," she says, "a remarkable and very interesting young man, very diminutive in person, which, to strangers, makes him appear insignificant; and so modest, and so very shy, that even now I wonder how he ever had the courage to address my brother by letter." It is obvious from these remarks that Dorothy and William had taken some trouble to bring De Quincey out of his shyness, had succeeded, and were charmed and fascinated by the result. Dorothy, with her impulsive, feminine sympathy, no doubt responded at once to De Quincey's appeal, instantly making

[1] II, 239.
[2] 1839.
[3] II, 242.
[4] *Ibid.*, and see p. 251.
[5] They were thirty-six and thirty-seven respectively.
[6] De Selincourt, *Dorothy Wordsworth*, p. 216.

him feel that she was his friend; while William, more cautious and reserved, and mindful, perhaps, of the letters he had written the young man, relaxed his solemn, rather humourless features in provisional approval, though his welcome was sincere enough.

On the whole, then, this first visit must be judged a success. De Quincey was delighted with everything—the landscape, the people, the life. Soon after his arrival, the whole party made an expedition to Ambleside in a farm cart. This mode of travelling seemed to De Quincey a little *infra dig.*, but "what was good enough for the Wordsworths was good enough for me." [1] Thence they proceeded over the Kirkstone Pass and down along Brother's Water to the Vale of Patterdale, Dorothy doing all the talking and receiving all the salutations from passers-by. At Patterdale they slept, and the next day went on beside Ullswater. Leaving Mrs. Coleridge and the children in the cart, at Ewsmere, De Quincey and Wordsworth walked on to Penrith, and that evening the poet read *The White Doe of Rylstone* aloud. The next day, Wordsworth, who had some business to attend to, left De Quincey to proceed alone to Southey's, at Greta Hall, Keswick, where he found the rest of the party already installed.[2]

Southey, whose fine, pronounced features may to-day be studied on the face of Mr. Aldous Huxley, appeared dressed in Tyrolese costume and struck De Quincey by "a remarkable habit of looking up into the air, as if looking at abstractions", and by an expression "even noble, as it conveyed a feeling of a serene and gentle pride, habitually familiar with elevating subjects of contemplation." But De Quincey's acute perceptions at once revealed to him Southey's chief fault: "an air of reserve and distance about him—the reserve of a lofty, self-respecting mind, but, perhaps, a little too freezing." [3]

Wordsworth arrived the next day, and the following morning, before the party left for Grasmere, De Quincey had the privilege of listening to the two poets discuss politics. He himself, who had been brought up on staunch Tory principles and an abhorrence of France, was too young to know anything of the libertarian enthusiasm with which men like Wordsworth and Southey had been carried away, in the early days of the French Revolution; and now he listened with amazement and something like dismay

[1] II, 307. [2] II, 307 ff. [3] II, 317.

to sentiments which seemed to him "absolutely disloyal."[1] For the two poets were contending that "no good was to be hoped for" until the royal family was expatriated, perhaps to New South Wales—a fancy which moved Southey to the composition of a ribald verse.

De Quincey now returned to Oxford with a feeling that something, at least, had been achieved. That his meeting with Wordsworth had been a slight disappointment is plain from the fact that, from now on, he tended to make Dorothy, not her brother, the chief confidant of his hopes and sorrows. Their correspondence alone shows this.[2] His relations with Wordsworth were to mature up to a certain degree of friendship and mutual esteem, from which they rapidly declined; but they were never really intimate. To Wordsworth friendship was never a "sheltering tree,"[3] and he had already reached the age when his desire for intimacy, which, in so self-sufficient a man, was never very great, had become fully satisfied by his wife and family. Even Coleridge, who was the most intimate friend Wordsworth ever had, was soon to feel the cooling of his affection—though the fault, in this case, was almost entirely Coleridge's own. It was not to be expected, therefore, that a young man of twenty-two, however brilliant, could play an important part in the life of a much older man who was, moreover, of too irretrievably masculine a temperament to have much patience for the difficult pleasures of friendship. As Keats once reported Wordsworth as saying of himself, he was "not one of those who much delight to season their fireside with personal talk."[4]

> The Human nature unto which I felt
> That I belonged, and which I lov'd and reverenc'd,
> Was not a punctual Presence, but a Spirit
> Living in time and space, and far diffus'd.[5]

De Quincey was never to be a "punctual presence" in Wordsworth's thoughts.

Moreover, the latter, with his sturdy, peasant independence, was not at all a subtle person, and his sensibility was not of the kind which produced involved and fastidious consideration of the

[1] II, 322. [2] The same is observable of Crabb Robinson.
[3] Coleridge, *Youth and Age*.
[4] Letter to John Hamilton Reynolds: 21 September 1817.
[5] *The Prelude* (1805), Bk. VIII, l. 760–63.

degree of his obligation to others—considerations which were paramount in the minds of Coleridge and De Quincey.

4

The chronology of these years of De Quincey's life is very confusing, because, although he was nominally resident at Oxford from 1804 till 1808, he was in fact continually moving about the country, and the only evidence we have that he was in a particular place at a particular time is contained in letters, and these are few and far between. However, we are able to fix the date at which he underwent the examination for his degree, by two hitherto unpublished letters which he wrote to Dorothy Wordsworth on the subject, in the spring of 1808.[1]

These letters are otherwise important because they indicate clearly the real reason why De Quincey abandoned the examination when he was already half-way through it.

The first letter was written in answer to one from Dorothy, which he had found waiting for him on his return to college:

> Ever since then however until within a day or two (either from having walked part of the way from London—frequently without my hat or from sleeping with my head too low) I have been wholly incapacitated from writing by a return of my complaint strengthened by an inability to sleep until about morning when mere exhaustion forces me into sleep: this attack would no doubt have yielded sooner to the remedies prescribed to me in London but that the anxiety which I could not subdue as to the public examination for a degree urged me perpetually to attempt reading though I found that I could read to no purpose; so that, finding the whole university on tiptoe for the approaching prize-fighting and myself in a state of palsy as to any power of exertion, I felt very much as in dreams which I recollect where I have been chased by a lion and spell-bound from even attempting to escape.

He continues with an elaborate explanation of his dislike to the kind of labour involved—the learning by heart "collections of unassorted details"—and one gathers from his statement that he will have to read 33 Greek tragedies in one week, that in his miscellaneous explorations into various literatures, in the last two

[1] Wordsworth Collection.

years, he had neglected at least some of the books specified by the Schools.

In the second letter, dated May 8th, he makes the appalling confession that he is reading eighteen hours a day and only goes to sleep on a sofa when he can no longer keep awake. "I am afraid you will think this very foolish; but having been treated with great kindness by my college, I cannot endure to disappoint their expectations if the time I have remaining will enable me to do what I have undertaken."

The signs of nervousness and cold feet are here unmistakable. At the same time it was only natural that De Quincey should have sought to give a more respectable reason for his strange behaviour, and long afterwards he did so. What happened was as follows. He did the first day's papers, which were in Latin, and Dr. Goodenough of Christ Church, who was one of the examiners, said afterwards to a colleague at Worcester: "You have sent us the cleverest man I ever met with; if his *viva voce* examination to-morrow correspond with what he has done in writing he will carry everything before him."[1] But he never turned up for the *viva voce*: he had quietly packed up and left Oxford the night before—for good. The reason he afterwards gave to Woodhouse was that the *viva* was to have been conducted in Greek, in which language he was looking forward to showing his proficiency; but that, at the last moment, it had been changed to Latin,* which so much annoyed him that, being in any case contemptuous of the method of examination as a proof of intellectual power, he had decided to go no further with it.[2]

There was no doubt some measure of truth in this explanation. De Quincey was not the first person, nor yet the last, who has found the examination method inappropriate to his technique of thought and no fair proof of his knowledge. It is, in fact, a truism that to do well in the Schools it is necessary to possess a particular type of mind—not necessarily the best type, but one which is capable of retaining a very large number of facts. This De Quincey had pointed out in his letter to Dorothy; but, though fully aware that his mind was of a more creative cast, he seems not to have realized that his astounding memory would certainly have been sufficient in itself to have carried him triumphantly

[1] Woodhouse, in Hogg, p. 109. [2] *Ibid.*

through the whole examination. Nerves, illness and insomnia, and the effect of opium (he had taken a dose before going in to the examination),[1] combined with the melancholy defeatism which never failed to attack him on occasions like this, prevented him from facing the risk of the intense mortification to which failure to reach the very highest standard would have exposed him.

It was probably the memory of this sudden moral collapse and regret for the missed opportunity which caused him to speak so bitterly of Oxford in after years. "Oxford! ancient Mother! . . . I owe thee nothing! Of thy vast riches I took not a shilling, though living amongst multitudes who owed to thee their daily bread." This is certainly an exaggeration, and De Quincey seems conscious of it, for he immediately adds: "Not the less I owe thee justice . . ." [2] and, a few pages later, he shows, in a finely expressed passage, that he had not entirely missed the point of Oxford:

> A collegiate incorporation, the church militant of knowledge, in its everlasting struggle with darkness and error, is, in this respect, like the church of Christ—that is, it is always and essentially invisible to the fleshly eye. The pillars of this church are human champions; its weapons are great truths so shaped as to meet the shifting forms of error; its armouries are piled and marshalled in human memories; its cohesion lies in human zeal, in discipline, in childlike docility; and all its triumphs, its pomps, and glories, must for ever depend upon talent, upon the energies of the will, and upon the harmonious co-operation of its several divisions.[3]

De Quincey certainly failed to make the most of his university career, partly for reasons outside his own control, such as ill-health and poverty, partly from constitutional ill-adaptation to the life. But it cannot be said that he wasted his time there. A restless desire for knowledge drove him into intellectual excesses in the course of which a certain wastage was inevitable, but at the ultimate gain of a fine technical balance between the imaginative, and the logical and analytical faculties, which constitutes his genius as a writer. But at this stage the furniture of his mind was as a sediment whirling muddily in a carrying fluid, and many years passed before it settled down sufficiently to allow him to start

[1] Dr. Cotton (Provost of Worcester) in Hogg, p. 110.
[2] II, 10. [3] II, 18.

out on his career as a writer. As he once confessed, in the *Letters to a Young Man*, one of the chief distresses of his youth was the thought—common to most men of genius—that the length of life was ludicrously ill-proportioned to the vast number of books, music, people and experience that he would have wished to assimilate.[1] In the course of coming to terms with life, he was to find it even more narrowly obdurate than he had expected.

[1] X, 28.

CHAPTER IV

TOWARDS HAPPINESS

I

It had originally been De Quincey's intention, on leaving Oxford, to travel in Germany.[1] But, like all his other projects for seeing something of foreign countries, this one came to nothing—no doubt for lack of funds. For his pecuniary affairs had been going from bad to worse. While at Oxford, finding his allowance hopelessly inadequate to his needs, he had had recourse to repeated borrowing from Jews; and when he came of age, in 1806, his inheritance of £2600 was immediately docked of £600, to pay various debts.[2] The rest quickly dwindled, entirely owing to mismanagement, so that by 1815 not a penny of it was left.

In the autumn of 1807 he had returned to Bristol, and finding Coleridge in financial difficulties, conceived the generous, but in the circumstances deplorable, plan of coming to his help. With this end in view, he approached Joseph Cottle, the Bristol publisher and friend of the poet, and asked him if Coleridge would accept £100 or £200 [3] as an anonymous gift. Consulted on this head, Coleridge became agitated and said: "Cottle, I will write to you. We will change the subject." The next day he wrote Cottle an elaborate letter, complaining of his health and asking anxiously if the anonymous donor would be transgressing "no duty of morals or of prudence" in parting with the money; but it is plain that, having made his gesture, he intended to accept.

Cottle then told De Quincey that Coleridge was in a position of serious embarrassment, whereupon the former said: "Then I will give him £500." After some more whispering, in the course of which Cottle assured Coleridge that his benefactor was quite able to afford the money, Coleridge announced himself ready to accept whatever De Quincey offered—but as a loan, as he had

[1] Woodhouse, in Hogg, 99. [2] Letters, II, 112 ff. [3] Japp, 96 ff.

stated in his letter. Cottle, who knew Coleridge well and must have been aware of the futility of lending him money, seems to have had some twinges of conscience over his responsibility in the affair, for he now represented to De Quincey that a smaller sum than £500 would meet the case. De Quincey, however, insisted on giving no less than £300, which he forthwith handed over to Cottle, who gave him a receipt for it, in Coleridge's name.

This reckless piece of generosity, which reflects great credit on De Quincey's character, was, nevertheless, not only ill-timed from his own point of view, but ill-judged from that of the character of its recipient. For Coleridge was the very last person to whom indiscriminate gifts of this kind should have been made. To give money to such a man is about as useful as pouring it into the sea. The only way to save the Coleridges of this world—*i.e.,* those who, while possessing great and valuable gifts, are clearly unfit for the responsibilities of practical life—is to turn them into the objects of Trust companies. This was what virtually happened to Coleridge himself in later years (and also, incidentally, to Swinburne), but not before his fecklessness and fumbling had lost him the respect of his friends and of himself. Had these steps been taken on his behalf while he was still comparatively young, it is possible (though for other reasons unlikely) that he would have been able to make a more complete—a less wasteful—use of his life than he actually did.

In the case of De Quincey's gift, it would be unfair to blame Coleridge for taking the money, since Cottle had assured him that De Quincey could afford it. But, in spite of the fact that the latter had insisted, all through, on preserving his anonymity, one cannot resist the conclusion that Coleridge must have been able to guess who the donor was. Rich young men who are willing to give away as much as £500 (a very considerable sum in those days) to a starving genius, do not fall from the skies, and Cottle's description will have given Coleridge a very good idea whom he had to thank. His conscience must have suggested to him that it was an act of levity, at his age, to take so large a sum from a young man who was just starting out in life; but Coleridge's conscience, though exceedingly tender, possessed the protective ability to drug itself into believing what was convenient for it to believe at the moment. There is no reason to reject his assurance that he regarded the money as a loan, though he might have known by that time that he would never be in a position to pay back money lent to him; but the fact remains that he never did repay it. When, in 1821, De Quincey wrote to him under personal stress, to remind him, not of this sum,* but of monies disbursed in buying books at Coleridge's behest, in 1808, the latter was obliged to repudiate even this debt. De Quincey himself made no reference to the affair until, in 1834, when writing an article on the poet for *Tait's Magazine*, he casually mentioned it, but in veiled terms and as a perfectly natural act.[1] The statement provoked a furious reply from Archdeacon Hare, who apparently took it as an aspersion on Coleridge (who had just died); but many persons must have known of the whole affair long before.

De Quincey afterwards recognized the folly of his action. In a statement of his affairs, which he drew up for his mother's benefit in 1818, he admits that, though better than spending money in self-indulgence, "in strict morality . . . it was wrong; it was an act not for my fortune nor for my situation. . . ." [2] Yet the act was typical of his attitude to money throughout life. His charity, in this respect, was at all times extravagant and out of all proportion to his own assets at the moment. He disliked money intensely, with the kind of dislike generally reserved for human beings; he despised it,[3] and, apart from the necessity of buying books and, later, of keeping his family, might almost have existed without it, so absolutely unpretentious was his mode of life. This horror and incomprehension was of course only another symptom of his general practical inefficiency; and the root cause of it was, as I have already indicated, the oppressive influence which his mother had always exercised over him. From the earliest days, her letters to him were rarely without a demand for some statement of account; and this constant harping on the subject, which was particularly acute at all the important turning points in his life, bred a nervous horror of money and everything connected with it, as recalling the odious image of his mother's uplifted finger. The earliest sign of this morbid attitude of mind is his behaviour in connection with the forty-guinea letter; later examples are, from an observer's point of view, even comic, though they involved agony to De Quincey himself. Charles Knight recounts how, in 1825, De Quincey received a cheque and was astonished

[1] II, 163. [2] Letters, II, 112. [3] See letter to mother, p. 39.

to discover that he could not get the money till the cheque fell due, and was still more astonished when Knight announced himself willing to advance the money.[1] On another occasion, wishing to borrow seven and sixpence from a friend for some immediate use, he offered the friend a £50 banknote as security, without which he felt that his request might be refused.[2] His honourability was in fact so complete that it never occurred to him to protect himself from fraud: it was difficult to extract receipts from him for sums received, because he did not see the necessity of demanding them himself. As an old man, when he was scolded by one of his daughters (then a child) for paying his landlady £49, 10s. without asking for a receipt, he merely answered, with his habitual mildness: "My dear, it is quite right; Miss So-and-So is a lady."

In view of this transparent unworldliness, it is not wonderful that no one ever thought the worse of De Quincey for the pecuniary scrapes from which his later life was scarcely ever free. For the courage and dignity with which he invariably supported his troubles earned him the respect even of those who were obliged to come to his assistance, and these were always publishers who were in any case beholden to him for his labours on their behalf. There are, moreover, two kinds of borrowers: (1) Those who spend the money borrowed on necessities; (2) those who fritter it away wantonly, or spend it on caprices, and then borrow more for the necessities which remain outstanding. De Quincey belongs strictly in the first group, men like Coleridge and Leigh Hunt in the second; hence the difference of attitude observable in the friends of these three men.

2

After leaving Oxford, De Quincey spent the rest of the summer of 1808 mostly in London. His intention was still to take up the Law as a profession, but the desultory manner in which he went about it shows that his heart was not in the business and that a belated regard for his mother's and his guardians' wishes had more to do with it than his own desire. The references to any steps

[1] *Passages of a Working Life.*
[2] Thomas Hill Burton, in Hogg, 256.

which he may have taken towards entering the legal profession, are few and vague. In the 1818 statement to his mother he admits that his only object in taking up the law was "simply to get money",[1] and that he was quite indifferent to the honours of the profession. He seems, indeed, to have kept a few terms here and there in the next few years; but with his settlement at Grasmere in 1809, all real intention to pursue the course of his legal studies must virtually have ceased, though he continued for some time to pretend that he was still pursuing them. The desire for a literary career, which had always been at the back of his mind, had by this time definitely taken precedence of all others.

During this residence in London, De Quincey lived first at 82 Great Titchfield Street (the scene of his abortive rendezvous with Ann, six years before), and afterwards with a college friend, one Richard Smith, at 5 Northumberland Street, Marylebone. He seems to have spent a good deal of his time with Coleridge, who was living at the office of the *Courier*, in the Strand. Coleridge had evidently come to value De Quincey highly and now looked to him to support his failing spirits; for he was ill and overworked, and the lectures which he was giving caused him a deal of nervous misery. Thus we find him writing to De Quincey to implore his frank opinion on all occasions and confessing, with the searching self-pity which so exasperated his older friends: "It would have been indeed far, far better for me—in some little degree perhaps for society—if I could have attached more importance, greater warmth of feeling to my own writings. But I have not been happy enough for that."[2] Meanwhile the poor man's discomfort in his present lodgings was extreme. He was continually disturbed by the din of printing and took large doses of laudanum to steady his nerves. De Quincey gives a pathetically comic description of him emerging from his room, "enveloped in nightcaps, surmounted by handkerchiefs endorsed upon handkerchiefs", and shouting down the stairs to the woman who attended to his wants: "Mistress Brainbridge! I say, Mistress Brainbridge!" until even the noisy Strand rang with his wailing cries.[3] So great, moreover, was the lethargy induced by the

[1] Letters, II, 114.
[2] Unpublished Letters, I, 423.
[3] II, 188 ff.

opium, that he was hardly able to deliver his lectures at all. "His appearance was generally that of a person struggling with pain and overmastering illness," observes De Quincey, and adds the comment that the lectures themselves suffered in consequence.[1]

But in spite of illness, Coleridge was by no means always alone, and it was in his room that De Quincey made the acquaintance of other members of the literary world: Sir Thomas Noon Talfourd, the future serjeant and author of *Ion*, a dull and slow-moving tragedy which, however, had a considerable *succès d'estime* on its first production in 1836—a success largely due, one suspects, to the personal popularity of the author, who was an exceptionally well-disposed man; Bryan Waller Procter, the dramatist, who wrote under the pseudonym of 'Barry Cornwall'; Sir Humphrey Davy, the distinguished scientist; Godwin, the political philosopher; and that eccentric figure, "Walking" Stewart. De Quincey afterwards gave accounts of his impressions of some of these people. Sir Humphrey Davy seems especially to have appealed to him, probably because of his exquisite manners, though Coleridge, significantly enough, did not like him, thinking him frivolous and effeminate.[2] Men whose manners betrayed worldly reserve were never liked by Coleridge.

Of all these men, however, the one most designed to appeal to De Quincey's imagination and sense of humour was John ('Walking') Stewart, whose peculiarly English brand of eccentricity has been immortalized in one of De Quincey's most amusing essays.[3] This man, who appears to have travelled very extensively, had settled down in London to write the series of works in which he attempted to explain the universal scheme of things and to improve the human race. He lived on milk, fruit and bread, played the organ with passion, and sat about in a white hat in St. James's Park among the cows, "inhaling their balmy breath" in "trance-like ecstasy." He had a very high opinion of himself, and being persuaded that his books were marked down for persecution by the princes of future ages, he made De Quincey promise to translate all of them into Latin (as being the language likely to survive the longest) and bury them in the earth at a depth of eight

[1] Compare Crabb Robinson's remarks on Coleridge's 1811 lectures (Diary, December 14th, 1841) in which he reaches the same conclusions as De Quincey.

[2] II, 16.

[3] III, 93 ff.

feet, secured from damp. De Quincey agrees that he was mad, but contends that he was the most naturally eloquent man he ever knew: "His mind, like a shell taken from the sea, still echoed and murmured to the multitudinous sounds and forms amongst which his former years had been passed." But, alas, "he could not express his ideas on paper." A cursory examination of one of Stewart's works will convince anyone of the truth of this assertion. *The Apocalypse of Human Perfectuability* [*sic*], admittedly one of his less crazy books, is a rigmarole far worse than any De Quincey himself ever committed to paper; but, embedded in the verbiage, a real and individual mind is discoverable. The ideas are simple in themselves, but are concealed in grandiloquent phraseology. Occasionally, however, one comes across evidences of thought, as in the following: "The chaste man may be devoid of thought, sympathy, sincerity, etc., while the virtuous man must have that moral chastity that guards his sensual pleasures from doing injury to self or neighbours"—not perhaps a very clever remark, but at the same time not altogether a foolish one. Sometimes Stewart preferred to expose his ideas in verse form; *The Revelation of Nature*, for instance, is a didactic poem written in blank verse that combines the styles of Erasmus Darwin and Robert Montgomery. It opens thus:

> Awake my reason, from the mental eye,
> Impression's film and phantom's ichor wipe,
> Behold the sum of moral truth appears
> Thro' fogs of prejudice and faith dispell'd,
> Intellect's orient busts [*sic*] into a blaze
> And stars of science fade in wisdom's day.

It is easy to imagine what a delight this fantastic personage must have been to De Quincey, with his untiring curiosity, his sympathy with the strange and solitary, his disinterested love of the endless permutations of the human intellect.

Lamb also played his part in these gatherings, and De Quincey drew a little nearer to him than before;[1] but the approach was gingerly and it was not till a later period that he allowed himself to become really intimate with him. For this reason, I shall leave De Quincey's impressions of Lamb until a later chapter.

[1] III, 57.

The chief concern of De Quincey's life at this moment,[1] and one which engrossed not only his own attention, but that of the entire De Quincey family, was the antics of his brother Richard, who, having run away to sea in 1804 and been given up for lost, now suddenly turned up again. The story of his exploit, romantic and complicated, provides a curious parallel to De Quincey's own adventure as a boy, and the consciousness of being kindred spirits explains the deep affection that existed between the brothers, though De Quincey emphatically disclaims any influence over Pink.[2] The story, which extends roughly over five years, can be pieced together by combining De Quincey's own account of "My Brother Pink",[3] with Mrs. De Quincey's allusions to the affair in her letters to Thomas and Henry, of 1804–9.[4]

Pink possessed an engaging character which combined the qualities of his brothers William and Thomas. Of the elder he had the heartiness and independence of spirit, of the younger the imagination and delicate personal beauty, and the love of reading. Finding, as Thomas had done, that his mother's domination became after a time intolerable, he twice ran away from school and then finally to Gosport, where he was picked up, half starving, by the captain of a ship, whom he entreated to take him on board. The man, who was evidently a rascal and, suspecting Pink's real condition, probably hoped to make some money out of his parents, complied, and took Pink on a voyage as cabin-boy. After many adventures, in the course of which he was transferred on board a whaler, Pink became involved in a battle with some pirates, who massacred most of the crew, but spared Pink on account of the services which, as an educated man, they supposed he could render them.

For the next two years Pink remained with the pirates, "perpetrating unnumbered atrocities",[5] and unable to free himself because of his skill in reading chronometers. From time to time the ship would weigh anchor outside the Galapagos Islands, to procure supplies of wood and water, and Pink would be put ashore, alone except for the precious chronometers. Now it happened that these islands were haunted, and Pink, who, like most sailors,

[1] Letter to Wordsworth of June 9th. (Wordsworth Collection.)
[2] I, 310.
[3] I, 287 ff.
[4] Letters, I, 220–275, and II, 133–143.
[5] I, 298.

was deeply superstitious, suffered agonies of fright as the sun began to go down and leave him alone with darkness and with no companion save the chronometers. For regularly, as twilight deepened, would come the clear tap!—tap! of a ghostly woodcutter out of the depths of the forest. For some time the rhythmical sound continued, and then, suddenly, came the crash of the falling tree. After that silence returned, but only for a few moments; then the regular, far, but bell-clear tap of the axe would begin afresh. As the night deepened, the woodcutter seemed to come nearer, and at midnight the crashes were terrifyingly loud, so that Pink would creep out on to a rocky promontory, whence he could at least see the ship rising dimly out of the night. At last, as dawn began to grow, the tapping receded into the distance, and the crashes grew fainter, and with the rising of the sun the woodcutter was silent once more.

By 1807 Pink seems to have escaped from the clutches of the pirates, for the captain of the ship on which he then was wrote to Samuel Hall demanding money which Pink owed him, but failing to enclose a letter which the boy had written to his mother. Later in the year, however, Pink himself wrote to Mr. Hall, expressing his disgust with the life he was leading and asking help to return.

In 1808, therefore, he arrived in England, but hid himself, as Thomas had done, from his mother. The family expected to see him,[1] but in the end he faded away again without having seen anyone. In May 1809 he was again in England, ill and penniless, and wrote to Thomas,[2] stating his intention to stay for a time in Liverpool, for the sake of health and study, and asking his brother's advice about books. A later letter includes the following reference to the feelings which united him to his brother: "It is a great satisfaction to me that my Feelings and actions are intelligible to you, however mysterious and extraordinary they may seem to those who extend their ideas no further than to the common occurrences which come every day within their own observation."[3]

The rest of the summer and autumn of 1809, until November, were spent by De Quincey in his favourite fashion of restless alternation between Grasmere, Wrington, where his mother was now living, and London, where it was that he and Pink eventually

[1] Letters, I, 244. [2] *Ibid.*, 251. [3] *Ibid.*, 256.

met again. Pink's easy-going, straight-forward character appealed to him now, as it had in the past, and the young sailor's hard-bitten, tobacco-chewing manners and downright method of attack charmed him by their contrast to his own elaborate civility. Pink developed an enthusiasm for romantic pictures, especially those of Benjamin West, and it was at an exhibition of Salvator Rosa that Pink, who had met Lamb only once, behaved in a manner which made the conquest of that whimsical man. Seeing De Quincey and his brother standing together in front of a picture, Lamb came up to them and was about to speak, when Pink suddenly roared out: "Damn the fellow! I could do better myself," and ejected a stream of tobacco juice on to the frame of the picture. De Quincey was horrified at this deplorable lapse, but Lamb shouted with laughter and he and Pink became fast friends from that moment.[1]

But still Pink refused to see any member of his family except Thomas, so that Mrs. De Quincey became convinced that the shipping agent, Rogers, was impersonating her son for interested reasons. The story is an odd one, and a certain atmosphere of mystification hangs over this phase of it,[2] as over Thomas's experiences of 1802–3. But in the end Pink succeeded in proving his identity and by November seems to have rejoined his family.[3]

The rest of his story is quickly told. The romantic life he had led proved a stronger hold upon his temperament than the tamer inducements of a life on land, and he soon went back to the sea. Scattered references connect him with Admiral Keats in the Baltic, after which he disappears again into a further distance. He died in Jamaica, at the age of twenty-five or six. Report has it that he went on a sporting expedition into the Blue Mountains and was there probably killed by wild beasts, since he never returned.

3

Towards the end of the year 1808 the friendship between De Quincey and the Wordsworths entered upon a new phase. The necessities of a growing family had made Dove Cottage far too small for the Wordsworths, particularly as Coleridge and his two sons were apt to appear at a moment's notice to swell the house-

[1] III, 58. [2] See Letters, I, 261 ff. [3] *Ibid.*, 275.

hold; so in 1808 they had moved into Allan Bank, a fairly large house which had just been built at the north end of the lake. The owner was a self-made man from Liverpool called Crump, and while the house was building, the Wordsworths could find no words too bad for the barbarian who was threatening the beauty of their beloved Grasmere. "Wretched in name and nature," Wordsworth calls him,[1] and adds that Crump has been "goaded on by his still more wretched wife." But directly Allan Bank was finished, they pocketed their pride and took a lease of the house from Mr. Crump, who seemed in no hurry to take up residence there.

Allan Bank is not, as a matter of fact, as bad a house as the Wordsworths were pleased to make out. The exterior, with its twin gables, is harmless if rather clumsy, and inside the rooms are large and light. A good deal of the present house was added after Wordsworth's time, but even then the space must have been ample. And the view from the front of the house, down across the lake towards Rydal, is almost fiercely picturesque in its beauty. But in spite of these advantages, William and Dorothy soon had complaints to make. The house was, as De Quincey admits, cold and damp, and—to make matters worse—the chimneys smoked. However, as he rather caustically adds, Wordsworth, who was a shrewd business man, made these defects an excuse for beating Mr. Crump down over the rent—almost, indeed, to the extent of paying none at all.[2]

It was at Allan Bank, then, that De Quincey came to stay towards the end of 1808. His correspondence with Dorothy had created a sense of ease and trust between them; William was still his idol; Mrs. Wordsworth and her sister, Sara Hutchinson, who followed the lead of William and Dorothy, continued to regard him with placid approval. But with no adult member of the household was De Quincey so much *persona grata* as with the children. Johnny, aged five, and Catherine, who was only a month or two old when De Quincey arrived at Allan Bank, were his special favourites, while Coleridge reserved his affection mainly for Thomas and little Dorothy. Playing with children is a special talent, which cannot be learned, any more than best-sellers can be written with the tongue in the cheek; a perfectly sincere

[1] De Selincourt, *op. cit.*, 214.

[2] II, 359.

WILLIAM WORDSWORTH
From a drawing in plumbago by Henry Edridge, 1805
By courtesy of Mrs. E. F. Rawnsley

DOVE COTTAGE ABOUT 1805
By courtesy of the Trustees of Dove Cottage

enthusiasm, as from equal to equal, is the essence of this talent, and it is clear that De Quincey possessed it in the highest degree. Johnny he loved, but the baby Catherine he adored. Dorothy, writing to Mrs. Clarkson in June of the following year, says that De Quincey " has made us promise that he is to be her sole tutor, so that we shall not dare to show her a letter in a book, when she is old enough to have the wit to learn. . . . If, however, he fails in inspiring her with a love of learning, I am sure that he cannot fail in one thing. His gentle, sweet manners must lead her to sweetness and gentle thoughts. His conversation has been of very great use to John. . . ." [1] Thus one may put a tick against the eleventh of his *Constituents of Happiness*—' The Education of a Child.'

So enchanted was he by the landscape of Grasmere and by the company of the Wordsworths that he decided to take a lease of Dove Cottage, which had stood empty since the Wordsworths had vacated it. It was still their property, however, and had been left in the care of an old woman called Mary Dawson, who remained as De Quincey's housekeeper, when he moved into the cottage. Meanwhile, the interior needed attention, and when he returned to London in February of 1809, Dorothy undertook to superintend the necessary repairs (which included the construction of shelves for De Quincey's already considerable library) and generally to make the cottage ready for his return at the earliest possible moment.

Besides the household at Allan Bank, De Quincey left behind him two new friends, one of whom was of supreme importance in his life. We will take the less important first. This was Charles Lloyd, a talented but mentally unstable man, who lived with his family at Low Brathay, at the north end of Windermere. He was considerably better off than most of his friends, being the son of a Birmingham banker who was also a Quaker, and though he lavished hospitality upon the literary lions of the neighbourhood, he never succeeded in making himself really liked by them. This was partly his own fault, for he was at once snobbish, self-conscious and unctuously humble to those whom he looked upon as his intellectual superiors. Moreover, the violent paranoia which was later to land him in a lunatic asylum, was already, in 1809, inter-

[1] De Selincourt, *op. cit.*, 242.

mittently apparent in exhibitions of groundless suspicion and acts of hysterical mischief. De Quincey, who understood him better than the other members of the circle, puts us in complete possession of this unfortunate man's not uninteresting character.[1] Lloyd was fully aware that Wordsworth and Coleridge despised him for his shivery sensibility, his feminine desire for approval, and the importance he so obviously attached to " the conventional usages amongst the higher circles." This consciousness and the annoyance it produced was no doubt responsible for the pointlessly malicious act which lost him the friendship of Coleridge. The latter had written to Lloyd illustrating the difference between talent and genius by the example of himself (Coleridge) and Lamb; upon which Lloyd promptly showed the letter to Lamb, who was not unnaturally vexed. This caused a coolness between Lamb and Coleridge, which was not forgiven Lloyd, either by the parties concerned or by their friends. Yet he had a genuine talent and considerable personal charm. "He was," says De Quincey, "somewhat too Rousseauish; but he had, in conversation, the most extraordinary powers for analysis of a certain kind, applied to the philosophy of manners, and the most delicate *nuances* of social life."[2] His poems, some of which were published in a joint volume with a series by Lamb, have a certain melancholy individuality, but they are tenuous, conventional in diction and purely autobiographical: poor Lloyd was never able to escape the approaching shadow of his madness, of which he was acutely conscious. His novel, *Edmund Oliver,** is a lachrymose affair told in a series of Richardsonian letters, in which the "*nuances* of social life" play an insistent part. De Quincey professed to derive pleasure from it, but it does not permit itself to be read to-day. There is, however, a deep pathos in the story of this tormented man, which De Quincey understood. Sympathy and understanding drew the two near together throughout 1809 and 1810.

John Wilson—" the Admiral of the Lakes ", as he called himself —was superficially a very different sort of person, though it will afterwards become apparent that he had certain fundamental traits in common with Lloyd. Tall, extremely handsome, intensely 'Nordic'; with a mane of fair hair and piercing blue eyes;

[1] II, 381 ff. [2] II, 201.

bursting with crude vitality and a schoolboy sense of fun; rowing, sailing (he kept seven yachts on the lake, a ten-oared Oxford barge, and several lighter boats), striding over the mountains, praying aloud for sixteen miles on end, making the landscape ring with his gigantic laughter, wrestling, jumping twelve yards in three jumps, with a heavy stone in each hand, reading voluminously and without method—here was a man peculiarly fitted to appeal to De Quincey's sense of romance and his need of hero-worship. Here was William all over again—but with oh, how welcome a difference! For Wilson, instead of despising and bullying De Quincey, admired him openly for qualities which he himself lacked, while at the same time providing his friend with an endless fund of vicarious energy.

The two met first in Coleridge's room at Allan Bank, though De Quincey had previously admired Wilson's appearance at a dance given by Lloyd. Wilson was his exact contemporary.[1] The eldest son of a rich gauze manufacturer of Paisley, he was left fatherless and well-off at the age of eleven. After spending six years at Glasgow University, he went to Magdalen College, Oxford, at the age of eighteen, in the same year as De Quincey matriculated at Worcester. But, as was perhaps natural, the two never met during their 'Varsity careers. After leaving Oxford, Wilson had bought the estate of Elleray, on Windermere, and settled down there. On this first occasion of their meeting, it was Wilson's conversation rather than his appearance which impressed De Quincey, "the points which chiefly struck me being the humility and gravity with which he spoke of himself, his large expansion of heart, and a certain air of noble frankness which overspread everything he said. He seemed to have an intense enjoyment of life; indeed being young, rich, healthy, and full of intellectual activity, it could not be very wonderful that he should feel happy and pleased with himself and others; but it was somewhat unusual to find that so rare an assemblage of endowments had communicated no tinge of arrogance to his manner, or at all disturbed the general temperance of his mind." [2]

Carlyle, who knew Wilson well at a later date, describes him in roughly the same terms as De Quincey uses, but with a more

[1] De Quincey makes him a year or two younger than himself; but this is a mistake.
[2] V, 268.

critical eye that discovers the fundamental weakness of this fascinating man. "What struck me most was the glance of those big blue eyes, stern yet loving, pointing so authentically to something far away—a human character of fine and noble elements, thought I, but not at one with itself; an exuberant enough, leafy and tropical kind of tree rather exhaling itself in balmy odours than producing fruit." [1]

But not at one with itself . . . Carlyle had put his finger on the essential point. It was easier for him to do so at the time when he wrote that passage; the self-distrust, the moral cowardice, the dilettantism, the self-indulgence in sentimental poses, the inability to acquire an adult view of life and social behaviour, had already gone far to change Wilson from the glittering Elizabethan of twenty-four into the raucous, second-rate practical-joker of the early Blackwood period. But at the moment when the friendship between himself and De Quincey broke into triumphant flower, this deterioration had not yet set in. Throughout those first years at Grasmere Wilson kept De Quincey in a continual state of delighted amazement and—what was more—of joy in living. Their mutual admiration provided the basis for an uncritical intimacy which restored to each those aspects of experience which his temperament had made difficult of access, steadying the blow-pipe flame of Wilson's erratic energy with the hand of scholarly judgment and enlivening the visionary fantasy of De Quincey's fearful soul with the thrill of animal enjoyment.

4

Those portions of the spring, summer and autumn of 1809 which De Quincey spent away from Grasmere are laced together by a busy correspondence with Dorothy, and a still busier and more voluminous one with Wordsworth himself. In Dorothy's letters the domestic affairs of the Wordsworths alternate with gossip about the district and news of the progress of the repairs to Dove Cottage (" Ned Wilson has made deal Bookcases, but in consideration of your having mentioned Mahogany for the Book-shelves, we have got all the rest of the furniture of Mahogany "),[2]

[1] *The Nineteenth Century*, vol. LXXXVII, No. DXV, 103–117.
[2] Letters, I, 201.

while De Quincey replies with humorous descriptions of his mother's household at Wrington and the self-importance of Hannah More. Throughout Dorothy's letters the theme of the children is constant: the progress of Johnny and Catherine; the former's affection for his friend and desire for his return;[1] De Quincey's unwarrantable extravagance in buying a new toy cart for the boy, when the one he has will do quite well;[2] Catherine's first efforts to pronounce De Quincey's name ("Ah! Kisleea; ah! Kisleea").[3] Dorothy has her anxieties too: Sir Michael le Fleming, of Rydal Hall, is quarrelling with Mr. North over the right to lop the trees on Nab Scar, a process which, whoever may perform it, causes great pain to the Wordsworths; the chimney at Allan Bank continues to smoke with unabated vigour; Coleridge, "though not noisy himself, makes a bustle in the house"[4] and generally disorganizes the household by sitting up all night and then staying in bed most of the next morning; worst of all, William has financial worries and may have to turn to journalism—a thought which Dorothy dislikes for him even more than he dislikes it for himself.[5]

But the chief concern of this time was Wordsworth's pamphlet on *The Convention of Cintra*, which De Quincey had undertaken to revise, punctuate and see through the press, while he was in London. It would seem surprising that a man of such sturdy independence of judgment as Wordsworth should have turned to a young man like De Quincey to edit one of his works, if we had not already had evidence that Coleridge entertained an equally high regard for De Quincey's critical faculties.[6] In 1814, moreover, Wordsworth again turned to De Quincey for advice about the poem *Laodamia* and pressed him, as Coleridge had done, to be more detailed in the expression of his opinion.[7]

The *Cintra* pamphlet really only concerns us here in so far as De Quincey may be said to have influenced the effect of its periods by his revision of the punctuation and phrasing; but, since he also evidently agreed with its burden, it is not out of place here to state briefly what that was. Wordsworth's main argument is that Wellesley's convention, by allowing Junot's army to retire unmolested from Portugal, with the plunder it had acquired, dealt

[1] Letters, I, 201. [2] *Ibid.*, 185 [3] *Ibid.*, 211.
[4] *Ibid.*, 192. [5] *Ibid.*, 194. [6] See p. 100.
[7] Japp, 135.

a disgraceful blow at the legitimate Nationalist aspirations of the Peninsula. But this contention was only the occasion for what is in fact a tract in favour of Nationalism as a valid gospel for all countries, and in this fact lies its historical importance and originality. Wordsworth's idea of nationalism resolves itself into a simple and instinctive attachment of simple men to the soil on which they were born—a view to which he was led less by any profound knowledge of the Westmorland Dalesmen than by an introspective analysis of his own relations with Nature. This being so, it is not remarkable that he should not have foreseen the horrors to which the gospel of Nationalism was to give rise, in the course of the next century and a half; for he based his theory on another which was a relic of his Jacobin days: the natural goodness of man. It was the recognition, in middle age, of this fallacy,[1] which caused him to turn his back on his early revolutionary principles and won him the thoughtless hatred of minds too unstable for useful meditation on experience, or of those who, like Byron and Hazlitt, were permanently embittered by their own inability to come to terms with society. As Mr. Crane Brinton has put it: "If the Revolution in ideas meant the natural goodness of man, the Revolution in fact meant the supremacy of an ill-educated middle class";[2] and the later conservatism of Wordsworth, Coleridge and Southey was due to the conviction, borne in upon them by time and experience, that the objects of Liberty are not necessarily new, are indeed more likely to be those goods which—man being what he is—experience has proved to be attainable in practice.

The pamphlet is in itself a fine piece of polemical writing. True, Coleridge blames the obscurity of the style—a fault which, he contends, was made worse by De Quincey's "strange and most mistaken system of punctuation. . . . The periods are often alarmingly long, perforce of their construction, but De Quincey's punctuation has made several of them immeasurable, and perplexed half the rest. Never was a stranger notion that , ; : and . could be made logical symbols, expressing all the diversities of logical connection."[3] But these strictures seem to me unduly severe.

[1] See Wordsworth's Prose Works (Grosart), I, 254.
[2] *Political Ideas of the English Romantics*, p. 59.
[3] Letter to Daniel Stuart, June 13th, 1809.

The punctuation is perhaps rather fussy, but that is surely a fault on the right side, especially in theoretical prose, where clarity of meaning is paramount. To a present-day reader, at any rate, the pamphlet presents no difficulties from this point of view.

The amount of trouble which De Quincey took with the preparation of this little work testifies both to his admiration of the author and the importance which he already attached to the question of literary style. The correspondence in which he and Wordsworth indulged on the subject is mountainous and makes such exceedingly dull reading that, were I to quote a single one of these letters, I am persuaded no one would read it through.[1]*

If Wordsworth was satisfied with the result of these joint labours, he can hardly have been pleased by the pamphlet's reception. De Quincey, however, continued for some time rather pathetically to hope that it might become a best-seller. In July he writes to Dorothy, from Wrington:

I could not help expecting that a second edition might be called for; and that then something might be made out of it in the money way—to make Mr Wordsworth amends for so much trouble and anxiety spent upon it; indeed I sometimes hope (particularly from its good reception, as I hear, in the army) that it may become the *rage*—and produce some thousand pounds. . . ." [2]

This optimism was far from being justified. The pamphlet seems, it is true, to have been read in a few cases with appreciation: Canning thought its contentions true in the main, Crabb Robinson reviewed it favourably in the *London Review*, and the *British Critic* spoke approvingly of "the generous spirit which this pamphlet breathes." [3] But, for all that, it fell under the table.[4] The elaboration of the style, and the way in which the topicality of the argument tends to be obscured by its more general implications—these are qualities which make it more interesting to us to-day, but made it less effective at the time it was written.

[1] Those who are interested can consult Letters, I, 148–175. The rest of the correspondence is in MS. in the Wordsworth Collection.

[2] Wordsworth Collection.

[3] Crane Brinton, *op. cit.*, p. 99.

[4] It is a curious fact, significant of the ephemeral and capricious nature of public feeling, that when, in the previous year to that in which Wordsworth's pamphlet was published, Brougham launched a similar attack on the "French Usurpation in Spain", in the *Edinburgh Review*, it was greeted with a storm of indignation and its author condemned as grossly seditious. (See G. T. Garratt: *Lord Brougham*, p. 31.)

5

As we have seen, from the last-quoted letter, De Quincey spent the late summer of 1809 at his mother's new home, Westhay, at Wrington, in Somerset. The extremely amusing and malicious letters which he wrote to Dorothy and Mrs. Wordsworth from this place show that he was in unusually high spirits at this time. Mrs. De Quincey was in her element, for the house was all but uninhabitable owing to the activities of a swarm of workmen and builders:

When I first came here [writes De Quincey] we had below stairs only one room habitable, besides the kitchen; and in every other part of the house workmen of every class—stone-masons, carpenters, painters, plaisterers, bell-hangers, etc; and even after the bedrooms were finished, it was impossible to make use of them in the daytime; for there being no front stairs yet erected—and there being no road to the back stairs but through the hall which the workmen used as a workshop, there was no getting upstairs without displacing all their benches, etc, which was a complete ceremony and process; and, being up, one was a complete prisoner—which did not suit me at all:—since then we have migrated successively into a parlour of a neighbouring farm-house;—into a greenhouse with no floor;—into a room with a floor but no ceiling;—into a closet 6 feet by 6;—and finally, after having been hunted round the house by the painters and paperers, we have resolved into our original sitting-room—with the library adjoining—completely finished. The effect of living in the house under these circumstances will have been to get it finished in one third of the time that it would otherwise have taken. . . ."[1]

He adds, significantly, that his mother is the only person in the neighbourhood who likes the *Friend*, the magazine which Coleridge was publishing at this time.

De Quincey was highly contemptuous of his mother's whole entourage at Wrington; but most of his sarcasms are directed at Hannah More and her sisters, with whom the De Quincey family were in daily contact:

As I have received a civil message from Holy Hannah (as Dr Beddoes called her) through my sister, I must go (I believe) and

[1] MS. in Wordsworth Collection.

see [*MS. torn*] great aversion to the elder sisters from all that I hear about them. So convinced are they of the incurable Jacobinism of Mr Wordsworth and Mr Coleridge—that none of them but Hannah, I am told, will suffer you to say a word about them: but for Mr Southey they have all a little kindness—enough to make them wish him out of such corrupting society—'he was such a Strephon!' they say, when they saw him in Bristol.[1]

Follows his opinion of Mrs. More's latest novel, *Coelebs*:

Such trash I really never did read . . . I could not have believed that even the reputation of H. M.'s godliness could have sold nine editions . . . I could not find a sentence with any thought in it; and the grossest errors in propriety and good sense in every page.

This is amusing enough; but in the last letter of this series, which is addressed to Mrs. Wordsworth,[2] De Quincey fairly lets himself go, in a passage which, for humour and psychological acumen, is worthy of Jane Austen. The attitude of the Wringtonites, first to the subject of Spain (they were "hostile to the Spaniards to a man"), secondly to the *Friend*, which they found "so obscure", irritated De Quincey so much that, singling out Hannah More as usual, he transfixes her with a skewer, thus:

She has described herself sufficiently in her books . . . her conversation (for that she thinks her forte) is just like them—aphoristic; epigrammatic—nothing been thought to be said well at Barley Wood[3] but what is said pointedly; full of trite quotations—hardly ever introduced to confirm—or illustrate—or because they might adequately convey the feeling—but as cold ornaments and garnishings; or, when she does sometimes make a formal quotation in proof of what she says, it is always—for fear of being thought 'a learned lady'—ushered in with an affectation of doubt as to the author—as 'I think, it is my lord Bacon who says'—etc. Then everything must be 'improved'; as, if Westhay stand on low ground—and Barley Wood on a hill—then 'what a benevolent dispensation of *Providence* it is that—when there were but two pieces of land to be sold in the valley for so many years, *that* should have been put up for sale when the old wanted to purchase which made it unnecessary to climb hills for a walk—and on the other hand, when the young who could climb hills wanted to purchase,

[1] MS. in Wordsworth Collection.
[2] *Ibid.* The letter is dated September 20th.
[3] Mrs. More's house.

that only should have been to be had which made it necessary for them to take the exercise necessary for their health before they could find any good walks.' Moreover she is restless until every thought is brought into such a shape that she can translate it into some of her received positions; and thus every avenue is shut up against gaining or communicating anything in her company; since, if she finds that the case is desperate and that you will not permit what you say to be lopped down into some of her own previous thoughts, then she makes no further answer but by bowing her head. On the whole, her house would be the very dullest place I ever was in (since generally everybody thinks it a duty to sit silent until she has some literary anecdote or formal sentiment to offer)—but for the endless succession of visitors . . . and but that, as all the 5 sisters knew everybody of any celebrity in the last age, I always draw one of them into an account of Louisa the lady of the haystack—Edmund Burke—Garrick—Mrs Montague and her society—Dr Johnson etc.

After these fireworks De Quincey reverts to the scandal of the success of *Coelebs* and concludes his diatribe thus:

I see, on looking back, that I have omitted the best that can be said of her—viz: that she is very courteous in her manners—as far as she can be so, not being benevolent;—but then I had also omitted the worst thing—viz. that she is, as you know, a horrid bigot—censorious—and greedy of flattery to any amount under cover of a frequent disclamation of all merit—and with all the forms and phrases of profound humility.

All this is much more outspoken than anything in De Quincey's published articles on Hannah More; yet that which he wrote for *Tait's Magazine* in 1833 [1] adds considerably to his virulent portrait of the lady, though at the same time he admits compunction at not having been more tolerant to her in his younger days. From the very first she antagonized him by her view of English and French generalship, and by her avowed hatred of philosophy—though she made him give her an explanation of Kant's system and tried to set him and Lord Londonderry by the ears on the subject of the existence of God. Recalling such incidents, one does not wonder at the glee with which De Quincey describes Mrs. More's snobbish embarrassment at being found *en tête-à-tête* with

[1] XIV, 94.

Joseph Cottle when some royalty called upon her, or the unspiritual determination with which she forced the man who had jilted her at the altar to disgorge £400 a year.

As De Quincey's visit to Westhay lengthened, his amusement at the follies of the Wringtonites gave way to irritation. One feels that he only managed to contain himself by unburdening his feelings in letters to the Wordsworths.

Walter Scott's last novel—*The Lady of the Lake*—is the grand subject of prate and chatter hereabouts [he complains]. I have read it aloud here, to oblige my mother; and a more disgusting task I never had. I verily think that it is the completest magazine of all forms of the *Falsetto* in feeling and diction that now exists; and the notes, as usual, the most finished specimen of book-making (alias swindling). . . . Yesterday at a dinner-party I had a hornet's nest upon me for only observing that the true solution of Walter's notoriety was to be found in this—that, whereas heretofore if one could read novels one must do it under the penalty thereunto annexed of being accredited for feeble-mindedness and *miss*iness, now (by favour of W.S.) one might read a novel and have the credit of reading a poem. An excellent joke is that all these good people think *The Lady of the Lake* infinitely superior to *Marmion*. . . . 'Strange that such difference should be 'Twixt Tweedledum and Tweedle-dee '.[1]

This is now the general opinion of Scott's poems; but it needed considerable critical perspicuity, as well as independence of mind, to reach such a conclusion in 1809.

De Quincey concludes this letter with a statement of his intention to return to Grasmere sometime in the following week, *i.e.* at the beginning of September. He seems to have fulfilled this intention, for it was in that month that we find him and Wilson projecting an expedition to Timbuctoo, to discover the source of the Niger. The suggestion will have come from Wilson, but De Quincey seems to have welcomed it at first. But doubts quickly supervened: "The trackless forest, the unbridged river, the howling wilderness, the fierce Mahometan bigotry of the Moor, the lawlessness of the pagan native, the long succession of petty despots . . . all these chances of ruin, with the climate superadded, leave too little of rational hopefulness to such an enterprise for sustaining

[1] MSS. in Wordsworth Collection.

those genial spirits without which nothing of that nature can prosper." [1] Moreover De Quincey did not think Wilson suited to such an expedition. That may have been true; but what is more obvious is that De Quincey was even less of the stuff of which explorers are made. In any case, the difficulties proved too great, and Wilson suggested Spain instead. This trip was to have included the Mediterranean Islands, Greece, Constantinople, Syria, Egypt, "and perhaps Nubia." [2] This time it was Coleridge who, consulted on the subject, rushed in to damp De Quincey's ardour with a long letter of elaborate dissuasion. His stay in Spain will not be long enough to enable him to acquire the language, especially as he will always be with two other English people (who the third member of the party was to be does not transpire) and the country is in a most uncomfortable state, from which danger to his health is to be apprehended.[3]

Whether De Quincey regarded this advice or not, we do not know, but the project was put an end to by a more portentous figure than Coleridge—Napoleon himself, whose movements made such a journey at that particular moment almost impracticable. This is to be lamented, for the enrichment of De Quincey's mind and the stimulus to his imagination, which this journey could not have failed to produce, is incalculable, and might well have changed the entire aspect of his subsequent writings. For it cannot be denied that the range of interest to be found in these, though astoundingly wide, suffers from a certain insularity of outlook largely attributable to the fact that their author never once, in the course of a long life, found it possible to go outside the British Isles. The harm done to De Quincey by this lack of opportunity is immediately apparent in the article on *Modern Greece* written in 1842, in which the Englishman's passion for the landscape of the south is sourly attributed to Radcliffian romanticism, and in which De Quincey betrays his inevitable ignorance of the essential qualities of that landscape by denouncing the traveller for "leaving a real Calabria in Montgomeryshire or Devonshire, for dreary, sunburned flats in Bavaria, in Provence, in Languedoc," [4]—hardly a good description of either Calabria, Devonshire or Bavaria, and particularly strange in view of the fact that he goes on to point out, in a most acute passage, how inconceivable to the Latin mind

[1] V, 291. [2] V, 283. [3] Letters, I, 140. [4] VII, 350.

is our northern habit of assimilating a landscape to our own moods.[1] That De Quincey realized this curious fact, but was able at the same time to express a contempt for " mere scenery "—an attitude which accords ill with his youthful passion for the Lake District—suggests that, as regards foreign travel, he suffered in middle age from a feeling of ' sour grapes.'

But it was now November, 1809, and as at last he entered into possession of Dove Cottage, his delight was too great for long regret at the collapse of a plan which, however alluring in itself, must have removed him from the spot which held so varied a prospect of delight.

[1] VII, 351.

CHAPTER V

THE DECLENSION

I

DE QUINCEY was happy at last. He had still sufficient money for his needs; he was immediately surrounded with an ever-growing mountain of books and—less immediately—by the friends he loved; he was living in a cottage consecrated for him by the fact that it had enshrined Wordsworth on the occasion of their first meeting. His health, though it still required the support and stimulus of opium, was better than it had been for many years and seemed, moreover, to be improving. "It gave me great pleasure to see how much stronger you seem," remarked Coleridge, in a letter of this date. "Your constitution is evidently strengthening, and with care and regular Exercise, I have little doubt that in another year you will have left all your complaints behind you." [1]

Coleridge need not have used that capital E. De Quincey, who had always been devoted to pedestrian exercise, now developed the habit of walking fourteen miles a day and more, either alone or in the company of Wilson or Ritson, the wrestler. To the opium-addict such exercise is absolutely necessary to preserve health; but De Quincey enjoyed walking for its own sake. The combination—so peculiarly English—of homeliness and romance in the landscape of Grasmere and the surrounding district, exactly fitted the mould of his imagination. The small details of nature—the grey tangle of a root clutching a bank, the drops of yesterday's rain still left in the cup of a flower, the oddly memorable shape of a patch of rock which has worn through the grass of the hillside—these were not De Quincey's preoccupation, in the sense that they were the chief source of Wordsworth's delight. De Quincey's pleasure in country scenery

[1] Letters, I, 143.

was of a more macroscopic kind; he used it, in fact, as a backcloth for his moods, arrogating the various aspects of mountain, field and lake to himself as the symbolic furniture of his mind. Grasmere made this method easy, for its landscape manages, within an actually very narrow scope (in comparison, say, with an Alpine valley), to provide the sensibility of the observer with all the characteristic images of nature, from the bleakly ferocious to the blandly domestic. In concentric rings, fitted with the nicety of Chinese boxes and coloured with the gradual shades of England, the black peaks of the mountains modulate into the tawny colours of the upper pastureland, down through belts of ash and fir and rank bracken, to the vivid green of the lower fields, the luxurious tints of oak and beech, and, at last—like a plain jewel in an elaborate mount—the oval lake itself, with its "ark-like" island. De Quincey himself noticed the peculiar flatness of the Westmorland valley bottoms; [1] perhaps it is partly this feature, combined with the comparative nearness of the mountains, which helps to make so vivid the impression of concentrated, rock-garden-like greenness in the immediate vicinity of the lake itself—that look of a specially and capriciously favoured tuft, planted with selective care and lovingly watered, in the midst of a whole field of reckless grass. It was this compendiousness—this giving of easy and rapid access to all the moods of nature, so that a man can pass, in the space of an hour or two's walk, from Alpine gloom, solitude and danger, to the clustered bird-song, the dappled gaiety and safety of a landscape garden—which inspired Wordsworth's poetry with that quality of comprehensive reverence and gave so lively a satisfaction to the imagination of De Quincey. This construction of the lakeland landscape finds a curious parallel in De Quincey's dreams, which are similarly 'ringed'—the outer confines being those of terror and despair, while, as we approach the centre, warmth and the graciousness of tender memories gradually supervene.

But it was not only, or chiefly, in the daytime that De Quincey's enormous walks were taken. The mysterious night, its solitude and silence, its rapt attention to the unspoken thoughts of the lonely vigilant, moved him, as on the night of his first meeting with Coleridge, to examine the nature of that secret cadence in which the life of day descends and merges into the life of sleep.

[1] XIII, 127.

The sense of adventure, not yet quite dead within him; the love of solitude; the sense of power conferred by threading, his brain still aglow with life, between the habitations of sleeping people; filled De Quincey's heart with a secret excitement.

What I liked in this solitary rambling was, to trace the course of evening through its household hieroglyphics from the windows which I passed or saw: to see the blazing fires shining through the windows of houses, lurking in nooks far apart from neighbours; sometimes, in solitudes that seemed abandoned to the owl, to catch the sounds of household mirth; then, some miles further, to perceive the time of going to bed; then the gradual sinking to silence of the house, then the drowsy reign of the cricket; at intervals, to hear church-clocks or a little solitary chapel-bell, under the brows of mighty hills, proclaiming the hours of the night, and flinging out their sullen knells over the graves where 'the rude forefathers of the hamlet slept'—where the strength and the loveliness of Elizabeth's time, or Cromwell's, and through so many fleeting generations that have succeeded, had long ago sunk to rest.[1]

And one night he came upon the huge, motionless figure of a farmer whom he knew, sitting in his garden in shirt-sleeves, under the cold moon of March, calmly taking snuff.

The walking habit remained with De Quincey till quite the end of his life. He affirmed, indeed, that it promoted the dreaming faculty,[2] and for this reason his nocturnal walks always gave him the most pleasure. His neighbours, seeing the tiny figure flit past their windows, with body, head and arms held rigid and only the legs flickering in rapid movements, thought him mad; but he did not care. Dove Cottage was a safe refuge from the eye of curiosity, an ivory tower for the activity of his endlessly busy brain. The house which nowadays stands in front of the cottage had not then been built, so that De Quincey's view of the lake was uninterrupted. It must have been particularly good from the room which he used as a study—the room on the right at the top of the stairs. This had been the parlour in Wordsworth's day and now, lined with the bookshelves which Dorothy had taken so much trouble about, and with an ever-increasing overflow of books all over the floor and chairs, it resisted even the well-meant

[1] II, 325. [2] XIII, 335.

efforts of old Mary Dawson to tidy it. But the little room is cosy and charming even now, as indeed is the whole of the cottage, partly because the lattice windows are astonishingly large for the size of the rooms, which are consequently much lighter than those of most cottages; partly because of an indefinable dignity and proportion which are generally found only in much larger houses. Dove Cottage, the exterior of which, apart from the windows, is in no way remarkable, possesses the most un-pokey interior imaginable for so small a space.

Here then, in the little room from the window of which could be seen the village of Grasmere and the church, with its curious, prick-eared tower; above and a little to the left, the gabled façade of Allan Bank; and beyond, the soft contoured cleft of Easedale, De Quincey would sit, reading, endlessly reading, with a decanter of laudanum by his side. He was busy filling in the gaps in the education which he had mapped out for himself at Oxford and which visits to London and Westhay (continued all through this period) interrupted but did not spoil. The ambition to produce a world-shaking system of philosophy still hovered in the back of his mind and guided the course of his reading; but it was becoming fainter with the realization that his talents lay elsewhere, in the regions of more various and imaginative interpretation. He had not as yet ventured to publish anything, feeling that it would be better to wait yet a little time for the tangled meditations of his brain to resolve themselves into some definitive form; and pressure of poverty had not yet made it necessary for him to drive his pen willy-nilly through a desert of hack journalism.

Meanwhile the laudanum decanter, though, to be sure, it was always there, was not emptied more rapidly as the days passed. The series of events which led to a sudden increase in De Quincey's daily consumption of opium, had not yet begun. At present he was only taking enough to quiet the nerves of his stomach and stimulate his mind to the pitch where he could work incessantly and with profit.

Besides the Wordsworths, Lloyd and Wilson, De Quincey had a number of acquaintances in the neighbourhood of whom he gives an entertaining account in the series of articles entitled *The Society of the Lakes*.[1] There were, for instance, the Misses Cullen, who

[1] II, 348 ff.

lived in high-nosed neglect of the poets who dwelt near them, in deference to the opinion of the *Edinburgh Review*. There was Monsieur Simond, a French American whom the Revolution had driven into exile and who had married a niece of John Wilkes. He was a convinced materialist and Wordsworth, who now loathed all things French, despised his opinion so much that he would not even trouble to contradict him. There was Miss Elizabeth Smith, a philological scholar and translator of Klopstock, and Thomas Wilkinson, whose verses, though feeble in poetic power, contained touches of feeling that caused Wordsworth to read them aloud with pleasure. And there was the Sympson family, celebrated in the *Excursion*, and Mr. K., a farmer upon whom Wordsworth looked with an unfavourable eye as a planter of the larches which were beginning to disfigure the landscape of Grasmere. But De Quincey probably had little truck with these minor figures of the Grasmere scene; an occasional visit, made in company with Wordsworth or Wilson, will have been sufficient for his slender social needs.

Southey can hardly be described as a minor figure of the scene, but De Quincey never sought out his society or became in the least intimate with him. "For the next ten or eleven years [*i.e.* from 1808] . . . I might, in a qualified sense, call myself his friend"[1] is not an enthusiastic statement, and though all De Quincey's references to Southey are informed by respect, it is plain from them that he could feel no affection for the man. The atmosphere of conscious rectitude dispensed by Southey must have been galling to almost anybody, let alone those who, like Coleridge and De Quincey, were conscious of considerable weakness of temperament which, they may have been sure, would receive short shrift from Southey. But the latter, though not a clever man, seems to have been not unconscious of De Quincey's abilities, for he remarked that he "is a singular man, but better informed than any person almost that I ever met at his age."

De Quincey at once noticed the lack of any real feeling of friendship between Wordsworth and Southey, and afterwards took a rather malicious pleasure in recording it.[2] Southey's female fussiness irritated Wordsworth—he called it "finical." The difference between the two men is well illustrated by their several

[1] II, 339. [2] II, 303 ff.

attitudes to books: Southey loved them as objects, whereas Wordsworth had no feeling whatever for them, apart from their contents. De Quincey reports his own and Southey's horror at the sight of Wordsworth cutting the leaves of De Quincey's own copy of Burke with a knife that had just been used to butter bread. To Wordsworth such an action seemed quite natural, because he "lived in the open air" and was without the instincts of the scholar or the bibliophile; but Southey "lived in his library, which Coleridge used to call his wife", and anyone who has seen one of his manuscripts—exquisitely written, with hardly an erasure, on tiny pages—will not be surprised by his indignation at Wordsworth's sacrilegious act.

A much more valued friend was Coleridge, who spent the greater part of 1810 at Allan Bank, where he occupied himself, with sighs and groans and a complete lack of method, with the publication of the *Friend*. It was already plain to everyone but the editor that this periodical was a failure, being both too 'stiff' to appeal to a wide public and so full of ill-expressed metaphysical speculation that it annoyed the intelligent for whom it was designed; but, as usual, Coleridge persisted for a time in evading the obvious truth. He saw De Quincey daily, finding the latter's library a great convenience. Indeed, he would accumulate as many as five hundred books at a time; but he treated them very conscientiously, inscribing De Quincey's name in each and adding the designation 'Esquire', which embarrassed their owner so much that he afterwards spent some weeks in rubbing out of each volume the offending title, "which else had the appearance to a stranger of having been conferred by myself".[1] Unless Coleridge's treatment of De Quincey's books was very different from his treatment of his own and other people's, we may take it as certain that De Quincey found a good many of the borrower's marginalia in the books, as well as the inscription.*

This was also the year in which the estrangement between Wordsworth and Coleridge, which, unknown to the latter, had been maturing for some time, came at last to a head. Wordsworth had by now become convinced of Coleridge's incurable feebleness of will, his inability to finish what he had begun, and his shilly-shallying method of conducting his life. To his irritation with

[1] II, 191.

these weaknesses was now added that of harbouring in his own house a man who upset the entire family by his inconsiderate habits, used Sara Hutchinson as a secretary, and made impossible demands upon the sympathy of everyone by his perpetual lamentations and sudden bursts of equally unreasonable optimism. It is easy for us to see that these contradictory transports were perfectly sincere, each at the moment it was indulged in; but a man of Wordsworth's temperament can hardly be blamed for finding the aggregate result intolerable. Thus the painful misunderstanding which arose out of Wordsworth's revision of feeling towards Coleridge, involved behaviour on the former's part which cannot be thought unreasonable or treacherous by a disinterested observer. The occasion of the quarrel was the fatal remark, made by Wordsworth to Basil Montagu, who had invited Coleridge to stay with him in London, that the latter was a "perfect nuisance" in the house, coupled with the no less disobliging opinion that he had "rotted out his entrails with drugs." In view of what Wordsworth had had to endure, this was a perfectly justifiable warning and must have represented but the irreducible minimum of what he felt. But Montagu was, as Carlyle said, "an honest-hearted goose,"[1] and his tactless blurting out, and exaggeration, of Wordsworth's remarks caused Coleridge, who alone knew how true they were, to fly into a passion and accuse Wordsworth of underhand and unfriendly dealing.[2]

What De Quincey thought of this affair is not known; but he must have heard of it, and it was open to him to regard it as a warning. It is this last point which mainly concerns us here. For, with his acute psychological instinct, De Quincey could, from the progress of the Coleridge imbroglio, have deduced several facts about Wordsworth's character that were, six years later, to have a bearing on his own case. The ostensible reasons were different, but the fundamental causes that led Wordsworth to give up Coleridge as a bad job, were responsible for the change in his attitude to De Quincey at the time of the latter's marriage.

[1] Froude, *Carlyle*, I, 258.
[2] See de Selincourt, *op. cit.* p. 250 ff. and *Unpublished Letters of S. T. C.*, II, 79.

2

De Quincey spent almost the whole of 1811 at Grasmere, and in the summer of that year received a visit from his mother and his two sisters, Mary and Jane. Mary seems to have been a sweet, rather colourless girl, but Jane's letters show her to have been made of the same tart stuff as her mother. " Pray explain to me," she challenged her brother, " why Milton dares to make Eve inferior to Adam before the fall, when we *know* that they were created equal. . . . Allow me to observe that this is a mistake which only man, proud man, could have made." [1] Moreover, she disapproved of her brother's making his sitting-room upstairs and wanted it, in defiance of his known income, to " open on a sloping lawn, buried in the shade of venerable beeches." [2] And in another place she styles herself an " Anti-spring-ist ",[3] severely preferring the autumn.

De Quincey himself has left no record of the feelings this visitation inspired in him; but I think we are justified in assuming that on the whole he was glad when it was over. During these years he was weaning himself, quietly but assiduously, from the influence of his family—especially of his mother; and whatever feelings of filial obligation may have remained with him, the fact is that he deliberately saw less and less of her as time went on. The correspondence continues of course, in a one-sided fashion,—now faintly pathetic, as from a mother who feels herself neglected, now acrimonious, whenever the question of money crops up, or the foolish independence of Henry or Thomas in daring to take a wife without asking their mother's advice. But it is significant that, though De Quincey's later letters to his mother are full of grateful affection, he pointedly ignores her efforts to interfere in his private life.

Wilson, who had just married a Miss Jane Penny, continued to provide his main source of pleasure, apart from study. Marriage seems to have made no difference to Wilson's life, for he still went dashing off into the country for days at a time, alone or in De Quincey's company, fishing and challenging tinkers to wrestle with him. De Quincey viewed this robust behaviour with a

[1] Letters, II, 7. [2] *Ibid.*, 2. [3] *Ibid.*, 12.

mixture of admiration and a rather prim disapproval; but it is plain, from his account of Wilson dealing with a runaway bull,[1] that he found the man's high spirits irresistible. In later life De Quincey used to tell a story of a row which he once witnessed, between Wilson and a Frenchman, in a theatre. Wilson announced that they would settle the quarrel outside. "Then," said De Quincey, gazing vaguely and mildly into the distance, "the Professor closed both the little Frenchman's eyes, and, his vision being eliminated, the conflict ended." Had the aggressor been anyone but Wilson, De Quincey would have had some tart comments to make on this act of violence, which also indicates one of the reasons why Wordsworth came to dislike Wilson so much, after a preliminary disposition in his favour.

In March, 1812, De Quincey left Grasmere for London, where he stayed until the summer, pursuing his legal studies in a half-hearted way. On April 16th he wrote to Wordsworth: "I called on Dr. Stoddart the Monday after I arrived in London. He was very friendly and communicative: so that I got all the information that was necessary to me in forming a judgment on the Civil Law as a profession; indeed quite enough to make me anxious for no more. I have now determined to enter at Gray's Inn. . . ."[2] The time was soon coming when De Quincey relinquished for good this vague but distasteful dream of becoming a lawyer.

While in London, he made a few excursions into society, in the course of which he met the notorious Lady Hamilton, whom he heard recite a scene from *Macbeth*. He amiably supposes her guiltless of illicit relations with Nelson and thinks her, with Madame Catalani, "the most effectively brilliant woman he ever saw."[3] Another, no less important, but to De Quincey much less sympathetic figure, whom he met at the house of Basil Montagu, was Dr. Samuel Parr, the famous scholar and the Edmund Gosse of his day. Parr was in many ways an excellent and, at heart, a very kind man, but his faults were glaring and of a sort calculated to prejudice such a temperament as De Quincey's against him from the start. De Quincey describes how, hearing a loud laugh proceed from an adjoining room, he expected to find a man of Johnsonian proportions, but saw instead "a little man, in a most plebeian

[1] II, 269. [2] Wordsworth Collection. [3] II, 209.

wig ",[1] who lisped, grimaced and gesticulated in a manner that put De Quincey in mind of a " little French gossipping abbé ". The description proceeds with a virulent imitation of Parr's absurd diction, frivolous preoccupations and undignified, giggling address. It is not difficult to guess the root cause of the contemptuous horror with which Dr. Parr inspired De Quincey: he saw in this " lisping . . . pedant, without personal dignity or conspicuous power of mind ",[2] a perfect caricature of all those superficial qualities which he abhorred as inconsistent with self-respect, and which he had spent so much time and trouble in eradicating from his own character. Thus, in spite of a fine passage[3] summing up Parr's literary talent, De Quincey, in the violence of his dislike, quite fails to explain how it was that, if Parr was really as tasteless, as mannerless and as meretricious a person as he makes out, his friends and correspondents were so many, so various and so distinguished.

Amyot once told Crabb Robinson a story about Parr which shows us that side of the great scholar which must have been peculiarly irritating to some people. Asked his opinion on politics, the Doctor answered " with an affectation of mystery and importance . . . 'I am not fond of speaking on the subject. If I were in my place in the House of Lords, I should', etc., etc." It is easy to see how this sort of snobbish pomposity and self-importance must have offended De Quincey; and on occasions of this kind he was in the habit of allowing his dislike to overwhelm his judgment.

In June, while he was still in London, news arrived from Grasmere which threw him into such a frenzy of grief as he had not known since the death of Elizabeth. Little Catherine Wordsworth—his favourite, the treasure of his imagination, the future object of his educative dreams—suddenly fell ill and died. She was not quite four years old. The illness was a mysterious one, but was said, unthinkably enough, to have been brought on by the eating of new carrots. Writing in 1839, De Quincey accused Sarah Green, one of the Wordsworths' servants, of causing the child's death by neglect;[4] but there is no evidence that the parents shared this view. But, whatever the cause, the event produced in De Quincey's soul an upheaval that seems a little exaggerated, considering that

[1] V, 16. [2] II, 208. [3] V, 115. [4] XIII, 147.

the child, however fond he may have been of her, was not his own and was, one would have thought, as yet too young to have had time to develop a personality distinct enough for its dissolution to cause a real sense of deprivation: " So small a child to leave so great a sorrow."[1] Yet, taking into consideration his intense love of children and the fact that he had as yet none of his own, one acquits him of exaggeration. The letters which he wrote to Dorothy on the occasion are proof enough of the violence of his grief. Crabb Robinson was with him when he met Wordsworth in London, just after the tragedy, and records that De Quincey, overcome by the pathos of the circumstances, burst into tears at the sight of the poet. But, as usual, it was to Dorothy that he turned in order to confide his grief:

Yesterday morning I received your letter with its bitter, bitter tidings. Oh that I might have seen my darling's face once again! Oh what a heavy increase of affliction to me and to her parents is this! What a bitter pang that we might not see her blessed face again. I parted from her in cheerfulness, and had no misgivings; but I cannot bear to think of this. My dear friend,—write to me as circumstantially as you can; it cannot add to your grief to do this; and it will be an inexpressible consolation to me. Particularly her father and I wish to know when she is buried. Do not, my dear friend, omit anything that you remember. . . .[2]

Three days later, unable to prevent his mind from dwelling, in an ecstasy of unhappiness, upon every detail of his last moments with Catherine, he wrote again to Dorothy:

Nobody can judge from her manner to me before others what love she showed to me when we were playing or talking together alone. On the night when she slept with me in the winter, we lay awake all the middle of the night—and talked, oh, how tenderly together: when we fell asleep, she was lying in my arms; once or twice I awoke from the presence of her dear body: but I could not find in my heart to disturb her. Many times on that night—when she was murmuring out tender sounds of endearment, she would lock her little arms with such passionateness round my neck, as if she had known that it was the last night we were ever

[1] Paul the Deacon. Carmina, XXIV.
[2] June 12th. MS. in Wordsworth Collection.

to pass together. Ah, pretty, pretty love, would God that I might have seen thy face and kissed thy dear lips again. . . .[1]

And he adds a private note to the effect that Mary Dawson has reason to have a heavy conscience, for the harshness with which she sometimes spoke to Catherine. De Quincey was no doubt thinking of the nurse who had been cruel to his own sister Jane, shortly before her death, and the thought was intolerable to him that perhaps Catherine might have suffered in the same way.

Six days later, the vision of the dead child was still terribly clear to him, so that he tortured himself with imaginary pictures of her suffering. "What anguish to us all if she had called upon our names in delirium, and fancied that we would not come to her relief!"[2]

What the Wordsworths thought of these transports is not revealed; but they cannot have failed to be touched by such evidence of the affection he bore to them all.

The profounder—and, curiously enough, the less personal—cause of De Quincey's suffering under this tragedy is perhaps to be sought in a passage in which he afterwards recalled his feelings for the dead child. "Over and above my excess of love for her, I had always viewed her as an impersonation of the dawn and the spirit of infancy; and this abstraction seated in her person, together with the visionary sort of connection which even in her parting hours she assumed with the summer sun, by turning her immersion with the cloud of death with the rising and setting of that fount of life—these combined impressions recoiled so violently into a contrast or polar antithesis to the image of death, that each excited and heightened the other." And he records his constant vision of the little girl, on the opposite side of some field to which he had resorted with the express object of having the vision. Her figure would *grow* out of the objects of the landscape—be composed of them, as it were.[3]

This habit of systematizing his emotions into symbolical constructions, in order to make bearable what would otherwise have thrown him off his balance by the extreme poignancy of its attack, had declared itself as early as the death of Elizabeth. Now the

[1] Wordsworth Collection. [2] *Ibid.* [3] II, 443.

parallel was close enough to call it forth again: Death and Summer—once again they had come together against him, in the flaunting beauty of their combined symbols, re-creating in his mind the old images of childhood, desolation, decay, and the tall lights of summer. And since those earlier days he had taken to himself the strongest of all stimulants to the creation of symbolical visions—opium, that winding fluid element, in which the muddled stuff of life crystallizes into significant images of satisfying power. Reading, when still a child, the story of Aladdin, De Quincey invented the conceit that the magician had selected Aladdin as recipient of the lamp by listening for the special sound of his footsteps—a gloss which is not to be found in the original story at all. "He had the power, still more unsearchable, of reading in that hasty movement an alphabet of new and infinite symbols; for, in order that the child's feet should be significant and intelligible, that sound must open into a gamut of infinite compass. The pulses of the heart, the motions of the will, the phantoms of the brain, must repeat themselves in secret hieroglyphics uttered by the flying footsteps. Even the articulate or brutal sounds of the globe must be all so many languages and ciphers that somewhere have their corresponding keys—have their own grammar and syntax; and thus the least things in the universe must be secret mirrors to the greatest." [1]

A mind which works in this way can never be broken by the accidents and the brutalities of life: there always remains for it, when the worst comes to the worst, the escape into symbolism—into art, in fact, where the spirit is purged of its affliction by the perfect formal beauty of its own fantasies. Thus the real Catherine, as De Quincey had known her and clasped her in his arms that livelong night, melted gradually into a beautiful image—part of the permanent furniture of his mind. The abrupt manner of his spiritual convalescence is equally remarkable. "I suffered an unaccountable attack of nervous horror which lasted for five months, and went off in one night as unaccountably as it had first come on in one second of time." Thus he wrote to Miss Mitford, describing a similar attack in 1846. On the earlier occasion, the symptoms were exactly the same and they left him in the same abrupt way, "suddenly with a nervous sensation of sickness," says Japp.[2] And the agony, once past, was not renewed. When,

[1] I, 129.

[2] *Op. cit.*, p. 129.

later in the same year, Thomas Wordsworth died of measles, De Quincey showed very little emotion.

The story ends appropriately on the physical note; for the mental strain imposed by the shock and the subsequent grief was responsible for a sudden increase in the nervous dyspepsia which, though by now chronic, had remained in a state of stability since 1809.* This of course meant increasing the dose of laudanum, and thus started the declension which was to end in the stress and agony of the years 1817 and '18.

3

The years 1813–15 were on the whole uneventful in De Quincey's life. He was still happy under the spell of Dove Cottage and the Wordsworths, a spell which frequent absences in London and Wrington did not destroy. Nor had his indulgence in opium yet reached the stage where pleasure passes over into pain.

In July 1813 he wrote to Wordsworth as follows:

I spent last night with Mr. Coleridge and the ladies in Berners St. He seemed uneasy and out of spirits when anything was said to draw his thoughts upon himself or his family; but as well able as usual to abstract his mind from such thoughts, and, on the whole, I thought pretty well in health as far as I could judge from his looks. I asked him, at parting, if he could not contrive to go down to the North in a few weeks; and I would join him on the road: but he only said that he would take some opportunity of speaking to me on that subject. . . .[1]

The quarrel between Coleridge and Wordsworth had been patched up in 1812, by the good offices of Crabb Robinson; but the reconciliation was never much more than a formal one, and this letter must have shown Wordsworth that his old friend had not changed his ways.

Indeed, Coleridge's nerves were going from bad to worse. In August De Quincey wrote that the poet was refusing to be seen, flinging a note down the stairs to Mrs. Morgan, his landlady, to the effect that the gout had mounted to his stomach and that if he

[1] Wordsworth Collection.

were disturbed or agitated it would speedily attack his brain. A night or two later, however, Mrs. Morgan and her sister, looking out of the window and seeing smoke rolling round the corner of the street, ventured to call Coleridge, who immediately " tripped downstairs with her as lightly as ever." [1]

To these years belong the mild orgies of opium and music combined, in which De Quincey confesses that he indulged when in London.[2] These debauches did not take place more often than once in three weeks (at any rate up to 1812: after that he might call every day for " a glass of laudanum negus, warm, and without sugar "), and generally on a Tuesday or a Saturday night, for it was only then that opera was to be heard, at the King's Theatre. Strung up, by twenty-five ounces of laudanum, to the necessary pitch of nervous receptivity, De Quincey would take a seat in the gallery and wait, " shivering with expectation ", for the entrance of Grassini, the famous contralto, whom he particularly admired. " Shivering I rose from my seat, incapable of rest, when that heavenly and harp-like voice sang its own victorious welcome in its prelusive *threttánelo-threttánelo*."

De Quincey's enjoyment of music does not appear, oddly enough, to have been of the purely sensuous variety one might expect from a person of such a temperament as his. " Now opium," he says explicitly, " by greatly increasing the activity of the mind, generally increases, of necessity, that particular mode of its activity by which we are able to construct out of the raw material of organic sound an elaborate intellectual pleasure." [3] This method of listening to music is a highly sophisticated one and presupposes a considerable technique; so that we can be sure that De Quincey spent a good deal more time in listening to music than he has actually put on record. As we shall see, the method of construction of his imaginative prose is frequently nearer to that of music than is that of any other writer of the day—or indeed of any other writer at all. He gives a special reason for this predilection for musical forms in literature: " a chorus, etc., of elaborate harmony displayed before me, as in a piece of arras-work, the whole of my past life—not as if recalled by an act of memory, but as if present and incarnated in the music; no longer painful to dwell upon, but the detail of its incidents removed, or blended in some hazy abstraction, and

[1] Japp, p. 133. [2] III, 389 ff. [3] III, 391.

its passions exalted, spiritualized, and sublimed." [1] The distinction described here is a very subtle one and shows how deeply De Quincey had meditated on the philosophy of music, making of it the very stuff of his life for some years before he ever put pen to paper with a serious view to publication. As for the music itself to which he listened, in those years, we do not know for certain what it was; but, from the admirations which he afterwards expressed, we can suppose that it consisted mainly of Mozart, Bellini, Paisiello, Cherubini, and perhaps a little Beethoven, for whose music he later expressed a particular admiration.

Music was not the only accompaniment to De Quincey's opium debauches. On some Saturday nights, after taking his dose, he would sometimes wander out into the by-ways and alleys of London, seeking out the markets and all the places where he could watch the life of the poor going on under his eyes. These expeditions were the complement of those long night walks which so much astonished the people of Grasmere; and he undertook them for the same purpose—that of mixing, in the state of serene and indifferent good humour induced by the drug, with his fellow-men; so that, by talking to them and entering into the hopes and fears of their lives, he might gain insight into the perpetual mystery of human personality and feel himself for a brief space at one with the souls of ordinary people. From these observations he drew the conclusion that "the poor are practically more philosophic than the rich; that they show a more ready and cheerful submission to what they consider as irremediable evils or irreparable losses." [2] Sometimes, so wrapt was he in the interest of what he saw and heard, that he would wander further and further from home and eventually get lost in the maze of sordid alleys in the very heart of London, so that his only way out "lay through a man's kitchen; and, as it was a small kitchen, you needed to steer cautiously, or else you might run foul of the dripping-pan." [3]

At Wrington, where he still continued to visit his mother from time to time, he met Mrs. Siddons in the company of Hannah More. He admired the famous actress's recitation of Shakespeare, but not her reading of Milton; but the most interesting part of the essay in which De Quincey recounts this meeting is devoted

[1] III, 391. [2] III, 393. [3] III, 394.

to the description of the unfortunate man in whose house Mrs. Siddons was staying. This was a Dr. Wh——, a tall, bilious and melancholy man, who had once been a member of the Lichfield circle and had just built himself a magnificent and hideous villa, a mile from Miss More's, with a view to lightening his sadness. But he only succeeded in deepening it, for he married an impostress, who was burdened with debts and a lunatic brother; between them they ruined the poor man, and he ended his days in a lodging-house on the Riviera.[1]

We now come upon an indication that, in spite of Catherine Wordsworth's death, De Quincey's interest in children was as strong as ever. There is, among the Baird-Smith collection of De Quincey's letters, an undated scrap of paper, which I am inclined to attribute to these years. It is headed Westhay and it reads as follows:

Sir,

I know a great many of the roads and the way to the wood which you just spoke of. I will get up as soon as soon as [*sic*] I am awake and will take you to the wood the first fine morning there is a fine hill to go up before we have got half round it which I daresay you will like, and we will write a book and name as you said but we must remember all the particulars so that we may make it as large a book as we can. I think you said it was to be two volumes quarto. Patience is a virtue.

Your affectionate friend,

Saturday. C. Buchanan.

It is open to anyone to construct what picture he pleases from this letter: the possibilities are many. What is certain is that De Quincey, hastening up that hill in the summer dawn, can have made no incongruous companion for his little friend, whether girl or boy. A like smallness of stature, a common light in the eyes, will have distinguished them both.

In 1814 De Quincey was again in London, established in lodgings on the south side of Waterloo Bridge, near the Surrey theatre. He seems to have had a predilection for this rather squalid neighbourhood, for he returned there in 1825. This time, however,

[1] II, 447.

his sleep was disturbed regularly every night by an explosion in the theatre, set up during a scene which involved the burning of the Kremlin—no doubt some ancestor of *Michel Strogoff*, that piece which draws thousands yearly to the Châtelet theatre in Paris. The noise of the explosion woke the cocks, who in their turn woke the dogs of the neighbourhood, so that it was some time before De Quincey could get back to sleep. He seems, however, to have been more amused than annoyed by this shindy, which provided him with a story after his own heart.

Then Paris was captured by the Allies, and he assisted at the festivities and processions which followed in London. His own rejoicing at the event was unmixed; but Lamb's was not, and this vexed De Quincey, who, like most people, could never suffer gladly a political opinion contrary to his own.[1] His tours of the London streets brought him a sight of the Czar, who impressed him unfavourably, and of Blücher, who appeared at intervals of five minutes throughout the day, on a balcony in St. James's Street. But what astonished him most was the Cossacks, who disorganized the London night by drinking the oil out of the street-lamps:

I, and others, my companions, returning from a ball . . . saw a mimic sketch of the decaying Oracles. Here, close to the hetman's front door, was a large overshadowing lamp, that might typify the Delphic shrine, but (to borrow a word from kitchen-maids) ' black out '. It was supposed to have been tapped too frequently by the hetman's sentinels who mounted guard on his Tartar Highness. Then, on the other side the street, was a lamp, ancient and gloomy, that might pass for Dodona, throwing up sickly and fitful gleams of *undulating* lustre, but drawing near to extinction. Further ahead was a huge octagon lamp, that apparently had never been cleaned from smoke and fuliginous tarnish, forlorn, solitary, yet grimly alight, though under a disastrous eclipse, and ably supporting the part of Jupiter Ammon. . . . And in the midst of all these vast and venerable mementoes rose one, singularly pert and lively though not bigger than a farthing rushlight, which probably had singly escaped the Cossacks, as having promised nothing; so that the least and most trivial of the entire group was likely to survive them all.[2]

[1] III, 62. [2] VII, 99.

4

And now financial disasters overtook both De Quincey and Wilson, almost simultaneously, forcing upon them a decision which they chose to make a common one. In 1813 Wilson lost his entire fortune through the dishonest administration of an uncle. It says much for his character that he accepted this reverse of fortune with great cheerfulness. Losing no time in futile lamentation, he left Elleray on the spot [1] and began to make arrangements for taking up his practice at the Bar in Edinburgh. This must have meant a very considerable sacrifice on his part, for it must be remembered that his was a fiercely independent nature; De Quincey himself remarks, *à propos* of this moment, that but for necessity Wilson would never have consented to limit his liberty by regular work.[2] Meanwhile De Quincey, with his usual generosity, immediately lent Wilson £200,[3] which he could now afford even less than in the days when he had made his ill-advised gift to Coleridge. No sooner had he done so, moreover, than he himself lost most of the small remainder of his capital, through the failure of a business into which it had been put. Colonel Penson wrote kindly from India, sending a small sum; but the mischief was now complete: De Quincey was all but penniless.

In these straits, he decided to throw in his lot with Wilson and accompany him to Edinburgh. It is not clear whether or no De Quincey, in taking this step, had any idea of earning his living by literary means. At all events, he did not do so; which leads one to suppose that he must still have had just enough money on which to scrape along for the time being. His own legal career was still hanging fire, and must in any case have been pursued in London—not in Edinburgh, where he had no legal connection. But these considerations do not seem to have worried him at the time. Perhaps Wilson's high spirits and easy optimism were infectious: these were cues which De Quincey was at all times prepared to take from his friend; and it was in hope, rather than despair, that he and Wilson arrived in Edinburgh, towards the close of 1814.

[1] He did not sell it at once, but returned there at intervals for some years.
[2] V, 281. [3] See Letters, II, 30 ff.

The northern Athens was now reaching the height of its reputation. The intellectual circles, which had been founded in the eighteenth century by legal lights such as Ferguson and Lord Kames, and by philosophers like Hume and Dugald Stewart, were now taking on a more specifically literary tinge under the growing influence of Walter Scott and Francis Jeffrey, the founder and editor of the *Edinburgh Review*. The Napoleonic wars had given a further fillip to the intellectual life of the city, by causing its university to be sought by many foreigners and by young Englishmen who would otherwise, in times of peace, have been making the Grand Tour. The end of the war brought the city to a sudden sense of the position it had acquired, and there was a wave of civic self-importance, conducted by a sort of legal aristocracy culled from the enormous and characteristic plethora of lawyers which Edinburgh has always harboured.[1]

One of the best descriptions of Edinburgh society at this time is given by Susan Ferrier, in her novel, *Marriage*:

> The circle is so confined, that its members are almost universally known to each other; and those various gradations of gentility, from the cit's [2] snug party to the duchess' most crowded assembly, all totally distinct and separate, which are to be met with in London, have no prototype in Edinburgh. There, the ranks and fortunes being more on an equality, no one is able greatly to exceed his neighbour in luxury and extravagance. Great magnificence, and the consequent gratification produced by the envy of others being out of the question, the object for which a reunion of individuals was originally invented, becomes less of a secondary consideration. Private parties for the actual purpose of society and conversation are frequent, and answer the destined end; and, in the societies of professed amusement, are to be met the learned, the studious, and the rational; not presented as shows to the company by the host and hostess, but professedly seeking their own gratification.[3]

This might be the picture of some famous Paris salon, before the Revolution. Simplicity was the keynote, and the values

[1] See Miss Elsie Swann's account of Edinburgh in her life of "Christopher North" (John Wilson).

[2] Abb. of *citizen* = townsman or shopkeeper (O. E. D.).

[3] *Marriage*, I. 177 (Blackwood, 1818).

which obtained were strictly intellectual—not snobbish or arising from considerations of mere prestige.

Wilson and De Quincey, arriving together, immediately created a circle of their own, on the above pattern. Its chief figures were Sir William Hamilton, Lockhart, William Allan (a painter, afterwards president of the Royal Scottish Academy), Robert Pearse Gillies, James Wilson (brother of John), Colonel Mitchell (biographer of Wallenstein and expert on strategy), Captain Thomas Hamilton (brother of Sir William and author of a novel, *Cyril Thornton*, after which he was nicknamed).[1] Raeburn and Wilkie were also members of the set, though De Quincey himself does not mention them.

Of all these people, of whom, with the exception of Hamilton, Raeburn, Wilkie and Lockhart (who had not yet sprung into fame), little is now remembered, Gillies is not the least interesting to us, partly because of De Quincey's affection for him, but chiefly for the admirable record he has left of the former's conversation. He was a gay, intelligent man, feckless and perpetually in financial difficulties of the most desperate order. De Quincey used ever after to think of him " with a sigh of inexpressible sadness, such as belongs of right to some splendid Timon of Athens, so often as, on the one hand, I revivify to my mind his gay saloons, resonant with Music and festive laughters . . . and, on the other hand, shudder at the mighty shadows of calamity, of sorrow, of malice, of detraction, that have for 30 years stalked after his retreating splendour, and long since have swallowed up the very memory of his pretensions from the children of this generation."[2] It is clear that De Quincey had a special sympathy for this man, whom he felt to have been troubled by the same weaknesses and to have been so often met by the same ultimate incomprehension as himself. Both found it necessary, at different periods, to seek sanctuary from their creditors in Holyrood. When Gillies had resort to this course and wrote to tell De Quincey of it, the latter replied: " I will be with you on Monday, D.V.; but on Tuesday, D.V. or not."*

De Quincey created a great stir in the literary society of Edinburgh. It seems probable that Wilson, on earlier visits to the capital, had taken the opportunity of warming his friend's place

[1] V, 322. [2] V, 322 (written in 1852).

for him, for the moment De Quincey arrived, he found himself, for the first time in his life, lionized. The prodigious learning which his photographic memory had enabled him to acquire astounded and fascinated these men, all of whom were comparatively young and fond of intellectual acrobatics.

In order that he might give of his best, the meetings of the circle took place chiefly late at night, for De Quincey, who was at this time approaching a climax of opium-eating, was always at his best in the small hours. Then, indeed, his anxious listeners could be sure of an astonishing display. His tiny body perched on the edge of a chair, his hands clasping and unclasping nervously between his knees, his face pale and tense beneath the steep wall of his forehead, his eyes an intense, unfathomable, drug-laden depth of blue, he would slide gently—almost imperceptibly—into the conversation, with a kind of whisper—low-toned, weird and musical. And at once the talk would be lifted—ingeniously, tactfully, with the utmost good manners—out of the candle-light into an iridescent, kaleidoscopic half-world lit by a livid gleam of the talker's own making and peopled with the half-recognized creatures of his extraordinary genius. "The talk might be of 'beeves', and he could grapple with them, if expected to do so, but his musical cadences were not in keeping with such work, and in a few minutes (not without some strictly logical sequence) he could escape at will from the beeves to butterflies, and thence to the soul's immortality, to Plato, and Kant, and Schelling, and Fichte, and Milton's early years and Shakespeare's Sonnets, to Wordsworth and Coleridge, to Homer and Aeschylus, to St. Thomas of Aquin, St. Basil and St. Chrysostom. But he by no means excluded them from real life, according to his own views of that life, but would recount profound mysteries from his own experiences—visions that had come over him in his loneliest walks among the mountains, and passages within his own personal knowledge, illustrating, if not proving, the doctrines of dreams, of warnings, of second sight and mesmerism. And whatever the subject might be, every one of his sentences (or of his chapters, I might say) was woven into the most perfect logical texture, and uttered in a tone of sustained melody."[1]

Yet—and this was the ultimate marvel which distinguished

[1] Gillies: *Memoirs of a Literary Veteran*, II, 220.

De Quincey's conversation from, and thus far raised it above, that of Coleridge and Carlyle—his talk was never a monologue. As he himself claimed, " above all things, I shunned . . . Coleridge's capital error . . . of keeping the audience in a state of passiveness " ; [1] and all through his life there are witnesses to the justice of his claim.[2] However fantastic the castle he built, he would always pause in the building to invite advice and suggestions, before proceeding to a further stage; then, when he had made others talk, he would gather up what they had laid out and, like a conjuror with a folded piece of paper, twist them in a moment into the oddest and most unexpected shapes. But those who listened never felt that they were a mere audience: De Quincey was always, as a friend [3] said of him in later life, a good listener.

But to return once more to what he has himself told us of his conversational methods, he had " the advantage of a prodigious memory . . . *a logical instinct for feeling in a moment the secret analogies or parallelisms that connected things else apparently remote* [4] . . . an inexhaustible fertility of topics . . . a prematurely awakened sense of *art* [5] applied to conversation. I had learned the use of vigilance in evading with civility the approach of wearisome discussions, and in impressing, quietly and often times imperceptibly, a new movement upon dialogues that loitered painfully, or see-sawed unprofitably." [6] This is not conceit, but the considered judgment of one who knew his own powers and their exact extent. The passage I have italicised, moreover, describes the essential quality which has distinguished all the world's greatest talkers,—a quality, too, which De Quincey elsewhere notes Coleridge as possessing in the highest degree.[7]

Since this subject is of high importance in De Quincey's life, it will not be out of place here to quote one more passage, this time from his brilliant essay on *Conversation*, from which we can realize, with even greater clarity, the peculiarly original quality which he brought to the art. It appears that as a young man he had viewed conversation as one of the dull necessities of life, but that maturer thought on the subject had " pointed to an absolute birth of new insight into the truth itself as inseparable from the

[1] III, 331. See also *Posth. Works*, II, 7 ff. (*Conversation and Coleridge*).
[2] See Japp, p. 249.
[3] The Revd. Francis Jacox.
[4] My italics.
[5] Italics in the original.
[6] III, 332.
[7] V, 204.

finer and more scientific exercise of the talking art. It would not be the brilliancy, the ease, or the adroitness of the expounder that would benefit, but the absolute interests of the thing expounded. A feeling dawned on me of a secret magic lurking in the peculiar life, velocities, and contagious ardour of conversation, quite separate from any that belonged to books—arming a man with new forces, and not merely with a new dexterity in wielding the old ones. I felt . . . that in the electric kindling of life between two minds,—and far less from the kindling natural to conflict . . . than from the kindling through sympathy with the object discussed in its momentary coruscation of shifting phases,—there sometimes arise glimpses and shy revelations of affinity, suggestion, relation, analogy, that could not have been approached through any avenues of methodical study. Great organists find the same effect of inspiration, the same result of power creative and revealing, in the mere movement and velocity of their own voluntaries." [2]

Music again! De Quincey went back and back to this analogy, whenever he was under the necessity of expressing the deepest and most complex processes of his thought. The fascination of conversing with him, then, must have consisted in being made to feel that one was taking part in a double improvisation, in which the subsidiary player started by mere vamping and then, as he caught the trend of the virtuoso's harmony and perceived the interlocking of the various themes, was gradually emboldened to take them up and use them himself, weaving his own inspiration ever more closely together with that of the other, until the music sailed away, at last unified into a triumphant whole.

But these performances, wonderful as they were, were a terrible expense of spirit to De Quincey; they exhausted him mentally and physically, thus exposing him further and further to the insidious effects of the drug. For he had now become a confirmed addict. The effect of the spiritual crisis through which he had passed at the death of Catherine Wordsworth, followed quickly as it was by the worry connected with his financial disaster, had produced an "appalling irritation of the stomach", accompanied by a "revival of all the old dreams." [2] Then it was that, weighed down by the

[1] X, 268. [2] III, 398.

misery of depression and the horrible sense of an immitigable fate, he gave up the struggle and abandoned himself to the daily solace of opium. By 1815 he had increased the dose to the extent of 320 grammes (8000 drops of laudanum) per day.[1] This was little more than half of what Coleridge was taking at the time; but it must be remembered that opium-eating is much more harmful to the system than opium-smoking,[2] and the above dose was quite sufficient to plunge a highly-strung man like De Quincey into the depths, and raise him to the heights, of which he has left so poignant a description. No one now knew better than he the death-in-life which he was thus preparing for himself. He had been at least half way there before, had peeped over the edge and had recoiled in time. But now the dull weight of sadness—so much harder to bear, in the long run, than sharp grief or violent anxiety—proved altogether too much for him. As he pathetically confesses, "I hanker too much after a state of happiness, both for myself and others: I cannot face misery . . . with an eye of sufficient firmness: and am little capable of encountering present pain for the sake of any reversionary benefit."[3]

It is at least doubtful whether anything could have saved De Quincey at this juncture. Everything had conspired against him, with bewildering suddenness, in the very midst of the calm happiness which he had shaped for himself with a sculptor's care. All had melted away, proving, inexorably, the fatal flimsiness of his workmanship, when it came to the building up of his own life; and instead of all that might have supported him, nothing remained but a perpetual twisted devil of pain, gnawing at his stomach, tweaking the centres of his nerves, and driving an iron wedge into the top of his skull, until all his thinking was deafened by the knocking pulse of agony.

What wonder, then, that he took the only certain way out of which he knew? Those midnight conversations in Edinburgh, so vital to him in his long literary apprenticeship (they assembled and clarified his ideas, they sorted the accumulated learning of years, they prepared the stress and rhythm of the prose he was soon to write), but reinforced the deleterious effect of the drug, by pressing,

[1] Japp, p. 143.

[2] "Eating" here includes both eating and drinking: opium can be either eaten in crude form, or in pills, or else drunk as a tincture.

[3] III, 399.

so to speak, upon the spring that would soon fly back and deal him a stunning blow.

Such a mode of life cannot be pursued indefinitely. At the end of the year, hopeless, resigned, De Quincey said farewell to his new friends and took himself back to Grasmere, there to shut himself up once more in Dove Cottage, alone.

CHAPTER VI

THE DARK IDOL (I)

I

BUT he had not yet reached the nadir of his declension. Somewhat to our surprise, we find De Quincey stating positively that the year 1816 was the happiest of his life, though he admits at the same time that it was but a parenthesis between years of unparalleled gloom.[1] This temporary equilibrium was partly due to the fact that he suddenly found himself able to reduce his daily consumption of laudanum from 8000 drops to 1000. "Instantaneously, and as if by magic, the cloud of profoundest melancholy which rested upon my brain, like some black vapours that I have seen roll away from the summit of a mountain, drew off in one week."[2] Relieved of the burden, he once more threw himself into study, opening Kant again, but with the same result as before.

An impression of greatly increased isolation from general society disengages itself from the story of De Quincey's life in this year. This isolation had begun to make itself felt before he left Grasmere for Edinburgh, in the previous year. The gradual estrangement from the Wordsworths, which was the chief feature of De Quincey's new solitude, seems to have arisen originally from an unpleasantness created by old Mary Dawson, who denied Wordsworth the right to make use of Dove Cottage when De Quincey was away,[3] though the latter had given her express orders to the contrary. The Wordsworths were now living at Rydal Mount, into which they had moved in 1813; but it had always been understood between them and De Quincey that, when he was away, Dove Cottage, which still belonged to Wordsworth,* should be available for the latter's children or guests, should he require it. The misunderstanding was a trivial one, and could, one would have thought, easily have been put right, with a little good will. But unfor-

[1] III, 401. [2] III, 402. [3] III, 201.

tunately the good will was absent, on the Wordsworths' side: De Quincey's habits had begun to offend them. Then, too, his absence in Edinburgh made a break in the continuity of his relationships in Grasmere—a break which, unlike former ones, was not bridged by correspondence. The atmosphere of the new world which he had entered still clung round him, shutting him off in some sort from his older friends; besides which, a new preoccupation, presently to be described, had already begun to fill the whole of that part of his mind and time which was not given over to books.

But one day De Quincey's solitude at Dove Cottage was broken into by a visitor so strange and grotesque that his passing left its impress on De Quincey's dreams. As he sat reading in his upper room, a servant, a beautiful girl called Barbara Lewthwaite, came up in agitation to say that a sort of demon was waiting below to see him. Descending, De Quincey found a Malay, dressed in native clothes, with a turban on his head, standing in the dim light of the hall, his fantastic form thrown into relief by the dark panelling on the walls. Knowing no word of Malay, De Quincey tried the man with the Arabic word for barley and the Turkish word for opium, but with no visible result. However, all the man appeared to require was rest, for after sleeping for an hour upon the floor, he got up and went upon his way. Before he started, De Quincey gave him various presents, among them a piece of raw opium, which the Malay, to his surprise and alarm, proceeded to swallow at a mouthful. De Quincey fully expected to see the man drop down dead on the spot; but, on the contrary, the drug seemed to have no effect upon him whatever, and he departed wrapt in the same impenetrable mystery as that in which he had arrived.

This incident seems to have been the only interruption to the studious monotony of De Quincey's days, at this time. His evenings, however, now began to be spent in a different manner. On the present road between Grasmere and Ambleside, on the banks of Rydal Water, stands a long low farmhouse with Gothic windows. This farm, called the Nab, belonged to one William Parke, who lived there with his daughter Mary and her husband, John Simpson, a massive, reserved man, of pronounced Jacobin views. These two had a family, among whom was a daughter,

Margaret. How she and De Quincey first became acquainted is not known; but before the year 1816 was far spent De Quincey was paying constant visits to the Nab, in search of her company. Writing to Dorothy Wordsworth in 1817,[1] Lamb recalls how De Quincey, on a visit to London, had broached the subject of his infatuation. "O how funny he did talk to me about her, in terms of such mild quiet whispering speculative profligacy." The description of De Quincey talking is graphic, but the statement is otherwise dark: it is difficult to tell exactly what feelings he entertained for the girl. But, however he may have felt in the beginning, a strong attachment soon grew up between the two of them. There is no evidence that the Simpsons regarded him with disfavour, or that they put any obstacle in the way of his meeting Margaret as often as he wished, though, in a letter to Wordsworth of March 29th, 1818, *à propos* of the Kendal election, De Quincey refers to John Simpson as a "pure malignant towards the nobility—gentry—clergy—magistracy—and institutions of the land",[2] and adds that the man's wife and eldest son share his convictions. At all events, before the winter was over the two young people (she was about eighteen, he thirty-one) had become lovers in the fullest sense of the word. In November, Margaret gave birth to a son (afterwards christened William); and, whether or no De Quincey had by then made up his mind on the question of Margaret's suitability as a wife for him, it seemed to him that now he was left with no choice in the matter. In February 1817, therefore, the couple were somewhat obscurely married in Grasmere church.

Before entering into the complications with the Wordsworths which this affair entailed, it will be as well to try, with the very slender material at our disposal, to reconstruct the shadowy but particularly attractive figure of Margaret de Quincey. Indications are few, but such as they are they point to an outward appearance of great beauty and a character whose solid peasant virtues are curiously combined with a wistful and pathetic charm.

The first glimpse we are vouchsafed is that of a little girl standing at the door of her home during a hailstorm and holding out her hand to catch the hail as it fell.[3] Apart from this, we have no

[1] Letter of November 21st. [2] Wordsworth Collection.
[3] Dorothy Wordsworth: *Grasmere Journal* of 1802 (unpublished section).*

certain reference to her personal appearance, unless the following passage may be (as I think) agreed to contain one.

Though in the first order of tall women, yet, being full in person and with a symmetry that was absolutely faultless, she seemed to the random sight as little above the ordinary height. Possibly from the dignity of her person, assisted by the dignity of her movements, a stranger would have been disposed to call her at a distance a woman of *commanding* presence, but never after he had approached near enough to behold her face. Every thought of artifice, of practised effect, or of haughty pretension fled before the childlike innocence, the sweet feminine timidity, and the more than cherub loveliness of that countenance, which yet in its lineaments was noble, while its expression was purely gentle and confiding. A shade of pensiveness there was about her; but *that* was in her manners, scarcely ever in her features; and the exquisite fairness of her complexion, enriched by the very sweetest and most delicate bloom that ever I have beheld, should rather have allied it to a tone of cheerfulness.[1]

Now I am fully aware that to dig about in an author's avowed fictions for portraits of real persons is a hazardous, and for the most part unjustifiable, proceeding. But in this case the presumption that De Quincey was painting a portrait of his wife, is very strong indeed. To begin with, the story in which this passage occurs is the only fiction of its kind for which he drew entirely upon his own imagination, and not upon some German original. And secondly, the nature of the story,[2] and the circumstances under which it was written (circumstances of stress and unhappiness, in which De Quincey felt that every man's hand was against him and his) indicate that he is here relieving his feelings against those whom he regarded as the persecutors of himself and his wife, by a fiction designed to symbolize his wretched state. And the few dim memories of Mrs. De Quincey's personal appearance which have been handed down to her granddaughters, confirm the portrait drawn in the above passage. Moreover, he describes the wife in this story as " daughter of the hills ".

But the extreme pliability and sweetness that informed Margaret's manner was evidently set off by a character of solid common

[1] *The Household Wreck:* XII, 165.

[2] For a detailed account of it see p. 264.

sense and very touching fidelity to an accepted fate. If she was naïve enough to be surprised when informed that the events described in the *Vicar of Wakefield* had never actually taken place,[1] she was fully capable of dealing with those quotidian problems which threw her husband into such woeful perplexity. As he himself testified: " Without the aid of M., all records of bills paid, or *to be paid*, must have perished; and my whole domestic economy, whatever became of Political Economy, must have gone into irretrievable confusion." [2] In another place, in commenting on Shakespeare's marriage, he indirectly justifies his own choice of a wife against those who accused him of marrying beneath him. " It is a noticeable fact," he says, ". . . that the abstract image of womanhood, in its loveliness, its delicacy, and its modesty, nowhere makes itself more impressive or more advantageously felt than in the humblest cottages, because it is there brought into immediate juxtaposition with the grossness of manners and the careless licence of language incident to the fathers and brothers of the house " [3]—a passage which also indicates De Quincey's disapproval (elsewhere expressed) of his father-in-law's opinions.

The pre-marital relationship between De Quincey and Margaret Simpson, proved by the premature birth of their first child, may seem surprising, in view of De Quincey's expressed opinion on sexual matters, his excessive but quite real shrinking from physical relationships, his ' respectful ' attitude to all women whom he held in affection, and his extreme timidity of address on all observed occasions. The explanation, I cannot help thinking, is that the seduction was more Margaret's doing than De Quincey's. At the least, she must have met him more than half way, responding to the hesitant ardour of his admiration with a straightforward ignorance of moral scruple in allowing her love to express itself in the simplest, fullest manner she knew. Large and motherly, she was attracted by the little man's loneliness and helplessness and childlike beauty, even as she accorded to his mental attainments the gaping admiration which only the intelligent illiterate can feel for the unimaginable activities of the furnished brain. Perceiving what he wanted, better than he perceived it himself, and aware, perhaps, that without some movement on her part, matters might remain indefinitely where they were, she gently assumed the active

[1] XIII, 238. [2] III, 433. [3] IV, 47.

part and, seizing the nearest opportunity, drew him down to her. . . .

There is no question, I think, of Margaret's having 'caught' him, in the vulgar sense; for he was not, even from her point of view, a 'catch', being both poor and in delicate health. Her simplicity and integrity, amply attested by the unwavering love and care with which she treated her husband from the day of her marriage to that of her early death, are proof enough that her character was entirely without meanness or calculating ambition. Moreover, though she remained the simple farmer's daughter to the end, her intelligence was keen enough to permit of considerable education at her husband's hands (" the Education of a Child "). The only extant letter of hers [1] tells us nothing of her from its actual content; but it is neatly expressed, and the handwriting, though somewhat unformed, is not ungainly.

In September 1816 the news that her son was contemplating marriage reached Mrs. De Quincey, who instantly took up her pen and wrote to him, asking incredulously if the news was true and managing to imply that, if it were, it ought not to be.[2] De Quincey's reply, supposing he made one, is not extant; but in the long and interesting letter which he wrote to his mother in 1818, and from which I have already quoted,[3] he describes the circumstances which attended his courtship and marriage, excuses himself for omitting to tell his mother of it, on the grounds that the social position and prospects of his bride would have given her pain, and concludes the passage thus: " In justice to my wife, I must say she is all I could desire, and has in every way dignified the position in which she stands to me." [4] This continued to be his opinion throughout their married life, and Margaret certainly did everything to deserve it.

2

It is now necessary to enter in detail into the complicated and painful subject of De Quincey's estrangement from the Wordsworths. As I have already pointed out, there are signs that this

[1] MS. in British Museum. Addressed to the publisher Hessey, on June 12th, 1824, it apologizes for delay in sending De Quincey's address.
[2] Letters, II, 109. [3] See p. 41. [4] Letters, II, 216.

coldness began some time before the affair with Margaret Simpson came to a head. Sara Hutchinson wrote, in the previous November, that Wilson had been back at Elleray for a fortnight and that he was "tolerably steady, though De Quincey was often tipsy. . . . He doses himself with opium and drinks like a fish and tries in all other ways to be as great a gun as Mr. Wilson."[1] The unfriendly tone of this passage is obvious, and indicates clearly that the feelings of the female part of the Wordsworth household had undergone a change towards De Quincey. Already spiteful, Sara was also, I cannot help thinking, inaccurate. De Quincey, who was at all times most abstemious where alcohol was concerned, can never have been guilty of "drinking like a fish"; but it is an accusation which women, when they are annoyed with a man, frequently make on the smallest, or no, provocation.

When De Quincey's visits to the Nab began to cause gossip in the neighbourhood, the Wordsworth ladies were by no means unready to bear the tale. This seems to have annoyed De Quincey more than anything. Crabb Robinson, writing to Wordsworth in October, after a visit to the Lakes, says that he found De Quincey "in a sore state", talking of the estrangement between himself and the Wordsworths, and "imagining comments" on himself. As we have seen, the comments were not merely imagined; and some months later, when De Quincey was married, Dorothy herself—his faithful, beloved Dorothy—could write of him in this strain:

Mr De Quincey is married; and I fear I may add he is ruined. By degrees he withdrew himself from all society except that of the Sympsons[2] of the Nab. . . . At the up-rouzing of the Bats and the Owls he regularly went thither, and the consequence was that Peggy Sympson, the eldest daughter of the house presented him with a son ten weeks ago, and they are now spending their honeymoon in our cottage at Grasmere. This is in truth a melancholy story! He uttered in raptures of the beauty, the good sense, the simplicity 'the angelic sweetness' of Miss Sympson, who to all other judgments appeared to be a stupid heavy girl, and was reckoned a dunce at Grasmere School, and I predict that ere this all these witcheries are removed, and the fireside already dull.

[1] De Selincourt, *op. cit.*, p. 303.
[2] There seems to be no general agreement about the spelling of this name.

They have never been seen out of doors, except after the day was gone. As for him I am very sorry for him—he is utterly changed in appearance and takes largely of opium.[1]

The hard, flippant unkindness of this letter comes strangely from the warm-hearted woman who wrote it. One can only suppose that a deep and wounding disillusionment by the young man to whom she had given so much affection, was responsible for the unwonted asperity and lack of generosity with which Dorothy now viewed his behaviour. The letter also shows a complete misunderstanding both of the people involved and of their feelings: Margaret was neither stupid nor heavy, the witcheries were never removed, and the fireside was anything but dull, as we shall see.

De Quincey afterwards expressed his anger at the behaviour of the Wordsworth ladies in the article which he wrote on the subject of the estrangement. "I was provoked to wonder," he says, "that persons, of whom some commanded respect and attention simply as the near connexions of a great man, should so far forget the tenure on which their influence rested as to arrogate a tone of authority upon their own merits"[2]—a snub, in the circumstances, not unduly severe.

Wordsworth himself, on the other hand, took no part in the crossfire of gossip that so much agitated De Quincey. Aloof and dignified as ever, he contented himself with silent but massive disapproval. Never having cared deeply for De Quincey, the latter's delinquencies caused him none of the painful disenchantment which had stung Dorothy into that bitter outburst. All that he saw was a young man, formerly a pleasant enough acquaintance and disciple, now committing follies and excesses which rendered him socially impossible. Surprise he may have felt, since he had never cared to plumb the depths of De Quincey's nature, nor taken thought for the peculiar difficulties and problems which beset one of a temperament so different from his own. Surprise, no doubt, but not pain: for Wordsworth was too deeply self-centred to allow his imagination to play with profit round the psychological complexities of other people: he had enough to do, unravelling his own; and the emotional thriftiness involved by this spiritual programme was

[1] Letter to Mrs. Clarkson of February 15th, 1817. Quoted by De Selincourt, *op. cit.*, p. 304.
[2] III, 203.

bound to appear to others as a fundamental failure in magnanimity. All through Wordsworth's life friends and acquaintances were not lacking whom this attitude of lofty indifference and impermeability irritated beyond endurance,[1] so that they made him aware of the way in which it affected them. But their anger made not the slightest difference to Wordsworth: he simply did not care what anyone thought of him. In a man of lesser calibre, this obduracy would have been comic, or merely disgusting; but Wordsworth was of the great, and his character commands the exercise of a larger criticism, in the light of which his lack of sympathy with particular individuals is justified by the general magnitude of his preoccupations.

His withdrawal from close friendship with De Quincey had made itself felt early in the year; in September, Crabb Robinson, in his *Diary*, reports a walk which he took with the poet up Nab Scar, at the end of which Wordsworth left him at the door of Dove Cottage, where De Quincey was living, but did not go in, thus indicating the state of his feelings. But it was no doubt the birth of Margaret's child that finally determined him to drop the friendship. Though it was, and is, an immemorial custom, in country districts, for marriage to be conditional on conception, and though Wordsworth himself had behaved in an exactly similar manner to De Quincey, twenty-five years before, at the time of his own liaison with Annette Vallon, his circumstances had changed and he did not now feel himself obliged to be tolerant to others on the same score. He had an unmarried sister and sister-in-law living in his house, and children who were growing up: these facts, it appeared to him (and to his wife too, no doubt), made it impossible that he and his family should continue on intimate terms with a man who was known to have lived in sin with a peasant girl in the neighbourhood. The result was that—in the smug words of Coleridge describing the way in which himself and Wordsworth had thought fit to treat Hazlitt on the occasion of the latter's Keswick scrape—Wordsworth now took the line of a "quiet withdrawing from any further connection with him (and this without any ostentation, or any mark of shyness when (he) accidentally met him)." Wordsworth did, of course, have further connection with De Quincey;

[1] See, for example, the Letters of Keats, *passim*. Even Crabb Robinson realized that Wordsworth did not care much for talk ("Keep quiet or go away," he would say to visitors).

but it was, as we shall see, more in the way of literary business than of friendly intercourse.

To modern ears, this behaviour on the part of Wordsworth must sound very callous. But we must beware, once again, of judging him by standards which not only he himself, but the whole society of his day, would have considered quite inadmissible. For the attitude which he took up was in fact unavoidable by anyone who pretended to a life based on the principles current in provincial society at the time; and Wordsworth did accept those principles—was in fact one of those chiefly responsible for the transition from the laxity of Regency morality to the stricter discipline of the Victorian age. It is idle to urge that a poet—a man of imagination—should have shown greater generosity and breadth of sympathy, for Wordsworth never pretended to either of these qualities. Had his own affair with Annette come to light at this moment, he would not have expected to be treated with greater clemency than he was showing to De Quincey. Our contemporary criticism of men like Wordsworth errs fatally by taking as its standard some isolated figure who happens to be more sympathetic to us personally. Judged from the point of view of Shelley or Byron, Wordsworth's morality of course seems cautious and hypocritical. Faced by such an accusation, he himself would doubtless have objected—and with perfect justice—that the do-as-you-please method of life may be natural in an adolescent (though not, for that reason, admirable or to be imitated), who has not had time to learn the nature of the individual's debt to society,—and all very well in a disgruntled exile who has never learnt the meaning of the word responsibility; but that it has no application to a poet of middle age who conceives it his highest duty to devote his genius to the consolidation of a system of society which experience has led him to consider the best.

Apart from this general consideration, Wordsworth had warned De Quincey, at the very outset of their relationship, not to expect too much of him, because he had only a limited fund of affection on which to draw. This is exactly what the younger man had refused to recognize, and now that he was being forced to realize the results of disregarding the shallowness of that fund, he cried out that Wordsworth was treating him meanly. This failure to see that the poet had in fact been consistent from beginning to end attenuates the value of De Quincey's self-justification and robs the article, which he afterwards wrote on the subject, of persuasiveness. Our sympathies to-day naturally go out to De Quincey, both because of the suffering which it entailed upon him and because the end of the story was not that which Wordsworth had reason to suppose it would be. But to argue that Wordsworth *ought* to have been kinder to De Quincey, is to vitiate the perspective.

There is, too, another side to the question of the estrangement—a side which has nothing to do with Margaret Simpson and has hitherto escaped attention: I mean De Quincey's increased indulgence in opium, which began in the last months of 1815, the date of the beginning of the estrangement. The letter of Sara Hutchinson, already quoted, shows that the Wordsworths were by now fully aware of this unfortunate feature of their friend's life, and their dismal experience with Coleridge will have determined them to avoid a repetition of any such embroilment in future. "For heaven's sake, let us have no more drug-addicts!" Some such thought must have occurred very forcibly in all their minds; and those who have any experience of drug-addicts will scarcely blame them. If the poor man was going to become a hopeless slave to laudanum, then let those nearest to him—his family; the Simpson girl, if she felt so inclined—see to it; they, the Wordsworths, all things considered, did not feel called upon to sacrifice themselves a second time, particularly as such vexations interrupted the poet's work and jarred upon the nerves of the whole household.

Some inkling of this must have entered De Quincey's own head, for he carefully avoids mentioning his opium habits when giving his own interpretation of the altered feeling of Wordsworth towards himself. A sense of guilt on this score (the Coleridge affair must at this moment have recurred to his mind) probably prevented him from giving a more vocal expression to his grievance against Wordsworth himself, at the time. There was no excuse for the malicious tittle-tattle of Sara, of Dorothy, of Mrs. Wordsworth, and he said so freely. But the poet himself was great enough to create his own standard and in any case had taken no part in the gossip: De Quincey had to acknowledge the distinction. At all events, he never attempted to defend himself to Wordsworth or to renew the shattered friendship he so much regretted. Apart from the question of pride, which no doubt played its part in preventing De Quincey from making the first advances, there is evidence that he judged the task of patching up the friendship a futile one. As he remarks, with some bitterness, Wordsworth was not amenable to argument on subjects upon which he had made up his mind. In such cases, explanations from the other side were regarded by him as " fending and proving ", as he called it, and he took no notice of them.[1]

The shock of finding himself cold-shouldered was a terrible one to De Quincey and was certainly responsible for much of the gloom and misery of the next two years of his life. The disapproval of his friends drove him back upon himself and fanned the ever-smouldering suspicion that the world was against him. As Dorothy testifies, he and his wife kept to the cottage, not caring to expose themselves to the sneers of their neighbours; and there, cooped up day after day with the grinding bitterness of his thoughts, De Quincey entered upon the most frightful experience of his whole life—the dark reverse of the medal whose bright side had brought him such exquisite pleasures—the grim despair of the body crying out at last under the tightening grip of an insidious drug—the " Pains of Opium ".

3

During the first months of the marriage, all went well at Dove Cottage. Relieved from the intolerable weight of loneliness, De Quincey was able to forget for a time the coldness of the outside world in the firelit warmth of a cosy interior graced by his beautiful wife and child. For such a form of refuge to be successful, it is necessary that all the exterior symbols should be present; so De Quincey, in recalling this early domestic rapture, is careful to evoke the rigours of winter, rather than the easier circumstances of spring or summer. Winter, then, and with it the appurtenances of cosiness so delightfully catalogued by the poet Cowper (De Quincey had read him first in the library at Greenhay), as well as several of his own invention: " Candles at four o'clock, warm hearth-rugs, tea, a fair tea-maker, shutters closed, curtains flowing in ample drapery on the floor, whilst the wind and rain are raging audibly without. . . ."[2] Only the sofa remains unmentioned; but instead, a very un-Cowperian object—" the real receptacle . . . as much like

[1] III, 199.

[2] III, 407.

a sublunary wine-decanter as possible . . . a quart of ruby-coloured laudanum; that, and a book of German metaphysics placed by its side. . . ." [1]

This sinister note, far from fading, as the rest of the passage might lead one to expect, only grew in volume with the appalling realization that the snake within him had not been scotched after all. In spite of every effort to distract his mind, the nervous pains increased and with them the daily quantity of opium. But this time it was not relief only which the drug brought; sleep itself became a menace, for the frightful visions with which it crowded the chambers of his brain. Margaret read aloud to him, chiefly poetry; at other times, probably when his distress was most acute, he read aloud himself; it was an accomplishment of which he was proud and with which he now attempted to restore the failing sense of his own reality.[2]

But it was all of no avail: the years 1817–1818, begun in happiness and hope, soon darkened into the grimmest of De Quincey's whole life. He became totally incapable of work, could not even write a letter. In an ecstasy of self-contempt he calls himself "a mere football of reproach".[3] Without Margaret he might well have sunk to that depth of indulgence where despair, become chronic, ceases to be an enemy to be fought against, and is at last embraced —as Baudelaire embraced it—as the only condition of living. But Margaret, whose ceaseless vigilance and uncomplaining love (her own health was none of the best) raise her to heroic status and establish her claim to our unstinted admiration, saved him in the end. "My Eumenides . . . were at my bed-foot and stared in upon me through the curtains: but, watching by my pillow, or defrauding herself of sleep to bear me company through the heavy watches of the night, sat my Electra; for thou, beloved M—— . . . thoughtest not much to stoop to humble offices of kindness, and to servile ministrations of tenderest affection; to wipe away for years the unwholesome dews upon the forehead, or to refresh the lips when parched and baked with fever. . . ." [4]

But the end was very long in coming, and meanwhile neither wife, nor children (a daughter, Margaret, was born a year after William), nor reading aloud, were spells strong enough to exorcize the visions which came thick and fast, pouring over him in a relent-

[1] III, 410. [2] III, 429. [3] II, 339. [4] III, 377.

less, suffocating stream. As often before, incidents of his childhood—of things seen or merely read of—incidents ultimately more real to him than any other in his life—returned now in distorted and fantastic forms, but poignantly recognizable to him, as if he had been about to die by drowning.[1] Elizabeth, twin-sister to the Daughter of Lebanon, leaned out of heaven towards him; ladies, dressed in costumes of the time of Charles I, rehearsed a stately dance upon the tapestry of darkness. Then, suddenly, a cry of "Consul Romanus!" and the dance would melt into a company of centurions, a procession studded with brazen shouts of war.

In the next phase, human figures gave place to huge architectural constructions, cloud-formed palaces and ruins of Piranesian grandeur, which moved restlessly and changed their shapes, toppling impossibly higher and higher, room rising upon room, more agonizingly unsupported than the storeys of a card-castle, sustained only by the fearful efforts of the creating brain, yet never, never falling.

Then this "pomp of cities and palaces" sank and disappeared, and in their place spread quiet lakes and "silvery expanses of water." But the tranquillity of this horizontal vision did not last long; soon, the calm mirrors of water were churned up and expanded into endless seas and oceans, upon which floated "innumerable faces, upturned to the heavens; faces, imploring, wrathful, despairing; faces that surged upwards by thousands, by myriads, by generations. . . ." It was the long-lost face of Ann that so tyrannized over his dreams—a dead face, multiplied a thousand times and floating bodiless on the enormous sea. "Infinite was my agitation; my mind tossed, as it seemed, upon the billowy ocean, and weltered upon the weltering waves." [2]

The horror and intensity of these visions was greatly increased by the fact that De Quincey seemed to himself actually to be *seeing* what he imagined—not only, that is to say, in the dark depths of his mind, but with his physical eyes themselves. And however grand and noisy the processions, however wonderful the cities and palaces, everything appeared steeped in the deepest melancholy, like the world seen through the leaden window-pane in Poe's tale of *Ligeia*. Space too, and time, expanded, like pulled elastic, to enormous and terrifying dimensions: "I sometimes seemed to have

[1] III, 434 ff. [2] III, 441.

lived for seventy or a hundred years in one night ";[1] and again, depriving these vast extensions of all sense of personal triumph: " Over every form, and threat, and punishment, and dim sightless incarceration, brooded a sense of eternity and infinity that drove me into an oppression as of madness."[2]

After a whole year of his own life—and, still more poignantly, of his wife's—had passed by in this haunted twilight, the mysterious Malay paid De Quincey a second visit, but not in the flesh. A far more terrifying figure than he had been in life, the dark stranger appeared to him now surrounded with all the cruel trappings and circumstances of oriental religions, and with him he brought—in one single grotesque circus—all the birds, beasts, plants and trees of tropical lands, whether of the east or of the west. China was there, Egypt and Hindostan. " I was stared at, hooted at, grinned at, chattered at, by monkeys, by paroquets, by cockatoos. I ran into pagodas, and was fixed for centuries at the summit, or in secret rooms; I was the idol; I was the priest; I was worshipped; I was sacrificed. I fled from the wrath of Brama through all the forests of Asia; Vishnu hated me, Seeva lay in wait for me. I came suddenly upon Isis and Osiris; I had done a deed, they said, which the ibis and the crocodile trembled at. Thousands of years I lived and was buried in stone coffins, with mummies and sphinxes, in narrow chambers at the heart of eternal pyramids. I was kissed, with cancerous kisses, by crocodiles, and was laid, confounded with all unutterable abortions, amongst reeds and Nilotic mud."[3]

Bad as were the other living objects of this eclectic inferno to their tortured creator, the very worst of them—the almost comic worst—was the crocodile. " I was compelled to live with him; and (as was always the case in my dreams) for centuries. Sometimes I escaped, and found myself in Chinese houses. All the feet of the tables, sofas, etc., soon became instinct with life: the abominable head of the crocodile, and his leering eyes, looked out at me, multiplied into ten thousand repetitions; and I stood loathing and fascinated."[4]

And then, all of a sudden, he heard voices in his sleep, piercing through the horrid fantasmagoria that was persecuting him, and

[1] III, 434 ff. [2] III, 443.

[3] III, 442. The conclusion is rresistible that Oscar Wilde peeped at this passage, before writing *The Sphinx*.

[4] III, 443.

woke up, and found his children standing hand in hand beside the bed, soliciting attention to their new frocks.

Once only, the threatening fury of his dreams was interrupted by a vision which, though sad enough, recalled past emotions of love and beauty, instead of those of fear.

It is Easter morning—a late Easter, in May; for the old fantasy of Death and Summer must have its place in De Quincey's visions. He is standing at his cottage door, in the early morning light; before him is the lake and beyond rise the mountains, higher far than in reality; great lawns stretch in between, and in the distance, round the church and the grave of Catherine Wordsworth, cattle are lying. "I will walk abroad," he says to himself; "old griefs shall be forgotten to-day; for the air is cool and still, and the hills are high, and stretch away to heaven; and the churchyard is as verdant as the forest lawns, and the forest lawns are as quiet as the churchyard; and with the dew I can wash the fever from my forehead; and then I shall be unhappy no longer." He turns to go, but is arrested by seeing that on his left has appeared the landscape near Jerusalem, as he once saw it when sitting round the nursery fire at Greenhay, huddled over a picture-book with his sisters, in far-off days. And there, under a palm, a woman is sitting, outlined against the dim background of the holy city; and the woman is Ann herself. "And I said to her at length, 'So, then, I have found you at last.' I waited; but she answered me not a word." She seems to him the same, and yet not the same, with the pathetic, unseizable beauty of something lost long ago and never to be found again, except in dreams. And before he can fix the new aspect of her face in his memory, cloudy vapour begins to dim her features, rushing in across the vision until his eyes are completely darkened. When he can see again, he is back in the Oxford Street of eighteen years ago, with the Ann he knew once more by his side.[1]

But this springtide intermezzo (reading the passage, one all but hears it as music) is no sooner over than the awful sounds of innumerable feet in "multitudinous movement" surge up again, filling De Quincey with the dread of some appalling, indecipherable catastrophe, which he longs, but is powerless, to avert. "Some greater interest was at stake, some mightier cause, than ever yet

[1] III, 444 ff.

the sword had pleaded, or trumpet had proclaimed. Then came sudden alarms; hurryings to and fro; trepidations of innumerable fugitives, I knew not whether from the good cause or the bad; darkness and lights; tempest and human faces; and at last, with the sense that all was lost, female forms, and the features that were worth all the world to me; and but a moment allowed—and clasped hands, with heart-breaking partings, and then—everlasting farewells! and, with a sigh such as the caves of hell sighed when the incestuous mother uttered the abhorred name of Death, the sound was reverberated—everlasting farewells! and again, and yet again reverberated—everlasting farewells!" The terror and despair, rising in a crescendo, were still denied their climax, for he "awoke in struggles, and cried aloud, 'I will sleep no more'——"[1]

This truly appalling cry, which makes the reader go cold with horror, should, one feels, have heralded the end of De Quincey's martyrdom. But sleep, which he had courted so long as the release from his tortures, had now turned itself into their instrument and kept him for many months suspended over the ultimate abyss of madness:

At length I grew afraid to sleep; and I shrank from it as from the most savage tortures. Often I fought with my own drowsiness, and kept it aloof by sitting up the whole night and following day. Sometimes I lay down only in the daytime, and sought to charm away the phantoms by requesting my family to sit round me and to talk, hoping thus to draw an influence from what externally affected me into my internal world of shadows; but, far from that, I infested and stained, as it were, the whole of my waking experiences with the feelings derived from sleep. I seemed indeed to live, and to converse, even when awake, with my visionary companions much more than with the realities of life. 'Oh, what do you see, dear? What is it that you see?' was the constant exclamation of M. by which I was awakened as soon as I had fallen asleep (though to me it seemed as if I had slept for years.) My groans had, it seemed, awakened her; and, from her account, they had commenced immediately on my falling asleep.[2]

Comment on this terribly graphic passage is needless. De Quincey had reached a crisis of opium-eating, from which escape

[1] III, 446. [2] Quoted by Japp, p. 146.

in one of two directions had somehow to be made: into madness and death, or through another disintoxication back into life.

Luckily for him, two outside agencies, apart from Margaret, operated to distract his attention from the imminence of physical disaster, and thus for a time to abate its rigour. The first of these was the *Westmorland Gazette*, a newspaper founded in 1818 to oppose "the infamous levelling doctrines diffused by Mr. Brougham"[1] and the *Kendal Chronicle*.* De Quincey roused himself so far as to contribute to the paper from its inception and eventually became its editor in July of the same year, a position which he kept until he voluntarily resigned it in November 1819.[2]

It cannot be said that De Quincey was a success as an editor. His bent of mind was altogether too far removed from sympathy with the ordinary interests of the common reader. As Crabb Robinson noted: "With great talents he could not do the common things for the periodical press";[3] and, though he fulfilled his post conscientiously and to the best of his ability, not only were his own contributions to the paper absurdly learned and above the heads of the general public, but the matter which he included from other sources was altogether too idiosyncratic to meet the taste and requirements of his subscribers. The latter complained, in a mild fashion, suggesting that De Quincey address himself more to the unlearned, and in particular that he drop the habit (very characteristic of him, as it seems to us) of stuffing each issue with reports of murders and other Assize cases of a revolting nature. But this sensible complaint only produced the irrelevant reply that to be a gentleman and to have had the advantages of education was a great thing in an editor, for which reason a great future was to be predicted for the paper, especially as contributions were confidently expected from London, Paris, Vienna, Canada and Hindostan![4] To which his correspondent might well have answered that that was all very interesting, no doubt, but not what was wanted, which was something more modest. In fact, in the light of his own notion of the art of editorship, De Quincey's strictures on Coleridge for the subject-matter of the *Friend*, lose something of their force.

[1] Letter to Colonel Penson. Japp, 153.
[2] Note by Masson, in XIII, 95.
[3] *Diary*, I, 377, note 1.
[4] Japp, 159.

But at least one public event occurred during De Quincey's connection with the *Westmorland Gazette* which roused him to a perfect frenzy of excitement quite unconnected with his own troubles. This was the Kendal election, which took place in the spring of 1818, Henry Brougham competing in the Whig cause against the local candidate, Colonel Lowther. This election, and in particular the manner in which Brougham conducted his campaign, aroused a tempest of indignation and virulence in the breasts of the local Tories that reminds us abruptly that man—even as represented by such examples as De Quincey and Wordsworth—is indeed a political animal. Some of De Quincey's hysteria, as revealed in the diffuse letters which he poured out to Wordsworth [1] on the subject, may perhaps be ascribed to the state of his nerves at the time; but the same explanation is hardly valid for William and Dorothy, who, as their correspondence shows, completely lost their heads, giving vent to a vindictiveness of feeling to which neither would have subscribed at any other time. Some years later, Wordsworth revised his opinion of Brougham; but there is no reason to suppose that De Quincey ever did so.

Apart, however, from the height at which Tory feeling ran, the sand-paper personality of the Whig candidate must have had much to do with the coarse violence with which the election was conducted, as well as with the hatred and contempt with which De Quincey and Wordsworth (their personal estrangement temporarily in abeyance, in the face of an attack which they felt as common to them both) regarded Brougham. Exceedingly clever, hard-headed, seething with valuable ideas and the power to express them in oratory, Henry (afterwards first Lord) Brougham was an insensitive man, crafty, unscrupulous, and the kind of opportunist whose methods aroused something more than dislike in a country deeply imbued with an aristocratic tradition. He rode rough-shod over everybody; and although a good case can be made out for his justification in so doing,[2] he had not the personal charm for the sake of which such behaviour is often forgiven.

The crux of the Tory feeling against him is acutely expressed in De Quincey's letter to Wordsworth of April 8th.:

[1] MSS. in Wordsworth Collection.
[2] See Garatt, *op. cit. passim.*

What you say of Brougham—that you 'firmly believe that he is a man who would stop at nothing to make himself of more consequence than he now is' . . . *I*, who draw my belief in this point from no source besides his own vagrant harangues, do also firmly believe. The violence and frantic intemperance of these has, I confess, gone much beyond what I expected: for, as he did not want any free recommendations with the mob, he might safely (I thought) have attempted *now* to conciliate the gentry; whereas on the contrary . . . he has throughout his remarks abused by wholesale every class, order, division and subdivision, of people in this country—from the Lord Lieutenant [1] downwards —excepting only the Yeomanry (whose votes he may have thought likely to be influenced by his speeches), and the Rabble who constituted his audience.

And later in the same letter he makes even clearer the fundamental reason for the abhorrence in which he and Wordsworth viewed Brougham. Referring to the latter's gibe at the local gentry for "licking the dust beneath the feet of Lord Londsdale", he comments: "Surely Mr B. cannot have any of the customary feelings of a gentleman: else, for his own sake, he would not have imagined as a bare possibility an intercourse of this kind going on at Lowther. . . ."

Here De Quincey lets the cat out of the bag: it was Brougham's disregard for the limits of gentlemanly behaviour in conducting his campaign, far more than the political views which he represented, that so scandalized De Quincey and Wordsworth. They were no doubt right in their contention that Brougham's attempt to "change the character of elections, by introducing the methods of Sansculotterie," [2] should be vigorously resisted and denounced; but they were unfair in their assumption (held, however, by most Tories at election time) that anyone voting in the Whig cause must necessarily be an out-and-out Jacobin. This misconception was much stronger in De Quincey's mind than in Wordsworth's, for the reason that, where political subjects are concerned, the former never exercised his intellect at all. Wordsworth had reached his present position by long experience, in the course of which he had seen reason to change his convictions. But De Quincey received his political (and to a lesser extent his religious) opinions ready made, and—

[1] Lord Lonsdale. [2] Letter of April 8th.

such was his subjection in these respects to the influence of his upbringing—he never seems to have questioned them for a moment, in the whole course of his life.

In the event, the result of his exertions on Colonel Lowther's behalf brought De Quincey a good deal of satisfaction, besides that which he must have reaped from the eventual triumph of the Tory cause; for, in a letter to Wordsworth of April 19th, he announces himself as scarcely knowing how to express " the sense which I have of the disproportionate honor (*sic*) done by the Committee to my Paper "—a reference, I suppose, to a vote of thanks proposed to him.* No thanks for the success of the Tories were, however, due to Wordsworth, who must have been one of the worst canvassers who ever lived.

De Quincey's rival, the *Kendal Chronicle*, indulged in repeated attacks on him, couched in language the violence of which recalls the early numbers of *Blackwood's*. But, whatever he may have felt at seeing himself described as a " scurvy pedant ", he never lost his temper with the offensive paper, contenting himself with reasonable and dignified replies.

The improvement, too, in his relations with Wordsworth, brought about by the Kendal election, lasted for some time, as is proved by a letter which De Quincey wrote to the poet on June 14th. 1819,[1] acknowledging receipt of a copy of *Peter Bell*. He approves the alterations in the Prologue, but is not sure about those in the body of the poem. Still, " in common with All Englishmen who know anything on the subject of poetry,—I feel more and more how great a debt of gratitude is owing to you for the vast services which you have rendered to the literature of the country and eventually to the interests of Human Nature." I seem to feel that in paying this tribute De Quincey was making a tentative effort, not to reinstate former relations, which he must have felt to be impossible, but at least to let Wordsworth know that his old admiration for him remained largely unimpaired.

One of the major difficulties with which De Quincey had to contend in the performance of his duties as editor of the *Westmorland Gazette*, arose from his natural desire to be in two places at once. On the one hand, it was extremely painful to him to have to spend days at a time away from his wife and family; on the other, the

[1] Wordsworth Collection.

distance from Grasmere to Kendal made it out of the question for him to make the journey to and fro daily.* He does not seem to have solved the problem very satisfactorily, either to himself or to the paper, for he complained much of the fatigue entailed by such constant journeys, on which his wife ended by accompanying him,[1] while at the same time the paper suffered continually from delayed production. This difficulty, as well as his eventual realization that he was not cut out to be an editor, certainly contributed to his decision to resign the post.

Even these tiresome journeys, however, brought him a characteristic pleasure, just because they meant movement in a wheeled vehicle. Alone with Margaret in the swiftly moving coach, with the night glimpsed through the window, he was able to recapture the excitement of his boyhood. "Sometimes the nights were of that pitchy darkness which is more palpable and unfathomable wherever hills intercept the gleaming of light which otherwise is usually seen to linger about the horizon in the northern quarter; and then arose in perfection that striking effect when the glare of lamps searches for one moment every dark recess of the thickets, forcing them into sudden, almost daylight, revelation, only to leave them within the twinkling of the eye in darkness more profound; making them, like the snow-flakes falling upon a cataract, 'one moment bright, then gone for ever."[2]

But it was another night journey, on a return from Wrington, where he had been paying a visit to his mother in the late summer of 1817 or '18, which provided De Quincey with the slight, but poignant adventure that, thirty-one years later, resulted in one of the most astounding literary fantasias ever written.[3]

The night was fine but not particularly warm for August; so, during a change of horses at Manchester, De Quincey took some opium to protect him against the chill of early dawn.[4] When the coach started off again, he seated himself next to the driver and settling down gradually into the state of calm, mildly hallucinated reverie induced by the drug, amused himself by watching the driver, who now appeared to him as a kind of Cyclops, fall asleep at his post. This seems to have caused him no immediate apprehension, for he noticed, with his usual intense appreciation, the

[1] II, 355.
[2] II, 356.
[3] *The English Mail-Coach*, XIII, 304 ff.
[4] See XIV, 275.

especial silence of the night, in the hour just before dawn, the mysteriousness of the deserted roads, the faint mist spread over the fields. . . . They were ten miles south of Preston and going a good thirteen miles an hour.

Suddenly, in the distance far ahead, De Quincey heard the sound of wheels approaching, and in a flash his hypersensitized brain apprehended the whole catastrophe that was about to happen, as it were a single gesture of fate.

The driver was asleep, the coach on the wrong side of the road. Rousing himself to action, De Quincey began to climb back over the mail-bags, to warn the guard, and even tried to seize the latter's horn, with some idea of uttering the warning himself. But, just at that moment, the coach turned a corner, and there, framed by the trees which bordered the road on either side, he saw to his horror a " frail reedy gig " ambling slowly towards them, and in it a young man and a girl, tenderly leaning towards one another, wrapt in the oblivion of love.

Immobilized by fear, De Quincey shouted once—twice. The young man looked up and saw the danger that was upon him in the headlong speed of the driverless coach. (" Ah! what a sublime thing does courage seem when some fearful summons on the great deeps of life carries a man, as if running before a hurricane, up to the giddy crest of some tumultuous crisis from which lie two courses, and a voice says to him audibly, ' One way lies hope; take the other, and mourn for ever! ' ")

De Quincey saw the young man start up and pull his horse's head hard round, which brought the gig at right angles to the coach (" Oh, hurry, hurry, my brave young man! for the cruel hoofs of our horses—*they* also hurry! ") Most of the gig was by now safely out of the way of the coach, but the back was still in danger to the breadth of a second (" Glance of eye, thought of man, wing of angel, which of these had speed enough to sweep between the question and the answer, and divide the one from the other? ").

The coach dashed past and, in so doing, just caught one of the back wheels of the gig, but only to the extent of causing a slight shock to it. But De Quincey, gazing back as the coach swept round another corner out of sight, had time to catch a glimpse of the girl, as she sprang to her feet in wild affright:

Oh, heavens! will that spectacle ever depart from my dreams, as she rose and sank upon her seat, sank and rose, threw up her arms wildly to heaven, clutched at some visionary object in the air, fainting, praying, raving, despairing? . . . From the silence and deep peace of this saintly summer night—from the pathetic blending of this sweet moonlight, dawnlight, dreamlight—from the manly tenderness of this flattering, whispering, murmuring love—suddenly as from the woods and fields—suddenly as from the chambers yawning at her feet, leaped upon her, with the flashing of cataracts, Death the crowned phantom, with all the equipage of his terrors, and the tiger roar of his voice.

The moments were numbered; the strife was finished; the vision was closed.

But no: the coach pursued its wild way, and De Quincey's mind dashed off at right angles to it, after the gig and its occupants. The dream and the reality now became one in his hallucinated mind, superimposing themselves one upon the other, like two photographs taken upon the same piece of film. And, with the speed of the racing coach, the whole elaborate system of fantasy which he had built up through his dream-saturated life, rushes into place, carrying him away into a dubious heaven where he himself, now become the lover, floats with the girl upon a summer sea ("Lo, it is summer—almighty summer!"), wafted, she in a fairy pinnace, he on an English three-decker, which weave their way between islands alight with flowers, vines, music and echoing laughter. The vessels slowly drift together, and De Quincey is just about to come face to face with the girl, when suddenly everything crumbles, like Klingsor's garden, winter sweeps in from the weather side and with it a frigate, which bears down upon the defenceless pinnace. Coach or frigate, she wheels past in safety, and the pinnace plunges off into "desert spaces of the sea; whilst still by sight I followed her, as she ran before the howling gale, chased by angry sea-birds and by maddening billows; still I saw her, as at the moment when she ran past us, standing amongst the shrouds, with her white draperies streaming before the wind. There she stood, with hair dishevelled, one hand clutched among the tackling—rising, sinking, fluttering, trembling, praying. . . ."

De Quincey watches her disappear, a mere point in the distance of the raving sea, while malicious laughter comes down around him in a storm of rain. His mind becomes dark for a moment, so that the scene may have time to change; but the music continues, transferring his consciousness from one part of the vision to the next—a music of "Sweet funeral bells from some incalculable distance, wailing over the dead that die before the dawn"—and the returning light reveals him to himself lying in a boat moored to a shore. Looking up, he sees the girl, dressed as for some festival, running in panic along the deserted stretch of sand. He leaps ashore and shouts to warn her of the quicksands which she is fast approaching. But in vain; she rounds a promontory, out of sight; and when he comes again in sight of her, it is too late: only her head, crowned with white roses, and one arm, are visible above the sand. She sinks further, and the dreadful cadence returns once again to the music, as he watches her arm "tossing, faltering, rising, clutching, as at some false deceiving hand stretched out from the clouds". . . .

De Quincey sinks down and weeps tears "to the memory of those that died before the dawn, and by the treachery of earth, our mother." But he is not left long alone with his grief, for a music of victory comes gradually nearer, out of the distance, and claims him for a triumphal progress, surrounded by companions, on the coach transformed into a car of victory which is destined to spread abroad the news of "Waterloo and Recovered Christendom!"

All garlanded with laurel, the coach dashes off and two hours after midnight reaches the gate of a cathedral, the great doors of which reach to heaven—even as the trees, at the entrance to the fatal stretch of road, had seemed to reach up and join with the blackness of the night sky. At the shout of triumph, the doors fly open and the coach enters the aisle at a flying gallop. "Headlong was our pace; and at every altar, in the little chapels and oratories to the right hand and left of our course, the lamps, dying or sickening, kindled anew in sympathy with the secret word that was flying past." And everywhere—in the galleries, on pillar and pinnacle and fretwork of stone—the whole interior of the cathedral is incrusted with white-robed choristers singing of joyful deliverance.

As the vision proceeds, the cathedral opens out into the night, and a vast necropolis heaves in sight, at first a mere purple stain on the horizon. But the immense distance is covered in a second by the flying coach, and De Quincey beholds, stretching into depths of shadow on either side of the aisle—which still remains, though set now in a city of towers and terraces—turretted sarcophagi of purple granite, sculpted with bas-reliefs of long-forgotten battles. "Where the terraces ran, there did *we* run; where the towers curved there did *we* curve. With the flight of swallows our horses swept round every angle. Like rivers in flood wheeling round headlands, like hurricanes that ride into the secrets of forests, faster than ever light unwove the mazes of darkness, our flying equipage carried earthly passions, kindled warrior instincts, amongst the dust that lay around us—dust oftentimes of our noble fathers that had slept in God from Créci to Trafalgar."

As the coach rounds the last of the sarcophagi, De Quincey sees coming towards him—as before, from a great distance—a carriage, "frail as flowers" and dimmed by the mists that had hovered above the night-locked fields. It is drawn by fawns and in it rides the girl, now returned to childhood (Elizabeth! Catherine! Margaret!), all girt about with the shells and tropical flowers of the island in that summer sea from which she and De Quincey had been so rudely torn away. And again, he sees himself bearing down upon her, the unwilling instrument of her death: "Oh, baby! . . . shalt thou be the ransom for Waterloo?" He springs up as if to seize the guard's horn; but before he can do so, the figure of a Dying Trumpeter rises out of one of the bas-reliefs and, with a final effort, lifts his stone trumpet and blows the warning —once, twice. "Immediately deep shadows fell between us, and aboriginal silence." Then the trumpet sounds a third time, and life, arrested suddenly, as at an eclipse of the sun, bursts out again in all its former joy of movement and sound.

The child has disappeared during the last scene of the drama; but now three windows rise enormous at the limit of sight, and above them an altar of alabaster. In the dawn light, the girl's figure appears again, for the last time, but grown now to womanhood (Ann! Margaret!). She is clinging to the altar, "sinking, rising, raving, despairing"—the leading motif transfigured at last —for behind her rise a fiery font and the shadow of her oft-repeated death. But beside her is her angel, the efficient cause of the final triumph that now breaks out, choir and organ uniting in a tremendous figure:

Oh, darkness of the grave! that from the crimson altar and from the fiery font wert visited and searched by the effulgence in the angel's eye—were these indeed thy children? Pomps of life, that, from the burials of centuries, rose again to the voice of perfect joy, did ye indeed mingle with the festivals of Death?"

It forms no part of my present intention to attempt a Freudian assault on De Quincey's opium dreams. Their general provenance will, however, be fairly obvious to anyone with a little knowledge of psychology: the prevalence throughout of anxiety, the suspicion of persecution, the feeling of dread, of irrevocability, above all of guilt—in short all the preoccupations, expressed in easily recognizable symbols, which harassed his waking mind in moments of unhappiness, or when the outside world exerted pressure upon his consciousness to the extent of demanding from him action.

Again, in the fantasia which I have just described in detail, the translation of real events, which immediately preceded the vision, into a stylized world of imaginative, 'literary' fantasy, the scaffolding of which is clearly derived from Jean Paul Richter, is so direct and transparent as to be immediately clear to the reader, without the exercise of the smallest interpretative ingenuity. And even where symbols occur which refer to some older, more deeply buried source of experience (the girl-symbol of Elizabeth and of Ann, as well as of Margaret; the boat and the triumphal car—symbols, not only of that particular coach but of all those De Quincey had ever travelled in, right back to that never-to-be-forgotten carriage in which his father was brought home dying; the religious motifs, harking back to childhood days at Greenhay), they leave the student of De Quincey's life in no perplexity. Indeed, the whole contents of his dream-emporium are from first to last exceptionally transparent, though not, for that reason, in any sense superficial. Doubtless all the sources necessitated by his temperament were tapped; it is only our knowledge (which we owe in large measure to his own searching analysis) of his early life, that enables us to fit the image to its original with at any rate such an appearance of ease. And that is as far as his biographer need go, even if he has the ability (which I lack) to go further.

4

I mentioned two agents as operating to rouse De Quincey from his opium-stupor to a renewed interest in life; the first was the *Westmorland Gazette*, his work on which I have already described. The second, and (curiously enough) by his own account far the more powerful, was his discovery, early in 1819, of Ricardo's *Political Economy*, which was sent him by a friend in Edinburgh. The to most minds comic inconceivability of being reimbued with a desire to live by a work on economics (of all subjects!) gives the measure of De Quincey's temperamental separation from the generality of mankind. The things which give acute pleasure to most people—frivolous conversation, all the various forms of play, and so on—meant little or nothing to De Quincey at any period of his life, so that as time wore on he became the very type of the pure intellectual, whose sole pleasure, apart from a rigidly canalized affection, consisted in arranging and rearranging (in accordance with accrued information) the complex furniture of his brain. When this is realized, his excitement on reading Ricardo will not seem extraordinary. To him the subject was neither dismal nor new; but here was light upon it which revolutionized all his former conceptions. "Wonder and curiosity were emotions that had long been dead in me. Yet I wondered once more—wondered at myself that could once again be stimulated to the effort of reading; and much more I wondered at the book." [1]

His brain once again alive with new ideas, he pulled himself together and projected a "Prolegomena of all Future Systems of Political Economy", which was to be written in algebraic formulæ—with the long-suffering Margaret as amanuensis! The idea was a remarkable one, but was only carried out in part (and not in algebraic formulæ); for, no sooner had he set to work, than the opium cloud descended, hiding him from himself and defeating all attempts at concentration. Like Coleridge, De Quincey stood confronted by the fearful moral paralysis of the drug-taker; and, like Coleridge, he fully realized the state he was in. "The opium-eater loses none of his moral sensibilities, or aspirations; he wishes and longs, as earnestly as ever, to realize what he believes possible, and feels to be exacted by duty; but

[1] III, 432.

his intellectual apprehension of what is possible infinitely outruns his power, not of execution only, but even of power to attempt." [1] This is admirable and shows how successful De Quincey could be in self-analysis. But the knowledge of the vicious circle in which his spirit was revolving did not—it never does—preserve him from agonies of conscience. "I had the power, if I could raise myself to will it; and yet again had not the power, for the weight of twenty Atlantics was upon me, or the oppression of inexplicable guilt." [2] This passage refers to a dream experience; but, as we have had ample opportunity to observe, dream and reality were almost interchangeable for De Quincey, during this period, and are thus equally valid for a review of his life.

This slight rift in the clouds, then, closed once more with no hope of finer weather in sight, even to one who should sweep De Quincey's horizon with hand-shaded eyes. He continued to shun Grasmere society—even though it seems to have remained more open to him than he imagined—thus making it possible for Mrs. Coleridge to report to Poole [3] that he "does not visit any of his *old* friends", the reproachful emphasis on 'old' seeming to imply that he had made new ones whom he preferred. But if this charge is true, we do not possess any proof of it. Strangers who might well have interested him came and went; but he did not meet them. One day in June 1818, Keats walked past the door of Dove Cottage,[4] but he was not acquainted with De Quincey and so did not go in. Had he done so (Wordsworth might easily have provided him with an introduction, had he considered De Quincey in a fit state to receive visitors), we might have been spared the rubbish De Quincey afterwards wrote about him—not out of spite, but (one would suppose) from pure ignorance, and prejudiced, perhaps, by Wordsworth's poor opinion of Keats.

Shelley, too, spent a short time in the Lake District in these years, as De Quincey himself recounts. But, though Woodhouse asserts [5] that the latter made the young poet's acquaintance at the time, the passage in De Quincey's [6] article is oddly ambiguous and leaves us in some doubt whether they actually met or not.

Even poor Charles Lloyd, to whom De Quincey had always

[1] III, 433. [2] III, 446. [3] June 4th. 1819.
[4] See Letters of Keats (Forman Edition), I, 171.
[5] In Hogg, 91. [6] XI, 369.

felt drawn in friendly sympathy, began about this time to exhibit definite and alarming symptoms of madness and was accordingly shut up in an asylum near York. But he succeeded in escaping back to Westmorland, where De Quincey one day met him, wandering about in a lonely district. He stopped and asked De Quincey if he knew who he was, then continued at once: "I dare say you think you know me; but you do not, and you cannot. I am the author of all evil; Sir, I am the devil!" De Quincey endeavoured to get Lloyd to explain his reasons for this conclusion, but the latter only replied: "I know who you are; you are nobody, a nonentity; you have no being. You will not agree with me, and you will attempt to argue with me, and thus to prove that you do exist; but it is not so, you do not exist at all. It is merely appearance, and not reality. There is, and there can be, but one other real being besides myself." [1]

Academically interested though De Quincey may have been by this curious exhibition of semi-solipsism, Lloyd's final speech cannot have failed to strike a chill to his heart, so perfectly did it chime with his own impressions of himself at this time. Deprived, for the first time in his life, of the power to work, despair and self-contempt were inevitable; the sense of personal identity, strong though it might be in him, was gradually being undermined by the disruptive force of the drug. By a tremendous effort, he saved himself from final dispersal; but the effort cost him his youth. In 1821, at the age of thirty-six, when he finally succeeded in disintoxicating himself to the point where, though he might be unable altogether to give up the use of opium, he could nevertheless feel that he was no longer on an ineluctable slope, he had, by the same token, irretrievably entered middle age.

5

There is always a chance that spiritual agonies, if nothing is done about them, may solve themselves. But no such optimism is possible with regard to financial ones. Even De Quincey was now becoming aware that he must take some drastic step, if he wished to remain even partially solvent. Alone, as I have already

[1] Woodhouse, in Hogg, 78.

pointed out, he might have drifted along indefinitely on the meagrest and most intermittent earnings. But with a wife and growing family, this kind of fecklessness was out of the question: some stability must be sought, at all costs.

For his position at the end of 1820 was a parlous one. In 1819 Kelsall had gone bankrupt, taking with him some of the De Quincey family's money—though luckily not very much, for Mrs. De Quincey had been prudent enough gradually to withdraw £7000 from his control. As a result of the long letter which De Quincey wrote to her in 1818, she sent him £160;[1] but in his present position this sum did not—indeed could not—last long, and towards the end of 1819 he sent a long statement of his affairs to Colonel Penson.[2] From this it appears that the editorship of the *Westmorland Gazette* brought him in £160, but that out of this he was obliged to pay a clerk £109, 4s., to avoid the expense of constant journeys back and forth, because, owing to the fact that his wife was ill at the time, he was unable to live in Kendal. He also states that he is writing for *Blackwood's Magazine* and the *Quarterly Review*, but from other sources it is clear that this statement indicated, at the time of writing, a pious hope rather than an actuality. It is true that William Blackwood had entered into an agreement with De Quincey for a regular series of articles; but, as late as August 1820, not a word of these had been forthcoming, so that Blackwood wrote in some irritation: "It is a remark warranted by reason . . . that 'Hope maketh the heart sick'. I shall still, however, hope against hope that you will yet fulfil your long bygone engagement to the Magazine."[3]

The upshot of all this is that De Quincey begs his uncle to guarantee him a bill for £500. Whether Colonel Penson complied or not does not transpire; but, in view of his invariable kindness to his nephew, it seems likely that he did. In the same letter De Quincey repeats his intention, now rather stale and bedraggled, of proceeding to London to take up the Law at last. But, since he had expressed the same intention in a letter to Wordsworth of April 14th. 1818, as to take effect in a year's time, it seems clearer than before that his fundamental disinclination to the legal profession was as strong as ever.

[1] Letters, II, 119. [2] Japp, 153.
[3] William Blackwood, I, 424.*

At the end of 1820, however, various circumstances conspired to place Edinburgh again in a light that determined De Quincey to make a second attempt to live there. Blackwood was becoming more and more insistent, no other prospect of making money was in sight, Margaret and the children must be provided for. Moreover Wilson, one of the few people with whom De Quincey remained on terms as cordial as ever, now sent an appeal for help. *Maga*, committed to a policy of facetious, thumb-to-nose squibs at the expense of all and sundry, frowned on by the more responsible writers (Scott included), and deprived, in the preceding year, of the support of its London editor, John Murray, was going through a difficult period. Wilson complained, with the shrill bitterness he always assumed when the world showed signs of looking askance at him, that he and Lockhart were finding it daily more difficult to write practically the whole paper themselves, and begged De Quincey, in fine, to come up and help them on the spot.

The appeal moreover, extended to a private object. In 1820 Wilson was elected to the chair of Moral Philosophy in Edinburgh, in spite of the strong disapproval of his predecessor-but-one, the celebrated Dugald Stewart, and also of James Mill. Their opposition was well founded, for the post should have gone to Sir William Hamilton and would no doubt have done so, had the famous scientist not been a Whig. Wilson was, moreover, flagrantly ill-fitted for the job: he had really no notion of a Moral Philosophy himself and was absurdly under-read in the subject. So that, as the time of his inaugural lecture approached, he became more and more nervous, and flooded his friend Alexander Blair and De Quincey with hysterical demands for help and advice. " What should I treat of in the Senses—appetites and bodily powers? —It seems to me . . . that I should have a lecture on ' The Origin of Knowledge ' when treating of the senses. What are the books? and what theory is the true one? And your objections to Locke." Further on: " What does, in your belief, constitute moral obligation? and what ought to be my own doctrine on that subject? "[1] And so on. It seems clear that a man who finds it necessary to ask somebody else what should be his view of moral obligation has no business to accept a post as lecturer on that subject. Yet his first lecture, when he came to make it, was an undoubted

[1] Letters, II, 44.

success, and he continued to hold the chair for many years—thus proving, once again, that a gift for thunderous rhetoric can blind a willing audience to complete lack of original ideas and of cogent reasoning, and to fundamental ignorance of the subject in hand. Yet some saw through him. A Glasgow student remarked, after hearing Wilson lecture: "I think that man is a fool; and that if he were na sic a *big* fool, he would be laughed at." That he was not in fact more generally discredited was largely due to De Quincey and Blair, whose information and arguments he used as a schoolboy uses a crib held under the desk.

William Blackwood received De Quincey's first article on December 18th.,[1] and for a short time the latter continued to furnish matter for the paper. But his relations with the editor were not cordial, owing to his own tactlessness and also, perhaps, to some misunderstanding on Blackwood's side. Now and for ever, De Quincey was constitutionally incapable of handing in his copy up to time. Dorothy had written of him in 1815, that he was "eaten up by the spirit of procrastination"; [2] and Blackwood's natural irritation at these perpetual delays was not reduced by his contributor's jaunty assumption that he was "the Atlas of the magazine."[3]*

De Quincey's second Edinburgh sojourn was distinguished by the same social gatherings as the first had been—gatherings at which he did his best to live up to the high standard which he had created for himself on his first visit. But circumstances were inauspicious: he was ill and exhausted, and his brain was struggling painfully under the drug, as under a heavy tarpaulin; so that, as a solution to his practical problems, this second visit was not more successful than the first—perhaps less so; and in the early spring of 1821 he again returned to Grasmere.

[1] W. B., I, 424. But examination of the early numbers of *Maga* for 1821 reveal no traces of De Quincey's hand. Perhaps Blackwood held the articles over for a later date.

[2] Letter to Mrs. Clarkson, April 15th. [3] *Ibid.*, 427.

CHAPTER VII

CRISIS AND SOLUTION

I

NOT, however, for anything in the nature of a stable residence. Having failed to borrow any more money from Wilson, upon whom it appears that he had already drawn more than once,[1] De Quincey decided that there was no help for it and that he must endeavour to turn his pen to profit in the metropolis. Why he supposed himself likely to succeed better in London than in Edinburgh is not clear, for he had no immediate connections with editors there and the question of his legal studies does not arise again. Yet even in these circumstances of stress, he could not make up his mind to live permanently in London, so painful was it to him to be severed, for any length of time, from his wife and family. So for the next four years (1821–24) he continued to return for short visits to Grasmere.

But not to Dove Cottage. De Quincey had now three children —William, Margaret and Horace—and the cottage was beginning to be too small for them all. So a slightly larger house at Rydal, called Fox Ghyll, the property of John Simpson of the Nab, was taken to accommodate the family in his absence, and himself when he could snatch a few days to join them. The evidence of his way of life at Fox Ghyll is meagre but unequivocal. Edward Quillinan, who had taken Spring Cottage (now The Stepping Stones), next door to Fox Ghyll, and to whom De Quincey had lent his stables, reported that he saw little of him, "for he (De Q.) remained in bed all day, and only took the air at night, and then was more shy than an owl;"[2] which, considering that Quillinan was committed to the Wordsworth family, by virtue of his infatuation with the poet and his aspiration to the hand of the poet's daughter, is not surprising. Dorothy, too, writing to Quillinan

[1] Letters, II, 46.

[2] MS. in Wordsworth Collection.

in 1822,[1] communicates the following dismal, almost sinister, impression: "De Quincey . . . shut up as usual—the house always blinded—or left with but one eye to peep out of—he probably in bed."

Silence and darkness . . . that comfortless, uninhabited look acquired by houses in which people drag out a twilit existence, under the shadow of illness—or that of a still darker idol. . . . It does not do to dwell on Margaret De Quincey's state of mind in these years. Her own health was too precarious to allow her to accompany her husband to London. Besides, there were the children to consider, and the everlasting question of money. Simple and direct, she was entirely engrossed by the needs of her family and more than a little worn out by the perpetual effort—as much spiritual as physical—of keeping up her husband's spirits and assisting at the spectacle of his agony, which even her absorbing love was powerless to dispel.

Thus he lay; and thus she moved about his bed day after day, behind drawn blinds, asserting a desperate hope against the dreadful cries of his misery. "Oh, what do you see, dear? What is it that you see?" So she would try to probe the horrible mystery of the visions which pursued him; unable, in the last resort—it is the tragedy of their love—to understand, even when he told her.

His London life, though painful enough, was at least preferable to the living death at Grasmere, for the simple reason that it meant activity, of one kind or another. He had found lodgings at number 4 York Street, Covent Garden, which he occupied intermittently for the next four years, writing feverishly. For at last he had settled down to the business of journalism, which was to be inexorably his for the rest of his life. It was not a deliberate decision: circumstances forced him into the life; he entered it tentatively, with a provisional air, but after a time accepted it as the only possible solution to his problem. It came about in this way. Soon after arriving in London, De Quincey again met (at Lamb's?) Sir Thomas Noon Talfourd, who, with his usual serviceableness, introduced him to Messrs. Taylor and Hessey, the publishers of the *London Magazine*. The result was a contract which set the seal on De Quincey's career.

The tentative, provisional air which we have just noticed, hangs

[1] November 19th.

round the composition of the *Confessions of an Opium-Eater*, which was De Quincey's first contribution to the magazine. Seated all day long in a little room in a building[1] which stood in a yard behind the house in York Street, he set himself to the construction of the *ballon d'essai* which was to decide his fate in the world of letters. The writing of the *Confessions* did not take him long; begun in the early autumn of 1821, they appeared in the *London Magazine* for October and November of the same year. The reason for this speed was that De Quincey had, as he stated later, composed the dream section beforehand, "at wide intervals of time, according to the accidental prevalence, at any particular time, of the separate elements of such dream in my own real dream-experience."[2] The narrative section, on the other hand, was written very quickly, at the time of putting the whole together. But this speed was only achieved at the price of large doses of laudanum, which De Quincey found necessary to produce sleep, while working at such high pressure.

The serial publication of the *Confessions* aroused so much interest that Taylor and Hessey brought out the whole in book form in 1822. This edition was soon reprinted, and in the same year a second appeared, with an appendix giving the author's account of the disintoxication which he had undergone in the summer of that year.

Though the little book caused considerable excitement by its extraordinary novelty and frankness, and Sir James Mackintosh wrote a letter praising it, doubts were cast in various quarters on its genuineness, notably by the poet James Montgomery,[3] and by the *North American Review*. Instead of flying into a passion, De Quincey replied—in the *London Magazine* itself—with a long and affable letter which is worth quoting for the light it throws on his conception of the duties of an autobiographer. He protests his absolute sincerity and accuracy, except where "delicacy towards some who are yet living, and of just tenderness to the memory of others who are dead, obliged me, at various points of my narrative, to suppress what would have added interest to the story, and sometimes, perhaps, have left impressions on the reader favourable to other purposes of an autobiographer. In cases which touch too

[1] No longer standing.

[2] III, 76.

[3] Not to be confused with Robert Montgomery, the butt of Macaulay.

closely on their own rights and interests, all men should hesitate to trust their own judgment: thus far I imposed a restraint upon myself, as all just and conscientious men would do; in everything else I spoke fearlessly, and as if writing private memoirs for my own dearest friends. Events, indeed, in my life, connected with so many remembrances of grief, and sometimes of self-reproach, had become too sacred from habitual contemplation to be altered or distorted for the unworthy purposes of scenical effect and display, without violating those feelings of self-respect which all men should cherish, and giving a lasting wound to my conscience." [1]

Most readers of the *Confessions* to-day will, I think, find De Quincey's claims justified and his explanation satisfactory. At any rate, his letter would seem to have convinced the contemporary world, for no more aspersions were cast on the author's veracity. When, at the end of his life, he again took up the book and added enormously to it, sufficient time had by then passed for him to feel himself justified in inserting various facts which he had before suppressed, and in printing in full some of the names which had formerly appeared merely as initials.

But if the *Confessions* brought him notoriety, he was in no mood to exploit it. He was, indeed, still acutely miserable. "I began," he says, "to view my unhappy London life—a life of literary toils, odious to my heart—as a permanent state of exile from my Westmorland home. My three eldest children, at that time in the most interesting stages of childhood and infancy, were in Westmorland; and so powerful was my feeling (derived mainly from a deranged liver) of some long, never-ending separation from my family, that at length, in pure weakness of mind, I was obliged to relinquish my daily walks in Hyde Park and Kensington Gardens, from the misery of seeing children in multitudes, that too forcibly recalled my own." [2] The opium, which had, in days gone by, stimulated his faculties to make work easier, now made it all but impossible. Yet he worked harder now than he had done since leaving Oxford.

Again, as in 1812, he looked to nocturnal walks to bring relief from overmastering depression; but even these only served to renew impressions which, once so bright and keen with pleasurable sensations, now increased his sense of difference by a slow film of

[1] III, Appendix, 465. [2] III, 71.

sadness. His old haunts—the opera-house, the suspicious purlieus of Holborn, even Oxford Street and Soho Square—instead of adding to his store of experience, merely evoked memories of the days when opium had brought him pleasure, instead of this roving, inescapable pain.

In this state of mind and body, De Quincey found himself little able to tolerate—far less take pleasure in—any kind of society. There were several houses in which he was always welcome, but the prospect of facing anything in the nature of a gathering was for the present intolerable to him.[1] Crabb Robinson, that indefatigable and entirely reliable Social Register of the literary circles of his day, makes no mention of De Quincey as having been present at the parties he himself attended in the years 1821–4; and Talfourd,[2] in giving account of Lamb's gatherings, does not mention him either. Yet the Lambs were the only people whom De Quincey took pains to visit, at this time—chiefly, no doubt, because, realizing the state of his nerves, they were kind enough to invite him alone, without the rest of their friends.

It was in these intimate sessions that De Quincey came finally to appreciate the lovable depths—the generosity, the fundamental seriousness—of Lamb's character. Though still apt to be jarred upon by the teasing way in which Lamb would refer, in his presence, to opium and Oxford Street—subjects on which he was, not unnaturally, extremely sensitive—De Quincey's last defences broke down before Lamb's disinterested kindness, his "regal munificence", and the perennial virtuosity of his charm, which lay in his large tolerance of, and sympathy with, the weaknesses (especially the *secret* weaknesses) of others. For there was nothing in the least censorious in the man: he could be counted upon never to read one a lecture, whatever one confessed to him. And his jesting would, one knew, always drop off him if one were really in trouble. It was only the pretentious people, the pontifical (Wordsworth), the snobs, and those who took themselves with humourless seriousness, who found him invariably and mercilessly flippant. De Quincey belonged in none of these categories and so could be sure always of bringing out what was deepest and most genuine in Lamb, who could always be relied on to sympathize with anyone who was downsides with the world.

[1] III, 78 and 126; V, 251.

[2] *Final Memorials of Charles Lamb.*

De Quincey has left us an unforgettable description of one of those evenings spent in the intimacy of Charles and Mary; of Lamb's virtuoso stammering, which ended always in a 'settling', at long last, upon the key word of the joke (generally a pun). While realizing the dubious quality of many of Lamb's puns, De Quincey evidently suffered them more gladly than Keats,[1] for he says: "The mercurialities of Lamb were infinite, and always uttered in a spirit of absolute recklessness for the quality, or prosperity of the sally. It seemed to liberate his spirit from some burden of blackest melancholy which oppressed it, when he had thrown off a jest: he would not stop one instant to improve it; nor did he care the value of a straw whether it were good enough to be remembered, or so mediocre as to extort high moral indignation from a collector who refused to receive into his collection of jests and puns any that were not felicitously good or revoltingly bad." [2]

Thus Lamb in the midst of his friends; but when alone with his sister and De Quincey, he did not stand upon ceremony. Having drunk a good deal of wine at supper, he allowed himself to sink gently into sleep. His guest, far from being offended by this, took a careful impression of Lamb's appearance at these moments (one remembers his painter-like description of Grasmere),[3] and afterwards retailed it in the following beautiful passage:

It (sleep) descended upon him as softly as a shadow. In a gross person, laden with superfluous flesh, and sleeping heavily, this would have been disagreeable; but in Lamb, thin even to meagreness, spare and wiry as an Arab of the desert, or as Thomas Aquinas wasted by scholastic vigils, the affection of sleep seemed rather a network of aerial gossamer than of earthly cobweb—more like a golden haze falling upon him gently from the heavens than a cloud exhaling upwards from the flesh. Motionless in his chair as a bust, breathing so gently as scarcely to seem certainly alive, he presented the image of repose midway between life and death, like the repose of sculpture; and, to one who knew his history, a repose affectingly contrasting with the calamities and internal storms of his life. . . . It could not be called a transfiguration that sleep had worked in his face; for the features wore essentially the same expression when

[1] See letters of Keats, I, 170. [2] V, 253.
[3] Quoted on p. 84.

waking; but sleep spiritualised that expression, exalted it, and almost harmonised it. Much of the change lay in that last process. The eyes it was that disturbed the unity of effect in Lamb's waking face. They gave a restlessness to the character of his intellect, shifting, like northern lights, through every mode of combination with fantastic playfulness, and sometimes with fiery gleams obliterating for the moment that pure light of benignity which was the predominant reading on his features.[1]

Those evenings at Lamb's must have done much to mitigate De Quincey's loneliness in London and his dislike at being separated from his family. Without providing him with a substitute for his home—Lamb was too genuine and individual a person to perform so self-effacing an office—he and his sister lightened the burden of the little man's sadness by showing him, in the discreetest way, that his vision of himself as outcast and pariah was not entirely well founded, and reminded him, moreover, that the pleasures of congenial society are at no time to be despised.

2

In the summer of 1822, yielding to the necessities of work, where the persuasions of misery had proved insufficient to move him to action, De Quincey submitted himself to a rigorous system of disintoxication, of which he gives the details in the Appendix to the third edition of the *Confessions*.[2] Since he had been in the habit of taking between 170 and 500 drops of laudanum daily, he began the experiment by limiting himself to 130. He continued this for three days, then plunged down suddenly to 80 drops, but, finding the reaction intolerable, was obliged to retrace his steps. After a month of this régime (130 drops), he attempted another plunge—this time to 60 drops—and the following day took none at all. This freedom lasted for ninety hours, after which he was again forced to recur to the drug—he does not say to what extent. In the end, he was able to abstain totally for one whole day, on condition he took 25 drops the next; and so on, alternately.

De Quincey's body, however, angered by this disturbance of its habits, now took its toll in various distressing symptoms: nervous

[1] V, 252.
[2] Reprinted in the Appendix to Vol. III of the Masson Edition.

irritability of the system, cramp in the stomach, restlessness, lack of sleep, ulcerated mouth, swellings of the lower jaw, violent and continuous sneezing. These secondary symptoms are perfectly in order; the pains in the shoulder and stomach, which De Quincey imagined to be rheumatic, as well as the ulceration and swelling, will have been caused by poison from the liver, which was now in a chronic state of disease, both from the continued use of opium and from lack of sufficient walking exercise.[1] The irritation of the mucous membrane, such as would result in perpetual sneezing, is also a well-known symptom of the body's craving for the drug, as De Quincey was himself aware.

This heroic effort nevertheless brought its reward in a greatly increased ability to concentrate on work, and also in a flood of new ideas.[2] True, he was unable to control these, which eluded him as fast as they came; yet the mere fact of their arrival in his mind was a comforting reassurance that his powers, far from having failed, had only been dormant. The realization had the strength of a revelation: "During the whole period of diminishing the opium, I had the torments of a man passing out of one mode of existence into another. The issue was not death, but a sort of physical regeneration."[3]

This mutation of the phoenix resulted, for the next two years (1823–24), in a burst of literary activity of an important kind. Under constant pressure from Taylor and Hessey, De Quincey enriched the *London Magazine* with the *Letters to a Young Man whose Education has been Neglected,* the essay *On the Knocking at the Gate in Macbeth,* two essays on Malthus, the article on the Rosicrucians, a series of *Analects from Richter,* the *Dialogues of Three Templars on Political Economy,* two articles on the *Education of Boys in Large Numbers,* two translations from Kant (*On National Character* and the *Idea of a Universal History*) four tales adapted from German originals (*Mr. Schnackenberger, The Dice, The King of Hayti, The Fatal Marksman*), as well as several shorter articles of less importance.[4]

[1] III, 71, and Hogg, 213 (Letter to Hessey). [2] *Confessions* (1823), p. 195.
[3] III, 448. And III, 73.
[4] To this period also belongs the absurd story of *Walladmor.* This clumsy German fiction had been evolved to meet the taste for novels in the style of Scott, and was indeed produced as a "translation" of a novel by that author. Called upon to review this in the autumn of 1824, De Quincey did so, exposing the hoax

But if the disintoxication from the drug renewed his ability to work, it did not relieve his depression of spirit or improve his qualities as a social figure. His liver, left in sole possession of the field, remained obstinately sluggish, inflicting tortures of gloom and effectually distorting his view of all those with whom he came in contact. In fact contemporary evidence, aided by correspondence, points to the fact that De Quincey was, during these years, what he was at no other time, *i.e.*, cross. Dilatory as ever in preparing his articles for the press, in perpetual anxiety over money, a prey to suspicions of persecution from creditors, he conducted a wrangling correspondence with Taylor and Hessey (chiefly the latter), which makes very painful reading.[1] For, in spite of the sympathetic co-operation of Thomas Hood, who was now, at the age of twenty-one, sub-editor of the *London Magazine*, De Quincey was entirely unable to accommodate himself to the routine of journalism. The above-mentioned letters are one long complaint of ill-usage, in which the accents of petulance and of a desire to placate are mingled to most unpleasing effect. He accuses Hessey of deliberately confusing the characters of friend and man of business to hurt him; complains bitterly that his editors do not realize the sacrifice he is making in exchanging " a Westmorland valley for a London alley " ; gives an unnecessarily minute account of how he spends his money and of the debts that burden him (he complains that he has had to sell a portion of his library to pay off a relation of his wife's); protests that he is near to death; describes Hessey's answers as " unprovoked ill-temper and violence " ; but entreats him not to betray his address to anyone, lest his enemies find him out. Anger, elaborate pathos, wounded dignity, poured themselves out over the unfortunate publisher as from a superannuated actor who feels himself laid on the shelf. And all because Hessey had accused him of " cruel delay " and demurred at always being asked to pay in advance for articles that were not forthcoming when required. Yet, strangely enough—and it is greatly to the credit of Taylor and Hessey—the relations

and translating a selection of passages. The review so whetted the appetites of his readers that a complete translation was called for; whereupon De Quincey, with inward groans at the " forests of rubbish " with which he was faced, proceeded to rehandle the whole thing, turning it into a sort of parody of *Guy Mannering*, in which guise it met with the approval of Dora Wordsworth. The story is told in an article which De Quincey wrote for *Tait's Magazine* in 1838. (XIV, 132.)

[1] MSS. in British Museum.

between editors and contributor remained on the whole good. De Quincey seems at moments to have realized that Hessey was really exercising considerable forbearance towards him, for on one occasion we find him writing: "I am greatly indebted to you for your kindness about time."

Here depression seems for once to have broken down De Quincey's principle of dignified reserve, where his own affairs were concerned; for he now complained to everyone he met of the wretched state of his health and made his acquaintance free of his wranglings with Taylor and Hessey, so that Lamb, ready as usual with a pun and too impatient to see that it might lay him open to a charge of unkindness, said that De Quincey ought rather to employ "Pain and Fuss" (Payne and Foss were a contemporary firm of publishers).

Back at Fox Ghyll, on one of his flying visits, De Quincey wrote to Wordsworth:

My dear Sir,

I feel so much pain at not having been able to express my sense of the favor you did me in calling—that I think it right to explain that the load of labor under which I groan, has continued to make it impossible for me to get out for one half hour even. . . . When I am not utterly exhausted, I am writing: and all is too little; so unproductive as to quality is ungenial labor.—Mere correction of proofs indeed, and corresponding with London on business, is almost enough to fill up my time: for, if all that I have lately written were published at once, it is a literal fact that I should more than fill the *London Magazine*. . . .[1]

We are reminded, in this last sentence, of De Quincey's claim to Blackwood that he was "the Atlas of the magazine", and of Blackwood's irritation at the impertinence. Yet there is no doubt that, given his state of health, De Quincey was in fact overworked.

Further evidence is not wanting that the impression he produced on strangers, at this period, was unworthy of him at his best. Procter ('Barry Cornwall') states that De Quincey appeared at only one of the *London Magazine* dinners, on which occasion "the expression of his face was intelligent, but cramped and somewhat peevish. He was self-involved, and did not add to the cheerfulness

[1] MS. in Wordsworth Collection.

of the meeting."[1] Hazlitt, who made De Quincey's acquaintance at this time, certainly received the same impression, though he did not record it. De Quincey, on his side, was perplexed and repelled by Hazlitt; he admits that he "felt depressed by the spectacle of a mind constantly in agitation from the gloomier passions",[2] sees in his manner "the peevishness of a disappointed man", and opines that "the original vice of his character was dark, sidelong suspicion, want of noble confidence in the nobilities of human nature. . . ."[3] To which criticisms, just as they were, Hazlitt might well have replied with a *Tu quoque*. The encounter has, in fact, its comic side, as a perfect illustration of the outraged annoyance which neurotic people always feel at the spectacle of others suffering from the same disease as themselves. Their diagnosis of each other's trouble is searching and correct; but each feels that it is *lèse majesté* for anyone but himself to suffer in that particular way. Moreover, in the case under review, Hazlitt and De Quincey met at a time when both were showing their least attractive side to the world. The latter was suffering, as I have shown, from ill-health, anxiety and homesickness, while the former, who had just published the *Liber Amoris*, was feeling himself an object of scorn and obloquy to the world in general. In these circumstances, De Quincey's primness, his elaborate politeness, and his Toryism, could not fail to irritate Hazlitt, who was highly conscious that his own manners were extremely bad, and who at all times regarded difference from himself on political and even literary matters as an insult.

Yet De Quincey really understood Hazlitt very well. In the pages which he devoted to him, more than twenty years later, he records not only what everyone who knew Hazlitt at once noticed—*viz*., his wilful enmity, his fantastic touchiness[4]—but points out also that these faults sprang from a sense not so much of what was due to himself as of what he conceived to be due to his principles and opinions—a more respectable position. "He loathed his own relation to the human race," says De Quincey, placing his finger with some subtlety exactly on the spot,[5] and shows an unexpected liberality in his opinion of the *Liber Amoris*, which he recognizes as an outpouring of frenzied unhappiness,

[1] *Life of Hazlitt*, by P. P. Howe, p. 329.
[2] XI, 347.
[3] III, 80.
[4] XI, 343.
[5] XI, 346.

and not, as to most people (both then and now) it has appeared—a mere piece of exhibitionism, an unpardonable washing of dirty linen. Indeed, the downright passion of that angry and unique little book impressed De Quincey deeply, "as showing him to be capable of stronger and more agitating passions than I believed to be within the range of his nature."[1]

Another cause of pain to De Quincey, at this time, and a most gratuitous strengthening of his sense of grievance against the world in general, was the publication in the *Kendal Chronicle* of a grotesque parody of the *Confessions*, containing a gross libel against Margaret De Quincey and referring in equivocal terms to the premature birth of her first child. De Quincey took this coarse attack very much to heart and did his best to discover the perpetrator of it, with a view to calling him out for what he characteristically describes as "prurient solicitations to the libidinous imagination, through blanks, seasonably interspersed."[2] The spectacle of De Quincey as a duellist is not one that offers itself very readily to the imagination; yet there is no reason to suppose that he meant less than he said. In many small ways a man of the eighteenth century, he was at all times very sensitive to the point of honour (one recalls his fury with the Bangor landlady, who had suggested that he might be a swindler), and, though physically very small, he was nothing of a coward. As it turned out, however, the utterer of the libel succeeded in concealing his identity, so that De Quincey was unable to carry out his threat.

Mention must be made here of the translation of the *Confessions* made by Alfred de Musset (then a boy of eighteen) in 1828. This astonishing production must, if De Quincey ever read it, have confirmed him in his low opinion of the French. Where the original is followed, the translation is quite good; but the capricious departures from the text, which are many: the false and tendentious title (*L'Anglais, Mangeur d'Opium*), which was, to do Musset justice, forced upon him by the publisher: and the interpolation of an entirely invented *Introduction à la quatrième partie*; make the whole thing one of the greatest literary impertinences ever committed.

The alterations are very typically French. The passage on prostitution and the attitude of the English law,[3] for instance,

[1] III, 79. [2] III, 176. [3] *Confessions* (1823), 49.

which in the original is reasonable and moderate, is rendered by the translator in one sentence, thus: "On ne peut nier qu' à Londres la classe élevée en général ne soit dure, cruelle et repoussante." And the final page of the London section [1]—the fine exordium in which De Quincey bids farewell to the image of Ann—is omitted altogether, no doubt because it does not fit in with the ludicrous twist which Musset afterwards gives to the story. This twist takes the form of a continuation, according to Gallic ideas of how such things happen. Patrolling Oxford Street as usual, in search of Ann, De Quincey is represented as meeting an officer of his acquaintance, who takes him to a ball. Once there, he behaves in the Byronic manner expected of an Englishman of the period: "Moi, vêtu de noir, et les bras croisés, je m'en allai m'appuyer sur une colonne tout au fond de la salle." The next moment Ann appears, all Dame aux Camélias, pale and dripping with diamonds. She makes shy advances, which he repulses with suitable scorn: "Plutôt que de voir Anna devenir la maîtresse d'un marquis de C. . . . j'aurais voulu la voir morte!"

After the ball is over, Ann sends for him to come to her, which he does, though reluctantly, and greets her coldly. She tells him her story—the hardships she has endured since the day on which he last saw her, how she was eventually taken up by the Marquis de C, who keeps her in magnificence, while at the same time treating her with coarse ferocity.

At this moment their tête-à-tête is violently interrupted by the supervention of the marquis himself. "'Mort et damnation!' s'écria-t-il." A duel takes place on the spot, in which De Quincey is victorious. After which he carries Ann off to a safe retreat, where they live happily ever afterwards. This passage is joined on, with the utmost impudence, to that in which, in the original text, De Quincey compares his wife to Electra; so that in Musset's version it is Ann who is made to invigilate over her lover's opium crisis, while poor Margaret De Quincey is quietly pinched out of the story!

This derisory invention is interesting if only because it shows so clearly the impossibility that any Latin—at any rate at that date, for the French later accepted our pure-flower-on-the-dunghill tradition with passionate enthusiasm—should understand the sort

[1] *Confessions* (1823), 49.

of relationship which existed between De Quincey and Ann. Musset was unable to entertain the idea that these two could have been associated in anything except an ' affair '; and even if he had been able to divine the true state of the matter, the French public would never have accepted it.[1]

3

I have already stated my conviction that this latest plunge into, and recovery from, opium constituted De Quincey's farewell to youth; it is now time to look more precisely into this assertion. I do not contend that the signs of this change show any marked degree of intensity: on the contrary, a cursory glance does not reveal them at all. Yet the signs are there—subtle, almost impalpable, like everything else about the man. The surprising thing about them is the suddenness with which they appear.

It is important to seize the full implications of this fact. In De Quincey's case, careful scrutiny of letters, of recorded speech and behaviour, show no gentle lapse from youth, no gradual and continuous dimming of lights on the stage of his faculties. The descent into middle age was in his case abrupt, like a sudden shelf of rock. The fiery enthusiasm which glitters in every page of the 1803 diary; the impatient urgency of his early letters to his mother, to Wordsworth; the jauntiness and ardour displayed in his pursuit of Margaret Simpson: all these disappear on a sudden. They are not replaced by opposites of an obvious kind—cautiousness, cynicism; they simply make themselves conspicuous by sudden absence. When we look upon De Quincey again, after he has awoken from his long opium sleep, it is—inevitably, perhaps, but most completely and abruptly—a different man whom we find. The essential qualities are of course what they always were; it seems probable, indeed, that at quite an early age (already reached by about 1809), his mind, which had developed so much faster than normal brains, ceased to alter its contours and merely con-

[1] Musset's version of the *Confessions* had at least one repercussion: it inspired Berlioz with the idea for the *Symphonic Fantastique*. And, though no proof exists, it seems obvious that Gérard de Nerval's posthumous *Le Rêve et la Vie* (1855) was influenced by it. The first paragraph of this little work reads like a direct translation from De Quincey, and the whole atmosphere of the book is deeply impregnated with the Opium-Eater's peculiar kind of imaginative fantasy.

tinued to amass and compare new stores of information. But the signs of an altered attitude to his own life are discernible in his relations with other people, though the alteration does not take the form of a radically new direction. It is rather that his former, instinctive attitude to the people with whom he is brought into contact, now appears as hardened (by gathering sadness? by loss of the larger hope?) into a deliberate method of behaviour. His business relations (including those with his mother) remain on the same old footing of procrastination and apology; but the youthful, almost light-hearted professions of hope now give place to a tone of querulous resignation, of take-me-or-leave-me regret. His exquisite manners and elaborate scrupulousness, though they never altogether lose their quality of innocent appeal, now crystallize, for the attentive observer, into a slightly overdone politeness (of the kind so strikingly exhibited, in our own day, by Proust) of the shivery person who prefers to keep everyone at arm's length, but lacks the independence of mind to allow others to draw their own conclusions from a perfectly natural method of address. It was a mild form of duplicity accompanied, too, by a certain heavy-lidded sadness, an extra degree of reserve, a subtle withdrawnness which gives a sense of finality, of surrender to what he has at last learnt to recognize as the more inexorable features of his character.

The emphasis, I repeat, is not on the degree of the change, which is slight, but on its suddenness. The De Quincey of the years with which we have henceforth to deal—the literarily productive years, when the vast accumulations of his reading and experience at last broke their dam and poured out in a swift and continuous flood over a space of nearly thirty-eight years—is a man prematurely aged by pain, by prolonged anxiety and sorrow, and by the deceptions of a gentle romanticism.

Carlyle, who met De Quincey first in 1826, gives, in his *Reminiscences*, an impression of him which, fundamentally contemptuous though it is, lays just emphasis on those features which I have indicated as characteristic of his emergence from youth:

He was a pretty little creature, full of wire-drawn ingenuities; bankrupt enthusiasms, bankrupt pride; with the finest silver-toned low voice, and most elaborate gently-winding courtesies and ingenuities in conversation: 'What wouldn't one give to have him in a Box, and take him out to talk!' (That was *Her* criticism of him; and it was right good.) A bright ready and melodious talker; but in the end an inconclusive and long-winded. One of the smallest man figures I ever saw; shaped like a pair of tongs; and hardly above five feet in all: when he sat, you would have taken him, by candlelight, for the beautifullest little Child; blue-eyed, blond-haired, sparkling face,—had there not been a something too, which said, '*Eccovi*, this Child has been in Hell——' . . . His fate,—owing to opium, etc—was hard and sore; poor fine-strung, weak creature, launched *so* into the 'literary career of ambition, and mother of dead-dogs.'

This would not have been an accurate picture of De Quincey in 1816.

4

At the beginning of 1825, it again becomes clear, De Quincey's affairs were reaching a complex crisis. His debts had become so pressing that he found it necessary to go into semi-hiding, changing his lodgings frequently in order to evade his creditors. A letter from his mother,[1] dated January 13th. and addressed to 4 Eccleston Street, Pimlico, throws some light on De Quincey's later relations with that lady. It appears that Colonel Penson had lately returned from India, with something less than a fortune, in spite of which, with his sister's mania for building, he was already engaged in building a new dining-room in place of the old greenhouse at Westhay. Proceeding to more important topics, Mrs. De Quincey states that her income is now £600 a year, out of which she is prepared to make Thomas an allowance of £100, as also to his brother Henry—who had disappointed her quite as much as Thomas had done, marrying an expensive smart woman and contracting debts which he expected his uncle (to the latter's fury) to pay. Mrs. De Quincey concludes with a reference to Thomas' profession, thus: "I cannot expect that your literary productions either as a Translator or an Author will rise in moral tone to my point, for I suppose you must please your Readers, and unfortunately little is required, and much will be lauded to the skies, and that by *Churchmen*, sadly at variance with Christianity."

De Quincey must have read the last sentence with a wry smile for the rigid consistency of his mother's point of view—to say

[1] Letters, II, 128.

nothing of her style, which had not weakened with the years. But the offer of help must have been exceedingly welcome to him. We do not know if he accepted it; presumably he did, for he was hardly in a position to refuse. In February, however, he was evidently still in a parlous condition, for he writes to Wilson as follows: "To fence with these [liver affections] with the one hand and with the other to maintain the war with the wretched business of hack-author, with all its horrible degradations, is more than I am able to bear. At this moment I have not a place to hide my head in. Something I meditate—I know not what. '*Itaque e conspectu omnium abiit.*' With a good publisher, and liberty to premeditate what I write, I might yet liberate myself: after which, having paid everybody I would slink into some dark corner—educate my children—and show myself in the world no more." And he warns Wilson to send letters either to Rydal Nab, where his wife is at present living (Fox Ghyll having been sold), or else 11 King's Bench Walk, c/o M. D. Hill, the author of a pamphlet on the education of boys in large numbers, which De Quincey had reviewed at great length in the *London Magazine*.[1]

One seems to see in this letter a hint that the writer would consider with favour a renewed offer from Blackwood; but for the moment nothing further was forthcoming from Wilson, who was finding life quite difficult enough on his own account, what with the unruly dragon of *Maga* to keep down on one side, and the chair of Moral Philosophy on the other.

At this juncture, while De Quincey was darkly meditating something, he knew not what, a 'friend indeed' turned up in the person of Charles Knight, an editor and publisher whose indefatigable efforts provided the nineteenth century with that typically modern convenience—potted information on all sorts of subjects, in easily assimilable forms.[2] He was at this time engaged in founding *Knight's Quarterly Magazine*, to which he invited De Quincey to contribute. At the same time, being a generous person of fairly ample means, he opened his house in Pall Mall East to the harassed little man, as a temporary haven of refuge.

De Quincey contributed only two pieces of importance (*The*

[1] See p. 213.

[2] *Penny Magazine* (1832–45), *Penny Cyclopædia* (1833–44), *Pictorial History of England* (1837–44), etc., etc. (*Dic. Nat. Biog.*) The impetus towards these publications came from Brougham and his Society for the Diffusion of Useful Knowledge.

Incognito, a story from the German, and *The Love-Charm*,* a translation from Tieck) to the magazine, but he lived for some months in Knight's house, a wan, eccentric presence, who astonished the servants and his host by the convolutions of his etiolated sensibility and his exaggerated idea of the *comme il faut*. Years later, Knight recalled how De Quincey's sensibility " was so extreme, in combination with the almost ultra-courtesy of a gentleman, that he hesitated to trouble a servant with any personal request without a long prefatory apology ; "[1] so that once he found the little creature sitting in a draught without his shirt, because he had not liked to require the servants to wash his linen, in the absence of Mrs. Knight.

On another occasion, he showed surprise at Knight's willingness to advance him money on a post-dated cheque. Just before this incident, expecting money from his mother, which was to enable him to return to Grasmere and which had not arrived, he worked himself into a state of mind from which the delay appeared to him as his own fault—as a deliberate swindle to deceive Knight. So, taking advantage of a moment when his host was from home, he snatched up his belongings and rushed out of the house, to take lodgings once again in his old haunt on the Surrey side of Waterloo Bridge, where Knight eventually discovered him and advanced the necessary sum.

After De Quincey's return to Grasmere, his friendship with Knight seems gradually to have lapsed ; but it was revived again in 1829, when De Quincey invited him to stay, in a letter that waxes lyrical over the excellence of Westmorland food.

Wilson, meanwhile, had not forgotten the hint conveyed in De Quincey's last letter to him. Out of sight, but by no means out of mind, De Quincey had been figuring, under the title of " Thomas Papaverius ", in the *Noctes Ambrosianae* with which Wilson had for the last three years been enlivening the now less vitriolic pages of *Maga*. These strange lucubrations are dialogues written largely in Scottish dialect, containing scraps of news and comments on topical events and characters—a sort of gossip-column, in which the protagonists are " Christopher North " (Wilson himself), James Hogg (" The Ettrick Shepherd ", not the publisher), De Quincey, " Timothy Tickler " (Robert Sym) and others. The dialogues scarcely make interesting reading to-day, but the fact of De

[1] C. Knight, *Passages of a Working Life*, I, 329.

Quincey's introduction into them (under a transparent pseudonym) serves to show that he was at last generally known in both capitals.

In November Wilson wrote to De Quincey, soliciting his collaboration on the *Quarterly Review* which was about to change hands—from John Coleridge's to those of Lockhart. De Quincey's contributions were not, at any rate at first, to be a one-man affair: he was merely to act as ' ghost ' in assisting Wilson to write a review of Brown and Welsh's lectures on psychology, the work involved " to be acknowledged in the way of business, and felt in the way of friendship." As if conscious that his demand may seem impertinent, as well as unsuitable, in view of all the ' ghostly ' assistance which De Quincey had already rendered him in the matter of his moral lectures, Wilson addresses him in his old jocular tone (" My dear Plato "), which he had dropped of late years, and continues, in an ingratiating style, by admonishing De Quincey of the " certain moderated tone " demanded by the Quarterly. The letter ends—somewhat gratuitously, as De Quincey may well have felt—with the following sentence: " Thank God you are not now domineered over by circumstances, and may your noble nature never more be disturbed but by its own workings! " [1]

Wilson may conceivably have supposed that De Quincey's return to Grasmere indicated an improvement in his financial condition; but he should have known his old friend better than to imagine that the " workings " of his " noble nature " were not in themselves more than sufficient to cause him intolerable suffering. The suggestion was, to say the least of it, ill-timed.

The letter was followed, however, a year later, by an offer of a more substantial kind, namely, what De Quincey seems to have hankered after: a return to the staff of *Blackwood's*. Provisionally, therefore, and with his usual dislike of irrevocable decisions, De Quincey went to Edinburgh, in the autumn of 1826, to make a fresh start in the pages of *Maga*.

It is in these years that Dorothy Wordsworth once more makes a gracious entry upon the scene—the last, moreover, which she was to make, and at De Quincey's solicitation. His return to Dove Cottage, in the previous summer, had been made none too soon, for Margaret had reached an advanced stage of nervous ill-health, Perpetual child-bearing (she was already expecting her fourth child,

[1] Japp, p. 192.

Francis) had not improved her always delicate health, and her husband's continuous absences and the uncertain condition of the family finances added greatly to the burden she had to bear. Aware of this, De Quincey swallowed what remained of his pride and, preferring to recall the Dorothy of early days rather than the scornful gossip of later ones, wrote to beg her assistance in calming his wife's fears and alarms:

Saturday, July 16,—1825.

MY DEAR MADAM,

I am at this time in great agitation of mind; and I solicit your assistance in a way where you can give it effectually.—Call, I beg and pray you, my dear Miss Wordsworth, on my poor wife—who suffers greatly from a particular case of embarrassment affecting me just now. What this is, and how it arose, I began to explain in a very long letter: but repeated interruptions from the Press have not allowed me to finish it. Suffice it however here to say—that in a few weeks I shall be free from all distresses of this kind which have so long weighed upon me. Meantime, she writes me the most moving and heart-rending letters—not complaining, but simply giving utterance to her grief. In her very last letter she concludes by begging me "not to take her grief amiss": and in fact she disturbs my fortitude so much, that I cannot do half what I else could. For my fear is—that being thrown entirely upon herself, with no soul (unless her eldest sister) to speak a word of comfort to her—she will suffer her grief to grow upon her, and in her present uncomfortable situation will fret herself to illness. If that should happen, I know what I must look for next: and I shall never have any peace of mind, or a happy hour, again. Assure her that all will be well in a very few weeks; and the greater part in a fortnight. What a sad thing then that she should give way to a momentary pressure, just at the time when I have first a prospect of for ever getting over any pressure of that kind. . . . Oh! Miss Wordsworth,—I sympathised with you—how deeply and fervently—in your trial thirteen years ago:—now, when I am prostrate for a moment—and the hand of a friend would enable me to rise before I am crushed,—do not refuse me this service. But I need not conjure you in this way: for you are full of compassion and goodness to those whose hearts are overburthened with long affliction.—What I wish is—that you would give my wife the relief of talking over her distress with one whom she can feel to be sympathising with her—To do this with less constraint, perhaps you will be so good as to go over and drink tea with her. And let me know, if you please, how she is in health:—Direct to me—To the care of Chas. Knight Esq., Pall Mall East,—London.

Say whatever you can think of to raise and support her spirits: beg her not to lie down too much, as she is apt to do in states of dejection, but to walk in the fields when it is cool; and to take some *solid* food, which she is very apt to neglect.—She is amused by newspapers: perhaps you could lend her a few just for the present, until I am able to send one down.

. . . If I had any cheerful news from home,—I am now in a condition to extricate myself in 28 days.

God bless you, my dear Miss Wordsworth,—stand my friend at this moment.[1]

This important and hitherto unpublished letter stands quite by itself: no evidence exists that Dorothy did as she was asked, at the time. She must have received the letter, for she was certainly at Rydal Mount throughout the summer of 1825.[2] However, we are justified in assuming that she did in fact visit Mrs. De Quincey, for in the autumn of 1826, after De Quincey had gone to Edinburgh, Dorothy suddenly wrote him a long letter of news combined with advice, which reads strangely like an answer to his own letter of the previous year:

. . . I called at your cottage yesterday, having first seen your son William at the head of the schoolboys; as it might seem a leader of their noon-tide games, and Horace [3] among the tribe—both as healthy-looking as the best, and William very much grown. Margaret was in the kitchen, preparing to follow her brothers to school, and I was pleased to see her also looking stout and well, and much grown. Mrs. de Quincey was seated by the fire above stairs with her Baby [4] on her knee. She rose and received me chearfully, as a person in perfect health, and does indeed seem to have had an extraordinary recovery, and as little suffering as could be expected. The Babe looks as if it would thrive, and is what we call a nice Child,—neither big nor little.

Mrs de Quincey seemed on the whole in very good spirits; but, with something of sadness in her manner, she told me you

[1] MS. in Wordsworth's Collection.
[2] See De Selincourt, *op. cit.*, p. 365.
[3] De Quincey's third child.
[4] Francis, De Quincey's third son.

were not likely very soon to be at home. She then said that you had at present some literary employment at Edinburgh; and had, besides, had an offer (or something to this effect) of a permanent engagement, the nature of which she did not know; but that you hesitated about accepting it, as it might necessitate you to settle in Edinburgh. To this I replied 'Why not settle there for the time at least that this engagement lasts? Lodgings are cheap in Edinburgh, and provisions and coals not dear.' Of these facts I had some weeks experience four years ago. I then added that it was my firm opinion that you could never regularly keep up to your engagements at a distance from the press; and, said I, 'Pray tell him so when you write.' She replied, 'Do write yourself.' Now I could not refuse to give her pleasure by so doing, especially being assured that my letter would not be wholly worthless to you, having such agreeable news to send of your Family. The little cottage and everything seemed comfortable.

I do not presume to take the liberty of advising the acceptance of this engagement, or of that—only I would venture to request you well to consider the many impediments to literary employments to be regularly carried on in limited time, at a distance from the press, in a small house, and in perfect solitude. You must well know that it is a true and faithful concern for your interests and those of your Family that prompts me to call attention to this point; and, if you think that I am mistaken, you will not, I am sure, take it ill that I have thus freely expressed my opinion.

My brother and sister do not know of my writing, otherwise they would send their remembrances. . . .[1]

The importance of this kind and sensible letter lies, not so much in the excellent advice which it contains, as in the glimpse it affords us of Mrs. De Quincey as she now was, after ten years of marriage. "Do write yourself": those three words conceal—or reveal—the whole of Margaret's hard-won experience of married life and of the husband whom she adored and pitied, but of whom she still stood in some awe. There is a charm, a confidence, a profound sense of humility in face of a character she did not pretend fully to understand, in this appeal to a woman whose words, she knew, would carry more weight with her husband than her own. She knew that Dorothy was her intellectual superior and that she had

[1] De Selincourt, *op. cit.*, p. 372.

once enjoyed De Quincey's intimacy; therefore—looking up from the baby on her knee—she was prepared unjealously to resign her own influence for the sake of her husband's good, to one who had not always treated either him or herself with generosity.

Dorothy's advice probably clinched the matter in De Quincey's mind, though he did not actually settle in Edinburgh for good until 1830. In the intervening years he still returned from time to time to the Nab,[1]* drawn back doubtless, by the poignant associations (he was, after all, as much of a sentimentalist in such ways as Hazlitt) of so many years, during which the landscape and the little cottage had had time to become saturated through and through with memories of every kind, memories lined with dreams and fantasies both beautiful and terrible, but dear by virtue of the intensity with which they still lived on in his imagination, to quicken it for the years which still remained to him. So the weaning could not but be gradual. But by 1830 it was complete: after this date, De Quincey never went back to Grasmere.

During the interim period, 1828-30, he lived, while in Edinburgh, in Wilson's house, number 8 Gloucester Place, as the owner was spending most of his time at Elleray during those years. In order to mitigate his sadness and produce around himself the sensation of home life, without which screen he was liable to feel the chilly draughts of despondency, De Quincey took with him to Edinburgh his two eldest children, William and Margaret, now eleven and ten years of age. As he was only too obviously unsuited to look after them himself, his old friend Captain Hamilton (" Cyril Thornton ") and his wife kindly took charge of them—no doubt to their mother's secret relief. At the same time, this lightening of her familiar burden must have meant a good deal to Mrs. De Quincey; the hardships and miseries of her life had given her health no opportunity to improve, and the time was soon to come when she would relinquish the struggle altogether.

[1] See invitation to Charles Knight, July 1829. Affairs at the Nab had been going badly for some time. John Simpson had involved himself in litigation and found himself obliged to sell the house. De Quincey, rushing into the breach, raised a mortgage on the estate and left his father-in-law in possession. By 1833, however, funds were again at an end, and the house fell to the mortgagee. After which John Simpson went to live with his daughter and son-in-law in Edinburgh.

The tenancy of Dove Cottage was not surrendered till 1834.

5

The ten years from 1818 to 1828 form the most critical phase of De Quincey's life. It was not that he had never before been faced with an important choice: there had been his elopement from Manchester, and later from Oxford; there had been his marriage. Indeed, if one cares to adopt the dramatic view of life, then De Quincey's can colourably be regarded as a series of flights—from authority, from himself, from convention, from physical pain. But this view, attactive as it may be, is far too expensive: it lays too much emphasis on the negative aspect of De Quincey's experience, and fails to take account of the strong, if generally latent, directive strain in his character. For the carpet of his youth is not one in which it is difficult to distinguish a 'figure', though the ultimate results in work, dictated as they were by circumstance, must be said to lack that particular distinction. This figure, blurred in its inception and defaced in places by many a false start, erased and written over like one of his own manuscripts, is simply the passion for knowledge—as learning, not as mere information—to be acquired primarily as a source of inner, individual power, and secondarily as a foundation for the communication of that power in literature. Indeed, after the romantic plans laid down in the 1803 diary had failed to fructify, it seems as though literature, in the sense of art, had been relegated to a place behind the creation of some imposing philosophic edifice, the enormous and elaborate façade of which must effectively have concealed any structures relying for their effect on the subtlety and delicacy of artistic treatment. But in course of time this programme, as is the way of programmes, became modified out of recognition. In his arresting distinction, made in one of his earliest published essays, between the Books of Knowledge and the Literature of Power [1]—comprehending, under the first heading, everything conferred by the *informative* authority of words, and, under the second, the entire world of art—De Quincey expressed a dichotomy of which, in his own works, he was to give but few clear examples; for there are few writers in whom it is harder to distinguish the point at which information and argument cease, to give place to the deliberate

[1] *Letters to a Young Man*, X, 47. This distinction was, as far at least as vocabulary goes, probably derived from converse with Coleridge.

creation of artistic effect. So that, if it was originally knowledge, in a narrower sense, which he aspired to give to the world, it was Power—not in the sense of artistry so much as the integration of his own spiritual life—which formed the fundamental intention of his early years, working obscurely in the boy who mused behind Mr. Clowes's stained-glass windows at Manchester, and becoming clearer and more deliberate in the studious recluse of Oxford and Grasmere.

But, just as he failed to reckon with the pressure of circumstance, so he failed to reckon with his own temperament. Tortured by his body, he tried to defeat it by ignoring it, and by attempting to live shut up in the airless structure of the sole intellect. The result was of course a stalemate,—a gradual but obdurate slowing-down of his intellect under the protest of his body, until, in 1818, it ceased to function in accordance with his will, but went off at a tangent into a fantastic limbo of its own, the furniture of which lay about in a freedom of association that could not be put to the uses of living, though it might—and did—provide the material of poetry. Here, then—in the convulsions artificially induced by opium, which forced to the surface the raw stuff of a nature fundamentally poetic but at the time consciously leaning away from the development of that one among his faculties—lies the explanation of the 'set' of his work towards the forms and effects of art which, instituted by the striking uprush of the *Confessions*, remained to inform all the rest of his work, more or less apparently, and which peeps through the joints of even his most drily expository periods. The question, to what degree De Quincey was ever a conscious artist, is one which I shall examine in detail later, when the whole body of his work lies before me; here it is only desirable to indicate the origins of the artistic element in his writing and to lay emphasis on the curiously fortuitous nature of its insurgence. For, however much the romantic imagination of the boy may have turned towards the creation of poetic literature, under the influence of Wordsworth, Coleridge, and the Gothic novelists, there is little doubt that, by the time De Quincey left Oxford, his mind had turned away from such ambitions towards what seemed to him more solid achievements in philosophy and interpretative literature. It was the incidence of physical ill-health and its concomitant, laudanum, acting with increasing force over a long period of years, which inserted between eye and object (whether incident of childhood, contemporary or historical figure, or process of logic) the spectacles of artistic vision, saturating that object with peculiar and persuasive colour. As he rather dangerously remarked, at the outset of his literary career: Never pay any attention to the understanding, when it stands in opposition to any other faculty of the mind.[1] But reason and intuition were both strong in this strangely constituted brain; throughout his career as a writer, he gave the preference, now to the one, now to the other faculty. But had no stimulus arrived from without, to goad him into expression in spite of himself, there is good reason to fear that his mind would have spun itself willy-nilly away into the incommunicable darkness of a solipsistic world.

The prising open of his brain by circumstance is therefore a matter for gladness. What is deplorable is the fact that the leverage, from that moment (1818) until the end of his life, never let up for one instant, thus forcing him to expend the whole of his spiritual capital in one continuous stream, without intervals for further accumulation and assimilation of material. Carried thus further and further out to sea by the inexorable current of financial pressure, De Quincey soon lost sight of land altogether—of the shores on which stood the half-finished city which he had been building so painstakingly, stone by stone, in jealous solitude, and in the dim distance of past years. It was the pace at which life urged him on—its treadmill threat—which so flustered and enraged him. For he had intended his building to be slow, trusting to time to dictate the form of the eventual edifice. Hence his protesting indignation at being rushed by outward circumstances into hack-journalism, which, he felt, impaired the value of what he had to say; left, so to speak, his unfinished, unroofed city to the mercy of the winds and waters.

That, I believe, was the shape of his crisis, the solution of which, in its first and tentative form, was the *London Magazine*, and in its second, firmer and more permanent, *Blackwood's*. For after his settlement in Edinburgh, in 1830, De Quincey never again attempted to look back. He knew himself committed now, for good or evil, to the life of a journalist, and he resigned himself consciously to making what he could out of the wreckage of his former building.

[1] X, 389.

He was forty-five, had known middle-age for the last ten years, and had learnt to make the usual compromise with life. The process involved a permanent complexion of sadness, darker perhaps than most men acquire, but not more inevitable; and relieved, quite as permanently, from the sordid and the dismal by the presence of a delightful family—his own. For the part which his marriage played in the most important spiritual crisis of his life is not minimized by the fact that, as an emotional event, it took place on its own plane, which was not and never could have been that of his intellectual life. This proceeded as before; but its roots reached down into the depths of his emotional nature, whose life, profoundly enriched and modified by the experience of Margaret's love and sacrifice, and by the exquisite comedy of fatherhood, sent up a sap that nourished his brain and fortified it against exhaustion and the aridity that lies in wait for those who deny the natural man. In this he differed profoundly from Wordsworth, who, in his self-sufficiency, remained astoundingly unmodified by marriage and fatherhood and was obliged to turn back to Nature and Memory for the emotional nourishment of his work.

As well, then, as providing the actual occasion of his crisis, by making his worldly condition so acute as to demand active decision, De Quincey's marriage secreted the antidote of its own poison.

6

Turning, for a brief appraisal, to the relatively small but important body of work which De Quincey composed during the period of crisis which I have been describing, one is struck at once by one of the most outstanding aspects of his whole work: the width of its range. Autobiographical fantasia (the *Confessions*), literary criticism (articles on Richter, Herder, Walking Stewart, Goethe, Lessing), translations (German tales, essays by Kant), Political Economy (*Dialogues of Three Templars*), Philosophy (*On Suicide, Notes from the Pocket-book of a late Opium-eater*), History (the *Rosicrucians* article, the *Falsification of English History*), problems of the day (*Education of Boys, Letters to a Young man*): in this first series of articles De Quincey lays out a full prospectus of his powers. Given what we know of his preparatory reading, and considering also the diversity of subjects on which reviewers have at all times been expected to deliver themselves, this width of range is perhaps not so surprising; yet we must remember that as yet De Quincey had undertaken none of the more strictly biographical and historical essays on a large scale—none of the literary theory, and little of the criticism, with which he later diversified his work.

On the other hand, apart from the *Confessions*, the list contains four of De Quincey's best efforts: the two tales, *Mr. Schnackenberger* and *The King of Hayti*,* the imaginative interpretation of the *Knocking at the Gate in Macbeth*, and the highly amusing account of the *Last Days of Immanuel Kant*; and, in the first part of the essay on *Murder Considered as One of the Fine Arts,* one of the strangest, most original and characteristic—if not on the whole one of the most successful—of his fantasies.

The first two show De Quincey in a comic-fantastic vein derived from Smollett and the Gothic novelists; they are the heirs, suitably desiccated by maturity, of all the romantic projects mentioned in the diary of 1803. Mr. Schnackenberger is a sort of latter-day Don Quixote, the pathetic butt of a whole town, and, in particular, of a Princess's practical jokes, but who emerges triumphant in the end by sheer force of amiability and insouciance. In describing his hero, De Quincey exhibits the same combination of allusive skill with the painter's piercing eye, which he brought to the description of his friends:

Upon a little, meagre scarecrow of a horse, sate a tall, broad-shouldered young fellow, in a greatcoat of bright pea-green, whose variegated lights and shades, from soaking rains and partial dryings, bore sullen testimony to the changeable state of the weather for the last week. Out of this greatcoat shot up, to a monstrous height, a head surmounted by a huge cocked hat, one end of which hung over the stem, the other over the stern of the horse: the legs belonging to this head were sheathed in a pair of Monstrous boots, technically called 'field-pieces,' which descending rather too low, were well plaistered with flesh-coloured mud. More, perhaps, in compliance with the established rule, than for any visible use, a switch was in the rider's hand; for to attribute to such a horse, under such a load, any power to have quitted a pace that must have satisfied the most rigorous police in Poland, was obviously too romantic. Depending from his side, and almost touching the ground, rattled an enormous back-sword, which suggested to the thinking mind a salutary hint to allow free passage, without let or unseasonable jesting, to Mr Jeremiah Schnackenberger, student at the University of X——. He that might be disposed to overlook this hint would certainly pay attention to a second, which crept close behind the other in the shape of a monstrous dog, somewhat bigger than the horse, and presenting on every side a double tier of most respectable teeth.[1]

The whole story is an admirable example of that English nonsense-humour in which De Quincey and Lamb both delighted—the kind of joyous fooling which was to produce *Alice in Wonderland* and the verses of Edward Lear. The imaginative source which produced it is essentially of the same order as that which has been tapped in our own day (but with conspicuously less success) by the French *Surréalistes*. The description of Mr. Schnackenberger calmly lighting his pipe from the flames of the burning house, before looking for means of escape,[2] is an equally perfect subject for Lear's pencil, for the *photo-montage* of Max Ernst, or for the prose of André Breton. In all cases, it involves the use of the private dream, though De Quincey, in making this use, was always at pains to clarify and arrange his associations, that his magic might be communicable to the reader.

The King of Hayti is amusing and fantastic in the same manner as the foregoing tale, but the intrigue is even wilder and more reminiscent of E. T. A. Hoffmann and his modern counterparts. Both these stories make one regret that De Quincey did not carry out any of his early projects, at a time when his imagination was flaring from the blow-lamp of adolescence. A complete romance on the lines of these short tales might well have equalled, in extravagant beauty, the best work of Jean Paul Richter. As it is, we have to content ourselves with the comparatively meagre excellence of *Klosterheim*, De Quincey's only extended fiction.

It may be mentioned in passing that his skill as a translator is considerable. Though these two stories do not pretend to be anything but free adaptations, *The Love-Charm*, which also belongs to this period,[3] is a closer translation, from the German of Ludwig Tieck, and reads at least as well as the original. The tale is in any case a remarkably fine one, full of a sinister, rhetorical power, and working up to a climax of very real horror.

[1] XII, 314. [2] XII, 319.
[3] It was published in *Knight's Quarterly Magazine*, in 1825.

In the essay on *Murder*, the later and most successful parts of which were not written until 1839 and '54, and in the short commentary on the *Knocking at the Gate in Macbeth*, De Quincey launches out into a type of imaginative criticism of which he was to become the acknowledged master and which had only been adumbrated before he made it so peculiarly his own. In the case of Shakespeare, Coleridge and Hazlitt had been before him; but this, his single contribution to the criticism of Shakespearean detail, as distinct from that of the man himself, does not suggest the influence of either of those writers. It is a piece of pure impressionism, in which the experience of the protagonists in the drama of the murder of Duncan is related as if it were a part of the writer's own experience. The method is essentially that of the novelist. In order to point out the source of the vivid sensation which we receive from this particular piece of Shakespearian stage-craft, De Quincey produces a parallel evocation of the scene, in poetical prose, thus:

In order that a new world may step in, this world must for a time disappear. The murderers and the murder must be insulated—cut off by an immeasurable gulf from the ordinary tide and succession of human affairs—locked up and sequestered in some deep recess; we must be made sensible that the world of ordinary life is suddenly arrested, laid asleep, tranced, racked into a dread armistice; time must be annihilated, relation to things without abolished; and all must pass self-withdrawn into a deep syncope and suspension of earthly passion. Hence it is that, when the deed is done, when the work of darkness is perfect, then the world of darkness passes away like a pageantry in the clouds; the knocking at the gate is heard, and it makes known audibly that the reaction has commenced; the human has made its reflux upon the fiendish; the pulses of life are beginning to beat again; and the re-establishment of the goings-on of the world in which we live first makes us profoundly sensible of the awful parenthesis that had suspended them.[1]

This is criticism of a high order, since it wrings the utmost significance out of what it describes; but it is also highly 'subjective' and as such touches the borders of fiction—of poetry. Both here and in the elaborate reconstructions of actual murders which he undertakes in the essay on *Murder* (in the story of the

[1] X, 393.

Baker of Mannheim, in the facetious 'history' of murder), De Quincey lays the foundations of what has come, in our day, to be known as *biographie romancée*—that dangerous, attractive, almost impossible art. In the case of this last essay, the method is further complicated by a stilted *parti pris*, designed, by its violently paradoxical nature (the admirable, artistic quality of a beautifully executed murder) to startle the reader into a double interest in the material and to give a fantastic twist to the descriptions of the murders themselves. The result, it must be admitted, is, in spite of the extraordinary bravura displayed in the writing, too strained to be successful.

But if its point of view excludes the essay on *Murder* from doing more than indicate the province of the *biographie romancée*, the vastly entertaining *Last Days of Immanuel Kant* lies well within its borders. This essay is in reality much more than the mere loosely strung together series of anecdotes which a superficial reading might announce it as being. The whole thing is in fact a very cunning *résumé* of the chief German authorities on the subject*; but De Quincey's affection for, and knowledge of, his subject, coupled with his inspired ear for significant gossip, has produced an organic whole in which the man Kant assumes the vivid life of a character in a novel by Dickens. Yet he is true in both senses, real and artistic; and so is the material by which he is created and illustrated. Indeed, this piece is one of the best examples of De Quincey's narrative power, of his ability to relate actual facts in such a way that they assume for us the strange and comically violent definition of actions in a dream. The deliciously slow description of Kant getting into bed,[1] where the movement of the prose imitates closely the meticulous movements of the old man himself (a favourite trick of De Quincey's); the parallel passage—even more impressive—which describes, with macabre care, the gradual dissolution of the philosopher:[2] both remind one of events related in the *Confessions* and the *Autobiographic Sketches*, in which actual facts have undergone that dreamlike transformation which De Quincey's peculiar perception conferred on everything he described, whether real or imagined. Though he never saw Kant, he brings the man before us as vividly as he brings, for instance, the figure of his own dying father.

[1] IV, 338. [2] IV, 374 ff.

It is this quality, of course—this raising to the level of general, illuminated significance, of what has actually happened—which has brought the *Confessions* their high renown and placed them, until imitations arose, in a class apart from other autobiographies. Other intimate narratives have startled by the extraordinary and outrageous nature of their material, but this one remained to impress and enchant succeeding generations, as much by its poetical qualities as by the charm and sincerity of the author, and the pathetic appeal of his story. At once franker and more exquisitely reserved than Jean Jacques Rousseau, that other great exponent of the artistic autobiography, De Quincey achieved a narrative of dreamlike fascination which yet convinces one of its substantial truth. The reason for this lies, no doubt, in the fact that, unlike most autobiographers, he had no axe to grind. He did not write to justify himself as an opium-eater (though incidentally he may do so, that was not primarily his object), nor yet to prove himself a better fellow than others thought him. He wrote simply because it seemed to him that his experience was peculiar and interesting and not too far removed from that of most men to be connected at vital points with what they had themselves been through; and he performed his task with a candour [1] and an intensity of memory ("emotion recollected in tranquillity") that gave it a universal validity which a moment's lapse into self-deception or self-pity would have destroyed—as it destroys the validity of so much of Rousseau's outpourings. For however terrible, however intimate, however personal De Quincey's confessions, they never descend to the level of what newspapers call 'revelations.' Rousseau's, on the other hand—with their sensationalism, their vulgar bragging of unpleasing personal traits, their underdog whine—are the parent of the 'Stories of My Life' with which *déclassé* aristocrats, worn-out demi-mondaines and convicted swindlers nowadays turn a dishonest penny by contributing to the Sunday Press. De Quincey is not tarred with that brush. His sense of what he owed to himself, his dignity, his irreproachable manners, saved him from all charge of

[1] I am aware that I have myself impugned the validity of De Quincey's account of his financial position during the *Confessions* period. But the affair of the forty-guinea cheque belongs mainly among the events narrated in the *Autobiographic Sketches* and, strictly speaking, scarcely concerns the story of the *Confessions* themselves, which forms an enclave in the larger work and is, therefore, not sufficiently concerned with the tenebrous affair to receive the latter's equivocal shadow.

vulgarity, then and now. When one considers that the story he had to tell was essentially of the kind which would nowadays produce interviews in the yellow press, entitled "How I escaped from Hell: Full Revelations of an Opium-Fiend", this avoidance, even allowing for the difference of period, must be accounted something of a feat. And here a word on the current continental reputation of De Quincey is in season. French and German writers, whose knowledge of De Quincey is mostly confined to the *Confessions*, unite in including him under the rubric of such figures as Huysmans and Beardsley, and treat his work as if it were a kind of pendant to *Les Fleurs du Mal*. The i's of this preposterous point of view have lately been sharply dotted in England itself by the otiose illustrations to an *édition de luxe* of the *Confessions*, which represent De Quincey in exactly this light. Nothing could be more at variance with the facts. To regard him as a decadent, *fin-de-siècle* figure is fundamentally to misconceive the nature of his being.

Having removed the plums from this early portion of De Quincey's work, we must do him the justice to examine some pieces of lesser interest which he contributed to the *London Magazine* during these years. Apart from the dialogues on Political Economy and the essays on Malthus, which I shall discuss in a later chapter, when the more important *Logic of Political Economy* comes up for consideration, the only pieces of any importance are the *Letters to a Young Man whose Education has been Neglected,* a review of the *Education of Boys in Large Numbers*, an introduction to the *Analects from Richter*, an essay on the *Falsification of English History*, and the two articles on Lessing.

The *Letters to a Young Man,* besides their intrinsic value, which is considerable, are of especial interest to the student of De Quincey's life; for they embody what amounts to a valuation of his own University education and the general principles he deduced from it. The scheme of education which he here outlines proceeds from Logic, through Languages, to what he calls the "arts of memory", by which he seems to mean mathematics. Emphasis is placed on the necessity of combining the study of literature (the "Literature of Power" as distinct from the "Books of Knowledge") with that of some more analytic, and therefore astringent, subject, in order to avoid befuddling the intellect (he adduces the example of

Coleridge).[1] At the same time (and here De Quincey's love of paradox again emerges), languages *as such* are characterized as "the dry-rot of the human mind",[2] "a barren and ungenial labour". The reason given for this strange opinion is the no less erroneous one that the rules of all languages are arbitrary and therefore give no scope to the systematizing intellect! And De Quincey follows this up by predicting that within the next two centuries all languages will be reduced to four, viz.: English, Spanish, Portuguese and Russian. He gives no ground for this extraordinary list, and I cannot help feeling that some sudden attack of self-destructive spleen, such as he was at all times liable to, must have been responsible for this irrational attack on a study which had been of such signal service and absorbing interest to himself. What is most valuable in the letters is the defence of a classical education, on the ground, again, that it communicates Power, which De Quincey describes as "the case in which I should be made to feel vividly, and with a vital consciousness, emotions which ordinary life rarely or never supplies occasions for exciting, and which had previously lain unawakened, and hardly within the dawn of consciousness,—as myriads of modes of feeling are at this moment in every human mind for want of a poet to organize them."[3] In the essay on Richard Bentley, De Quincey puts forward the same argument, apologizing, however, more succinctly for a classical education on the grounds, simply, of its liberalizing effect.[4] In either case what is meant is the widening, deepening, and subtilizing of the mind by the comparative study of literature,—not an original view but one which slips very neatly into its place in a reconstruction of our author's character. It is essentially the same point of view as that which Coleridge expressed in a letter to young James Gillman, in 1827. "Believe me, my dear James! it is no musty old saw but a maxim of life, a medicinal herb from the garden of experience, that He alone is *free* and entitled to the name of gentleman, who knows himself and walks in the light of his own consciousness. But for this reason nothing can be rightly taken in, as a part of a liberal education that is not a means of acquainting the learner with the nature and laws of his own mind. . . . All knowledge, I say,

[1] This programme is virtually the same as that outlined by Giambattista Vico. See *The Life and Writings of Giambattista Vico*, by H. P. Adams, p. 87.

[2] X, 35. [3] X, 48. [4] IV, 173.

that enlightens and liberalizes, is a form and a means of self-knowledge, whether it be grammar, or geometry, logical or classical."

In spite, then, of some exaggeration by the way and of paradoxes which are sometimes wanton, the *Letters* are still worth reading for their incidental felicities of argument, and for their acute remarks on Latin and German literature. Unfortunately for their total effect, they tail off and end abruptly with a digressive discussion of the appreciation of Kant in England—a journalistic fault which, through pressure of time and a natural tendency to divigation, appears all too often in De Quincey's work.[1]

The article on the *Education of Boys* shows De Quincey in a very advanced and sympathetic light. Rather surprisingly for so convinced a conservative, we find him here advocating reforms in teaching and school government which the nineteenth century was only very gradually to put into effect—and then only partially. Rule *by* the boys *for* the boys; a criminal court of boys for trying offences committed by their number (both adumbrations of the prefect system); abolition of corporal punishment; improvement in the methods of teaching, with a view to making the subjects more interesting and agreeable (knowledge and the love of it must be generated together);[2] cribs to be allowed for the construing of classical texts; no more learning of useless facts, as degrading to the memory. This is a remarkably liberal programme for the year 1824; and when we call to mind what schools were like in those days, and what they remained far on into the century, we must applaud De Quincey and the anonymous author[3] of the tract which inspired him, for the far-sightedness and humanity of their proposals.

The essays on Jean Paul Richter and Lessing are De Quincey's first attempts at critical appreciation, and both were designed to call the attention of English readers to two great writers of whom De Quincey rightly believed them to be all but entirely ignorant. The first, which was written as early as 1818, when De Quincey was at Grasmere,[4] establishes once and for all the type of criticism

[1] Lamb was sufficiently entertained by the *Letters* to produce a parody of them, entitled *Letters to an Old Man*, etc., which he sent to De Quincey with apologies for impertinence. It is to be supposed that De Quincey took the joke (not a very substantial one) in good part.

[2] XIV, 25.

[3] His name was M. D. Hill. See p. 195.

[4] Letter to Wordsworth, April 14th, 1818, in Wordsworth Collection.

in which he was destined to excel. It is, again, criticism from within. De Quincey explains the methods and effects of his author by entering his mind and looking outwards upon the objects which he has described, so as to give back, if possible, the peculiar *taste* of the experience of the writer himself. This is the method of De Quincey's most successful interpretative ventures, of his essays on Lamb, Pope, Shakespeare, Bentley, Herodotus, Milton, Greek Tragedy. A typically romantic method, its virtues are obvious and are almost better observed in the literary criticism of Hazlitt than in De Quincey's own; the former possessed the harder mind and was less liable to the cardinal error of the 'subjective' method, which consists in not keeping the eye firmly fixed upon the object. That De Quincey was very frequently guilty of that error explains the paradoxical oddity of emphasis and proportion which disfigures some of his critical essays and led him, for instance, to fritter away most of a long article on Shakespeare (intended for the *Encyclopædia Britannica*!) in an elaborate discussion of the poet's marriage, of whether or no he was a gentleman, and of his fame in his own lifetime—discussions which throw more light on De Quincey himself than on Shakespeare.

In the case of Jean Paul, however, De Quincey was fully justified in his method, if only because his subject did in fact so curiously resemble himself. Listen to this:

> John Paul's intellect—his faculty of catching at a glance all the relations of objects, both the grand, the lovely, the ludicrous, and the fantastic—is painfully and almost morbidly active: there is no respite, no repose allowed. . . . From his mode of presenting things, his lyrical style of connexion, and the prodigious fund of knowledge on which he draws for his illustrations and his images . . . his obscurity arises.[1]

If no name had been mentioned, one might have taken this for an extremely searching description of De Quincey's own writing. But if it is true in this sense, it is also true in the sense in which De Quincey meant it; for not even Carlyle appreciated so well the astonishing genius—now unfairly neglected—of Richter. For in his extraordinary, sprawling books the pathetic, the humorous and the fantastic are united as few writers except Shakespeare have

[1] XI, 267, 268.

united them. De Quincey is at pains to make this point (he instances Falstaff, in especial) and in doing so he again involuntarily draws our attention to the unique qualities of his own writing; qualities subtly different from those he is celebrating, though partaking of their essence; qualities less robust, more fastidious, and superficially at least more human than those of the author of *Titan*. Yet, while De Quincey was translating that 'Dream upon the Universe' which is the most remarkable of the extracts which he chose to represent his author,[1] it must surely have seemed to him, as it seems to us, that here was the origin of the dream-fantasies which were even then troubling his brain and which he was soon to give to the world in the *Confessions*.

This brings us round again to the point at which we inevitably started out on this critical excursion: the *Confessions* themselves. And now the obvious demands to be said: the work stands alone among De Quincey's writings; he never 'brought it off' again so completely. The *Autobiographic Sketches* contain much that is of enthralling interest, much that is beautiful, much that is entertaining; the *Suspiria de Profundis,* the *English Mail-Coach,* the *Revolt of the Tartars,* all contain passages that are, in themselves, equal to anything in the *Confessions*. But none of them attains the unity of the earlier work—at least in its first version; they lack the concentrated intensity, the ease, the passionate fluency, which make of the *Confessions* so astonishing, so eternally *fresh* a work of art. The reason is plain: nothing else that De Quincey wrote was so immediately the outcome of personal experience—in this case, of an overwhelming one. Unannounced, unprepared, it appeared quite suddenly, at the touch of a need simpler and more universal than that of artistic expression. Never was a great piece of literature less deliberate in its inception, whatever it may have become in its final form, when its author had had time to think over what he had written. Composed 'straight from the heart' (like that very much more considerable affair, the *Mass in D* of Beethoven), it has the spontaneous quality of a lyric poem; as such it has appealed to subsequent generations, and as such it deserves, in the last resort, to be judged.

[1] XI, 291.

CHAPTER VIII

THE FLAME IN SUNLIGHT

I

Blackwood's Edinburgh Magazine, soon to become familiarly known as 'Maga', was the outcome of a succession of circumstances which must concern us briefly at this point. Edinburgh, it was felt, had for too long been under the domination of London publishers. With a view to bringing this state of things to an end, the Edinburgh publisher Archibald Constable, in 1802, enlisted the help of such prominent Whigs as Sydney Smith and Brougham in bringing to birth the *Edinburgh Review*. Its early policy was of the anonymous-ragging order which was afterwards imitated by *Maga*; but it quickly settled down into a graver tone and even instituted the system of paying its contributors—an arrangement which Brougham and Sydney Smith had waived. Constable's bookshop became the centre of literary society and, under the ægis of Francis Jeffrey, a Whig tone diffused itself pungently over the town.

After this had been going on for some time unchallenged, William Blackwood, a high-spirited young man of Tory opinions, who had already made his way as a bookseller (seller and publisher were often one in those days) in the teeth of Constable, moved his premises from the comparative obscurity of the South Bridge to 17 Princes Street and there speedily created a rival centre of attraction to the circle of the *Edinburgh Review*. Numerous barristers, including Wilson and Lockhart, joined the Blackwood circle, and the prevailing Whig odour of the town began to suffer increasing dilution.

But Blackwood's ambitions had by no means exhausted themselves. In 1811 he managed to snatch an important connection with the London publisher, John Murray, who had just severed his own with Constable. But Murray was overbearing and inclined to dictate Blackwood's policy to him; and when the latter, through a tactless error of judgment, failed to secure Scott for his list, Murray advised him to turn his attention to the younger writers. This suggestion was the germ from which *Maga* was eventually born. The Whig domination, under the *Edinburgh Review*, began to make itself felt as an irritant outside Scotland, and Murray, seizing his cue, started the *Quarterly* in London, as a rival. But this proved to be too tame. Then Blackwood came across two men, Pringle and Cleghorn, who wished to edit a magazine on Tory lines. Blackwood closed with them and, hastily sweeping Wilson, Lockhart and Gillies into a bunch, offered his first bouquet to the public in April 1817, under the title of the *Edinburgh Monthly*.

But the association of editors was not a success: there were quarrels, and Blackwood ended by buying Pringle and Cleghorn out. In the meantime, however, he had gathered new flowers into his bouquet, which now included, besides Wilson and Lockhart, Sir William Hamilton, Professor Jameson the geologist, Dr. Brewster the astronomer, Henry Mackenzie (the "Man of Feeling"), and James Hogg ("The Ettrick Shepherd"). The last named was fuel to the undisciplined fire of Wilson and Lockhart. Possessed of a touch of genius (his *Memoirs of a Justified Sinner* are a most remarkable attempt, on the part of the *Zeitgeist*, to produce a Dostoevsky novel before the latter's birth), but with no intellectual stamina to support it, Hogg was both conceited and quarrelsome—an unfortunate combination of qualities for a journalist to possess. Unsupported by the mischievous irresponsibility of Wilson and Lockhart, and kept in order by older contributors, his brilliant qualities of invention and entertainment [1] might have adorned any magazine. But the discreet urbanity of men like Sir William Hamilton was no match for the schoolboy humour of the three young scapegraces to whom Blackwood now looked to 'make' his magazine. They took matters into their own hands, and the result was a bombing attack which would have caused a panic in any literary League of Nations.

The first number of *Blackwood's Edinburgh Magazine* came out

[1] Allan Cunningham tells an amusing story of his cheeky self-possession. Hogg had put about some story of losses sustained by him at the hands of a bookseller named Gibson. When the latter came to him and expressed resentment at the aspersion, Hogg merely replied: "Ah, sir, I thought you were *dead*." This piece of effrontery is very much in the style of the early numbers of *Maga*.

in October, 1817. It included the first of the attacks on the "Cockney School" (in this case Leigh Hunt and, incidentally, Coleridge) and a hotchpotch entitled *The Chaldee Manuscript*, which consisted in a transparent satire on Edinburgh society. The idea of this lampoon had originally been Hogg's, but it was actually carried out by Wilson and Lockhart. The indignation aroused by the virulence, the tastelessness, and above all the personal nature of the attacks, was universal and violent; but, as with all publications of a scandalous kind about 'People One Knows', the public bought and asked for more. More was quickly furnished, in the shape of a machine-gun sweep, which attained Keats (who was advised to return to his chemist's shop and there to be "a little more sparing of extenuatives and soporifics in your practice than in your poetry"), Hazlitt (apostrophized as "pimpled"), Shelley, and Benjamin Robert Haydon ("The Cockney Raphael").

For a time the secret of the attackers' identity was well kept. The articles, which were written alternately by Wilson and Lockhart, were signed 'Z'. John Murray was sincerely shocked and wrote to Blackwood: "I cannot congratulate you on your victory; another such, says Pyrrhus, and we are ruined. Do as you would be done by. I will venture my existence that you are injuring your character in the opinion of everyone whose good opinion is worth having. I cannot perceive your object in literally running amuck at everyone; and I would not undergo your feelings for any worldly advantage. I am sure you are wrong. . . ."

But Blackwood paid not the slightest attention to this sensible warning; smiling sardonically, he let his bright young men have their heads, and the orgy continued. It was useless for those who were attacked to protest: they got no satisfaction. Poor Hazlitt, one of whose worst corns had been trodden upon by the cruel adjective "pimpled", wrote a reply which was not published, instituted proceedings, obtained damages—and then wrote the *Liber Amoris*, thus giving Wilson and Lockhart more food for ribald invective.

John Hunt, brother of the libelled poet, put a notice in his own paper, *The Examiner*, demanding the name of his brother's detractor. The answer was a letter giving the name of one John Graham Dalyell, a perfectly innocent person who had himself been pilloried in *The Chaldee MS.* What was this man's dismay and fury on receiving an abusive letter from John Hunt! The affair then proceeded through the medium of solicitors; but Blackwood, who was clearly enjoying himself, showed great astuteness in protecting his masked schoolboys, who continued to poke insulting letters, couched in the best 'Black Hand' style, at the indignant Hunt, from behind their editor's back.

Encouraged by the scandalized attention they were arousing, Wilson, Lockhart and Hogg gave free rein to their extravagant fantasy. The fun waxed ever faster and more furious. One catches echoes of irresistible *fou rire*. Deepening the atmosphere of facetiousness and mystification, they adopted numberless absurd pseudonyms. One would write an article in a parody of another's style, or several of them would combine to compose one article. Hogg signed with his own name; the others then wrote articles of their own and signed them "Hogg". A luckless dentist, Dr. Scott, had some jocular verses (written by Lockhart) attributed to himself, described as "the Odontist". He retaliated by accepting the attribution, but in private wrote pathetically to Blackwood: "How would you like it if I were to sit down and write a deal of stuff about you, Mr Galt, or Mr Wilson?" And to Galt: "I earnestly beg you not to delay a serious survey of the consequences to yourself, as well as to me and my friends who are exceedingly hurt. Surely strangers think me a poor silly chap, and I am afraid others think so likewise, otherwise this trouble might have been spared."[1] This is the ultimate cry of resentment, shorn of all dignity, which has always sprung to the lips of the victims of newspaper gossip and misrepresentation. But it generally stops short at the lips, few of the victims being naïve enough to admit that they resent being thought "poor silly chaps".

Blackwood ought certainly to have responded to such an appeal, if not to Murray's remonstrance. But he had allowed the thing to go too far now to put a sudden stop to it; it would have to die down gradually. Nevertheless, in the last resort, the responsibility was his: Wilson alluded to him as "The Monster", and it is clear that the whole business had his wholehearted support and his secret guidance. Years later, Lockhart tried to justify his share in the sport by palming off the responsibility on to Wilson; but the excuse will not hold. The explanation of the whole

[1] W. B., I, 212.

harlequinade on the ground that the Whigs had " had all the jokes to themselves for too long," may be allowed to suffice for the part which harmless facetiæ had played in the affair; but no excuse whatever is valid—except on 'satanic' principles—for the barbarous and withal stupid attacks on Leigh Hunt, Hazlitt, Haydon, Keats and *Adonais*. The mere violence of the animosity displayed is hard to account for. It is, for instance, difficult to conceive that a man of Lockhart's education could write that Hunt, Hazlitt, and others, were " by far the vilest vermin that ever dared to creep upon the hem of the majestic garment of the English Muse ". Bad style apart, the accusation is ridiculous and only explicable on the supposition that the whole thing was conceived, from the outset, as a practical joke. The spectacle of the Blackwood set sitting round after dinner and composing the next number of *Maga* on the principles of Consequences (the Biblical style in which many of the articles were written was an invention of Hogg's), gives sufficient colour to the assumption.

But a practical joke, however deliriously amusing to those who utter it, cannot continue indefinitely. The grave disapproval of Murray and Walter Scott, combined with a general atmosphere of deprecation, which deepened the moment the joke began to grow stale, set the tide running in the opposite direction, in spite of the fact that the Blackwood policy had already given rise to a number of similarly scurrilous, but even lower-toned papers, such as *John Bull* [1] and *The Beacon*. Then, in 1818, Wilson and Lockhart were at last unmasked by the anonymous author of a pamphlet attacking their methods, whom they were unwise enough to challenge, thus obliging themselves to come out into the open. In the next year, Murray withdrew his support altogether from the magazine and Coleridge, who had been asked to contribute, wrote a comically pompous reply, in his most estecean manner (" My belief was more strong in the *posse* than in the *esse* thereof"), gratuitously giving his views on how a magazine should be run and evidently expecting that his advice would be taken humbly by Blackwood.[2]

But the real end did not come until 1825, when John Scott, then editor of the *London Magazine*, challenged Lockhart to a duel and was killed at Chalk Farm by Lockhart's proxy, Christie.

[1] Edited by the notorious Theodore Hook.

[2] W. B., I, 408.

This tragic and futile affair, which Mr. Frederick Page, in his book on Coventry Patmore, declares to have been mismanaged by the poet's father, Peter George Patmore, gave an efficiently symbolic *coup de grâce* to the slapstick policy of *Maga*, which thereafter rapidly calmed down until, by 1830, it had become entirely innocuous and even accepted contributions from Lamb. After the affair of the duel, Lockhart, perhaps feeling the pricks of conscience, began to tire of writing for the magazine and told Wilson so. Shortly after this admission, Lockhart went to London to edit the *Quarterly Review*, thus leaving Wilson to some extent in the lurch, for his inspiration had, after all, been pre-eminent. But thirteen years had cooled his head and brought with them new desires and more moderate views: Lockhart had a hard head and—unlike Wilson—knew when an end must be made of going too far.

In 1834 Blackwood himself died, and Wilson was left to carry on the magazine for the owner's sons, until 1837. In 1850, James Hogg (the publisher) could speak of the younger literary set of the day as "plain-living and high-thinking", an earnest, if tame, brood hatched under the leathern wing of Carlyle. Only to Wilson, perhaps, with his undevelopable boyishness, will have come nostalgic thoughts and regrets for the enormous fun of that first year of *Maga's* scandalous blossoming.

2

It seems scarcely necessary to say that De Quincey played no part whatever in the repulsive blackguardism with which "Blackwood's Young Men" disfigured the first numbers of the magazine. That sort of thing would not have been at all to his taste. But certain features of this early policy remained as permanent characteristics of the magazine, and De Quincey ended by acquiring them. But of these more anon. What we are at present concerned with is the date and method of his inclusion among the contributors to *Maga*.

In 1822, when De Quincey had already become well known through the publication of the *Confessions*, Lockhart started, and Wilson carried on (under the pseudonym of "Christopher North" which he had originally invented for Blackwood's own use, as editor, in 1819), the *Noctes Ambrosianae,* to which reference has already been made.[1] The introduction of De Quincey into these dialogues, under the name of "Thomas Papaverius", served to bring his personality before the readers of the magazine; so that when he actually began to write for it, he had a certain reputation to draw on for attention. Meanwhile, during what we will agree to call his probationary period on the staff of *Maga*, two events of different interest attract our attention.

The first of these, which is of more importance in the history of *Blackwood's* than in that of De Quincey, is the critical articles which Wilson, in 1829, devoted to the subject of Wordsworth. Knowing what we do of Wilson's personal antipathy to the poet, these articles come as a surprise and increase our respect for the author of them. They were also of great importance to Wordsworth himself (much as the latter would have disliked admitting the debt), because they turned the tide of critical opinion, which had lain so long under the hostile thumb of Francis Jeffrey, in Wordsworth's favour. Wilson's motive in writing the articles can only have been disinterested admiration of the poet, for he disliked the man exceedingly and continued to do so. Wordsworth had always disapproved of him, and it was never his practice to conceal what he felt. Nor was Wilson the man to take lightly such an opinion of himself; he retaliated intermittently, and in a manner which makes plain the fact that his expressed contempt of the man was not disinterested. At the very time when he was publishing the articles in question, he was writing to Alexander Blair that "Wordsworth is entirely superannuate, wears a boy's fur cap . . ."; [2] and in 1850, when the poet died, Wilson, all his old bile reviving, dashed off an article of violent abuse of Wordsworth ("Fat, ugly cur") for the *Quarterly*, which Lockhart, naturally enough, refused to print. Yet he had had no hesitation, when canvassing his friends for testimonials at the time of his proposed election to the Chair of Moral Philosophy, in including Wordsworth in the list. The latter acceded to the request, and his testimonial is a triumph of slyness,[3] especially in view of the fact that he must long have

[1] See p. 196. [2] Swann, *op. cit.*, p. 204.

[3] ". . . But if the choice is to depend upon pre-eminence of natural powers of mind, cultivated by excellent education, and habitually directed to the study of ethics in the comprehensive sense of the word; upon such powers, and great energy of character with corresponding industry, I have no hesitation in saying that the electors, the university, and Scotland in general, must be fortunate in no common

been aware of Wilson's *Maga* activities. The 1829 articles must, therefore, have been written by Wilson as a sop to his conscience, which had been liberally abraded by Lockhart's defection, the gradual growth of public disapproval, and perhaps also by the memory of the attack which he had himself launched against Wordsworth, in *Maga*, four years previously. A certain generosity, flamboyant as everything else that belonged to him, but not without its roots in moral feelings, was, apart from the rhetoric, Wilson's sole claim to his university position.

The other event which I mentioned, directly concerned De Quincey himself. This was the beginning, in 1828, of his acquaintanceship with Carlyle. The meeting took place under the auspices of Wilson, who, suspicious as ever of intellectual superiority, was very definitely not at his ease with Carlyle, but tried to appear so by a semblance of flippancy that did not deceive that censorious eye. Carlyle considered Wilson a potentially great man who had missed his train, and in this year (1828) was writing of him: "Poor Wilson! It seems as if he shrunk from too close a union with anyone. His whole being seems hollowed out, as it were, and false and counterfeit in his own eyes. So he encircles himself with cloudy sportfulness, which to me often seems reckless and at bottom full of sharp sorrow." [1] So that it was with a jealous eye that Wilson watched the meeting between his own special friend and Carlyle.

The meeting was a qualified success. Carlyle was ten years younger than De Quincey; but, apart from a natural indisposition to humility of any kind, he was prejudiced in De Quincey's disfavour by a review which the latter had written of his translation of Goethe's *Wilhelm Meister*, four years before, in the *London Magazine*. This review is one of the worst, as well as one of the most violent, which De Quincey ever wrote; [2] and he had every reason to feel apprehensive of Carlyle's reception of its author. At the time of its appearance, indeed, the angry translator, who was in any case in one of his moods of acute misanthropy, described

degree if among the competitors there be found one more eligible than yourself."* Wordsworth's sense of humour was not always the minus quantity which it is generally supposed to have been.

[1] Froude, *Carlyle*, I, 427.

[2] He toned it down considerably in the Collected Edition.

* Swann, *op. cit.*, p. 136.

the review as by "the dwarf opium-eater" who "carries a laudanum bottle in his pocket, and the venom of a wasp in his heart," [1] but added relentfully, that "if I could find him, it would give me pleasure to procure him one substantial beefsteak before he dies." However, it is plain from Carlyle's letters to his brother John that he did not really think very much more highly of *Wilhelm Meister* than De Quincey himself; so that when he and his reviewer met, he was prepared to let bygones be bygones. He produced himself as a talker for the sake of De Quincey, of whose fame in this department he was doubtless not ignorant. "His conversation was at that time brilliant in the extreme, but spiced with paradox and tending to extravagance." Thus De Quincey, in 1852, to Mr. Fields of Boston (of Messrs. Ticknor and Fields, who published the American edition of De Quincey's collected works). The criticism, if true, might equally have been applied to the critic's own talk.

Carlyle, perhaps recalling the desire he had expressed with regard to the beefsteak, followed up the meeting by an enormous, egotistical letter [2] containing an invitation to Craigenputtock, expressed with typical Carlylean circumlocution: "I had a thousand things to ask concerning you: your employments, purposes, sufferings, and pleasures. Will you not write to me? Will you not come to me and tell? Believe it, you are well loved here, and none feels better than I what a spirit is for the present eclipsed in clouds." It is a kind, a sincerely friendly letter, and perhaps it was impossible for the writer not to show a certain degree of patronage—especially to one whose aspect proclaimed him so clearly in every way 'distressed'.

It does not appear that De Quincey followed up the invitation; but, whether or no, Carlyle soon afterwards called on him "about two o'clock and found him invisible in bed. His landlady, a dirty, very wicked looking woman said, if he rose at all, it was usually about five o'clock." [3]

The two were not destined to see very much of one another, nor can one regret overmuch that this was so. As a friendship, it did not hold any fruitful seeds. The feeling of contempt, as for a character all too ineffectual, which Carlyle was later to

[1] Froude, *Carlyle*, I, 263. [2] Japp, 206.
[3] Letter to John Carlyle, March 7th, 1828.

express for De Quincey, was already lurking behind his attitude of amiable interest; and on the other side, Carlyle's dogmatic emphasis, his uninterruptable sermonizing, must have jarred hopelessly on De Quincey's fine-spun nerves and offended his sense of intellectual good manners. An Airedale and an Italian greyhound do not as a rule make suitable companions for one another. I give this facile image for what it is worth, but hasten to place beside it the fact that when, in 1876, James Hogg gave Carlyle a message (of kind remembrance, one supposes) which De Quincey had entrusted to him at the end of his life, the Chelsea prophet was much moved, think what he might of De Quincey as a writer.

3

The state of affairs indicated by the last-quoted letter of Carlyle is a melancholy one; but we must get used to it, for it will be seen obtaining, with slight modifications one way or the other, during the next ten years—years in which the incidental accompaniments to De Quincey's life were one and all of a depressing, when not positively disruptive, kind. The threads of his existence, which up till now he had somehow managed to keep few and separate, now multiplied and became vexatiously tangled. Work, more necessary than ever now that his family had grown so large (Emily, his eighth child, was born in 1832), presented itself in two guises which were, it is true, firm and clear enough. These were *Blackwood's* and *Tait's Magazine*, the latter of which came to divide his attention from 1833 onwards; but neither brought with it the tonics and anodynes wherewith to render its performance adequate to time and needs. Friends were at hand to bless: Wilson (his temper less good than formerly, his eye less clear, his heart less carefree), Sir William Hamilton and his brother—the latter a great support in every way to the harassed journalist, who borrowed liberally from his library. But De Quincey was in no state in these years to get the best out of friendship; the careless give-and-take of early years was no longer possible to his excruciated nerves, nor was he in a position to assume again the rôle of genial talker with which he had captivated the Edinburgh of 1815. In fact, he had reached one of those stages in a man's life when help can come only from himself; friends can do little but sit in the background, watch, and occasionally put out a hand.

Yet self-help was the one thing of which he seemed incapable. His will-power was at no time destroyed by his addiction to opium: the fourteen volumes of the Collected Edition are a sufficient proof of this. But it was intermittently seriously impaired by it. More than ever now was he unable to face the question of money—of what he owed, of what was due to him, of how he could balance the family budget. The Coleridgean inability to rise from bed, too, indicated by Carlyle's letter, was probably responsible for much of the dilatoriness of which Blackwood complained—as bitterly as ever Hessey had done—in these years. And though the fourth and last opium crisis did not occur till 1844, the years which preceded it must be regarded as a preparation, in the sense that throughout that time physical ills and mental anxieties were working underground to undermine De Quincey's resistance, so that, when the moment came, with its stale burden of crushing grief, he was ready to crumple up into his own abyss.

At the end of 1830 his wife joined him in Edinburgh, bringing with her the younger children, Horace, Francis, Paul Frederick, Florence, and little Julius, the baby of a year old. She had been very ill with jaundice,[1] and the depression which is the invariable accompaniment to that disease must have made her feel that she could no longer bear to live apart from her husband. Moreover, there had been a disagreeable scene at Grasmere: the De Quincey children and those of the woman in whose house they were temporarily lodged, had quarrelled, and the mothers had taken sides, each with her own children. The result was that the landlady had been insolent, casting aspersions (one suspects) on Mrs. De Quincey's financial position, as well as, perhaps, harking back to the old scandal of her marriage. Informed of what had occurred, De Quincey had been so much worried that he was again late with his copy for *Maga*, and Blackwood was again annoyed.[2]

On the arrival of Mrs. De Quincey and the younger children, the whole family moved from Wilson's house, first to a house in Great King Street, then to one in Forres Street, and later still to Duddingston—three removals in four years, which exhibit once

[1] See W. B., I, 431. [2] W. B., I, 435.

again De Quincey's restless inability to stay in one place for any length of time. This agonized shifting of a body in pain was to find its ultimate and most fantastic expression in later years, when De Quincey kept going three or four sets of lodgings in Edinburgh at the same time, spending a week or so in each one of them and moving on when driven out by the spate of books and papers which steadily accumulated.

If we are to take literally a sentence in the essay on *Style* (written in 1840), De Quincey and his wife visited London in 1832.[1] The passage continues with an amusing description of a landlady (men of De Quincey's type are always at the mercy of landladies) who drove him in search of other lodgings by her appalling affability, which jarred his sensitive ears as much by the astonishing pomposity of its vocabulary as by its copiousness. It is difficult to know quite what to make of this story, for nothing that we know of De Quincey's life in 1832 gives him any reason or even excuse for going to London in that year. It is possible that, in the confusion of mind as to actual events in which De Quincey spent the year 1840 (when he wrote the passage), he may have merely mistaken the date, intending to refer to an earlier year —1825 or '26.

Of more importance is the work which, in spite of adversity, he managed to carry through at this time. For *Maga* he wrote on *Kant in his Miscellaneous Essays*, the important essays on Richard Bentley and Dr. Samuel Parr, the little novel of *Klosterheim* (published in book form), the six articles on *The Cæsars*, essays on Charlemagne, the *Revolt of the Tartars, The English Language, Miracles as Subjects of Testimony, Casuistry, On Murder Considered as one of the Fine Arts* (second paper), on the *Philosophy of Roman History*, and the *Casuistry of Roman Meals, On Milton,* and two tales (*The Avenger* and *The Household Wreck*).

The articles which he contributed to *Tait's* [2] in these years are, on the other hand, mostly reminiscential and as such are more widely read to-day than his purely speculative and critical essays. Under the former heading are to be included the *Autobiographic Sketches*, the controversial articles on Coleridge, Wordsworth and

[1] X, 150.

[2] This magazine was a Whig opponent of *Blackwood's*, but it kept its literary side separate from the political, thus enabling writers like De Quincey to contribute to it with an easy conscience.

Southey, the *Recollections of Charles Lamb, The London Reminiscences,* and the *Early Memorials of Grasmere.*

To these must be added the 'lives' of Goethe, Pope, Schiller and Shakespeare, which De Quincey wrote for the *Encyclopædia Britannica* in 1837 and '38.

The list is considerable: such an amount of work should surely have sufficed to keep its author out of serious financial embarrassment. *Tait's* alone paid him 20 guineas per sheet of sixteen pages,* whereas other contributors only received fourteen.[1] Blackwood was probably less munificent, and De Quincey certainly looked to *Tait's* as his main source of income for the seventeen years from 1833 to 1851, when he ceased to write for it. Yet, until the last fifteen years of his life, when his daughters firmly took the management of their father's affairs into their own hands, he remained chronically unable to make both ends meet. He was a byword—indeed a positive joke—for inability to finish his articles. One reason for this was the fact that he often wrote them twice or even several times over, though this must have been agony to him, for some strange inner uncertainty made him hate what he had just written—a hatred shared (no doubt for the same reasons) by Coleridge. "I also shrank," he says, "from treating any subject which I had much considered; but more, I believe, as recoiling from the intricacy and the elaborateness which had been made known to me in the course of considering it . . . than from any blind, mechanical feeling inevitably associated (as in Coleridge it was) with a second survey of the same subject." [2] And he adds the illuminating fact that opium habitually disturbed his judgment of what he had recently written. Besides this disability, it was impossible for him, in consequence of his ill-health, to work regularly. But, above all, it was his unerring misjudgment, both of the amount his work would bring him and of what was actually owing to him at any particular moment, that kept his affairs in a state of such resounding chaos. "How shattering to the power of exertion, and, above all, of an organ so delicate as the creative intellect . . . to know that instant ruin attends his failure," he wrote once, with autobiographical pungency, in the essay on Goldsmith.[3]

The spur was sharp, but not sharp enough to pierce the armour

[1] Japp, 223. [2] III, 76. [3] IV, 292.

(for that is what, paradoxically, it had become) of De Quincey's tortuous sensibility in regard to money. *Tait's* office-boy, by name James Bertram, recounted in after years how he had once taken De Quincey a letter containing money. "Rising from his chair, he said, 'This is a somewhat embarrassing sum of money for me to have here. Might I request you—there is a place of entertainment, it is called a public-house, almost at the door, and if you will have the kindness to go there and ask the lady of the house to give you lesser money for this note, I shall be extremely obliged to you; and if at the same time you will be so good as to ask the servant of the establishment to send me a small supply of the excellent brandy which is kept there, you will still further oblige me.'"[1]

It is called a public-house: the snirt of astonished amusement with which we read such a phrase recalls to us the "Lord Altamont's only child" of the letter to his sister Mary, written from Bath when he was fourteen. That kind of politeness, of shrinking from the grossness of contact with physical objects—whether people or money—is paralysing. What, for instance, did his friends *call* him? It is difficult to imagine them addressing him as anything but "My dear Sir"—as they did in their letters. No wonder servants (Charles Knight's, for example) were frightened of De Quincey, and that those who had to deal with him, in these later years, in any capacity save that of purely social intercourse, found their efforts as unsatisfactory as the grasping of a handful of air.

Once again, and rather against our will, we must turn to Carlyle to corroborate our depressing view of De Quincey at this time. In a letter to John Carlyle,[2] he reports the Opium-Eater as "living on game which has spoiled on the poulterer's hands, having made a bargain to that effect with him and even run up a score of fifteen pounds." And a month later, he wrote to John Stuart Mill:[3] "As for De Quincey, I have not seen him this winter; and no man, except Bailiffs, it appears, has for the last eighteen months: he is said to be in the uttermost unaidable embarrassment; bankrupt in purse, and as nearly as possible in mind. I used to like him well, as one of the prettiest talkers I ever heard; of great, indeed of diseased *acuteness*, not without depth, of a fine sense too, but

[1] Japp, 222. [2] March 29th. 1833. [3] April 18th.

of no breadth, no justness, weak, diffuse, supersensitive; on the whole, a perverted, ineffectual man." So the story of the high game was only hearsay, but it was of the kind which rings true. Reading this last letter, one stretches out one's hand almost mechanically for the salt-cellar which the reader of Carlyle must never be without. Of course it was not true that De Quincey was nearly bankrupt in mind, and we have Carlyle's own word for it that he had not seen the man for months; nor need the sneer at "supersensitiveness" surprise us in one of such obtuse sensibilities. But, with the salt duly sprinkled, we are left with the most uncomfortable impression—one, I had almost said, of decrepitude. Our only source of reassurance lies in the work which De Quincey produced throughout these years; and it is an all-sufficient one. To a man capable of writing the *Autobiographic Sketches,* the *Literary and Lake Reminiscences,* the *Revolt of the Tartars* (to name only the very best), phrases like "mentally bankrupt", "decrepit", "on the decline", "poor So-and-so" are essentially inapplicable. The flame was burning brightly enough, with its curious, secret intensity, only the general glare of sunlight prevented it from being generally visible.

Bearing this in mind, we must now contemplate him facing a further series of disasters—bereavements, this time. In 1833 the baby Julius died, of a fever, at the age of four. The next year swept away Lamb, Coleridge, Blackwood, and Colonel Penson—a queer miscellany of ghosts to have to entertain, and provocative, in De Quincey at least, of very varied feelings. In the same year his wife, again seriously ailing, returned to Grasmere. And in 1835, William, the hope of his father, the eldest son, who had shown great promise of brilliance, was carried off suddenly by what was evidently meningitis.

I shall not, I think, be accused of unfairness if I suggest that, in this cataclysm, the remoter figures left De Quincey relatively unmoved. It was not merely the pressing instance of grief for his own children, which was responsible for deadening his mind to sorrow for the eclipse of old friendships; it was the feeling, rendered almost absolute by present anxiety and the neutralizing effect of opium, that such people as Coleridge and Lamb, however much they had meant to him in the past, had now been dead to him for some time. No doubt the consciousness of their actual deaths added something to his present burden: De Quincey was too tender-hearted a man to be able to think of the death of anyone he knew without some increase of sadness. But a single sigh was all he could spare them now—a sigh of passing regret for hours of pleasurable intimacy, of which he had—alas!—long ago learnt the essential transience.

On the death of his uncle, his mother took up her pen once more and, after giving an account of the will, which left her in possession of £400 a year for life, to be divided between De Quincey and his sister Jane on the death of their mother, she allowed herself to express her feelings on the subject of her son's way of life:

> But I must now enter on some very painful subjects: 1st. I have heard and noticed before, though you replied not, that you are still an Opium-Eater, and this dreadful Drug, as it is its nature to ruin the unhappy recipient, thus acts on you, destroying alike both the will and the power to discharge all bounden duties to the full extent which the more common forms of intoxication effect! Well, with all you wrote *so well* before me, of poor Coleridge's dying opium misery, I am lost in the saddest wonder, and what I have further to say, however grievous, can be no wonder at all. That you write, in a disreputable Magazine, on subjects and in a spirit afflicting as I hear too, to your real friends, I suppose may be accounted for in this way, that to the last moment of opium delirium, you will not write where you might with honour and no compromise of your professed principles; money being spent, and no choice left, you take up with Mr Tait! Another report I rejected as quite incredible, namely, that your Children's education is neglected.[1]

This letter will have extorted another sigh, but of a different kind, from De Quincey: the days were indeed long past when he had cared what his mother thought of him. And now he could not even be bothered to correct her inaccuracies.

But in the previous year, unknown to him, Sara Coleridge, the poet's daughter, had written to Mrs. William Wardell, expressing the same views on De Quincey. This letter, which gives the impression of having been written more in anger than in sorrow, deserves extensive quotation:

[1] Letters, II, 173.

HAMPSTEAD. 13 October, 1834.

The Periodicals have been busy bringing out criticism of his (my Father's) writings and attempts at sketches of his life, the last extremely incorrect, as you may imagine. It is very wrong in Mr. de Quincey to publish so many personal details respecting my Parents in Tait's Magazine, his account is elegantly written, and does justice in most particulars to my Father's genius and to the benevolence of his nature, but there are many mis-statements in it, and a false colouring is cast over all the part which relates to domestic matters; but, my dear friend, is it not unjustifiable in any man to expose the recesses of a friend's home to the general gaze? and what person of delicate feeling can bear to see the characters of those near and dear to them commented on in print? Mr. de Quincey has shown little dignity in exposing himself as an *opium-eater*, and describes so many passages of his life, which are calculated neither to do himself credit nor his readers any good, for the amusement of the public; but we may do what we will with our own: this new sort of personality is at the expense of his neighbours; However, I believe, poor man, he will stoop to almost anything which will put a few guineas into his pocket with the least possible trouble to himself, and enable him to descend from his upper storey in Edinboro whence I am told he can never stir save on a Sunday for fear of falling into the clutches of a creditor. I was also told (but there may have been some mistake in the matter, for I well know how incorrect these hear-say reports generally are) that his wife is gone home in ill-health, and that his little Maggy manages all Papa's domestic concerns. She and the other children are sensible and good looking but have no regular education and are brought up in a bad shifting way; allowed to sit up late, to help themselves to laudanum and so forth. "How can you keep your eyes open, Maggy," said a gentleman to the little girl, "when you are kept up so late?" "O we get an opium pill and that makes us quite brisk and lively." However she added that this would have been displeasing to Papa, had he known of it. . . .

Not much credence can be attached to the last statements of this letter, dictated, as they so evidently were, by spite. It is, I think, out of the question that De Quincey, whose love and feelings of responsibility towards his children were almost painfully acute, should not have seen to it that his supply of the drug was not tampered with by the children. There has never been the slightest suggestion that De Quincey, in the manner of so many drug-addicts, indulged a desire to convert others to the practice; indeed there is every sign that he took the opposite course. Besides, apart from William and Julius, the rest of the family grew up into normally strong men and women, which would certainly not have been the case if they had been given recurrent doses of opium in childhood. The origin of the gossip was probably the story of how, when De Quincey's eldest daughter Margaret was sleepless as a child, he would bring her down to his study, give her pieces of sugar soaked in coffee, and allow her to cut the leaves of a book.

By the year 1835 his affairs had reached such a pitch of confusion that he was obliged to seek sanctuary from his creditors in Holyrood. This refuge requires a little explanation. Imprisonment for debt was of course still in force in Scotland; but the ancient law of sanctuary provided a way out, and a comparatively comfortable one. The rule was that the debtor must 'book' himself within twenty-four hours of the writ's being served upon him, and at the cost of two guineas. The whole business was in the hands of the Bailie, who was a magistrate appointed by the Keeper of Holyrood and who had to decide in court all questions relating to the debtors, to their affairs within sanctuary, and to the creditors' cases. If a debtor remained outside sanctuary for more than fourteen days, he was obliged to rebook himself in order to obtain re-admittance. On the other hand, the bounds of sanctuary seem to have been wide, and the debtor could move outside them on Sundays with impunity. Often he forgot the time and was arrested outside Holyrood after midnight on Sunday. But thrilling escapes sometimes occurred, and the debtor would attain sanctuary again for a further respite.

There would seem to have been no limit to the length of time debtors might spend in sanctuary. De Quincey remained thus 'attached' to Holyrood for five years (1835–40); but he actually spent little time inside the prescribed bounds, for there were many people who were prepared to offer him unofficial sanctuary in their own houses—and for as long as he wished to stay. Thus, if he found himself "after hours" in Ambrose's Hotel, he would simply remain there until the following Sunday. On other occasions, he would go to visit some friend—*e.g.*, his solicitor, Thomas McIndoe—and remain in the house for the next year or so.[1]

The system was not an unpleasant one—for the debtor; and if it was cumbrous, mediæval and fundamentally unjust, it was also a salutary offset to the horrors of the debtors' prisons, with their dreary eternities of hope and despair.

De Quincey made friends in Holyrood and continued to work in the usual way, writing many of his articles for *Tait's* there. At the same time, it is not impossible that, had some capable person been at hand to go thoroughly into his affairs, he need never have had resort to such a course at all. For, as Japp points out, at the very moment when he was flying from creditors as much money was in reality due to him from editors, had he only realized it, as he himself owed to others. Again, he was capable of forgetting money which he had received and put away. After his death, quite a sum was found straying among his books, the notes slipped between the pages, to smooth them out, the coins washed and put up in twists of paper. Yet, in spite of this care, such was his shrinking from the whole subject, that he preferred to enter sanctuary rather than face a thorough examination of his financial status. It may also be suggested, in this connection, that, to one suffering from De Quincey's particular neuroses, mitigated imprisonment, of the kind implied by sanctuary, would come as a positive relief from anxiety; he would feel that, for the time being, the odium of responsibility was lifted from his shoulders—that he was, in fact, paying in kind.

It was while De Quincey was still in sanctuary that the worst blow of all fell upon him: in 1837 his wife died. Nothing is known of the circumstances of her end, save the fact that the death of her eldest son seems to have deprived her—at long last—of the desire to live any longer. She had indeed had a hard life; incessant vigils by the vision-haunted bedside of her husband, constant anxiety, ill-health and attacks of depression (especially when De Quincey was absent), the bearing of eight children and the death of two of them. It is small wonder that her spirit, simple as it was and unused to the consolations of the intellect, should have been unable to stay the course. The

[1] Japp, 224.

wonder is rather that she managed to accomplish so much, in a sphere from which she never aspired to depart.

4

It was a time, for De Quincey, of utter despair. He had lost the two beings who were dearest to him in the world, and it was a loss which he felt that nothing could redeem. The last of his three muses was dead, and the sorrow threw open his soul to all the winds of autumnal sadness, all the sounds and colours of earthly transience. Into the obscure, dim, crepuscular existence in which he lived during these years, the long shadows of premature old age came creeping, bringing with them a wild host of memories. "Phantoms of lost power, sudden intuitions, and shadowy restorations of forgotten feelings, sometimes dim and perplexing, sometimes by bright and furtive glimpses, sometimes by a full and steady revelation, overcharged with light—throw us back in a moment upon scenes and remembrances that we have left full thirty years behind us." [1] Thirty years ago. . . . His first meetings with Coleridge, with Lamb, with Wordsworth; the brilliant figure of 'Pink'; early days in Dove Cottage; adventures of the mind . . . friendship . . . Dorothy. . . .

But Dorothy was no longer the same (did he know it?); the "subtle fire of impassioned intellect" had become smeared over and dulled by a fatal enfeeblement of mind; the fascination of her vitality, her impulsive generosity, had thinned away into petulance and restlessness. Yet sometimes the old, lyrical love of the world and living things returned to flood her mind with rapturous regret of the past. Some such mood must have been upon her when in 1838, she wrote her last letter—surely one of the most touchingly beautiful ever written.

My dearest Dora,

They say I must write a letter—and what shall it be? news—news—I must seek for news—My own thoughts are a wilderness 'not pieceable by power of any star'—News then is my resting place—news! news! Poor Peggy Benson lies in Grasmere Churchyard beside her once-beautiful Mother. Fanny Haigh is gone to

[1] II, 204.

a better world. My friend Mrs Rawson has ended her ninety and two years pilgrimage—and *I* have fought and fretted and striven and am here beside the fire. The Doves behind me at the small window—the laburnum with its naked seedpods shivers before my window and the pine-trees rock from their base. More I cannot write, so farewell! and may God bless you and your kind good Friend, Miss Fenwick, to whom I send love and all the best of wishes, Yours evermore

DOROTHY WORDSWORTH.[1]

This is indeed still the Dorothy whom De Quincey had so tenderly loved and so delicately allowed to pass out of his life—of her own will; a being among the very few to whom the much-abused epithet 'divine' exactly applies.

But "these are *positive* torments from which the agitated mind shrinks in fear; but there are others *negative* in their nature—that is, blank mementoes of powers extinct, and of faculties burnt out within us."[2] And it was these which De Quincey dreaded most and which now thrust their faces into his, as the monstrous old visions began to form themselves once more in his tired brain.

Fragments from tales which he wrote at this time weave themselves irresistibly into the tapestry of his life:

I never ridded myself of an overmastering and brooding sense, shadowy and vague, a dim abiding feeling . . . of some great calamity travelling towards me, not perhaps Immediately impending . . . but already dating from some secret hour. . . .[3]

And the following wonderful and frightful passage, which evokes a whole world constructed from the ultimate agonies of the soul:

. . . when one feels one's self sleeping alone, utterly divided from all call or hearing of friends, doors open that should be shut, or unlocked that should be triply secured, the very walls gone, barriers swallowed up by unknown abysses, nothing around one but frail curtains, and a world of illimitable night, whisperings at a distance, correspondence going on between darkness and darkness, like one deep calling to another, and the dreamer's own heart the centre from which the whole network of this unimaginable chaos radiates,

[1] De Selincourt, *op. cit.*, p. 396.
[2] II, 205.
[3] *The Household Wreck*, XII, 168.

by means of which the blank *privations* of silence and darkness become powers the most *positive* and awful.[1]

Yet there is one note that is conspicuously missing from the chromatic scale of De Quincey's agony: that of self-pity. Apart from these cries of distress, which he embedded discreetly in what purported to be fiction, no complaints reached the outer world. Tender, as ever, of his dignity, and sensitively aware that to burden others with one's private sorrows is an act of intrusion, and unwilling, perhaps, to emphasize the impression of pathos, which he was conscious in any case of giving, he wrapped himself in silence and the only solace left to him—unremitting work. "Grief does not parade its pangs nor the anguish of despairing hunger willingly count again its groans or its humiliations." [2]

Remained the purely practical issue. Had it not been for the presence of the two eldest of his remaining children, Margaret and Horace (now aged about twenty-two and twenty-one), there is no telling how long De Quincey might have continued to struggle about in the weedy shallows of insolvency. But the death of their mother seems to have impressed upon these two the necessity of taking family matters into their own hands. This they accordingly did, though De Quincey continued for some time to worry over the upbringing of the other four children—Francis, Paul Frederick, Florence and Emily (born in 1832).[3] But Horace and Margaret soon put an end to any anxiety their father may have felt, by the decision which they showed. Though there is no record of the straightening process, the fact emerges that from now (*circa* 1840) onwards, financial embarrassment ceased to play a part in De Quincey's life. Responsibility of all kinds—except in the matter of his work—was gently and tactfully lifted out of his hands; at first by the two elder children, later on by Florence and Emily. The business of living—that abhorrent ogre—was now faced by an efficient proxy.

As a final step in the disentangling process, Horace and Margaret decided that the family had better move out of Edinburgh itself to a distance at which peace might once more gradually gather

[1] *The Avenger*, XII, 236.
[2] See *ante*, p. 57.
[3] He left record of this anxiety in the *Letters from a Modern Author to his Daughters on the Useful Limits of Literature considered as a Study for Females.* (Not published in the Masson Edition.)

round the head of their dejected little father. The result of this decision was the leasing of Mavis Bush, a small house in the Greenhay style, at Lasswade, then seven miles outside Edinburgh. This was to be the last of De Quincey's permanent homes (if the word 'permanent' can properly be applied to anything connected with De Quincey). Though he left it frequently between 1841 and '47, which years he spent in posting to and fro, in his familiar fashion, between Lasswade and Glasgow; and though, even after his definitive return from the latter town, he preserved the system—so characteristic of his mind, both tortuous and possessed of its own complex order—of keeping several sets of lodgings in Edinburgh itself, as a kind of secret burrow; yet Mavis Bush remained his real home, in that his strongest ties with life—his children—were always waiting for him there, whenever he chose to return.

CHAPTER IX

CRITICAL RETROSPECT (I)

I

THE division of De Quincey's life into periods is valid only for outward events: as a writer, he sprang fully armed into the pages of the *London Magazine*, and the characteristics of style, of method, of thought, observable in the articles which he wrote for that paper, are substantially those which distinguish the later Blackwood-cum-Tait period. Certain accretions appear at the later date, but on closer examination, they prove to be mere accentuations of qualities already present in embryo in the earlier work. For De Quincey, in his published work, did not develop in any important sense: he started publishing too late in life for the various stages in the history of his style to be apparent. If we could examine the sentences which tried themselves over in his mind (as they try themselves over in the mind of every born writer) between 1803 and 1821, no doubt we should observe a growth in which the various stages would be as marked as those exhibited in the published work of Goethe, Meredith, or Henry James. But even then, I think that all we should observe would be the skeleton, so to speak, which a careful scrutiny now reveals to us, beneath the layers of acquired tissue. For nearly all writers develop by a system of inspissation; very few indeed show a sudden volte-face, in mid-career, and begin writing in a fashion totally opposed to that which they have favoured hitherto. The works of most writers (be they novelists, historians, poets or belle-lettrists) show a steady thickening of the qualities of vision and method over the original framework—the common-denominational factors, the general colour of which is borrowed from some other writer—until the process of saturation is complete and the mature work is left perfectly opaque with its author's organically evolved quality. The result is, therefore, something new; its success is in all cases proportionate to the skill which the artist has shown in adapting his personal material to the old framework, or in cunningly underpinning it in order to conceal the fact that he is really demolishing the framework itself, until the new structure is strong enough to stand by itself. The process may be compared to the substitution, in an existing building, of a new façade for the original one, without pulling down and rebuilding the whole. Scaffolding is erected, props are introduced before mullions are withdrawn, no piece can be moved without the substitution of another; but in the end the scaffolding disappears to reveal the new façade complete.[1]

A reading of the complete works of most great writers reveals this process in action: not so De Quincey's, and for the reason I have indicated. He has covered his tracks, preferring to unveil the finished style. Thus all his most striking notes sound as clearly in the early as in the late work. The first version of the *Confessions*, the *Knocking at the Gate, Mr. Schnackenberger*, the *Letters to a Young Man*, the economic *Dialogues*, the *Last Days of Kant*—run through the complete scale. Flights of fantastic imagination, incense-born rhetoric, cunning constructive effects lifted from the methods of music, humour, logical ability: all these are present and they are (to revert to an earlier metaphor) the immovable foundation stones of De Quincey's intellectual building. Even the lesser stylistic peculiarities are in evidence: the passion for Latin words, the frequency of inverted clauses, the vocative passages, the italics of old-maidish emphasis.

But there are four evil qualities which are very little in evidence in the *London Magazine* articles, but which begin to consolidate themselves—to preponderate dismayingly—in the writings of the second period: Pedantry, Digression, Prolixity, and Facetiousness. These bad fairies were present at De Quincey's birth, and they may

[1] In music, Beethoven is a perfect case in point. To take an example from still another art, the work of Turner shows the same process of gradual substitution in action; but his case is particularly interesting, because the development is from a style which contains many intricate elements to one which contains hardly any. The very late paintings of Turner in fact show a tendency towards the blurring and negation of definite factors, right out into the simply blended palette; so that the ultimate goal of this kind of painting would seem to be an unrelieved milky glow, whose perfection is unencumbered by shape of any kind. It is the straight piece of string into which the tangle of a cat's-cradle eventually pulls out. Any simile of new façades built into old buildings would be most inappropriate to illustrate so extraordinary an elimination of the material of art; yet the process by which it was arrived would seem to be the one I have described.

be said to have been largely successful in encompassing his ruin; for, if the bulk of his work is so little read to-day, the responsibility must be laid at their door. Yet, if they were indeed present at his birth, it was *Maga* who was the eventual agent of their spells—Maga, with her tradition of involved 'private' jokes, her tasteless flippancy in and out of season. The puerile facetiousness—the elaborate and so eminently un-funny quips (*e.g.*, calling Timbuctoo 'Tombuctoo'[1] and Tiedemann "Tedious mann"—to give the shortest possible examples)—which put the present-day reader under the depressing necessity of constant skipping; the divagations, the labouring of points which make him exclaim: "How this man does *go on*!"—these are faults only adumbrated in the earlier essays, but for which *Maga* provided precedents too tempting to be resisted. Again, the appalling levity with which, just in the middle of making his most important point, De Quincey will get up and go off on the track of some insignificant detail, leaving the reader in a state of agonized suspense, for page after page, found its sanction in the rococo fantasmagoria of the *Noctes Ambrosianae*.

These enraging lapses are so frequent in De Quincey's later writings that it would be wearisome to multiply examples of them. For typical cases of prolixity the reader may turn to the *Brief Appraisal of Greek Literature*, where De Quincey seems to be in a state of nervous garrulity owing to consciousness of the questionable nature of his main thesis—though, as usual on these occasions, he has much that is admirable to say by the way; or to the Shakespeare article, where he wastes fifteen out of the seventy-nine pages in disposing of the view that the poet was neglected in his own day. Further evidence is provided by the *Aelius Lamia* appendix to the *Cæsars*, where a great deal of space is expended on the resolution of an unimportant difficulty in Suetonius and the argument is further weakened by an untimely display of facetiousness. On occasions like these De Quincey becomes the absolute type of bore, displaying an incredible and devastating facility for meandering on and on, in pursuit of his own nose,—toying with his subject in what seems a spirit of pure silliness.[2]

[1] V, 282. A more extended example is given on p. 261 of this book.

[2] For a perfect late example of De Quincey's ability to write about nothing at all at any length, see the first of the *Memorial Chronology Letters* (XIV, 275).

Examples of digression are strewn even thicker on the ground, so that it is only worth while to mention the more obvious. One of the best occurs in the *Autobiographic Sketches*,[1] when De Quincey interrupts his account of Pink and the pirates to pursue the red herring of moral degeneration, which leads him, through Louis XVII, birth, and omens, to a footnote on Charles I. Again (the example is slight but significant), when drawing a parallel between the traditionless state of America and that of German literature, he must needs append a footnote pointing out the comparative modernity of the greater part of Africa! [2] Most of the more extended examples of digression occur in De Quincey's later work: the 1856 additions to the *Confessions,* for instance, consist of but little else. Very often, too, the consciousness that the printer's devil was waiting at the door caused him to break off an article before he had said all he had to say, as in the case of the Coleridge essay,[3] the fourth part of which, instead of ending, as De Quincey intended, with an examination of the poet's intellectual pretensions, wanders off into a defence of the war against Napoleon and closes, somewhat wildly, with one inadequate paragraph on Coleridge's political development.

These deplorable features of De Quincey's writings do, however, as we should expect, find earlier precedents than in *Maga*. The extreme facility, which is observable in his letters, from " Tabitha " days to that on which, towards the end of his life, he wrote to his second daughter: " O my dear Florence, I rattle in order to beguile my deadly nervousness ", made it possible for him to pour out words on any and every subject, undisturbed by monitions of the ordering faculty. Nerves are apt to make a man garrulous, when they do not render him dumb. And we must not forget that careful paring down and pulling together of what has been written are the observed results of leisure, not of the incessant hurry in which De Quincey habitually worked. Sometimes, indeed, his haste was so great that he told the same story twice in the same article, without noticing the fact, as when he repeats, at length, a description of Lamb reading aloud, which he had already given a few pages before.[4] When, at the end of his life, the Collected Edition gave him an opportunity carefully to revise what he had written at so impossible a speed, the bad habits bred of long necessity had got

[1] I, 299. [2] II, 85. [3] II, 225. [4] III, 83.

the upper hand; procrastination, alternating with jerks of hurry, continued to be the order of the day; and revision tended to lengthen and perplex what needed no alteration (*e.g.* the *Confessions*), and further to confuse, with enormous notes and digressive paragraphs, what was already too long.

Excuses, of course, abound. Continuing to enumerate them, we light on the fact that De Quincey had probably read too much—almost as bad a mistake, in its paralysing way, as under-reading; then, his memory was too good, plucking continually at his sleeve to notice some detail, some aspect not yet recorded—and yet again some further detail or aspect—until all relation to the matter in hand was lost in mists of digression. Thus the extraordinary range of his mind is to a large extent rendered nugatory, in the displaying of it, by his inability (or his lack of opportunity) to arrange his material in an acceptable form. Though one dislikes to harp continually upon this particular string, just because it is so resonant and lies so easily under the finger, yet it must at least be suggested that even here opium had its effects, in a kind of loosening or dispersal of the ordering faculty, with a corresponding tendency to increase the temptation of following connections too vague, between ideas, facts and personal impressions. In speaking of Coleridge, De Quincey does not mince his words over this particular fault: "There is the same imbecility in attempting to hold things steadily together, and to bring them under a comprehensive or unifying act of the judging faculty, as there is in the efforts of a drunken man to follow a chain of reasoning."[1] This does not mean that De Quincey is unconscious of possessing the same fault himself: on the contrary, he apologizes on several occasions for it, now in a quick aside—"I beg the reader's pardon for this disproportionate digression"[2]—now in a more cogent and persuasive form—"placing my reliance for the redress of any harsh judgment on the absolute certainty that each successive month washes out of the public mind every trace of what may have occupied it in any previous month."[3] The embittering persuasion that he was really nothing but a journalist, dulled the determination—originally as strong as that of any artist—that his work should be as good as he could make it. It is also possible, I think, that he derived a kind of humiliated satisfaction from this conviction.

[1] III, 77. [2] III, 268. [3] III, 100.

But he would not reform his practices, even if he was prepared to apologize for them; having made his excuse, he simply continues, *de plus belle*. And, as if the prolixities of his text were not sufficient, he must needs burden the reader further with a mass of enormous footnotes, in themselves often far longer than the passages to which they apply, and generally not more than indirectly germane to them.[1] If he had not been writing in a continual hurry, he would no doubt have worked the matter of the notes into the text itself, as he expressly states should be the practice of every writer;[2] the form, as it stands, is anomalous in the extreme and totally unreadable. Nevertheless, when the opportunity occurred, at the time of the Collected Edition, to "absorb the redundancies", the habit had become so ingrained that he only added to them.

The article on Sir William Hamilton is the most extreme case of De Quincey's divagatory manner. Though the essay does not belong to the period under discussion (it was written in 1852), it may be well to trace its crazy graph here, because it is so finely illustrative, both of its author in his worst moments and of a free associational kind of writing that was to have no parallel until James Joyce and Virginia Woolf systematized it into a method of deliberate art. De Quincey starts off with a preliminary explanation of his aggravating distance from the press, after which he wings the following course: the press harder to reach than Bokhara and its villainous sultan; the tortures of memory; Sir William Hamilton; Faust; Mephisto (facetiæ); Sir W. H. and conversationalists in general; slang; Magliabecchi (more facetiæ—Magliabecchi apostrophized as "Now, Mag"); useless talents; Sir W. H.; address to the reader and facetiæ *in vacuo*; the revolution of 1688; connecting the subsequent numbers of a paper by means of one article; discourse on youth and its relation to actual age; Sir W. H. and his Edinburgh circle; his character; athleticism reviewed and condemned; Sir W. H.'s work on Logic; some logical conundrums; Kant; Sir W. H.'s contributions to knowledge; a comprehensive Logic sketched; illogicalities in Scottish customs.[3]

To do De Quincey justice, it must be admitted that this sort of thing, if swallowed at a gulp, works a preposterous kind of charm. As criticism of a man and his ideas, it is grotesque; but it is certainly

[1] See, for instance I, 163 (note 2, on the shilling).
[2] X, 165.
[3] V, 303 ff.

literature of a kind, and can be enjoyed as such, in the sense that the more extreme and formless examples of post-Strauss tone-poem can be enjoyed as one kind of music, if listened to in an unprejudiced manner. "My way of writing is rather to think aloud, and follow my own humours, than much to consider who is listening to me."[1] It would be foolish to go to De Quincey *when he is in this mood*, for an accurate account (indeed for any account at all) of a person, an event, a theory: what he gives us is a kind of magic spell—a free improvisation on a theme, or a series of interlocking themes, suggested by the title of the essay. It would also be disingenuous to pretend not occasionally to be glad of some of these digressions,—as, for instance, when he interrupts an essay on Lamb to give a vivid impression of the London festivities of 1814[2]; or when he leaves direct examination of the subject of *Style* to pronounce a most illuminating discourse on Greek history.[3]

I italicized the words "when he is in this mood", for when he is in another, no one can paint a more brilliant portrait or distribute more acute and original criticisms round a figure of dispute, whether of ancient or modern days. De Quincey was capable, on occasion, of keeping his eye on the object, and this ability is best illustrated in the essays collected under the title of *Literary and Lake Reminiscences,* in passages of the *Autobiographic Sketches*, and in such single pieces as *Richard Bentley*, *Dr. Samuel Parr* (in spite of its jaundiced outlook), *Pope* (1838 article), and *Milton* (1839).

I have skimmed the cream from the *Autobiographic Sketches* in the quotations with which I have illustrated the narrative part of this book. It remains to say something of De Quincey's own attitude to it, as a significant introduction to the vexed question of his utterances on the subject of his distinguished contemporaries and friends.

Writing to his publisher, Hogg, in 1850, he gives as his opinion that "nothing makes such dreary and monotonous reading as the old hackneyed roll-call, chronologically arrayed, of inevitable facts in a man's life." Nobody will accuse De Quincey of this kind of dryness, nor of undue attention to facts. A passage in the general preface to the Collected Edition gives a more definite idea of his intention. "Generally they [autobiographies] pretend to little beyond that sort of amusement which attaches to any real story,

[1] *Confessions* (1823), p. 145. [2] III, 67. [3] X, 168 ff.

thoughtfully and faithfully related, moving through a succession of scenes sufficiently varied, that are not suffered to remain too long upon the eye, and that connect themselves at every stage with intellectual objects. But, even here, I do not scruple to claim from the reader, occasionally, a higher consideration. At times the narrative rises into a far higher key." This last contention is, as we have seen, amply justified; it is, indeed, exactly these passages (the deaths of Mr. Quincey and of Elizabeth; the description of the night in the inn at Shrewsbury; the account of Pink), together with the exquisite humour of "The Female Infidel", which constitute the unique value of the *Autobiographic Sketches.* For the original title is apt: De Quincey was well aware of the sketchiness of the work and sought to justify this feature by describing his procedure as "connecting the separate sections of the sketches, not by ropes and cables, but by threads of aerial gossamer." [1] This is evidently intended as a covert apology for his digressive habit in general; but while it may be allowed to pass for the work in question, we may be pardoned for feeling that an essay on Shakespeare should exhibit different characteristics—should be, in fine, closer knit. To repeat what has been said on an earlier page, these sketches, fascinating as they are, have not the concentration—the peculiar intensity—of the *Confessions*, with which they inevitably invite comparison. They are too diffuse, too casual, too much encumbered with asides, and too full of their author's latter-day preoccupations, to command the reputation enjoyed by the smaller work in its original form. Crabb Robinson called them "scandalous but painfully interesting." [2] This was the general opinion of the day. To us the scandal is no longer of moment, but the interest is still lively.

With the *Literary, Lake and London Reminiscences,* in which De Quincey summed up his memories and opinions of his most famous contemporaries, the ground shifts slightly; but we must not forget that we are still within the domain of autobiography. This realization will help us to assess correctly the irritation which these essays produced in those concerned—an irritation which would otherwise seem to us more than a little overdone.[3] We have

[1] I, 316.

[2] Diary, October 7th. 1821.

[3] It seems only just to add that contemporary opinion, even when it was not directly interested, was on the whole against De Quincey in the matter of these reminiscences. Thus Edward Fitzgerald: "The *Life* of Coleridge is indeed an

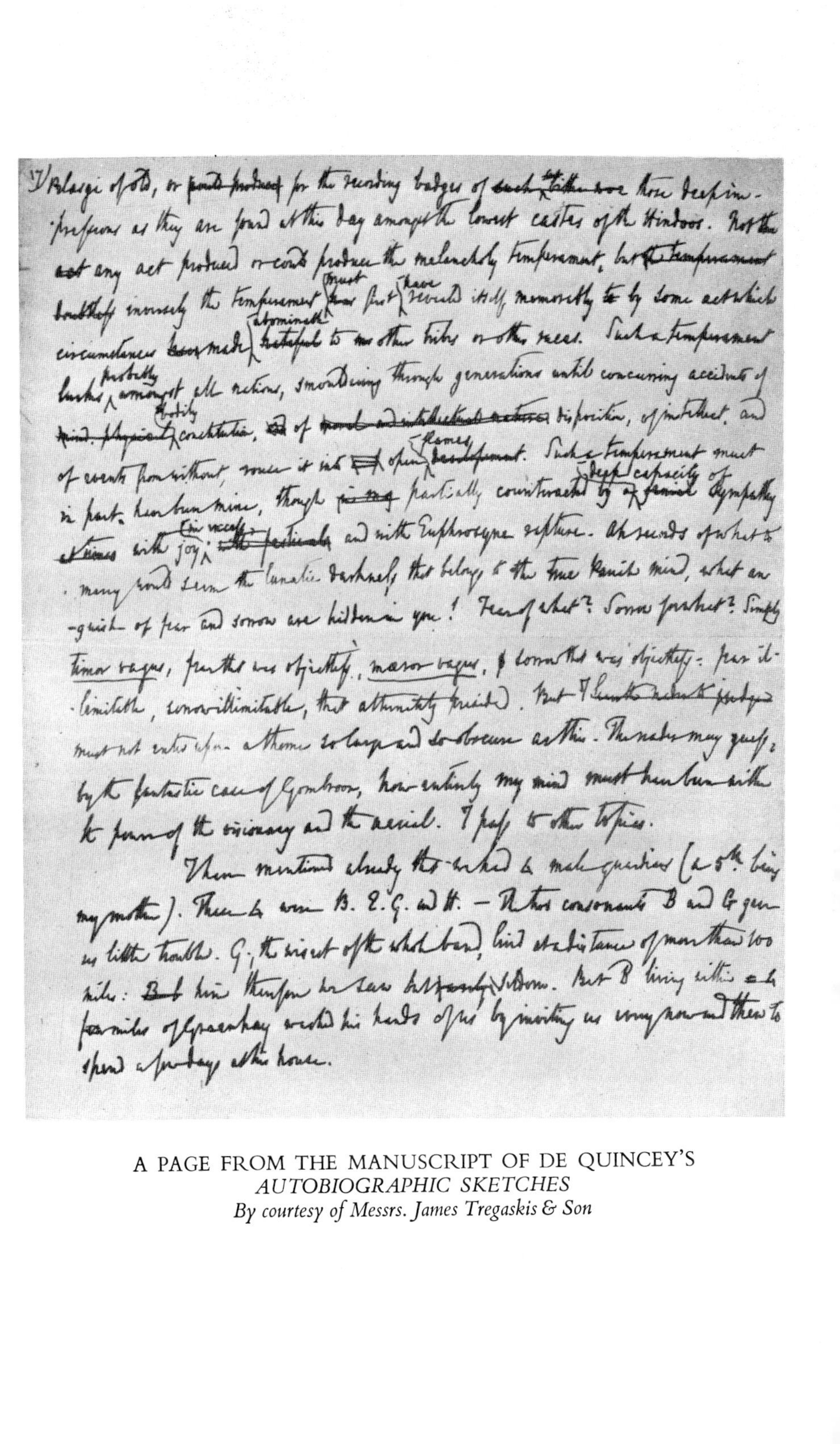

A PAGE FROM THE MANUSCRIPT OF DE QUINCEY'S
AUTOBIOGRAPHIC SKETCHES
By courtesy of Messrs. James Tregaskis & Son

already heard what Sara Coleridge and her family thought of De Quincey's account of her father. When we have added that Wordsworth's family and friends were equally annoyed on his account, we have no choice but to examine the grounds for all this displeasure.

There are five features of the Coleridge articles which, I conceive, must have been responsible for the feeling aroused: the references to Coleridge's marriage [1] and to the Wordsworth-Montagu imbroglio,[2] the charges of literary plagiarism,[3] the accusation of taking opium to produce "luxurious sensations",[4] and the revelation of the gift of £300.[5] In fairness to De Quincey it must be said at once that the main substance of what he says in these articles is true, and that the inaccuracies of detail (misquotations, wrong dates) by no means invalidate the conclusions drawn.[6] The burden, then, of the charge may be briefly summed up in the word "blurting". The treatment of Coleridge's marriage is shrewd and well-expressed, but it gave offence because, although the poet himself was dead, the other parties concerned were not. Dorothy Wordsworth, for instance, can hardly have liked to see herself referred to as possessing "no personal charms." This sentence again: "My own impression is, that neither Coleridge nor Lord Byron could have failed, eventually, to quarrel with *any* wife, though a Pandora sent down from heaven to bless him," if true, was not tactful: no member of the circle can have cared to see himself compared to Byron. It was felt that De Quincey's observations were an impertinent indiscretion, and in so far as a sniggering tone sometimes creeps into the style one must admit that the charge is justified. To make matters worse, De Quincey had added to the Montagu story by revealing the fact that the latter was driven to his angry outburst by discovering Coleridge entertaining one Captain Pasley to dinner *and wine*, which Montagu forbade in his house. The sting of these indiscretions must have been felt all the

unsatisfactory thing: I believe that everybody thinks so. . . . It seems to me to proceed from a kind of enervation in De Quincey." (*Letters of Edward Fitzgerald*, I, 34, Macmillan Edition.) The error here would seem to lie in regarding the articles as a "life", whereas they really consist in a personal impression—a very different thing.

[1] II, 166. [2] II, 207. [3] II, 143.

[4] II, 184. [5] II, 163.

[6] But in the *Posth. Works* (II, 16) he admits that he was never a "confidential" friend of Coleridge.

more sharply in that they were so amusingly related. De Quincey had not learnt the business of journalism for nothing, and this essay in particular sparkles with his dry, impish humour. At the same time, one cannot blame the Coleridge family for exclaiming that all this was no business of his.

The reference to Coleridge and opium was undoubtedly provoked by the poet's own animadversions against De Quincey on this subject;[1] in the circumstances, knowing what we do of both cases, we shall not blame De Quincey for retaliating. There was a good deal more glass in Coleridge's house than in De Quincey's. The latter was to point this out again, some years later,[2] when Gillman's *Life* revived the controversy. Here De Quincey emits the curious opinion that opium killed the poet, but stimulated the philosophizing faculty, in Coleridge; and he expresses resentment at the latter's boast that disintoxication was easy and rapid. *A propos* of this article he wrote angrily to Hogg, in 1859: "This is a description of S. T. C.'s person, not only accurate, but the sole accurate among many that are libellously false—drawn from my own knowledge, guaranteed defyingly by myself and sure to give pleasure in many quarters."[3]

As far as the matter of the £300 goes, the reference to it is so vague and ambiguous[4] that anyone unacquainted with the truth of the story would be quite unable to gauge the extent of the assistance given, or even its nature.

The accusations of plagiarism, on the other hand, are ill-founded, though there is no reason to suppose that they were made in bad faith or in a spiteful spirit. De Quincey claims to have discovered in Coleridge's writings traces of Milton, Schelling and Shelvorke (in *The Ancient Mariner*).[5] He admits that Coleridge denied this indebtedness, but does not withdraw the charge, which modern critics have shown to be beside the point. Coleridge may have 'taken his belongings where he found them', but in doing so he added so much that was indubitably his own, that the charge of picking becomes absurd.

De Quincey's critical estimate of the man himself is of permanent value, because, though scattered and at first sight not particularly

[1] His letters accuse De Quincey of spreading Opium-Eating by his works.
[2] *Coleridge and Opium-Eating* (1845).
[3] Japp, 356. [4] II, 163. [5] II, 143.

striking, it does in fact explain the main difficulty with which students of Coleridge are faced:

> Coleridge, to many people . . . seemed to wander; and he seemed then to wander the most when, in fact, his resistance to the wandering instinct was greatest—viz., when the compass and huge circuit by which his illustrations moved travelled farthest into remote regions before they began to revolve. Long before this coming round commenced most people had lost him, and naturally enough supposed that he had lost himself. They continued to admire the separate beauty of the thoughts, but did not see their relations to the dominant theme.[1] . . . However, I can assert . . . that logic the most severe was as inalienable from his modes of thinking as grammar from his language.

This is primarily a description of Coleridge's conversation, but it shows, by the same token, a profound insight into the fundamental processes of the poet-philosopher's mind—processes to which justice is only now being done.[2]

Some pages later, De Quincey points to the manœuvre that made friendship with Coleridge so difficult and, in the end, always so ephemeral. "It was, indeed, Coleridge's infirmity to project his own mind, and his own very peculiar ideas . . . upon other men, and to contemplate these reflex images from himself as so many characters having an absolute ground in some separate object".[3] De Quincey is here describing the essential fallacy of the romantic approach to friendship, with its insulting disregard of the 'otherness' of other people, its insistence on creating the friend according to a preconceived idea, the ultimate result of which is, of course, disruption. This is one of the reasons (there are, to be sure, others) why it is a life's work, being fair to Coleridge the man; and De Quincey is to be congratulated on coming through the labour with only a few scratches, and those mostly inflicted by others than Coleridge himself. For a man so eminently not estimable, it is necessary to be lovable, if he is to come off well in the long run, at the hands of his associates; and Coleridge was, most unfortunately, too superficially Pecksniffian, parsonic, and nebulous to be really

[1] II, 152.

[2] In Stephen Potter's *Coleridge and S. T. C.* and I. A. Richards' *Coleridge on Imagination.*

[3] II, 185.

lovable. The spectacle of him living his life is an unedifying one, look at it from what angle we will. A certain degree of irritation is almost always inseparable from pity, and those who were Coleridge's friends knew a double vexation at what seemed to them the peculiar gratuitousness of many of the emotions which Coleridge forced them to feel.

De Quincey is at pains to rectify the blunder made by contemporary critics in lumping Coleridge, Wordsworth and Southey together " under common views of literature "—[1] a blunder as foolish as most of the references to " Bloomsbury " in our own day; and his essays on the three men illustrate the fallacy at all points. That on Wordsworth is mainly read nowadays for the wonderful accounts of De Quincey's first approaches to and meetings with the poet and his sister, the bulk of which I have already quoted in a previous chapter; but the article is otherwise remarkable for the same brilliant humour as distinguishes the account of Coleridge. At the same time, the humour will have caused annoyance. There is, for instance, the delightful story of De Quincey and Dorothy walking behind William and Mr. J., a man of such imposing proportions that Dorothy was moved to exclaim: " Is it possible,—can that be William? How very mean he looks! " [2] And to illustrate Wordsworth's lack of humour, De Quincey tells a story of himself and the Wordsworths dining with a lady who ate the whole of a pheasant herself, after it had been passed round the table and the other guests had all refused it, thinking that, if they did not do so, there would not be enough to go round. Dorothy was much amused; but William remained grave: " A person cannot be honest ", he remarked, " positively not honest, who is capable of such an act." [3] Later, the same lady refused to dine with De Quincey a second time, as that would have put her under debt to him. " Very well," said De Quincey, " give me 3/- and that will settle the account." But still she refused.

The accusation of cattiness, which has often been levelled at De Quincey, receives some support from this article, as well as from that (written in the following year) on the *Gradual Estrangement from Wordsworth*.[4] Readers of this biography will have gathered, by this time, that De Quincey's was not essentially a spiteful nature. But Wordsworth had hurt him very deeply, and

[1] II, 172. [2] II, 243. [3] II, 349. [4] 1840.

he could not prevent his sense of injury from piercing through everything that he wrote about the poet. Thus: "I do not conceive that Wordsworth could have been an amiable boy; he was austere and unsocial . . . not generous; and not self-denying. I am pretty certain that no consideration would ever have induced Wordsworth to burden himself with a lady's reticule."[1] And a few pages later, he expresses astonishment that the poet should ever have brought himself to pay court to a woman.

All this is mightily offensive, written about a man who was still alive; and Wordsworth's friends were perfectly justified in protesting. Miss Fenwick, in particular, writing to Henry Taylor, furiously denied the charge of unchivalrousness. Wordsworth himself characteristically refused to read the articles; but no doubt Mary and Sara did so, in which case they will have seen Hazlitt's proposal to Dorothy published, and have failed to be amused by the extraordinary opinion that their sister-in-law would have been happier in middle life if she had taken to journalism![2]

The same sense of injury which produced these impertinences, deprives De Quincey's account of the estrangement of the force and cogency it might have had. His case is a good one, but he fails to make the most of it. He makes it plain that he understands Wordsworth's incapacity for dispersed affection, outside his family circle, but wastes the rest of the article in petty fault-finding—Wordsworth does not admire Harriet Lee's *The German's Tale*, therefore his mind must be one-sided; and so on. The truth was that De Quincey was consumed, not surprisingly, by envy of Wordsworth's easy lot in life; and he gives voice to this envy in a sentence which I shall quote, not more for its matter than because it is so magnificent an example of our author's prose at its finest and most elaborately balanced:

> Thus I have traced Wordsworth's ascent through its several steps and stages, to what, for his moderate desires and habits so philosophic, may be fairly considered opulence. And it must rejoice every man who joins in the public homage *now* rendered to his powers (and what man is to be found that, more or less, does not?) to hear, with respect to one so lavishly endowed by nature, that he has not been neglected by fortune; that he has never had the finer edge of his sensibilities dulled by the sad

[1] II, 262. [2] II, 300.

anxieties, the degrading fears, the miserable dependencies of debt; that he has been blessed with competency even when poorest; has had hope and cheerful prospects in reversion through every stage of his life; that at all times he has been liberated from *reasonable* anxieties about the final interests of his children; that at all times he has been blessed with leisure, the very amplest that ever man enjoyed, for intellectual pursuits the most delightful; yes, that, even as regards those delicate and coy pursuits, he has possessed, in combination, all the conditions for their most perfect culture—the leisure, the ease, the solitude, the society, the domestic peace, the local scenery—Paradise for his eye, in Miltonic beauty, lying outside his windows, Paradise for his heart, in the perpetual happiness of his own fireside; and, finally, when increasing years might be supposed to demand something more of modern luxuries, and expanding intercourse with society something more of refined elegancies, that his means, still keeping pace in almost arithmetical ratio with his wants, had shed the graces of art upon the failing powers of nature, had stripped infirmity of discomfort, and (so far as the necessities of things will allow) had placed the final stages of life, by means of many compensations, by universal praise, by plaudits reverberated from senates, benedictions wherever his poems have penetrated, honour, troops of friends—in short, by all that miraculous prosperity can do to evade the primal decrees of nature, had placed the final stages upon a level with the first.[1]

It is a complete elegy on De Quincey's own dreams, which he had been obliged to abandon in the bitterest detail. Wending our way through this marvellously managed sentence, which reminds us that the seventeenth-century divines were among the few French writers whom De Quincey admired,[2] we cease to wonder at his resentment at the very different treatment which he himself had received at the hands of life.

But when the envy and detraction has been accounted for, there remains a still larger portion of eulogy and—what is of greater interest—of acute criticism of Wordsworth. The pages [3] devoted to the poet's experiences in France, and the effect which they had upon him, are not only a fine piece of rhetorical biography, but tell the complicated truth at a time when few knew it. And some years later, when De Quincey's resentment against the man had still further died down, he wrote an admirable study of Words-

[1] II, 292. [2] X, 126. [3] II, 276 ff.

worth's poetry.[1] His criticism of the *Excursion*, for instance, is much in advance of his day, which either dismissed the poem with Jeffrey or accepted it as a revelation. De Quincey, on the other hand, while pointing out its grave merits,[2] criticizes the inadequacy of its plot, the unevenness of its construction, its lack of sequence, and the unpoetical nature of much of its material. He had never been an adherent of Wordsworth's theory of poetic diction, realizing its limitations and the fact that, although justified by the artificial language of the lesser imitators of Pope, it had no application to Shakespeare or Milton.

The third eminent contemporary to whom De Quincey devoted attention, in this series of articles, was Lamb; and although this essay is less good than that which he wrote ten years later, it contains one paragraph which proves once more his ability to sum up a remarkable man in such a way that all his most important qualities are conveyed:

> Considered as a man of genius, he was not in the very first rank, simply because his range was a contracted one: within that range, he was perfect. . . . But, as a *moral* being, in the total compass of his relations to this world's duties, in the largeness and diffuseness of his charity, in the graciousness of his condescension to inferior intellects, I am disposed . . . to pronounce him the best man . . . that I have known or read of.[3]

He was "Diogenes with the heart of a St. John",[4] and De Quincey searchingly describes Lamb's hatred of shams. Yet the description, as a description, is weakened by two enormous digressions (one on the London festivities of 1814, another comparing his own use of opium with that of Coleridge), and the subject of Mary Lamb's madness is danced round in such a way as to make it seem far worse than if he had simply said: "She was subject to intermittent fits of madness."

Humour, as I have already stated, is one of the most important characteristics of these sketches, and it is probably the one which will take most readers back to them. Mr. Coleridge senior at dinner, gradually stuffing the train of a lady's white dress into an

[1] XII, 294.

[2] See also *Posth.. Works*, II, 201 ff., where he defends Wordsworth's choice of the Pedlar as protagonist, against the criticisms of Coleridge.

[3] III, 48.

[4] III, 44.

aperture in his clothes, under the impression that it was a piece of his own shirt; Walking Stewart sitting among the cows in St. James's Park; Hannah More being surprised by Royalty *en tête-à-tête* with Cottle; the whimsical account of Lakeland society: these are De Quincey at his funniest. On other occasions, unfortunately, and particularly later in life, this true humour was replaced by mere facetiæ, or by a purely verbal fun, highly favoured by *Maga,* of which the following description of spitting is an example:

> The chief problem in this system of hydraulics being to throw the column in a parabolic curve from the centre of Parliament Street when driving four-in-hand, to the foot pavement right and left, so as to alarm the consciences of guilty peripatetics on either side.[1]

—a form of joke which most of us nowadays would agree to think only fairly funny.

As a critic of great men who were not his contemporaries—Shakespeare, Bentley, Pope—De Quincey was more hampered by the extreme peculiarity of his vision, in giving a generally acceptable description of their characters and work, than he was in dealing with those of his own day, whom he was in a better position to see roughly as they were. His essay on Shakespeare is a case in point.[2] De Quincey declares that he took more trouble with this article than with any other he ever wrote. That being so, we should expect to find it more carefully composed than those which were torn from his hands by the printer's devil while he was still at work on them. But we are disappointed, for at least half of it is as eccentric, in the way of criticism, as anything he ever wrote. As I have already stated, fifteen pages are virtually wasted in proving that Shakespeare was not neglected in his own day, and two in pointing out that it does not matter whether the bard was a gentleman or not. And before reaching the plays themselves, we have to submit to a long account of Shakespeare's marriage, for the simple reason that De Quincey felt an itch to tell us something about his own, but could not do so in a more direct manner.

[1] X, 265.

[2] It was written to discharge a debt (under £30) which Adam Black had paid for De Quincey, having found him helpless in the hands of the sheriff's officer.

(Here, by the way, he makes the acute remark that the unhappiness of Shakespeare's marriage and the poverty of his circumstances may not have been entirely unconnected with the work which we now enjoy, by throwing him back upon himself and his own resources.)

But when at last he comes to the plays themselves, De Quincey immediately becomes admirable, pointing out the beauty and complexity of the female characters and comparing Shakespeare's originality in this respect with the much more limited treatment of women by the Greek dramatists; though here he exaggerates in alleging that the Greek drama shows women only in circumstances that unsex them.[1] The criticism that the Greeks exhibited Man over against Fate, while Shakespeare shows him at grips with his own character, is probably an echo of Coleridge; but the passage describing the wonderful variety of the poet's dialogue has a perfectly authentic note:

> Every form of natural interruption, breaking through the restraints of ceremony under the impulses of tempestuous passion; every form of hasty interrogative, ardent reiteration when a question has been evaded; every form of scornful repetition of the hostile statement; in short, all modes and formulæ by which anger, hurry, fretfulness, scorn, impatience or excitement under any movement whatever, can disturb or modify or dislocate the formal bookish stuff of commencement: these are as rife in Shakespeare's dialogue as in life itself.[2]

It is interesting to compare this sentence, the vividness and power of which consist in its seeming to describe an actual event taking place in the presence of the reader, first with the more famous passage in the *Knocking at the Gate*,[3] and then with that describing the lucky course of Wordsworth's life.[4] The method will be found to be in all three cases the same, and it is a favourite one with De Quincey, learnt originally from the masters of seventeenth-century prose—Sir Thomas Browne, Jeremy Taylor—for whom he had an unstinted admiration.[5]

The 1838 essay on Pope, like that on Lamb, is slighter and less interesting than that which De Quincey wrote in 1848, when the disapproving fascination with which Pope inspired him dictated a

[1] IV, 57. [2] IV, 79. [3] See p. 208.
[4] See p. 251. [5] See, for instance, X, 105.

return to the subject. In the earlier article, his criticism is confined to contending that the *Dunciad* is superior to the *Essay on Man*, the 'millenniumism' of which seems to have afflicted De Quincey, and to pointing out that "Arcadian life is at the best a feeble conception, and rests upon the false principle of crowding together all the luscious sweets of rural life, undignified by the danger which attends pastoral life in our climate, and unrelieved by shades, either moral or physical."[1] Proofs are abundant that De Quincey never threw off the influence of Wordsworth, which was as much a moral as a literary one; and in this last sentence the master is clearly standing in his light. De Quincey might believe, and state, that he had never subscribed to Wordsworth's theory of poetic diction; but that he was obliquely affected by it, as by a widely diffused scent, is plain from this passage. Yet the rather worried interest which he at all times shows in Pope, who was one of his continual points of reference, is evidence that the eighteenth-century 'pull' was still strong in him, dragging him back to his earliest literary discoveries, at Greenhay and Manchester, before the nineteenth century, in the person of Wordsworth, had exerted its full sway over his mind and opinions.

The essays on Bentley and Parr may be considered as a pair, in that it was De Quincey's concern to show that, as he asserted in a letter to his daughter Emily, written in 1851, Bentley was all that Parr pretended to be. But while the account of the latter, because of its extended application to Whiggism in general and the added interest of its autobiographical material, will hold any modern reader's attention from beginning to end, that of Bentley is too specialized to have much appeal to-day, and will be turned to, if at all, for the brilliant narrative—almost as Gothic in style as a passage of Carlyle, but more grammatically strict—of Bentley's protracted wrangles with the governing body of Trinity College, Cambridge. It is possible that De Quincey, in his eagerness to discredit Dr. Parr, exaggerates the accuracy of Bentley's scholarship. Landor (himself no mean scholar), referring to the Master of Trinity's treatment of classical texts, accuses him of changing "whatever can be changed, right or wrong".[2] But Bentley's was a character which De Quincey could wholeheartedly respect, while for Parr himself, as we have previously noticed, he could feel nothing but an irritated contempt.

[1] IV, 259. [2] Landor, *Imaginary Conversations: Rousseau and Malherbes*.

Admiration in this case brought with it a greater degree of concentration on the object than De Quincey usually commanded; the essay is extremely well knit, and free of digressions, while the examination of Bentley's work gives a very good idea of De Quincey's own minute and anxious scholarship.*

Receding still further into antiquity, we come upon him examining the pretensions of Charlemagne and of the Cæsars. And here it becomes necessary briefly to review De Quincey's own pretensions as a historian. Thus the Charlemagne essay is mainly of interest for its preliminary discourse on the three kinds of historical writing—the Narrative, the Scenical, and the Philosophic.[1] From his work on the whole, in this field, it emerges that he was best fitted to approach history by the second of these methods—a fact which fits in well with what has otherwise been observed of his tenor of mind. His long preoccupation with Kant,[2] whose outlook (like that of Wordsworth) continued to influence De Quincey long after he had consciously ceased to subscribe to it, had set his mind along the line of " birds'-eye views ", large generalizations (such as would nowadays be called 'Spenglerian'), and a processional method of approach to historical events and characters which suited his own very special vision of the world. A perfect example of this method occurs in *The Philosophy of Roman History*:

> The Battle of Actium was followed by the final conquest of Egypt. That conquest rounded and integrated the glorious Empire; it was now circular as a shield—orbicular as the disc of a planet: the great Julian arch was now locked into the cohesion of granite by its last key-stone. From that day forward, for three hundred years, there was silence in the world: no muttering was heard: no eye winked beneath the wing. Winds of hostility might still rave at intervals: but it was on the outside of the mighty Empire: it was at a dream-like distance; and, like the storms that beat against some monumental castle, 'and at the doors and windows seem to call', they rather irritated and vivified the sense of security than at all disturbed its luxurious lull.[3]

It is very beautiful, very graphic, intensely *romancé*: phrases like " no eye winked beneath the wing ", and the sense of solemnity

[1] V, 354.
[2] *Viz.*, his translation of Kant's *Idea of a Universal History*, IX, 428 ff.
[3] VI, 430.

conferred by all those colons, make such passages a delight to read and to remember—to roll over on the tongue. The most obvious criticism which they arouse is that, *qua* history, they are inadequate—do not contribute anything to our knowledge of the subject. And that is doubtless true, if facts be our criterion. De Quincey's rigid and purely emotional political outlook, which brought him down automatically on the side of those who opposed the Reform Bill,[1] opposed the Catholic Emancipation movement,[2] opposed the Secession of the Church of Scotland,[3] and condoned the Peterloo Massacre,[4] made it out of the question for him to take any view of history according to the ideas of Progress which grew with the century in which he wrote.* His love of paradox, too, which led him to describe Oliver Cromwell as " exceedingly good-natured ", [5] and to posit a " total defect of heroic minds amongst the French of that [Bonaparte's] day ",[6] permitted him to ' rush in ', with frequently ludicrous effect, on subjects of which he had, to say the least of it, insufficient knowledge.[7] Here, though, he would have a right to urge the journalist's plea, that his capacity as reviewer obliged him often enough to criticize books which were essentially outside his range, wide as that was.

It is a pity, therefore, that Blackwood should have required him to review P. R. James's *History of Charlemagne*, for he simply used the book as a convenient stick with which to beat Napoleon. It is enjoyable to hear the latter described as " presenting in his deficiencies the picture of a low mechanic, and in his positive qualities the violence and brutality of a savage " [8]—an energetic expression of a half-truth; but the general indictment is carried to ridiculous lengths and is in any case an inadequate recompense to the reader who hoped to hear something more circumstantial about the man whose name stands at the head of the article.

Yet, even given the ' eye on the object ', De Quincey's attitude

[1] De Quincey discusses this question in some detail, in his *On the Political Parties of Modern England*. He considers the Reformers too divided on points of detail to form a whole of any value (X, 343) and censures the " habit of stating great public questions as lying between a party and the nation, when it is notorious that they lie between the nation and itself " (*Ibid.*, 318)—in fact, between what Disraeli afterwards called the " Two Nations ", though De Quincey would not have cared for the description. His disparagement of the value of the vote to the individual (*Ibid.*, 345) is, again, very specious.

[2] In the *Westmorland Gazette*.

[3] See his article, XIV, 219 ff.

[4] Also in the *Westmorland Gazette*.

[5] IX, 303.

[6] V, 365.

[7] See, also, p. 316 ff.

[8] V, 375, note 2.

to historical events, when he brought himself to examine them in detail, was far too casuistical and hair-splitting—a feature of the scholastic method which he had learnt at Oxford. It is typical of him, for instance, that in the early article on the *Falsification of English History*,[1] he tries to prove that, in the sentence " The King can do no wrong ", the Great Parliament altered the emphasis from " wrong " to " King ", so that the sentence should mean that Charles was not personally responsible for the acts of the Constitution—a piece of argument which is only interesting as a curiosity.

These odd kinks, which make De Quincey so inadequate an historian, were not lost upon the ineluctable Carlyle who, however, might have done well to look first for the beam in his own eye before dismissing *The Cæsars* in the following words: " Some papers of his on the Roman Cæsars in *Blackwood* are the last I know of him: Teufelsdröckh might well pause in amazement to find Nero and Commodus thus treated as having ' something sacred ' still,—in virtue of their purple clothes. De Quincey is one of the most irreclaimable Tories now extant: despising Poverty with a complete content; and himself, alas, poorer than Job was, who at worst never got gazetted."

There is always something terrifying in the square-toed conviction of Carlyle's utterances, with their capricious capital letters, their picturesque phraseology, and their angularity: terrifying, because their influence is so difficult to avoid. Yet Carlyle's is by no means the last word on *The Cæsars*, which occupies something of the same place in English literature as Montesquieu's admirable but now little read *Considérations sur les causes de la Grandeur et de la Décadence des Romains* occupies in French. The reason for the neglect of both these works is obvious; to a recommendation to read them most people would reply: " Why should I bother, when Mommsen and Ranke are so much more erudite, and Gibbon is so much more amusing? "

As far as facts go, this statement is unanswerable; but, as usual, De Quincey has his own very special contribution to make, even to a subject of which he is not wholly the master. The statistical, legal, the purely explanatory portions of this little book (the six articles dispose of some two hundred pages) are indeed very dull,

[1] IX, 295.

chiefly because De Quincey then assumes a style that reminds one of a literal translation of *De Bello Gallico*; but the moment he gets a chance to tell a story—the death of Nero, the sports of Commodus—all his best qualities as a writer flower out across the page. So that for the descriptive passages alone the book is well worth a visit; in these De Quincey works all his familiar magic.

Eccentricities, of course, we expect and find. Julius Cæsar is laboriously vindicated from the charge of atheism[1]—not, one suspects, because De Quincey had any respect for the Roman religion, but because atheism of any kind shocked him, and he happened to admire Julius Cæsar. Again, his horror of scandalous behaviour leads him to make the astonishing statement that "the Cæsars in themselves . . . are not interesting".[2] And six pages later we find him censuring Gibbon, not only for the arbitrary selection of Commodus as the point from which to date the decline of Rome (a possible contention), but also for failing "to notice the steps and separate indications of decline as they arose"—a quite unjustifiable accusation.

In order to realize how remarkable, on the whole, is De Quincey's grasp of Roman History, it is necessary to read, in conjunction with *The Cæsars*, the article on Cicero, which is chiefly interesting for its account of Roman judicial administration, and the excellent essay on the *Philosophy of Roman History*, both written some years later. Here he traces the essential contributions of Rome to civilization and dates her internal decline from the moment at which outside pressure on the empire ceased, *i.e.*, from the time of Trajan. The degeneration of Latin literature from this date was one of De Quincey's favourite theories, to which, as we shall see, he returned on numerous occasions. It is something of a surprise, however, to find him shaking his head over the rise of 'anecdotage'[3] in the Augustan History and calling the Goths and Vandals the "regenerators of the effete Roman intellect".[4] The latter theory has indeed been held at different times, but usually by 'advanced' persons in whose galley De Quincey would have shivered to find himself.

His only other contributions to Roman history in these years

[1] VI, 244. [2] VI, 355.
[3] See, however, *Posth. Works*, I, 85, where he returns to this charge.
[4] VI, 436.

is the *Casuistry of Roman Meals.*[1] This little piece of literary high spirits can be cordially recommended to those who wish to sample De Quincey at his intolerable worst. The burden of the argument is that the Romans ate very little for breakfast or luncheon; but this fact is buried in a facetious rigmarole, teeming with Latin and Greek phrases, mixed together, pudding-fashion, to produce an explosion of feeble puns. This is the kind of thing: "Dinner was an ugly little parenthesis between two still uglier clauses of a teetotally ugly sentence"[2]; or "Perhaps, as two negatives made one affirmative, it may be thought that two layers of moonshine might coalesce into one pancake, and two Barmecide banquets might be the square root of one poached egg. . . . But, probably, as a rump and dozen, in our land of wagers, is construed with a very liberal latitude as to the materials, so Martial's invitation, 'to take bread with him at eleven', might be understood by the συνετοι (the knowing ones) as significant of something better than ἀρτοσιτος. Otherwise, in good truth, 'moonshine and turn-out' at eleven a.m. would be even worse than 'tea and turn-out' at eight p.m., which the 'fervida juventus' of Young England so loudly deprecates."[3]

A good many English writers of the nineteenth century were capable of this kind of nonsense, among them Thackeray and Carlyle; but none of them had the impertinence or the lack of control (one hesitates which to call it) to pursue that vein uninterruptedly for thirty pages on end, and with a total disregard for propriety of occasion. As Professor Saintsbury has put it: "Swift did not put *mollis abuti* in the *Four Last Years of Queen Anne,* nor Thackeray his Punch jokes in the death-scene of Colonel Newcome. De Quincey would have done both."[4]

It is a relief to turn from such rubbish to other pages, where an acuter knowledge of the subject has produced a book-review that is also a spirited piece of historical writing—*The Revolution of Greece*. Apart from the interest of the subject matter, which is lively and well-knit, the article is remarkable for its fine peroration,[5] which is worth placing beside the examples already quoted of De Quincey's rhetorical method. Here the effect is built up by opposing

[1] VII, 11 ff. [2] VIII, 36. [3] VII, 26.
[4] *Macmillan's Magazine*, July, 1890. [5] VII, 317.

two contrasted sets of enumerations, which are thereupon resolved in a series of shorter, dramatic sentences.

It is in such passages—here and in the best pages of *The Cæsars*—that De Quincey comes nearest to reconciling 'the Books of Knowledge' and 'the Literature of Power'—passages in which the stylistic lesson of the seventeenth century is lightened of its burden of heavy latinity by some bright constellation of anglo-saxon words. The care with which their effect is calculated, too, reminds us that their author had studied Burke and sung his praises in a sentence which I shall quote in praise of De Quincey himself: "With what marvellous skill does he enrich what is meagre, elevate what is humble, intellectualize what is purely technical, delocalize what is local, generalize what is personal." [1]

With *The Revolt of the Tartars* we definitely cross the border into the 'Literature of Power'. This is admittedly one of De Quincey's finest pieces, and one of the few which are still read by those who know anything of his work. Grave doubt has been cast on the sources of the story which De Quincey tells,[2]* and the presence of the Emperor Kien Lung at the approach of the Tartar hosts is certainly a fiction, introduced for effect; but the question of historical accuracy, in a piece which is admittedly a rhapsodical vision, hardly arises. The story probably reached De Quincey in the merest outline, but it was one which he recognized at once as it were one of his own opium dreams, with its shadowy armies, its dusty and spectral agonies, and the voluminous speed of its events. In Kien Lung's vision of the Tartar host, and the subsequent combined rush of the Kalmucks and their enemies into the Tengis lake, to quench their thirst and then slaughter one another in the water, De Quincey achieves a glittering, symphonic splendour only equalled in the dream-fugue of the *English Mail-Coach*. His own phrase, "flying armies of thoughts", struck off in a letter to his daughter Margaret, perfectly describes the effect of this extraordinary prose-poem, for that is what it is. Rapid movement, the hurtling of bodies through space, tense with the danger of some sinister collision: the mere suggestion of such a theme was enough to put De Quincey on his mettle. As if under the baton of a master conductor, the phrases begin to rise on the air, weaving an elaborate counterpoint of magical images:

[1] X, 334.

[2] See Masson's remarks, VII, 422 ff.

Through the next hour, during which the gentle morning breeze had a little freshened, the dusty vapour had developed itself far and wide into the appearance of huge aerial draperies, hanging in mighty volumes from the sky to the earth; and at particular points, where the eddies of the breeze acted upon the pendulous skirts of these aerial curtains, rents were perceived, sometimes taking the form of regular arches, portals, and windows, through which began dimly to gleam the heads of camels ' indorsed ' with human beings —and at intervals the moving of men and horses in tumultuous array—and then through other openings or vistas at far distant points the flashing of polished arms. But sometimes, as the wind slackened or died away, all those openings, of whatever form, in the cloudy pall would slowly close, and for a time the whole pageant was shut up from view; although the growing din, the clamours, shrieks, and groans, ascending from infuriated myriads, reported, in a language not to be misunderstood, what was going on behind the cloudy screen.[1]

But quotations from this piece are not much more useful than the snippets of music printed in concert programmes. The symphonic poem must be experienced in its organic entirety. Yet the above quotation is worth examining, for the exactitude of its language (" pendulous curtains ", " was shut up from view "). De Quincey seldom, and never in his best moments, indulged in mere resonance of the kind into which Poe, for instance, frequently lapsed, when attempting musical effects in prose or poetry.[2] He remained ever severely conscious of the limits of language, which is another of the reasons why it is so foolish to class him among the ' decadents ', who imitated his methods but did not command his technique.

Before closing this chapter with some account of De Quincey's experiments in pure fiction, during this period, we must bestow a glance on the strange little fantasia entitled *The Toilette of the Hebrew Lady*. Personally, I should have been inclined to pass this over in silence, were it not that De Quincey, writing to Hogg during the preparation of the Collected Edition, gave as his opinion that " considering its *Biblical* relations, over and above its interest of curiosity, I really think this Hebrew Toilette—*with the*

[1] VII, 411.

[2] *Ulalume* is an almost perfect example of this kind of meaningless musical rumble.

exception always of some six or seven—the best in the collection." It is not easy to see why De Quincey held this view, for the piece, though certainly 'curious' and no doubt accurate enough, has none of its author's distinctively literary qualities. A kind of glorified notice of a Dress-Show, it contents itself with merely cataloguing the various articles of clothing, which it describes with poring minuteness, but quite without the poetic imagination and fantasy which we should expect from De Quincey in the circumstances. He corrected the wording of the original with minute care, when preparing the article for the Collected Edition, making more changes than he was accustomed to do; and the sense of the trouble he had taken perhaps led him to rate the result higher than its intrinsic interest warranted.

The Household Wreck, which De Quincey wrote in 1838, holds a peculiar place in his writings. It is the only avowed fiction of his which deals with the modern world, and its whole tone and treatment is entirely different from those of his other fictions, which are all eminently 'Gothic'. I have already, on an earlier page,[1] suggested that De Quincey had himself, his wife and his own affairs in mind, while writing this story, at a time when his mind was seriously affected by the bereavements which he had suffered (among them the death of his wife) and by his long persecution for debt. The story is exactly the sort of thing one would expect from a man in this state of mind; it concerns a plot laid by a villainous shopkeeper, who has failed in his advances to the hero's wife, Agnes, to frighten the latter into yielding by threats to expose her as a shop-lifter (using a stolen muff of her own as evidence). But the law goes too fast for him, and Agnes is condemned to ten years' penal servitude. The husband catches typhus during the trial and only recovers consciousness at the moment when the sentence is being passed. He succeeds in engineering her escape from prison, but she dies in hiding.

This odd affair is, as fiction, completely unsuccessful, partly because it is very slow and prolix (features which are conspicuously absent from De Quincey's other fictions), but—more interestingly—because of the violent sense of personal injury which glares hysterically out of the pages, disturbing and dividing one's attention. To read it is a most uncomfortable experience, not unlike listening

[1] See p. 149.

to the elaborate complaints of a friend whom one knows to be temporarily unhinged.

If I have left *Klosterheim* as the last work to be considered in this chapter of critical retrospect, the reason does not lie in indifference. It has been generally supposed that De Quincey omitted this book from the Collected Edition because he had come to despise it. I see no reason to believe this. The Collected Edition was by no means finished when he died, many pieces remaining to be revised which no one has ever suggested that he would eventually have rejected. Moreover, the order in which he revised his articles for the edition seems to have been entirely capricious—to have depended largely on that which happened to come next to hand, in the chaotic sea of manuscripts among which he was working.[1]

However that may be, it seems to me that he had no cause to regret having written *Klosterheim*, which remains one of the most generally acceptable of all Gothic novels, though connoisseurs of the latter almost invariably neglect even to mention it. Its style alone, apart from its matter, places it high in a *genre* not generally conspicuous for good writing. Coleridge admired it: " In purity of style and idiom, in which the Scholar is ever implied, and the scholarly never obtrudes itself, it reaches an excellence to which Sir Walter Scott . . . appears never to have aspired. . . ."[2] Whatever may be thought of the last assertion, the first will not, I think, be denied by those who take the slight trouble to read *Klosterheim*.

The plot centres round a town in Swabia, during the Thirty Years' War. There is a villainous Landgrave, who is in league with the Swedes, while the rightful Landgrave, Maximilian, whose father the villain has murdered, is fighting in the Imperial armies. A certain Countess Paulina, with whom Maximilian is in love, is seen journeying from Vienna to Klosterheim. Her journey is interrupted by a battle and the apparent capture of Maximilian. Immediately after this, a mysterious Masque makes his appearance in the town and carries out a series of terrorist activities, to combat which the Landgrave calls in the help of his confidant, Adorni,

[1] Masson suggests that the reason why *Klosterheim* was not reprinted in the Collected Edition was that Blackwood possessed the copyright. De Quincey, who was pressed for time, will have shrunk from the bother attached to acquiring it.

[2] *Unpublished Letters*, I, 419.

"a subtle Italian . . . who covered a temperament of terrific violence with a mask of Venetian dissimulation and the most icy reserve."[1] The result is a masked ball at which the Masque escapes, after threatening the Landgrave. The latter then abducts Paulina and, apparently out of pure fiendishness, endeavours to have her tortured; but she is saved by his own daughter, who is killed instead. The Masque then contrives the secret entrance into Klosterheim of the Imperial army, which takes possession of the town; he discovers himself to all as Maximilian, and the book ends happily.

The comic effect unavoidable in a mere *précis* of such a story, is not felt when the book is read as a whole. The sequence of events is very well managed and, in spite of the fact that we know at once who the Masque is, the atmosphere of suspense is admirably sustained. There are some very fine single scenes: the *adagio misterioso* opening, with Pauline in the coach at night watching a man creeping about in the light of a lantern hung in a tree; the masked ball *chez* Adorni, the central scene of the book, with its gate-crasher-preventing device of gold lattices and the game of Musical Chairs by which the presence of the Masque is sought;[2] and, finally the magnificently operatic finale in the chapel, loud with the brass of Meyerbeer, in which a dividing curtain is drawn aside to reveal the serried host of the Imperial army to the eyes of the terrified Landgrave.

Involuntarily comic effects, with which Gothic novels usually teem, are infrequent in *Klosterheim*. Only one occurs to me: "The restraints of high breeding, and the ceremonious decorum of his rank, involuntarily checked the Landgrave from pursuing [the Masque] with a hurried pace."[3]

It must be admitted that the characters—as characters—are of no interest at all: they are completely wooden. Only the sinister Adorni, with his nostalgic echoes of Manfred, Schedoni[4] and Melmoth, seems to emerge slightly from the flat and to behave in a way that is not quite mechanical. But this is almost of course: the livid flare and flicker of evil, from the days of the *Faery Queen* and earlier, has always stimulated poets—and the Gothic novelists

[1] XII, 49.
[2] What seems to be an early sketch for this scene occurs in the *King of Hayti*, XII, 406.
[3] XII, 84.
[4] In Mrs. Radcliffe's *The Italian*.

were essentially poets—to greater feats of imagination and virtuosity than the level beam of goodness, which requires a much rarer combination of gifts to establish its peculiar quality.

But this criticism does not much alter the quantity of pleasure to be got out of *Klosterheim*, though it may perhaps be thought to minimize its quality. For the book is essentially an adventure, a novel of action, pure and simple. That being so, one may regret that De Quincey used so restrained a method in treating his plot; for restraint is most unsuitable in such cases, as 'Monk' Lewis and Mrs. Radcliffe—to say nothing of smaller fry—had so marvellously shown. The more extravagant the better, the more Gothic. With Jean Paul at his fingers' ends, De Quincey might have contrived something a little more intoxicating than the almost classically sober tone with which he invests so very romantic a narrative. So that, in the last resort, the book cannot be called very characteristic De Quincey. Not that, were its authorship in question, attributions would vary much. Sundry touches in the opening scene, in the paraphernalia of the masked ball—above all the superbly dramatic conception, so unvulgar, in spite of its Meyerbeerian orchestration, of the final scene: here are indubitable signs of the master who dreamed through the experiences of his childhood and youth, who experienced the terrible dreams of manhood, who saw the Tartars drown in a lake of water and their own blood, and who felt, as it were the beating of his own heart, the knocks of Macduff and Lennox upon the gate at Dunsinane.

CHAPTER X

THE DARK IDOL (II)

I

CHAPTER VIII ended on a valedictory note which, if in the circumstances unavoidable, was a little misleading. For the comparative tranquillity, which was to lead gently down to death, did not set in until 1849. The relief from immediate personal responsibility which I have represented as occurring nine years before, is indeed remarkable as some kind of temporary end; but it was really no more than the cæsura in a line whose painful meaning required the addition of a final phrase. The movement of De Quincey's life had not ceased, as it may be said to have ceased in 1849; it had only suffered a brief suspension.

In 1841 it started to totter on again at an uneasy pace set by his usual vertiginous system of work, and now further complicated by an intricate network of personal relationships. There were his daughters, Margaret, Florence and Emily, who loomed ever more importantly in his life and to whom he wrote with fussy reiteration whenever he was separated from them ("How is Florence? I heard with anxiety that she was rather what people call delicate"); there were scattered and diverse friends—Mary Russell Mitford, Wilson, J. P. Nichol,[1] Professor Lushington;[2] there were his sons, Francis and Horace, whose careers occupied his attention; there were business relations—*Blackwood's, Tait's,* and various small demands on his patronage occasioned by his now considerable standing as a writer. Finally, there was Glasgow; but before proceeding to account for his association with that town, we must pause to disentangle the other threads.

[1] John Pringle Nichol (1804–1859), astronomer; rector of Montrose Academy, 1827; regius professor of astronomy at Glasgow University, 1836. (*Dic. Nat. Biog.*)

[2] Edmund Law Lushington (1811–1893), Greek scholar; of Charterhouse and Trinity College, Cambridge; professor of Greek at Glasgow, 1838–75; Lord Rector of Glasgow University, 1884; married Cecilia, daughter of Lord Tennyson. (*Ibid.*)

It was at about this time that De Quincey's second daughter, Florence, began to assume the upper hand in the management of her father's life. The first evidence of this is the fact that, soon after her mother's death, De Quincey began to make her a small fixed allowance for the family maintenance. All that we know of this daughter reconstructs a figure of much charm and beauty; she combined the four-square features of her mother's character with the delicacy, dignity, lovableness and humour of her father. What survives of her to-day, for those who did not know her personally, are above all her eyes, as they appear in the portrait of her as an elderly woman;[1] they are—one sees at once—De Quincey's eyes, infinitely deep and sad, with that strange, *washed* look, as if drained of colour by overmuch weeping; yet with an unearthly glitter, as if they were jewels set as central revelations among converging surfaces of age-old pain.

Beside this daughter, the figures of De Quincey's sons seem shadowy and remote. Indeed we know very little about them. William dead, it was Francis who acquired his father's most immediate interest. Horace had become an officer in the 26th Cameronians, and in 1840 made the China campaign under Sir Hugh Gough. He died out there in 1842. Paul Frederick likewise entered the army, but, more lucky than his elder brother, passed unscathed through the first Sikh war and later the Indian Mutiny. He afterwards became military secretary to General Galloway in the Maori War, received a grant of land in New Zealand and died there in 1894.[2]

The third son, Francis, at the period with which we are dealing, was clerk in a mercantile house in Edinburgh, but was pursuing medical studies with a view to becoming a doctor. De Quincey corresponded with him fairly frequently, as well as going to Edinburgh from time to time to coach him through the Latin preliminary examination; and the letters indicate that Francis, perhaps alone of the living sons, had inherited his father's intellectual tastes. In 1842, De Quincey wrote to him to set him right over the letters of Junius, which Francis had admired and which his father stigmatized as being stale as an out-of-date copy of a newspaper.[3] And later, in 1847, De Quincey wrote him a long letter

[1] By Sir W. B. Richmond (1886) (Bairdsmith Collection).
[2] See Hogg, p. 70.
[3] Japp, 238.

on the "Religious Objections to the Use of Chloroform",[1] which was the subject of Francis' graduation thesis. (The view expressed in the letter is a characteristic one, *viz.*, that there is no moral objection to the use of chloroform, because neglect to take such mediative steps as may avert death is tantamount to suicide, which is a sin.) Eventually Francis pursued his medical career in Brazil, where he died in 1861, of yellow fever.

A dark, a depressingly recognizable thread now emerges from the skein. A letter to Professor Lushington,[2] written in 1845, reveals this thread in a reference to the composition of the *Suspiria de Profundis*. "No man can have descended more profoundly than myself into the consolations of utter solitude, no man can ever have weaned himself more entirely from *dependence* upon sympathy; but, at the same time, perhaps, no man has ever felt it more keenly." This second set of visions and meditations on the past and its relation to the present and future, arose from another (the fourth and last) of those stealthy crescendos of opium-eating to which De Quincey succumbed, between 1840 and '48, in order to escape from the realities of sorrow. 1844 was the bottom of that difficult valley; in that year he reached the high dose (lower, however, than in the worst phases of 1817 and '21) of 5000 drops of laudanum per day.

Once again that awful echo from the past, which he had hoped to have heard for the last time, comes booming out into his life, "and the worm which was beginning to fall asleep is aroused again to pestilential fierceness."[3] By a frantic effort, in June of the same year, he managed to reduce the dose to 150 drops. The result was an agony which could not remain untold:

It is as if ivory carvings and elaborate fretwork and fair enamelling should be found with worms and ashes amongst coffins and the wrecks of some forgotten life or some abolished nature. In parts and fractions eternal creations are carried on, but the nexus is wanting, and life and the central principles which should bind together all the parts at the centre, with all its radiations to the circumference, are wanting. Infinite incoherence, ropes of sand, gloomy incapacity of vital pervasion by some one plastic principle, that is the hideous incubus upon my mind always. For there is no

[1] Printed in Vol. XIV of the Masson Edition.

[2] Japp., 253.

[3] *Posthumous Works*, I, 25.

disorganised wreck so absolute, so perfect, as that which is wrought by misery.[1]

And it lasted for several years. Thus he writes to Miss Mitford in 1846:

No purpose could be answered by my vainly endeavouring to make intelligible for my daughters what I cannot make intelligible for myself—the undecipherable horror that night and day broods over my nervous system. One effect of this is to cause, at uncertain intervals, such whirlwinds of impatience as precipitate me violently, whether I will or not,—into acts that would seem insanities, but are not such in fact, as my understanding is never under any delusion. Whatever I may be writing becomes suddenly overspread with a dark frenzy of horror. I am using words that are, perhaps, tautologic; but it is because no language can give expression to the sudden storm of frightful revelations opening upon me from an eternity not coming, but past and irrevocable. Whatever I may have been writing is suddenly wrapt, as it were, in one sheet of consuming fire—the very paper is poisoned to my eyes. I cannot endure to look at it, and I sweep it away into vast piles of unfinished letters, or inchoate essays begun and interrupted under circumstances the same in kind, though differing unaccountably in degree. I live quite alone in my study, so nobody witnesses these paroxysms. Nor, if they did, would my outward appearance testify to the dreadful transports within.[2]

This remarkable passage, besides opening a chink of light on to De Quincey's daily life at this time, reveals all the old demons back at his side, goading him into storms of reasonless irritation with those he loved, and filling him, as in years gone by, with destructive hatred for what he had written. But, together with the misery, something of that early sense of splendour returned to his haunted brain; so that, in the *Suspiria* which he wrote at this time, we find him reaching out towards a comprehension of new modes of being, of unexplored planes of the spirit:

Pain driven to agony, or grief driven to frenzy, is essential to the ventilation of profound natures. . . . A nature which is profound in excess, but also introverted and abstracted in excess, so as to be in peril of wasting itself in interminable reverie, cannot

[1] Quoted by Japp, 241. [2] Japp, 255.

be awakened sometimes without afflictions that go to the very foundations, heaving, stirring, yet finally harmonizing. . . . [1]

The realities of death, bereavement, and the hardness of the world, had now enriched him with a deeper understanding of life and of the mysterious possibilities that may open out in the spirit under the etherializing experience of pain:

> Turn a screw, tighten a linch-pin . . . and the Infinities appear, before the tranquillity of man unsettles, and the gracious forms of life depart, and the ghostly enters.[2]
>
> In point of awe a fiend would be a poor, trivial *bagatelle* compared to the shadowy projections, *umbras* and *penumbras*, which the unsearchable depths of man's nature is capable, under adequate excitement, of throwing off, and even into stationary forms. There are creative agencies in every part of human nature, of which the thousandth part could never be revealed in one life.[3]

Thus, the old ecstasy was renewed, by this second turn of the screw, and shapes of remembered beauty came flooding back into his mind. Elizabeth, framed in summer and vaguely confused with the figure of Margaret, appeared for a moment at the door of Dove Cottage, only to wave him away with a brief greeting.[4] Then Ann joined them and all three muses, robed as sisters of sorrow—Mater Lachrymarum, Mater Suspiriorum, Mater Tenebrarum—came wandering to the front of the stage, for their final trio.[5]

The first was "she . . . that night and day raves and moans, calling for vanished faces"—of Rachel, of the Innocents. "She, to my knowledge, sat all last summer by the bedside of the blind beggar, him that so often and so gladly I talked with. . . ."

The second "never scales the clouds, nor walks abroad upon the winds. She wears no diadem. And her eyes, if they were ever seen, would be neither sweet nor subtle; no man could read their story; they would be found filled with perishing dreams, and with wrecks of forgotten delirium. . . . This Sister is the visitor of the Pariah, of the Jew, of the bondsman to the oar in the Mediterranean galleys; of the English criminal in Norfolk Island. . . ."

[1] *Posth. Works*, I, 12. [2] *Ibid.*, 25.
[3] *Ibid.*, 9. [4] *Ibid.*, 17. [5] XIII, 365 ff.

The third "is also the youngest. . . . Her head, turretted like that of Cybele, rises almost beyond the reach of sight. . . . She is the defier of God . . . the mother of lunacies, and the suggestress of suicides. Deep lie the roots of her power; but narrow is the nation that she rules. For she can approach only those in whom a profound nature has been upheaved by central convulsions. . . ."

The first sister closes the vision with a strange blessing that is also a curse:

'Lo! here is he whom in childhood I dedicated to my altars. This is he that once I made my darling. Him I led astray, him I beguiled; and from heaven I stole away his young heart to mine. Through me did he become idolatrous; and through me it was, by languishing desires, that he worshipped the worm, and prayed to the wormy grave. Holy was the grave to him; lovely was its darkness; saintly its corruption. Him, this young idolater, I have seasoned for thee, dear gentle Sister of Sighs! Do thou take him now to *thy* heart, and season him for our dreadful sister. And thou,'—turning to the Mater Tenebrarum, she said,—'Wicked sister, that temptest and hatest, do thou take him from *her*. See that thy sceptre lie heavy on his head. Suffer not woman and her tenderness to sit near him in his darkness. Banish the frailties of hope; wither the relenting of love; scorch the fountain of tears; curse him as only thou canst curse. So shall he be accomplished in the furnace; so shall he see the things that ought *not* to be seen, sights that are abominable, and secrets that are unutterable. So shall he read elder truths, sad truths, grand truths, fearful truths. So shall he rise again *before* he dies. And so shall our commission be accomplished which from God we had,—to plague his heart until we had unfolded the capacities of his spirit.' [1]

The last of these sinister intentions was even then in process of being realized; but at what a cost! "This night, Wednesday, December 25,[2] about 7 p.m., has first solemnly revealed itself to me that I have long been under a curse, all the greater for being physically and by effort endurable, and for hiding itself, *i.e.*, playing in and out from all offices of life at every turn of every moment. Oh, dreadful! by degrees infinitely worse than leprosy —than—But oh, what signifies the rhetoric of a case so sad! Conquer it I must by exercise unheard of, or it will conquer me." [3]

[1] XIII, 368. [2] 1844. [3] Japp, 244.

The 'curse', as imaged in the vision of *Levana*, he evidently thought of as something deeper-seated and more irreducible than the mere laudanum on which he was obliged to live; it was a soul-sickness from which he could not hope, at this time of day, entirely to free himself. Melancholia is a habit. But his instinct was right: "exercise unheard of" was the only weapon left to him, and he used it unsparingly, tramping doggedly round and round a "space of forty-four yards in circuit, so that forty rounds were exactly required for one mile, [and] I had within ninety days walked a thousand miles." [1] He suffered from a perpetual feeling of hunger, but at the same time, owing to the weakening of his stomach, found nearly all food impossible to digest. Any change in temperature produced extreme discomfort: "Heat always untunes the harp of my nervous system"; [2] and cold was worse. In later years he told Hogg that he had never been really warm in his life and had at one time been reduced to scrubbing his back with a hairbrush, in order to produce a sensation of warmth.[3]

Dread lest his mind were finally giving way seized upon him, but the sovereign power of his intellect asserted itself again and again, proving itself, in De Quincey's as in so many other cases, man's last and best resource against the forces of disintegration. In the summer of 1847, to make matters worse, he caught a severe fever, while in Glasgow, and a friend,[4] going to his rooms to collect some copy which was late, found him lying on the hearth-rug in a stupor, clad only in dressing-gown and slippers.

But the next year, 1848, saw the end of his agony. It came, as such physical triumphs are apt to do, suddenly and unexpectedly. "*Mem.*—That this day, Thursday, Nov. 23, 1848—being my twenty-fourth day of abstinence—after having descended into utter despair, the 17th. to the 22nd. November having been days of profoundest suffering and utter hopelessness . . . to my utter surprise the misery passed off after breakfast, not fully and consciously until about one or half-past one; so it continued until after cocoa, when for an hour or so a reaction of misery set in, which again passed off; and now, half-past eleven at night, I am almost as well as before cocoa." [5] One is not surprised to read

[1] Japp, 243. [2] Letter to Margaret, June 10th. 1847.
[3] XIV, 275. [4] Colin Rae-Bronw. [5] Japp, 270.

that, for one whose stomach was in that state of weakness, cocoa should have induced a " reaction of misery ". No more unhealthy food-stuff can be imagined; nor can the large quantities of tea and coffee, taken to enable him to work at night, have improved the condition of his nervous system.

The abstention from laudanum, mentioned in the last quotation, was kept up for sixty-one days, after which he found it necessary to return to a moderate use of the drug. But he had had his last relapse, had conquered it, and had attained a balance of peace which proved lasting.

2

It is now time to explain the incidence of Glasgow in De Quincey's life between the years 1841 and '47. During the earlier of these years his only reason for visiting Glasgow would seem to have been the pleasure of seeing his two friends, J. P. Nichol and Professor Lushington, unless the strange passion for multiplying sets of lodgings may be considered a reason; for, after staying with his friends, he moved to a house in the High Street, and then to 79 Renfield Street, posting back constantly to Lasswade in the intervals. On later visits (1846 and '47) he stayed in Rotten Row, but afterwards returned to Renfield Street, because the landlady's son contracted scarlet fever. Yet, ever since a visit in 1843, and all through the Rotten Row period, he continued to pay for the lodgings in Renfield Street!

One of his reasons for this extravagant system of living was a desire to escape from the importunities of friends. Another, more important, was his dislike of throwing anything—books, papers, manuscripts—away, combined with an even more intense objection to having his belongings 'tidied'. In this he did not differ from most men of letters; but few even of them can have collected such literary snow-drifts as De Quincey managed to amass during the last years of his life. When tables, chairs, bed and floor were entirely encumbered, and even the narrow path between the door and the fireplace had become silted up, he would simply lock the door of the room and betake himself to another lodging, there to remain until once more driven on by a similar state of affairs. At his death, no less than six sets of lodgings were found in this condition.

Contact with Nichol, who was Regius Professor of Astronomy at Glasgow University, stimulated De Quincey's lively imagination in the direction of that science. "Dr. Nichol . . . has destroyed—utterly without mercy cut the lovely throat of . . . the Nebular Hypothesis," he wrote to Margaret,[1] in facetious excitement.

But developments in connection with his work, somewhere in 1845 or '6, added importance to these Glasgow visits. *Tait's Magazine*, from which he was now drawing most of his income, fell upon evil days and was bought by the *North British Daily Mail*, a paper which was edited in Glasgow and which eventually absorbed *Tait's* entirely. Its editor was one George Troup, a clever journalist and a Liberal agitator of some ability, but on the whole a reckless, wrong-headed man.[2] De Quincey, however, seems to have liked him and to have appreciated the difficulties through which he and his paper were passing; and though Troup experienced the usual trouble in getting De Quincey to produce his articles in time, relations between the two men remained good.

In 1846 De Quincey's mother died, in the last of her many homes—Weston Lea, near Bath. It was the kind of death which is invariably spoken of as a 'merciful release'—a purposely ambiguous phrase, which could, however, in this case have been given only one construction. His mother's death may have caused De Quincey a fugitive sadness, but he cannot really have regretted it. That she had ever been actuated by a real desire to promote the happiness of her children is beyond question. But a nagging spirit dwelt in her, born of some deep-seated uncertainty. It sought out the weak spots in those she loved, insisted cruelly upon them, and refused to listen to the other side of any question, only giving way when absolutely obliged to do so, and then with a bad grace and gloomy prognostications. Hers was a type of nature with which amicable relations are only possible *at a distance*. This De Quincey had long since discovered and put into practice, so that the separation was now made not much more complete than it had already been for many years. In death Mrs. De Quincey found a kind of absence which made the heart of her son grow fonder of her.

In the late autumn of 1847 De Quincey returned from Glasgow for good. For the last twelve years of his life he divided his time

[1] April 15th. 1846. [2] See Japp, 272 ff.

between Lasswade and 42 Lothian Street, Edinburgh, where the usual chaos of books and papers could be produced without interference from his daughters.

By the end of 1848 he had virtually wound up his connection with *Tait's* and the *North British Daily Mail*, afterwards only contributing an occasional paper to them. Otherwise, with the exception of the *English Mail-Coach* (*Blackwood's*, 1849), the few published articles which De Quincey wrote in the last ten years of his life saw the light in a magazine called *Titan*, or *Hogg's Weekly Instructor*. They are mostly of tertiary interest. In the main, his time and energies, during these last years, were devoted to the revision of his entire literary output for the Collected Edition launched by his new publisher, James Hogg, in 1853.

The list of his works between 1840 and '50 is sufficiently impressive,[1] but it is almost certainly far from complete. De Quincey's inveterate fecklessness in regard to his manuscripts; his multiplication of abodes; hints dropped by other people ("... De Quincey, for aught I know, may have written something for him, as he did write for all sorts of things"); [2] the number of his pieces attributed to each year, which is comparatively small when it is considered that he worked incessantly, at this time, in spite of nerves and ill-health: [3] these considerations leave us with the moral certainty that detached leaves of his later writings are still drifting about the country,[4] either in MS. or indecipherably buried in the unreadable depths of some forgotten periodical. Occasionally such leaves are blown into some shop, some library, some sale or other; but those I have come across have not, I must admit, been very rewarding,—in fact, they have convinced me that, in default of some immense 'find'—say, in an attic in Edinburgh—the best of De Quincey lies before us in the pages of the Masson edition. Whatever remains to be discovered may well contain sentences, even paragraphs, of characteristic rhetorical subtlety, of filigree argumentation, that recall unmistakably the unique personality of their author; but I should be much surprised if they revealed any important development, hitherto unsuspected, either of his art or of his intellect.

[1] See XIV, 379–81.
[2] J. P. Nichol, in Japp, 237.
[3] See also p. 287, note 1.
[4] It became his habit, as he grew older, to leave boxes and packets of MS. with waiters and shopkeepers, "to be called for later", and then to forget them entirely.

3

What Henry James calls "the glamour of reduced gentility and fallen fortunes" hangs over De Quincey in these last years. But the effect is not, as it so easily might be, one of squalor or of sordidness: his astonishing vitality of soul prevented him from ever losing heart altogether—from allowing a mere slovenly hebetude to describe the remainder of his days. Quite alone in the world, he might have been unable to resist the temptation just to fade quietly away into death, before it was time; but the love which united him to his daughters—the inspiriting tension created between his efforts to help himself and their efforts to help him—effectively lifts the spectacle of his later fortunes (as of his earlier) out of the merely dismal. Essentially and finally a lonely man, a soul whose solitary experiences of the terrible and the sublime had placed it to the *side* of (not necessarily *above*) that of other men, thus rendering the ordinary systems of communication impassibly difficult, De Quincey inevitably fell back, when friends had either died or failed him, on the kind of sightless, unified affection which only his children could give and receive.

In the latter connection it is noticeable that his attitude to women in general had undergone a change. The gradual experience of his daughters' practical efficiency no doubt inspired a passage which he wrote at this time stigmatizing the viciousness of viewing women as dolls—"the ladies", "my dear", and so on.[1] The false romantic outlook which had inspired his early passion for Miss Blake, here received its death-blow; woman was now seen to be something more than "nobly planned, to warn, to comfort and command."

How completely De Quincey became wrapped up in his daughters, in these last years, is best gauged by his correspondence. I referred just now to the "fussy reiteration" with which he wrote to them, even when only separated from them by the distance between Glasgow or Lothian Street and Lasswade. Readers may think this an unkind way of describing such a correspondence. But a glance at the letters themselves (I do not propose to quote any of them in full) will make my meaning clear. They are for the most part enormously long and in them De Quincey divagates after the fashion that lessens the value of so many of his essays. As

[1] *Posth. Works*, I, 203.

he himself confesses, after spending some 640 words on the description of the sheet of paper (an abnormally large one) on which he is writing—"O my dear Florence, I rattle in order to beguile my deadly nervousness"; [1] and the majority of the letters which he wrote to his daughters in these years could be described as "rattle", in which, however, a certain amount of information and criticism of current events and books are embedded. Sometimes the rattle is almost unadulterated, as in the following example:

MY DEAR EMILY,—I forward to you Mr Prof. Alexander's note to myself from the Coburg Hotel, in that tip-top quarter of London West, Charles Street, Grosvenor Square.

I shall write *to-morn's morn* to our new friend the Coburg—a theatre of that name I once knew, but never yet a hotel. Indeed I knew the theatre only too well—viz., by living in too close neighbourhood to its savage nightly uproars, and especially in those days to the midnight explosion of the Kremlin.

To return, however, from the Kremlin to the note of *to-morn's morn*, I shall say to Mr Alexander, that according to your original plan, if not miscalculated by me, your return to Lasswade would at any rate fall upon the longest day (June 21, 22) or thereabouts. To-morrow completes the first *ephthemeron*, or series of seven days in June. Now, in twenty-one days there is a first, a second, a third such phenomenon. One is gone, and pretty nearly irrevocable. A second would reasonably be consumed in exchanging kisses, summoning the washerwoman, and paying our 'little accounts'. So that the total controversy—— [2]

But if I continue this quotation any longer, 'the book will fall from the reader's nerveless fingers.' After making full allowance for the fact that, in the middle of the nineteenth century, people communicated with each other in a more leisurely manner than they do nowadays, there still remains the question of content, of communication. Few people, women not excepted, have explored the possibilities of pure verbosity to the extent to which De Quincey explores it, in these letters, so that even on those occasions when some definite arrangement was in question, it must have been difficult for Florence—or Emily or Margaret—to decipher exactly what it was their father wanted done. The sensation, in reading one of these passages (whether in the letters or in the essays), is one of suffocation: the reader feels that he cannot draw breath until

[1] Japp, 284 ff. [2] June 6th. 1858 (Japp, 289).

he has reached the point, which eludes him again and again, leading him down a series of false vistas, until at last he sinks down, bewildered and disappointed. Much of this discursiveness must be put down to the fact that De Quincey admittedly wrote these letters in bits, sometimes keeping half—or a quarter—or even wholly finished letters for days at a time before deciding to finish and send them off.

Actual facts, when they occur in the letters, are always of interest. In 1847 De Quincey sent his daughters to the south of England to visit their aunt Jane, and in Bath they made the acquaintance of Walter Savage Landor, who had, as it happened, just sent De Quincey a copy of his Latin poems, a present which had much gratified him.[1] Florence afterwards reported that Landor had admired her aunt's garden, but that, when the latter said that certain trees had looked better before they were lopped, he replied: "Ah! I would not lop a tree; if I had to cut a branch I would cut it down to the ground. If I needed to have my finger cut off, I would cut off my whole arm "[2]—an extravagant absurdity not uncharacteristic of Landor, whose 'atticising' was rigidly confined to his writings and never found its way into his life.

As years went on, the letters became ever wilder, more discursive, less consecutive. There are long discussions of the guilt of Palmer, the poisoner;[3] an account of De Quincey's new friends the Wilsons, and of how Miss Wilson had one day hurried upstairs and burst a blood-vessel in the middle of the drawing-room. This leads to a comparison with Lady Hester Stanhope, "that most odious of Pagan women", and the occasion when she had vomited blood.[4]

Fluttering the leaves back a little, one lights on the following and pauses for a smile:

Friday, February 9, 1855.

My dear Florence,—I heard with great concern from Ellen on (was it not?) Friday evening last—i.e., this day week—of your toothache sufferings. Every day I have been on the point of writing to you about the remedy; and I reproach myself heavily for having suffered my own miserable want of energy to interfere

[1] Letter to Margaret, September 8th, 1847.
[2] Japp, 283. [3] June 9th, 1856.
[4] Letter to Emily, November 6th. 1856.

with the *instant* suggestion of so much practical counsel as my own bitter experience enables me to offer. This counsel divides into three sections—A, B, C. A relates to the *cause* of toothache. I pass to B and C. B indicates what relates to *clothing*. Warm coverings for the feet (lamb's wool fleecy hosiery, etc.), and above all, for the chest and shoulders, are indispensable. . . . Have you and Emily muffs and fur tippets? C stands for diet——

And so on, with long paragraphs of curious, remote pedantry, which seems to deprive the advice of all practical application.

On another occasion,[1] it is the doctrine of Immortality which is thoroughly thrashed out for Margaret's benefit, with special reference to Plato's and Wordsworth's contributions to the subject, concluding with a summing-up after De Quincey's own scholastic heart ("A, B, and C" again.)[2] Or it is the wordy solution of a puzzle in the *Domitian* of Suetonius (also for Margaret's benefit), which debouches into an account of an evening party he had been to and of the appearance he presented—" a scarlet coat—no, by the way, it was brown; salmon-coloured trousers—no, on consideration, they were grey; buff waistcoat; a beard of six months' growth, which has won so general an approbation that I am shy of mowing it."[3]

But the most interesting and curious of these letters is that which recounts a dream he had in January, 1855.[4] It is worth while to give this in De Quincey's own words:

This morning, being Sunday . . . the hour (I should guess) 6 a.m., I had a dream, which dream was this. A door opened; it was a door on the *further* side of a spacious chamber. For a few moments, I waited expectingly, but not knowing *what* to expect. At length a voice said audibly and most distinctly, but not loudly, *Florence and Emily*, with the tone of one announcing an arrival. Soon after, but not immediately, entered Florence, but, to my great astonishment, no Emily. Florence wore a dress not as if coming off a journey, at least not a travelling dress, but a simple

[1] Letter to Margaret, November 1856.

[2] Compare the following passage, from the *Spanish Military Nun*: "For that scissors were bad, though Kate does not say so in her memoirs, I know by *a priori* argument, viz.: because *all* scissors were bad in that year 1607. Now, say all decent logicians, from a universal to a particular *valet consequentia*, the right of inference is good. *All* scissors were bad, *ergo some* scissors were bad." (XIII, 166.)

[3] Japp, 406.

[4] *Ibid.*, 370.

walking dress. . . . The prevailing hue . . . was white. Florence did not look back; and how she accounted for Emily's not following is best known to herself. A shadow fell upon me, and a feeling of sadness, which increased continually as no Emily entered the door, which, however, still stood open. . . . But it relieved my feeling of sadness that Florence, of whose features I had the steadiest view, seemed cheerful, though not smiling. I felt it strange that I could not question her, notwithstanding that she was obliquely nearing my position. If I could catch her eye I felt that I could speak to her—not else; and this I could not do. What Florence was making for must have been a garden, still, solitary, and rich to excess with flowers past all counting, and gayer than any I had ever seen. The garden was on my right hand; the positions, in fact, were these—

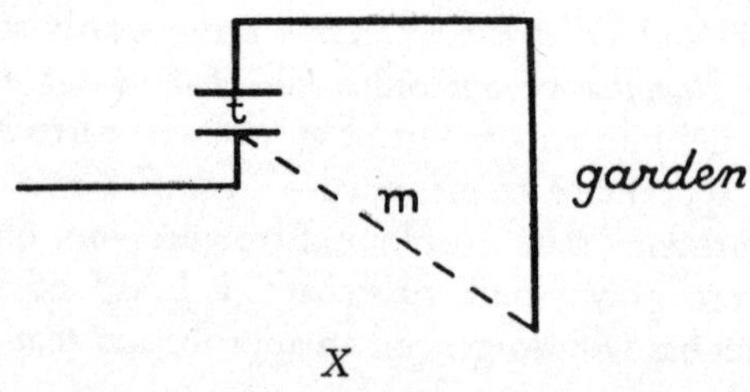

t is the door of entrance; *m* is Florence; *X* is myself in an unphilosophic mood of irritation, and, I fear, likely soon to become waspish if I should not succeed in arresting Florence's eye. However, I did *not* succeed; neither did Emily come so long as I staid, which might be six to eight minutes. Suddenly all vanished . . . and I was broad awake . . . I should mention . . . that although Florence continually advanced in the sense of widening her distance from the entrance door, nevertheless she never came nearer to me, for the chamber floor expanded concurrently with her steps. . . . The garden, I should add, *melted* into the chamber, through steps of transition that were indescribable.

The origins of this dream are buried too deep for it to be possible or profitable to attempt to fish them up. The appearance and behaviour of Florence are not especially remarkable: anxiety on behalf of her health, which De Quincey had already expressed, on another occasion,[1] are sufficient to account for the symbolism of her actions. But the dreamer's consciousness of Emily's non-appear-

[1] See p. 268.

ance is interesting, and the sadness associated with it, a sadness which links up with other female figures of his past life—Elizabeth, Ann, his wife—who, each in her different way, had caused him grief through some aspect of absence.

It is possible, too, that he may have been labouring under some general sense of desertion, for Margaret had married, two years previously, and Florence was just about to do so. The former had already departed to Ireland with her husband, a Mr. Craig. Miss Mitford described the marriage, in her prim way, as "a venture; but a genial young couple may, I think, find and make friends among the Irish." [1] Mr. and Mrs. Craig appear to have found no difficulty in achieving this modest ambition. There is no reason to suppose, moreover, that De Quincey regarded the marriage in the same qualified light. That of Florence may have caused him a greater sadness, for his prospective son-in-law, Colonel Baird-Smith, of the Engineers, was stationed in India, and De Quincey must have doubted whether, at his age (he was now in his seventieth year) and in his enfeebled state, he would live to see her again. He did not, in fact, do so.

His passion for children now became stronger than ever, recalling, in its union of mystic nostalgia, naïveté, and sentimentalism, the very similar attitude of another great figure of the nineteenth century—the composer Gustav Mahler, whose exquisite *Kindertotenlieder* are the *ne plus ultra* of the cult of childhood. De Quincey would walk round and round his tiny garden, day after day, with the four-year-old son of one of the maids, just for the pleasure of talking to him. Indeed, any and every child would do, as long as it was prepared to be a patient listener to the old man's endless, whispered rigmaroles, composed, one supposes, of a characteristic mixture of fairy-tales, odd bits of information, and moral disquisitions. It mattered little whether the child took in what he said or not: in his essential loneliness all he desired was someone to whom he could talk and who would accept unquestioningly the subtle fantasies of his restless brain. So that when, a year after her marriage, Margaret Craig gave birth to a daughter, De Quincey's delight was unbounded. He was glad that the child was a girl: boys, he said, were a nuisance. The question of its name provided the excuse for three of his longest and most elaborately discursive

[1] Japp, 309.

letters.[1] It is fascinating, and at the same time pathetic, this outpouring of tattered memories, of fussy distinctions and comparisons, as from an old drawer which its owner has never had time or leisure properly to sort out:

First of all, concerning what is just now first in importance, viz., dear little Eva. Glad I am that she has gotten herself a name, for really it is an awkward case, when giving the health at a dinner-party of a little lady, as one's own sole representative in the next generation but one, the advanced *vedette* on the frontier of posterity, plainly to confess that she is anonymous, and also a Pagan, or at least that the Pagan question is for her still an open question. *Any* name therefore was beginning to be an advantage. As to the particular name chosen, it is to my feeling a very pretty one. Two novels at the least have been written by men of high pretensions bearing this name for their sole title; one by Sir Edward Lytton, which perhaps I have not read, but certainly do not remember,—the other by a man whom I think of with even more respect, viz., Maturin. It was not, however, by any means among Maturin's better works. Still, being Maturin's, it could not be otherwise than interesting. Maturin's 'Eva', if I remember the story at all, is the subject of an odious persecution from some hyperbolical feather-bed of a *soi-disant* lover, who does not improve his position, or at all win upon the sulky reader, by being also a dissenting parson. His reasons for dissenting I do not know, but the reader's reasons are undeniable—'*first chop*'—for dissenting from the Rev. Featherbed; and, unfortunately for *him*, Eva's dissenting principles are equally strong; but then, unfortunately for *her*, the odious and reverend lover draws some iniquitous support from a dissenting aunt. The issue, I fear, is tragical. The true lover, he whom Eva and the reader countenance, is non-suited. Such, at least, is my fear. And it is a proof of Maturin's power that now, at this moment, though left behind me for thirty years, the tale and very name of Eva are nevertheless set and steeped in some indistinct haze of sorrowful impressions, whilst my separate remembrances of the fable are no more than what I have related. Simply through the power of Maturin, who was verily and indeed a man of genius, the name of *Eva* had shaped itself to my symbolising fancy in the shape of a white rose—overcharged (I do not say *surcharged* as suggesting odious thoughts of income-tax) with rain or heavy dews—dimly descried in a solitary garden through the very dimmest

[1] Japp, 361 ff.

twilight of earliest dawn upon a morning of June. Is this too much for a conscientious man to pack up into that one little triliteral name of *Eva*.

Much too much, Emily, to whom the letter was addressed, may well have thought—particularly as her father then proceeded, for another page and a half, to review the Miltonic significance of the name.

Yet, if a long breath is taken, previous to embarking on these later letters of De Quincey, it is possible to enjoy them, in the same way and for the same reasons that one cannot help being carried away by the high spirits of the article on Sir William Hamilton.[1] The sheer fantasy, the tone of the writer's voice—precise, clear, silvery, with a perpetual undertone of amusement at its own pedantry—bring the hands together in instinctive applause, at the end of each enormous paragraph. The allusive richness is preposterous, but it is of the type which afterwards made the stylistic fortune of George Meredith.

The years 1854 and '55 close the list of De Quincey's dead. In the former Wilson died. This was a considerable blow to De Quincey, for, to the very end, Wilson was one of the few people who had the power of rousing his spirits, when they became depressed. Apart from this, the last years of Wilson's life (after his wife's death in 1837) present a somewhat sad and dishevelled spectacle. Keeping up intellectual appearances told on him in the long run, especially when his iron health began to give way. Although now considerably tamer than he had been as a young man, his manner retained some of its Berserk qualities to the last. He would, for instance, pour out tea without tilting back the pot between the cups, so that a continuous stream ran all over the saucers and tray.[2] In 1851 ill-health had obliged him to retire from his position in the university, but with a pension of £300, granted him by the Queen. De Quincey, perhaps feeling that his own pretensions to such a grant were in reality greater than Wilson's, expressed indignation at the amount of the pension.[3] But this resentment cannot have survived the death of his old friend, whose wild spirits and enthusiastic personality had inspired him again and

[1] Analysed on p. 244.
[2] Nathaniel P. Willis, *Pencillings by the Way*, p. 395.
[3] Swann, *op. cit.*, 222.

again with the sheer lust of living and revealed to him the joys of intimate friendship, in those far-off days at Grasmere.

A last echo, extremely faint, of his friendship with the Wordsworths came to De Quincey in the news of Dorothy's death, on January 25th. 1855. Seven years previously, he had written a letter of introduction to Wordsworth for a young Greek called Neocles Jaspis Mousabines.[1] It is a stiff letter, though it ends " your faithful friend and servant " ; it expresses what was necessary to the occasion, and no more. That chapter was closed for ever. And so, when Dorothy died, De Quincey, if he felt any emotion, at all events did not reveal it. He records the mere fact in a letter to Florence,[2] quite without comment, but adds that he is " sincerely grieved " to read of the death of Miss Mitford.

This lack of comment is quite natural. At the age which De Quincey had now reached, the friends of youth, if they are not present, grow dim in the mind, and the thought of them, if it occurs, is apt to create sadness rather than pleasure, as recalling irrecoverable emotions. Recently acquired friends, who trail no cloaks of sorrow or regret, are thus often the most acceptable to old people, and the most regretted when they die or disappear.

4

Japp's assertion that " the last ten years embrace a period of quiet and steady activity " [3] is rather misleading. De Quincey's activity during this period was as steady as his health and habits would allow it to be, but it was certainly not quiet—if by 'quiet' is meant freedom from nervous exhaustion, an amount of work suited to his capacity, and the sort of tranquillity conferred by the easy sense of a well-spent life. In this sense, De Quincey's activity was never quiet. For one thing, his health, though free from the taut agonies of the opium crises, continued to give him every kind of trouble. In 1852 he complained of suffering continually from a stagnation of blood in the legs, resulting in a torpor so great that he was unable to hold a pen, while the sensation was accompanied by a " frightful recurrence of long-ago imagery and veriest trifles of the past." [4]

[1] Japp, 268.
[2] February 15th. 1855.
[3] Japp, 277.
[4] Japp. 298.

It was no doubt this terrible state of tension between desire and ability to execute which produced the following outburst at a mention of Wordsworth: "Heavens! had I but ever had his robust strength, and healthy stomach, and sound nerves, with the same glorious freedom from all interruptions and embarrassments! . . . But, in point of fact, never have I written but against time, pressed by overbearing anxieties, and latterly more especially pressed down by physical suffering."[1] The exaggeration in the first sentence is pardonable, when one compares the fate of the two men, throughout their lives.

He had attacks of lumbago and his eyes began to weaken; but he refused obstinately to wear spectacles and read habitually with one eye shut. That his state of health caused him acute worry emerges from the fact that once, when staying with a friend in Edinburgh and finding a lot of old medicine bottles in his room, with nothing in them but dregs, he drank them all, in the hope that one of them might do him good.

What seems to have done him most good, both late and early in the history of his attenuated martyrdom, was walking; and it was in this connection that there now occurred an incident most amusingly characteristic of his type of sensibility. It so happened that some labourers came to repair the road in the neighbourhood of Lasswade, on which De Quincey was accustomed to take his daily constitutional, up and down, up and down. The first men he passed called greetings to him and enquiries concerning the weather, which he answered as best he could. But after a time these exchanges became embarrassing to him, and he began seriously to worry over the propriety of answering questions on a subject of which he knew as little as they. He thought, at first, of buying a set of weather-calendars and presenting them to the men, but rejected the idea and attempted to carry on as usual, returning their friendliness to the best of his ability. But in the end he found that these conversations took up so much time that his walks were seriously curtailed, and he was therefore obliged to return with a sigh to the more circumscribed, but more private, space of his own garden.[2]

[1] Japp, 298, See also the reference, in the quotation on p. 271, to "inchoate essays begun and interrupted", which indicates a large mass of fragmentary matter.

[2] Japp, 335.

This story introduces, by an obvious link, the question of bores, which had not on the whole played much part in De Quincey's life up to the present time. But in the last ten years he was a firmly established celebrity and people of all sorts made the pilgrimage to Lasswade in order to catch a glimpse of him. His extreme courtesy obliged him to suffer bores with an appearance of gladness, but the novelist James Payn, who made his acquaintance at this time, perceived that he was acutely sensitive to them. "The association of commonplace people and their pointless observations were in fact intolerable to him. They did not bore him in the ordinary sense, but seemed, as it were, to outrage his mind." [1]

This fine distinction was suggested to Payn by a story which De Quincey told him, of his encounter with an old lady on a pier, at Tarbet, on Loch Lomond. "I felt," said De Quincey, "that she would presently address me; and she did. Pointing to the smoke of the steamer which was making itself seen above the next headland, 'There she comes,' she said. 'La, sir! if you and I had seen that fifty years ago, how wonderful we should have thought it!' Now the same sort of thing," added De Quincey, with a shiver, "might happen to me any day, and that is why I always avoid a public conveyance."

Visitors from America began to turn up, especially after the American edition of his works had been set going. Among these was Emerson, whom De Quincey admired but whose accent pained him. He complained a great deal of the nuisance and interruption which all these visitors caused him, but added that he felt obliged to let them in, since his daughters had no other amusement. No doubt those ladies wisely allowed him to think this, but will themselves have felt that the occasional society of strangers was as good for their father as it was for them.

But, whatever De Quincey himself might feel, the visitors can scarcely have regretted their trouble; for his conversation was as wonderful as ever, and his appearance sufficiently extraordinary to be worth beholding for its own sake. Time had been impotent to alter the beautiful shape of the head; but the lines of the face, which still shone delicately, as if lit from within, had become pinched and sunken, drawn by the asceticism of long suffering. The mouth, which had pouted so romantically in youth, had now

[1] *Some Literary Recollections*, p. 58.

lost its teeth, so that the upper lip all but disappeared and the lower projected like a little shelf. The steep cliff of the forehead was now deeply eroded; but below, the eyes, blue as childhood itself and of a fathomless imploring sadness, proclaimed the immutable innocence of his character. He seems, at one time, to have worn a beard, because shaving bored him and he could not stand the smell of a barber's fingers; but this phase did not last long and all the later portraits show him clean-shaven, except for slight downy whiskers.

He wore list shoes for preference, and the clothes which hung loosely on his tiny, child's body, as on a scarecrow, were very strange indeed. He had never taken the smallest care of his appearance and now, in old age, he obstinately refused to allow anyone to improve his inveterate untidiness. He bought his clothes, very much as he wrote his letters, in bits—never a whole suit at a time; and the ill-assorted, rag-and-bone-man appearance of the whole was so complete that, on one occasion, when he was visiting a friend, a child of the house, after gazing at him for some time in silence, suggested that he should "get a penny and go home".[1] If an idea came to him in the midst of dressing he would sit down to work without a coat, or minus one stocking; and if someone came to visit him, he would receive them like that.

Such, then, was the comic, pathetic figure which, perched on the edge of a chair, with a cup of tea in one hand and a small glass of laudanum in the other, could still make his visitors forget the comicality and the pathos by unfurling the silver-thread tapestry of his talk. There would be long, dreamy pauses, during which his heavy eyelids would sink slowly over his eyes, giving to his face an expressionless look, as of death. And then his eyes would open, and he would make a queer gesture with his arm, as if pulling out an organ-stop, and immediately the elaborate period would come murmuring and whispering out into the room, as if he were talking to a ghost, with the prim little emphases on certain words, which find their parallel in the italics of his written style. No question was too slight, no subject too trivial, to receive the garment of his extraordinary poetry. Thus, when Findlay feared a change in the weather: "Yes", said De Quincey, "but it will be

[1] Woodhouse, in Hogg, 252.

gradual. All the great operations of nature are slow, and the grand dome of fine weather which has hung over us for weeks is not to be lightly or suddenly broken up." [1]

Most of his writing was done at night, on repeated cups of tea and coffee. He went to bed in the early hours of the morning, rose at midday and spent the hours of daylight wandering about. In 1855 he was still walking seven miles a day—" not much, certainly, but as much as I can find spirits for." If unable to walk in the daytime, he would do so at night, as in his youth at Grasmere. In the evening, the whole family—or as much of it as remained—would gather round and De Quincey would give a digest of the day's newspaper, instead of reading it aloud; and this performance would be illustrated by lights of memory and old stories culled from his past life, and by the restless enquiry of his busy spirit. For, up to the very end, he never ceased to entertain projects for future work. He spoke to Francis Jacox of a history of England, which was planned to reach from the earliest times down to the point at which Macaulay's work begins; of an historical novel, which was to recount the fortunes of two prisoners in Austria during the reign of Maria Theresa; and of a work, begun but not finished, on the Human Intellect.

Mrs. Baird-Smith has made plain how fascinating and lovable a companion her father was, in these last ten years. Yet his habits were too irretrievably eccentric to permit of life in his immediate proximity being at all easy. I have already insisted sufficiently on his sciurine hoarding of books and papers; this must have made the house-work at Lasswade an arduous business, particularly as De Quincey, who was a born Bohemian and had no sense of appropriateness of use, even filled a bath, which had been temporarily left in his study, to the brim with manuscripts.[2] Then he was always setting things, including himself, on fire, by sheer inadvertence. Such incidents were so common, that it was quite casually that his daughter would look up and say: " Papa, your hair is on fire." But he did not look up himself. " Is it, my love? " he would say, vaguely, rubbing his head as he continued to read. But if it were papers to which he had set fire, he showed more

[1] J. R. Findlay, *Recollections*, p. 45.

[2] He used this bath as a kind of bran-pie, out of which to pick articles at random, when editors asked for them. (See *Sortilege and Astrology*, XIII, 251.)

concern, absolutely refusing to allow water to be thrown upon them, for fear of spoiling them; and often he would lock the door and extinguish the blaze himself, with a rug, in case he should be disobeyed. Nevertheless, a good many manuscripts perished in this way, including some of the opium dreams which were to have been included in the enlarged edition of the *Confessions*.[1]

As he grew older, music became more and more of a necessity to him. Though the expeditions tired him, he never missed an opportunity of hearing a good concert in Edinburgh; and at home Florence and Emily would sing to him, from the operas of Bellini. Listening, his mind would recur to those days in London, thirty and forty years ago, when he had sat in the gallery of the opera-house, on Saturday nights, his intellect and senses clear and alight with opium, and applauded Grassini and the music of Cimarosa, Cherubini and Mozart—his favourites to the end. Of later music, he seems only to have got pleasure from Beethoven; the single more recent composer whom he mentions is Mendelssohn, some of whose music he heard in 1846, at a performance of the *Antigone* of Sophocles. His verdict was unfavourable,[2] though he thought Mendelssohn on the whole a great composer. Like all truly musical people, he hated the sound of bagpipes.[3] To him the supreme instrument was the violin: "There is an *infinity* about the violin," he said to Hogg.

5

The gradual issue, during the 'fifties, of the American edition of his 'complete' works, by Messrs. Ticknor and Fields, of Boston, not only gave De Quincey great satisfaction, but caused his Edinburgh editor, James Hogg, to broach the subject of an English edition, to be conducted on the same lines as the American, but with the enormous advantage of being revised and corrected by De Quincey himself—a task which, so he had told Mr. Fields, his health precluded him from undertaking.

Hogg made De Quincey's acquaintance either late in 1849 or early in 1850,[4] and he seems quickly to have discerned exactly

[1] See III, 222. [2] X, 383. [3] Letter to Emily, May 1855.
[4] In Japp's book Hogg gives the earlier, in his own volume the later, date.

what difficulties he would have to deal with, if his project was to be carried out with any semblance of success. He was to prove, in fact, the kindest and most long-suffering of all De Quincey's editors. In order not to alarm the old man, he proposed at first to issue only a small number of volumes, to be entitled *Selections Grave and Gay*, and, though he worked at his task of revision for six years, De Quincey would seem never to have envisaged the possibility of a complete edition, since, when Taylor and Hessey claimed the copyright of the *London Magazine* articles, he would not have bothered to dispute the point, had Hogg not insisted on his doing so.

The manner in which De Quincey carried out his work of revision was worthy of a mediæval lunatic asylum. He was both dilatory and fussily conscientious over the correcting of proofs, writing ridiculously learned notes to the printers explaining his corrections, and making confusion worse confounded by writing his additions and notes on margins torn out of books, so that the printers frequently printed, not only what he had written, but whole sentences from the mutilated books themselves. In the monumental chaos of 42 Lothian Street he could never find any given article, when he happened to want it, and wasted further time in writing to Hogg to explain the delay. It says a great deal for the latter's character that he never lost patience, nor burst out in irritation when De Quincey held everything up to explain some new and utterly impracticable idea he had just had, for the scheme of the edition. Hogg kept his temper admirably, for six years, and on the whole his patience was rewarded.

Wrapt in an old military cloak lined with red, which his landlady, Miss Jean Stark, had bought for him, with tea and laudanum within reach, the harassed little old man would sit, hour after hour, surrounded by indescribable confusion, like a mouse in a blizzard—writing frantically on the extreme edge of the table, correcting, erasing, adding; substituting one word for another, then impatiently crossing out the substitute and replacing the original word, only to cross that out and replace the substitute once more; appending endless footnotes, and footnotes on footnotes; being interrupted repeatedly by the boy Roderick, the printer's devil, and interrupting himself quite as frequently to indite long, plaintive letters to Hogg: [1]

[1] Japp, 347, 350, 351.

MY DEAR SIR,—I am exceedingly sorry for the trouble I cause; and moreover I become painfully conscious that the article may not prove such as to justify being stayed for. But if it is stayed for the rest will certainly be ready by 10 a.m. to-morrow. . . . Being so overmastered as I find myself by nervousness, perhaps it will be better that I send myself to the press—to save loss of time to the press runner. I am at present greatly dependent on Tea; and as soon as I have had *that*, I hope to be a new creature.

It disturbs me to find that I have been constantly working at the wrong part. My notion was—an erroneous notion, it seems—that, when at any point I could not satisfy myself in the expression of a thought, then it was open to me to go forward, leaving a chasm to be filled up afterwards when it became necessary to make up the text into sheets. . . .

I am suddenly thrown into despair. All the Parr proofs . . . would have been by this time burned, but for the accident that some arrear of queries arose upon them. Hence, *not* burned; but so chaotically confounded with all other papers, that (if the press finds them indispensable) I must spend this night in searching for them. I have already found two packets, but discontinuous.

. . . working through most parts of the night, I have not yet come to the missing copy. I fancied that when the press sent for the notes, this implied that the whole of the text was received. But as it turns out that I was mistaken, I am going on with the search yet,—being walled in by superfluous furniture, in so narrow an area (not larger than a post-chaise, as regards the free space), I write with difficulty, and the *stooping* kills me.

The following is a typical programme of his day, at this time:

3.35 a.m. Awakes.
3.45–7.30 In great physical distress, not daring to stoop or stretch out his arm.
7.30 Breakfast.
8.0 Newspapers arrive, which irritate him, but which he reads carefully.
8.30 The post ('a letter from Tipperary that would require three laborious days for a commensurate answer.').
9.12 Writes and corrects.
12 Dinner.
12.12–3.10 Bothered by strangers.
3.10 Johnny comes for the proofs.
4.0 Still finishing the latter, when he falls asleep till 7.15—

—to be awoken by Miss Stark, who finds that he has fallen forward over the table and in so doing has upset the candle and burnt his clothes.[1]

No wonder that, by 1856, he was complaining that he was "somewhat weary of Lothian Street"! Not that Lasswade was not always there to provide a change; but even so, De Quincey's awkwardness in practical matters made communication between the two houses, whether by letter or in person, very wearisome. "It is easier for me," he explained, "to write a letter from Edinburgh to Astrachan, than from Lasswade to Edinburgh. In the former case you point a gun levelled directly at the object; but in the latter you shoot round a corner. . . . Such a labourer gives the letter to such a farmer. . . ."[2] And if it was a question of his spending some time at Lasswade, he would perform the journey to and fro on foot, returning at night with a little lantern, which invariably went out just as he came to the foot-bridge over the Esk.

Money was easier in these days. In spite of some small worries connected with taxation[3] and with the lease of Mavis Bush, De Quincey had said farewell for ever to financial embarrassment—rather late in the day, it may be thought. Yet he was far from insensible to the relief; in 1852, according to Miss Mitford,[4] he was filled with delight and surprise at receiving a cheque from Mr. Fields, for part of the proceeds of the American edition; and in 1857 he wrote to Hogg[5] to express thankful acceptance of the terms, "so exceedingly liberal", which the publisher had proposed for the absolute purchase of the *Selections Grave and Gay*.

6

Any view over De Quincey's character, as seen from this late point of vantage, must needs be dominated by a tall, four-branched tree, representing the four opium crises which he managed to overcome in the course of his long life. Through the dark and sinister tracery of these branches appear, doubtless, in the middle distance, not a few houses of the soul inhabited by incidents and characteristics which detract from the general impression of greatness. The very presence of the tree may in itself appear to some a

[1] Japp, 357. [2] Letter to Miss Agnes Duncan, March 5th. 1855.
[3] See letter in Japp, 342. [4] Japp, 309. [5] Japp, 352.

final symbol of condemnation. But, if the magnitude of the human soul be judged, not from a general aspect of fortunate brilliance, in which the inner and the outer worlds have chanced to coincide, to the enhancement of the individual effect, but rather by the power of the disabilities to which it has risen superior, then De Quincey's claim to greatness rests upon a secure foundation, quite apart from his achievement as a writer. Here, once more, emphasis must be laid upon the fact of his essential solitude, throughout life. The man who wrestles with terrors and weaknesses which lie hidden in the secret places of his soul, and *which are fundamentally incommunicable*, must rely upon himself alone. It is this truth which constitutes the 'figure' in all his imaginative writings—the "burden of the Incommunicable",[1] of the deeply cut lettering on the black wall which rises at the last limits of possible despair.

In spite, then, of friends, wife, children, De Quincey's life was essentially that of one who is vowed to the mortification of the flesh—of a monk, in fact. That he did not *intend* to give his life this direction, is nothing to the purpose: some lives have directions given to them, and then the light of final judgment plays exclusively round the integrity with which the performer conceives his part. It is this absolute integrity which makes of De Quincey so original, so sympathetic a figure. As I implied above, he demands to be judged by the Christian—not by the Greek—standard (he made it sufficiently clear, in his writings, which standard he believed in). Life was not conceived by him as a spectacle, a tragic drama, the value of which should consist in the symbolic grandeur of the heroism involved; it was of the Christian variety, which has ulterior motives. These motives, which require no enumeration here, were of paramount importance to De Quincey, and I think there can be no doubt that it was they which saved him from shipwreck. The spectacular ethic, which was not without its advocates in the days of his youth, when the romantic movement was in full swing, would quite certainly have let him down, as it has let down so many in our own day, whose pursuit of an artificial paradise has lacked the support of a belief in a mediate reality. De Quincey's unshakable and unreasoning reliance on the truth of the Christian ultimate, automatically freed him from the modern drug-taker's fatal attempt to achieve a reality which shall be *immediate*—fatal,

[1] III, 315.

because the minimum of experience teaches him that such an ultimate is in fact a contradiction in terms.

Thus despair, though it sometimes held him for long, could not hold him for ever, because, unlike most drug-takers, he believed in a reality outside himself, which was worthy of his efforts. And what efforts! For the victim of opium, in those days, there were no nursing-homes, no doctors experienced in the malady, no carefully worked out systems of disintoxication, with anodynes that spare the patient the very worst agonies:—there was nothing but the victim's unaided will. Four times, imprisoned in the haunted ruin of himself, De Quincey underwent the appalling ordeal, and not in vain. "Oh, what do you see, dear? What is it that you see?" I think it is no injustice to Margaret de Quincey to suggest that even her devotion, strained though it was to the limits of endurance, can have done little but touch the uppermost layer of his agony. And at two of these crises—the first and the last—she did not assist. Then his solitude was supreme, then it was complete.

In 1823 he could write that his life showed a surplus of happiness. Would he have been prepared to repeat this remark in 1853? I think so; and that is why his story, unless I have failed to tell it aright, should not leave an impression of final sadness on the reader. For the toughness of soul, the hold on life, the intense interest and curiosity, which enabled him, in spite of sorrow, poverty and pain, to live and work almost incessantly up to the age of seventy-four, are not qualities which lead their possessor to judge his life amiss. It will not have occurred to him, even at this stage, to say: Was this or that worth while? He accepted his life as a whole, with the absolute minimum of complaint which his standard of personal dignity permitted him; and when he knew that he must soon die, the knowledge came unaccompanied by fear. "I shall grieve to die, but not fear it," he had written to Hessey, somewhere about 1821;[1] and the words express exactly the attitude in which death eventually found him.

His Christian stoicism served him well to the last; but it is insufficient to account for his inexhaustible fund of spiritual vitality. A stupider man might have shown a like amount of courage, but it is unlikely that he would have lived as long. After De Quincey

[1] MS. in British Museum.

died, no specific disease was found in the body: he died of simple exhaustion of the system—of old age. The answer, then, lies in the majesty of the sole intellect: it was sheer cerebration that kept De Quincey alive for so long. Animal spirits, love of the world, of adventure, ambition and the intoxication of love, are noisy suns, in the blaze of which the quiet flame of intellect looks tame and poor. To live on them alone is also to live upon a capital which perishes with youth itself. But Thought is a dividend derived from capital which is inexhaustible. . . .

Aside from those aspects of his character which concerned himself alone, what was that which made him memorable to his friends, when they had nothing but his works to remember him by? Charm is an easy word and one which springs glibly into place in such a chronicle as this. Yet it seems that De Quincey undoubtedly possessed it in a very marked degree. His rich, fantastic talk, his fabulous manners (when presenting a manuscript to Hogg, he would first take out a little brush and carefully dust it), his comical pedantry—the sheer oddity of the tiny creature—were some of its ingredients. But not, I think, the chief one. For his was a charm founded, not, as in so many it is, on vanity and egotism, which lowers it to the level of a mere social technique, but on limpid goodness and purity of heart and the love of gracious relationships with his fellow-men.

And here we must leave him again, for a space, to examine the more tangible evidences of his genius.

CHAPTER XI

CRITICAL RETROSPECT (II)

IN this chapter, the amount of ground to be covered is much larger than that with which my former chapter of criticism had to deal, so that I propose, for the sake of clarity, to divide it into sections. Only thus will it be possible to treat adequately the various departments of De Quincey's work, which groups itself under the several rubrics of Reminiscence, History, Philosophy, Political Economy, Fantasy, and Literary Theory.

1. REMINISCENCE

The chief matter of interest in this department is of course the revision and enlargement of the *Confessions*, a task which De Quincey undertook in 1856. Apart from this, the only article of real importance is the 1848 essay on Charles Lamb, from which quotation has already been made.[1] This essay, which was written as a review of Talfourd's *Final Memorials of Charles Lamb*, is perhaps the best example of De Quincey's appreciation of a contemporary, not excluding the Coleridge and Wordsworth articles, of which it signally avoids the inaccuracies, the cattiness and the digressive tendency. As an 'introduction' to Lamb, it would be hard to beat.

The final form of the *Confessions* gave De Quincey much trouble, for its destiny necessarily lay nearer to his heart than that of any other of his works. In October 1855, he wrote to Emily: "It is almost rewritten and there cannot be much doubt that here and there it is enlivened, and so far improved. To justify the enormous labour it has cost me, most certainly it *ought* to be improved. And yet, reviewing the volume as a *whole*, now that I can look back from nearly the end to the beginning, greatly I doubt whether

[1] See p. 184.

many readers will not prefer it in its original fragmentary state to its present full-blown development. But if so, why could I not have felt this objection many weeks since, when it would have come in time to save me what has proved an exhausting labour?"[1] He had indeed felt it, but had continued with the task of enlargement, because the book in its first form was not long enough for its new price—7s. 6d. But he adds: "As a further reason for reading it I must mention, that as a book of amusement it is undoubtedly improved; what I doubt is, whether also as a book to *impress*."

Yet it had always been his intention, even in 1822, to expand the matter of the original MS., and if he did not do so at the time, it was because the disintoxication which he was undergoing, at the moment the proofs arrived, precluded it.[2]

The actual additions and divergencies which the 1856 edition comport are six in number, as follows:

(1) Additional notes, and one passage of text, to the original preface.[3]

(2) A new preface to the enlarged edition, in which he refers to the *Daughter of Lebanon* as the only one of many 'extra' dreams to be rescued from one of those little accidental conflagrations, which were so common at Lasswade and Lothian Street.

(3) A vast expansion of the Preliminary Confessions, which he now calls 'Introductory Narration'.[4] There is a defence of himself against the attack which Coleridge had launched in a letter, after the publication of the first edition. There is a long digression on the subject of guardians, which is extremely dull but has the single merit of telling us something about De Quincey's own guardians. When he comes to the Manchester period, he traverses a great deal of the ground already explored in the *Autobiographic Sketches* and which was hardly touched on in the original version. There is a detailed account of Mr. Lawson, a long comparison between Paley and Grotius, an estimate of English literature (*à propos* of its neglect at Oxford), an extended

[1] Japp, 387. [2] See *Confessions* (1823), 180 and 202. [3] III, 214.

[4] The first three pages of the first edition are omitted altogether.

account of the reasons for his flight from Manchester, including reference to the forty-guinea letter, the dream of the Whispering Gallery, and the events at Chester. The transition to the London episode is much extended (the reference to sleeping in the open air in Wales is omitted) and Brunell (now named in full) is treated to a much fuller description.

(4) Part I starts at the 'Pleasures of Opium' section, not (as in 1822) at the paragraph beginning, "So then, Oxford Street!" This section has been much less changed than the first, with the exception of unimportant stylistic amendments.

(5) Part III. The second paragraph of *The Pains of Opium* has been remodelled and now contains the interesting passage [1] in which De Quincey attributes both the opium and the dreams to his sufferings as a child. Also, the section dealing with the habit-forming propensities of the drug has been expanded in the light of increased knowledge. [2]

(6) The short fantasy, entitled *The Daughter of Lebanon*. It is difficult to see why De Quincey should have inserted this particular dream, which combines oriental matter, in the Moore-Byron style, with a seventeenth-century manner, at the end of the *Confessions*. Its place is clearly among the *Suspiria,* of which it was originally intended to form part.

When all these additions are examined together, I think it is impossible to avoid the conclusion that, in making them, De Quincey spoilt the book. His instinct, expressed in the letter quoted on page 298, was a right one: the enormous extension of the first section, which comprises most of the additions, not only spoils the book as an *artistic whole*, by ruining its proportions, but weakens the effect by a simple process of dilution. As he says himself, the book in its final form may be more amusing, but it is less impressive—and impressiveness was one of the outstanding qualities of the original. We cannot but be grateful for the Shrewsbury Inn episode, the fuller description of Brunell, and the dream of the Whispering Gallery, all of which are new; but we also cannot help regretting that De Quincey should have impaired

[1] III, 413. [2] III, 417, 429.

the concentrated poignancy of the earlier work, by overlaying it with so much that, even when it is not absolutely irrelevant, blurs what was sharp, dilutes the emotion communicated, and dims the passionate appeal which glows in the original pages. De Quincey has suffered for his error in expanding this work, for it has been perpetuated down to our own day, so that the modern reader, unless he can manage to get hold of a copy of the first edition, or of one of the reprints, knows the book exclusively from the second version. It is much to be regretted that the editors of some of the popular and cheap ' series ', in which the *Confessions* are reprinted, have not thought it worth while to include the short first version along with the second, so that readers might judge for themselves as to the merits of both.*

Yet the success of the new version was resonant—so resonant that a General E. B. Hamley published in *Blackwood's* [1] a parody entitled *A Recent Confession of an Opium-Eater*, a hideously clumsy and absurd piece of work which may be dismissed with a mere mention.

Baudelaire's *Un Mangeur d'Opium*, which was published in 1860 (the year after De Quincey's death) in the series of articles united under the title of *Les Paradis Artificiels*, is a very different affair. Though most unsatisfactory as a translation of the *Confessions*, it is nevertheless deserving of respect, if only for the beauty of its prose. Baudelaire's object in making his paraphrase is expressed in a letter to Poulet-Malassis: [2] " Il s'agissait de fondre mes sensations personnelles avec les opinions de l'auteur ", he says, and proceeds to make a cunning tesselation, composed partly of phrases, sentences and whole passages of De Quincey, and partly of his own commentary on the latter's story. Unfortunately, the two men occupied each a fundamentally different position with regard to the drug, Baudelaire taking the view succinctly expressed by his general title, while De Quincey, as I have tried to make clear, took opium primarily as a pain-killer and to the end regarded his dream-experiences as a secondary product. That being so, Baudelaire's paraphrase could not fail to be misleading. His skill as a translator was superior to Musset's, so that the work as a whole is worth reading, as a curiosity; but it is not, to say the least, a faithful rendering of the original. In one respect, however, it is a distinct advance upon Musset's version: Baudelaire, with his profound

[1] December 1856. [2] February 16th. 1860.

sensibility, fully understood the nature of De Quincey's relations with Ann. "Je voudrais," he says, "pour raconter dignement cet épisode, dérober . . . une plume â l'aile d'un ange, tant ce tableau m'apparait chaste, plein de candeur, de grâce et de miséricorde." He describes the episode accurately, mostly in *oratio obliqua*, and does not find it necessary to finish off the story *à la française*, as Musset had done.

It will be in place here to give some account of the *Suspiria de Profundis*, whose connection with the *Confessions* is as important as it is obvious. Of them De Quincey said, rather surprisingly, that they were "the *ne plus ultra*, as regards the feeling and the power to express it, which I can ever hope to attain." [1] In spite of the magnificent organ-notes of *Levana*, it is difficult to agree with this opinion. As regards fantastic imagination, subtlety of impression, fine passages of writing—even "the feeling and the power to express it"—the *Confessions* and the *Autobiographic Sketches*, to say nothing of the *English Mail-Coach*, have better to show. Besides the *Daughter of Lebanon* and *Levana*, the Suspiria are six in number; they are extremely fragmentary, and though interesting from the light they throw on De Quincey's curious psychological states, they are insufficiently worked out to support the pretension with which he burdens them. The first one, *Dreaming*, in which De Quincey declares that this faculty is impaired by "the too intense life of the *social* instincts",[2] should perhaps be read as an introduction to the *Confessions* themselves. The fifth, *Savannah-La-Mar*, which describes a Dantesque wandering in a submerged city, suggested by a passage in Milton, is very curious indeed; some allegory appears to be implicit in it, but what that is, escapes one, and the effect is one of complete inconsequence.

The *Posthumous Suspiria* [3] are on the whole more interesting, less for any displayed fantasy than for the indication they give that, at the end of his life, De Quincey was groping after a new method of expression: a new kind of rhapsody, more exact, less purely rhetorical, and more profound. It seems as if, like Coleridge, he were reaching out towards a new philosophy of life, a kind of super-Christianity:

[1] Letter to Prof. Lushington (Japp, 254).
[2] XIII, 335.
[3] *Posth. Works*, I.

Ah, reader, scorn not that which . . . is assuredly the reality of dreams, linking us to a far vaster cycle, in which the love and the languishing, the ruin and the horror, of this world are but moments —but elements in an eternal circle. The cycle stretches from an East that is forgotten to a West that is but conjectured. The mere fact of your own individual calamity is a life; the tragedy is a nature; the hope is but as a dim augury written on a flower.[1]

In him the wheel had come full circle, and what he sought now, in old age, was a new understanding of the whole, illuminated by a ceaseless meditation on the theme of childhood. "Thus, be you assured that though infancy talks least of that which slumbers deepest, it yet rests in its own transcendent solitude."[2] It is the quality of this solitude, which can only be realized on its return, at the other extreme of life, and which, if only we could seize it, would provide the clue to the secret rhythm of the whole.

2. History

This department comprises the important articles on *Homer and the Homeridae, The Philosophy of Herodotus,* and *Greece under the Romans*; the discursions on the *Essenes*, the *Pagan Oracles*, the *Theban Sphinx*, and *Secret Societies*; and the very beautiful rhapsody on the theme of *Joan of Arc*.

The first two essays, which were written in 1841 and '42, bring their author on to ground which is still highly controversial, and it says much for his historical sense, as well as for his scholarship, that his conclusions agree on whole with those of modern scholars, who have more material at their command than he had.

Since De Quincey's day, the Homeric question has been altered by three main factors: (1) the discovery of the site of Troy by Schliemann; (2) the study of other early epics, notably the Finnish, Slavonic and Russian; and (3) the increased knowledge of early Greek, from inscriptions, etc. De Quincey's criticism reposes only on the text of the poems and the literary tradition about them; but the fact that he knew these well and that he had a real sense

[1] *Posth. Works*, I. Compare also the following: "Christianity, merely by her settlement and fixing of truths, has disengaged and unfixed a world of other truths, for sustaining or for tempting an endless activity of the intellect." (*Posth. Works*, II, 233.)

[2] *Posth. Works*, 28.

of poetry, prevented him from making the characteristic mistakes of his century, which were (1) to regard Homer as an historian, (2) to regard the poems in the same light as primitive epics such as Beowulf, and (3) to divide them up by the method of false linguistic tests.

For these reasons De Quincey's essay can be read with profit, even to-day. It is especially remarkable that he should have realized so acutely the relation of the poems to the writing, contending that they were composed in the head, transmitted orally and written down in the sixth century B.C.[1] Again, though the point is still in dispute, it seems likely that he was right in assuming that Pisistratus edited the texts,[2] though the design of the poems seems to preclude the theory that he was also responsible for joining them together.

On the other hand, there are some bad mistakes, of a typically paradoxical sort. The *Iliad*, for instance, cannot, for archæological reasons, be dated earlier than 800 B.C. and may be as late as 700, whereas De Quincey confidently attributes it to the year 1000.[3] Then, his eccentric suggestion that the poems took their rise in Crete,[4] is fantastic: the linguistic objections are insuperable. The proposed derivations of Homer's name are equally wild: nothing is known of it except that it was a real name and was borne by other men than the poet.

On the question of metre and lexis, however, De Quincey is again on firmer ground. He realizes the great difficulties implied by as full a vocabulary and as rich a metre as Homer uses, at so early a time, and rightly contends that these are evidence that the poet came at the end of a long and ancient tradition.

The subject of Herodotus, again, is now in a very different position from that in which De Quincey found it. The recent excavations in the East and in Greece, the deciphering of hieroglyphs and cuneiform inscriptions, have put us in a strong position from which to criticize Herodotus, and, since Sayce published his edition in the 'eighties, there has been an almost complete reversal of opinion in favour of Herodotus' veracity. It is now clear that he preserved correctly some most valuable facts; that, even when he misunderstood them, the facts are still valuable and may be

[1] VI, 20 ff. [2] VI, 53 ff.
[3] VI, 27. [4] VI, 35.

corrected from other sources; and that he was plainly influenced by Greek scientific ideas of the time.

That being so, De Quincey's arguments are both sensible and acute; he understood very exactly the nature of Herodotus'[1] work, and his defence of the historian's chronology[2] and appreciation of his science[3] have since received many justifications and are still doing so. It is less clear how far De Quincey realized that Herodotus might be wrong while still reporting his authorities correctly, or that his book is admirably organized, not only as a story of the Persian Wars, but also as an account of the contrasted civilizations and the perennial conflict of East and West.

From the layman's point of view, this essay is of more interest than the former one, because it is less dry, less discursive, and more characteristic of its author. The opening pages, indeed, display De Quincey's historical style at its best. The personality of Herodotus obviously attracted him, by a curiosity and catholicity of interest which he felt to be akin to his own.

The essay on *Greece under the Romans* is likewise very typical of De Quincey. To derive profit from it, the actual course of events must be known beforehand, so that the extraordinary angle from which De Quincey views the subject may prove suggestive rather than merely eccentric. Of this, as of the essay on the *Essenes* and much of the *Cæsars*, the same thing may be said as De Quincey himself says of the historian whom he is reviewing:[4] "He rehearses ancient stories, not with the humble ambition of better adorning them . . . but of extracting from them some new meaning, and thus forcing them to arrange themselves . . . as illustrations of some great principle or agency now first revealing its importance."[5] The 'new meaning' which De Quincey manages to extract from the transfer of the seat of empire from Rome to Byzantium is the assertion that the Byzantine was the first empire to be based on Christian principles, because of the invention, by Constantine, of a system of Poor Relief. This peculiar piece of emphasis is used to usher in a long digression on Pauperism in England, for the apparent purpose of getting in a dig at Malthus ("the man of 1800"),[6] whose opinions afflicted De Quincey in his Christian feelings. But the ensuing argument, that Christianity is to be

[1] VI, 100. [2] VI, 109. [3] VI, 115.
[4] George Finlay. [5] VII, 253. [6] VII, 261.

praised for encouraging excessive populations, simply because these in turn gave rise to Poor Relief, is a cart-before-the-horse eccentricity that will appeal to few nowadays. Yet, in spite of the outrageous oddity of much of the argument, the whole essay has the fascination always conferred by extreme cleverness.

In the *Essenes* and *Secret Societies*—even more than in the foregoing essay—De Quincey's favourite bees buzz their loudest. The chief of these is Christianity itself which, when he came to apply it to events and controversies, and did not merely entertain it as a system of personal salvation, gave rise to the majority of his most destructive prejudices and misproportions. It led him, in the essay we have just been examining, to state categorically that Mahomet was not a great man, because he stole his main idea from Christianity.[1] In the case of the Essenes, it substituted Josephus ("the hound Josephus", sold to Rome)[2] for Malthus, as the villain of the piece, and produced a theory—as wild as that by which De Quincey attempts to prove the Cretan origin of the Homeric poems—that the Essenes were (1) invented by Josephus, in order to discredit Christianity by depriving it of its claim to originality, and (2) that the sect in fact consisted of the Christians themselves, masquerading under another name.[3] This theory had always been a pet one of De Quincey's, but it is none the less completely untenable, considering that Josephus is only one of three sources for the existence of the Essenes as an independent sect. The reason for De Quincey's passionate adherence to it, even after scholars had pointed out to him its demonstrable falsity,[4] is evidently the fact that he considered his argument "essential to the dignity of Christian truth."[5] His elaborate comparison of the Essene tenets with those of early Christianity indeed shows a startling similarity, but does not—as he wished it to do—prove that they were one and the same. But that a sect anterior to the Christian should have had as sound a moral basis, was more than he could bear. As a piece of special pleading of an extreme sort, the essay is persuasive enough in its cleverness, but unfortunately for De Quincey it has no foundation in fact.

The article on *Secret Societies* ought to have been one of its

[1] VII, 272 ff. [2] VII, 211.

[3] The last argument reposes largely on the fact that the breastplate of the high priest was called the *Essen*.

[4] See Postcript to Essay, VII, 169. [5] VII, 168.

author's best, if only because the subject, with its overtones of mystery and crime, lay so near his heart. Yet it is one of the most disappointing, because De Quincey has again allowed the wide claims of his subject to be drowned by the buzzing of the Christian bee. His account of the Eleusinian mysteries is thus hopelessly inadequate and lacking in understanding, while that of Freemasonry is distinguished by equal proportions of bad taste and ignorance. Apart from these nugatory excursions, the essay is swamped by a repetition of the Essene argument examined above. Our disappointment and irritation (for here we feel that De Quincey could easily have done so very much better) would be complete, were it not for a single passage which is a fine example of what one may call De Quincey's 'intermediate' style—intermediate, that is to say, between rhapsody and pure exposition:

The same principle in man's nature, the everlasting instinct for glorifying the everlasting, the impulse for petrifying the fugitive and arresting the transitory, which shows itself in ten thousand forms, has also, in this field of secret confederations, assumed many grander forms. To strive after a conquest over Time the conqueror, to confound the grim confounder, is already great, in whatsoever direction. But it is still greater when it applies itself to objects that are *per se* immortal, and mortal only as respects their alliance with man. Glorification of heaven—litanies chanted day and night by adoring hearts—these will doubtless ascend for ever from this planet. That result is placed out of hazard, and needs not the guarantee of princes. Somewhere, from some climate, from some lips, such a worship will not cease to rise. But, let a man's local attachments be what they may, he must sigh to think that no assignable spot of ground on earth, that no nation, that no family, enjoys any absolute privilege in that respect. No land, whether continent or island—nor race, whether freemen or slaves—can claim any fixed inheritance, or indefeasible heirlooms of truth. Yet, for that very reason, men of deep piety have but the more earnestly striven to bind down and chain their own conceptions of truth within the models of some unchanging establishments, even as the Greek Pagans of old chained down their gods from deserting them; have striven to chain the vagrant waterbrooks of Wisdom, lest she might desert the region altogether, into the channels of some local homestead; to connect with a fixed succession of descendants the conservation of religion; to root, as one would root a forest that is to flourish through ages, a heritage of ancient truth in the territorial heritage of an ancient household.[1]

In passages like this, where all the bees are silent, De Quincey rises above the somewhat petulant narrowness of his personal beliefs and achieves a grand, timeless serenity, in which his enormous knowledge, joined to the realized sources of his experience of life, sound out like bells submerged in the depths of the sea. The total effect, which is organic and amounts to much more than the sum of the actual sentences—in themselves of almost commonplace import—is not unlike that of the meditations of Seneca.

The Pagan Oracles, unlike this last article, fulfils our expectations from the title; it is a mine of curious and interesting ideas, of odd bits and pieces of knowledge, which are, however, not invalidated by untenable and paradoxical views. His main argument is that the Fathers were wrong in asserting that Christianity was an immediate death-blow to the oracles; they died gradually, like the London street lamps which De Quincey had watched go out, one by one, that night in 1814, when the Cossacks had drunk the oil from them.[2] The image is vivid and poetical, like the passage in which he compares the Greek temples to modern banks.[3] De Quincey was always at his best when some personal memory stimulated his mind to an entertaining parallel—to some strange and recondite joke, such as he indulges in in *The Theban Sphinx*. Here, however, the humour is overstrained and pedantic. The answer to the Sphinx's riddle was not, according to De Quincey, 'man', but 'Œdipus'—*i.e.*, a being who went on all fours as a helpless, abandoned babe; rose majestically on to two feet as a king; and ended with the necessary support of a third foot—Antigone.[4] A simple exclamation mark would seem the only suitable greeting to such a quirk; the contention is true enough, as far as it goes, but is it a point worth labouring? De Quincey's jokes sometimes smell too strongly of the schoolroom.

On the whole, one prefers him in serious vein. Yet the *Joan of Arc* would have been even better than it is if the rhapsody had not been split in half by girdings at Michelet for unfairness to England—a charge which comes poorly from De Quincey, who could hardly mention France without hyperbolous abuse. Still, the

[1] VII, 184. [2] VII, 99. [3] VII, 91 ff. [4] VI, 147 ff.

concluding pages are among the best that he achieved, in this style,—the flying, contrapuntal style of the *English Mail-Coach,* applied, with passionate and visionary conviction, to the actualities of history:

> Bishop of Beauvais! thy victim died in fire upon a scaffold—thou upon a down bed. But, for the departing minutes of life, both are oftentimes alike. At the farewell crisis, when the gates of death are opening, and flesh is resting from its struggles, oftentimes the tortured and the torturer have the same truce from carnal torment; both sink together into sleep; together both sometimes kindle into dreams. When the mortal mists were gathering fast upon you two, bishop and shepherd girl—when the pavilions of life were closing up their shadowy curtains about you—let us try, through the gigantic glooms, to decipher the flying features of your separate visions.[1]

The passage is too well known to need further quotation. Even in this first short paragraph one is thrilled by the lovely exactitude of the imagery—"kindle into dreams", "pavilions of life"; while the concluding passage, with its elaborate antiphony of question and answer, will always stand high among rhetorical visions.

3. Philosophy

De Quincey's later contributions to the various subjects assembled under this heading include the scattered articles on the *System of the Heavens, Plato's Republic, Casuistry,* and *Modern Superstition*; together with four essays having a more direct bearing on Christianity—*Miracles as Subjects of Testimony, Judas Iscariot, Christianity as an Organ of Political Movement,* and *Protestantism.*

Now it would be tedious to examine every one of these articles separately, since, with the exception of a paragraph here and there, they have in themselves no more than an interest of curiosity. For De Quincey, who started out in life with a magnificent training and a real aptitude for philosophical speculation, eventually allowed a narrow Christian prejudice, inculcated by his mother and stiffened by the influence of Wordsworth (whose philosophy was of the purely 'natural' order), to destroy his clarity of vision in these fields and block the way to all effective thought. I am not sug-

[1] V, 413 ff.

gesting that a belief in the tenets of Christianity need necessarily preclude any useful contribution to philosophy: that would be a very superficial view to take. But that it arbitrarily imposes certain full-stops is undeniable, and these full-stops operate with particularly paralysing effect in assessing the absolute value of pre-Christian doctrines.[1]

This was the difficulty which put De Quincey's nose out of joint with the whole of ancient—and more especially of Greek civilization; so that, with most of the equipment necessary for a unique understanding of the Greek genius, he failed to achieve a really profound or illuminating view and only revealed by scattered observations of extreme insight, how near he came to realizing his early intellectual objective. But the miss is not quite as good as a mile: De Quincey's analysis of the fundamental divergences between the Pagan and the Christian views of religion[2] is perspicacious enough for his final evasion of the point to be all the more astonishing. The crux of the situation is expressed in the following passage:

> All moral theories of antiquity were utterly disjoined from religion. But this fallacy of a dogmatic or doctrinal part in Paganism is born out of Anachronism. It is the anachronism of unconsciously reflecting back upon the ancient religions of darkness, and as if essential to *all* religions, features that never were suspected as possible until they had been revealed in Christianity.[3]

So far, so good. But now comes the snag:

> Pagan religion aimed at no distant prize ahead: it fled from danger immediately behind. *The gods of the Pagans were wicked natures. . . .*[4]

Here De Quincey is committing the very fallacy he has just been at pains to expose: the question-begging epithet 'wicked'

[1] De Quincey had the greatest respect for these full-stops. "Neither can I think that any man . . . ever could travel upwards into a very great philosopher unless he should begin or should end with Christianity. Kant is a dubious exception" (II, 155). And in 1850 he wrote: "Beyond the boundary and ring fence of an ultimate faith in the capital articles of revealed truth no man can trespass without a risk of losing his compass; he cannot speculate safely so far as that." (XIV, 311.)

[2] See VIII, 211 ff.

[3] VIII, 212. This point is made, at greater length and with more fruitful results, in Walter Otto's *Die Götter Griechenlands*, p. 5. This book is one of the best expositions of the subject in existence.

[4] VIII, 213. (My italics.)

proceeds straight from the point of view of Christian morality, and would not have been understood—far less accepted—in the sense in which De Quincey uses it, by a Greek. The Greek gods constituted an emporium of complex symbols from which a man might select the perfect example of the life-form on which he wished to place emphasis, for himself. They were images of a life here and now, not the ominous heralds of a life hereafter. To call Hera or Artemis 'wicked' is therefore to write yourself down incompetent to speak on the subject of Greek religion. The Greeks were a practical people (Hermes, for instance, is the god of business men, *par excellence*) and their religion had a pragmatic basis; but it is subtly untrue to say, as De Quincey says, that the qualities of their divinities "must have worked an extensive conformity to their own standard".[1] Here again he is putting the cart before the horse: the Greeks were far too much at home with their gods to be overwhelmed by their own creations, and their mythology was likewise far too closely bound up with things that were well within their control. It is exactly the beauty of Greek religion that it was not a slave religion, as Christianity necessarily was—in its origins, at any rate. Thus, severely practical in its essence though the Greek (and the Roman) pantheon may be, the people who invented it also understood—to an extent which has never been equalled—the heroic side of life. This operated through the idea of Fate, a quality, in Greek eyes, inherent in life itself; through it man was privileged to rise to heights of tragic grandeur, in which all that was most powerful, terrible and inexplicable in life found a reconciliation. It was this feature of Greek religion—this Fate and the gods directly concerned with the interpretation of its sterner aspects—which to De Quincey, muscle-bound by the Christian notion of 'test', seemed merely wicked, because apparently inhuman and indifferent. He could not stomach the notion of a conflict occasioned by man and resolved by man *alone*, with no help save that of his own conjugated faculties (the gods themselves within him, immortally imaged); the conflict, whatever its nature, had, according to his Christian belief, to be carried through with the eye always on a transcendent God who had sent it to 'try' man for an immortality proportionate to his success in the outcome. Hence De Quincey's insistence on the fact that not even Plato really

[1] VIII, 221.

understood immortality and that the Pagans were, moreover, incapable of grandeur, even in their gods.[1] He would allow no grandeur to the Pagan heroes, because the ethos in which their exploits cohered was not an other-worldly one. For the Christian hero, on the other hand, he cherished a passionate admiration; and his hatred of figures like Machiavelli[2] and Paley[3] clearly proceeds from the fact that the one stripped man of his pretensions to disinterested goodness and the other took what amounts to a pragmatic view of Christianity. Given the facts of his own life, it is scarcely surprising that De Quincey should have insisted so passionately on the necessity of conflict; but it was a conflict that had to be resolved through faith in an omnipotent wisdom, the operations of which were essentially beyond the range of human comprehension.

It was a faith in which revelation was of paramount importance, with Sin and its 'infinitizing' power[4] as a key dogma.[5] There, again, De Quincey entertained a sense (*i.e.*, that of sin) which would not have been comprehensible to a Greek.

Indeed, his entire faith rested on what Newman called the Illative sense—that inner revelation which 'proves' the truth of inspiration. De Quincey implies reliance on this sense, in all his later religious writings, and explicitly invokes it to prove the miracles of Grace and Prayer.[6] It is, of course, difficult to argue either in favour of or against this sense, since it necessarily withstands all tests from without. Other kinds of 'proof' are not wanting in De Quincey, but they are mostly of a sadly puerile order, as when, for example, he attempts to prove the superiority of the Christian sensibility by declaring that the "deep pathos in a sunset"[7] would not have been felt by Cicero or Plato; or when he conceives that the truths of science were not uttered by the founder of Christianity or the apostles, because to have done so would have been to distract attention from a revelation to what was already discoverable by the mere intellect, and therefore irrelevant to the higher truth of the former.[8]

This is all rather unhappy, and if the speculations of De Quincey

[1] *Posth. Works*, I, 33 ff.
[2] VIII, 143.
[3] VIII, 138.
[4] *Posth. Works*, I, 227.
[5] For De Quincey's hatred of eighteenth-century Deism, see the article on *Pope*, XI, 82.
[6] VIII, 168 ff. He pays tribute to Newman himself in VIII, 290.
[7] I, 190.
[8] *The True Relations of the Bible to merely Human Science*, VIII, 35 ff.

on the subject of religion had nothing but casuistry of this kind to offer, we should be justified in ignoring them. But, on the positive side, his conception of religion and deity was a good deal more complex and subtle, as the following two passages show:

He [the philosophic theist] demands, in the first place, something in the highest degree generic, and yet again, in the opposite direction, something in the highest degree individual; he demands on the one path a vast ideality, and yet on the other in union with a determinate personality. He must not surrender himself to the first impulse, else he is betrayed into a mere *anima mundi*: he must not surrender himself to the second, else he is betrayed into something merely human. This difficult antagonism of what is most and what is least generic must be maintained; otherwise the idea . . . of that august unveiling which takes place in the Judaico-Christian God is absolutely in clouds.[1]

I . . . profoundly believe that the Scriptures ascribe absolute and metaphysical eternity to one sole Being, viz., to God; and derivatively to all others according to the interest which they can plead in God's favour. Having anchorage in God, innumerable entities may possibly be admitted to participation in divine *æon*. But what interest in the favour of God can belong to falsehood, to malignity, to impurity? To invest *them* with æonian privileges, is an effect, and by its results, to distrust and to insult the Deity. Evil would *not* be evil, if it had that power of self-subsistence which is imputed to it in supposing its æonian life to be co-eternal with that which crowns and glorifies the good.[2]

The latter argument also led De Quincey to disbelieve in the accepted doctrine of Eternal Punishment. Here, the Bradleian conception of an Absolute which swallows up all contradictions, including Evil itself, seems near at hand; but there is a nebulousness, an effect of not being thought out to the end, which deprives of final importance De Quincey's contributions to these subjects. The problems of religion and philosophy demand a more concentrated attention than he was able to give them, especially at the time when such a task would have been most congenial to him. Yet, up to the end, he continued obstinately to believe in his vocation to the subject: "Not only is it false that my understanding is no

[1] VIII, 223.
[2] *On the Supposed Scriptural Expression for Eternity*, printed in Hogg, 293 ff.

measure or rule for another man, but of necessity it is so, and every step I take towards truth for myself is a step made on behalf of every other man." [1]

We shall hardly deny this generalized claim, which, in a thinker of De Quincey's calibre, is no more than just. Yet the value of his thought, which in other departments of knowledge depends on width and sweep, here, in the domain of religion, finds its most permanent expression in short, aphoristic phrases which tend to escape notice. "Men mistake God's hate by their own." [2] It is in such moments of brief inspiration, which, in their profundity and originality, recall the writings of Kierkegaard, that De Quincey strikes the shrewdest blows in defence of his faith.

4. Politics and Political Economy

As in the case of the philosophical essays, it is undesirable, at this time of day, to examine in detail De Quincey's contributions to politics and political economy, because here his thought is even less original than there; and, though he was in many ways an admirable expounder of the economic theories of his day, those theories have since been either proved false or else absorbed into some more up-to-date corpus.

The Political Economy articles are five in number, as follows: *Malthus on Population*; *Malthus on the Measure of Value*; *Dialogues of Three Templars on Political Economy: Chiefly in relation to the Theories of Mr. Ricardo*; [3] *Ricardo and Adam Smith*; and *The Logic of Political Economy*.[4]

The third and fifth of these pieces contain all that is considerable in De Quincey's thinking on the subject. It will be remembered with what excitement he first 'discovered' the sociological writings of Ricardo, at a time of the direst mental depression and physical debility. These essays were the direct result of that excitement and they bear the marks of its singular nature. To begin with, De Quincey was not widely read in Economics: apart from Ricardo, Malthus (whom he despised) and Adam Smith constituted his sources. This narrows his field of enquiry to only two or three of the fundamental problems concerned; his economic thought is in no

[1] *Posth. Works*, I, 196.
[2] *Ibid.*, 171.
[3] These three pieces all belong to the years 1823–4.
[4] 1842.

way creative, he establishes no new theorems and demonstrates no new relations. Thus his single claim to consideration lies in the skill with which he has interpreted his admired master, Ricardo; and, given the skill, what remains of permanent interest is the method which he employed. For, if any evidence is needed of the thoroughness with which De Quincey had absorbed Aristotelian logic during his years at Oxford, that evidence lies in the fascinating completeness with which he has applied that system to the problems of Economics. In so doing, he has not improved the doctrines, as set forth by Ricardo, but has thrown into sharp relief the logical relations which they present. He shows how thorough a grasp he had of the subject as a whole, by making it clear that Ricardo's system, though unsystematically presented, was coherent and self-consistent, and that Malthus, on the other hand, was a hopelessly muddled thinker. Once convinced of the truth of Ricardo's main theorems, De Quincey remained proof against sophistical objections to them.

On the other hand, he tends, especially in the *Logic of Political Economy*, to fall a victim to the illusion, under which the schoolmen themselves undoubtedly laboured, that, in simply re-stating someone else's theorems in scholastic terms, he was advancing knowledge. The process does, it is true, occasionally shed a fitful light on the problems, and it is certainly as fascinating to follow as the stages of a complicated puzzle. Yet the scholastic categories, as handled by De Quincey, appear fearfully cumbersome; and here again his old fault—prolixity—rears its head. His faultless syntax and literary power carry the reader on and even raise a sense of excitement; but if he could perceive in Ricardo a natural inaptitude for the task of simplifying knowledge,[1] he was himself equally unable to attain to first-rate lucidity in exposition.

The passages that come nearest to forming a new contribution to the subject are those which deal with Value in Use.[2] De Quincey appreciated the fact that Ricardo had treated this topic in too off-hand a manner and felt that something should be done to make it an integral part of the system. In this he was truly prophetic, for thirty years later the theory of political economy made an enormous advance in the hands of Jevons,[3] whose formulation of the concept

[1] IX, 246. [2] See *Dialogues* I and IV, and *Logic*, I, Section VI.
[3] *Theory of Political Economy* (1871).

of *marginal* value in use made it possible to show the general relation of value in use to value in exchange. But De Quincey himself did not arrive at the marginal concept. He struggled with the problem and said a few interesting things by the way—as was his wont; but the final solution escaped him.

The quaint violence of some of the judgments expressed in these pieces will surprise no one who is acquainted with the rest of De Quincey's work; nevertheless it betrays a mind unused and unsuited to the caution and diffidence necessary in dealing with scientific subjects. His logical preoccupation leads him to mete out the severest castigation for theories whose actual fault of substance is small, but whose form offends his scholastic principles. And though he was undoubtedly right in insisting on the importance of Ricardo's discoveries, his denunciations of everyone else as being totally erroneous, are naïve.

This is perhaps hardly an occasion on which to raise the question of readability; but, if this be done, we are bound to give the first place to the *Dialogues*, in which the argument is fascinatingly developed and the illustrations are simple and adequate (a great virtue in a scientific treatise). And this in spite of the fact that, as De Quincey himself pointed out, with some inconsistency,[1] the dialogue form is fundamentally unsuited to the subject of political economy. Reading what he chose to cast into that form, we feel bound to agree with him; the method of the Socratic dialogue, as applied to a scientific subject, has certain superficial advantages; but De Quincey has managed to nullify them by a series of interruptions, *politesses*, etc., which, whatever their 'literary' appropriateness, hold up the argument when the reader's attention is necessarily stretched to grasp a point, and generally attentuate the force and astringency of the whole.

. . . . .

De Quincey's specifically political articles, on questions of contemporary interest, need not detain us long. As I have already pointed out,[2] on political questions he was all too ready—from Tory prejudice, from sheer ignorance, and from the curious ferocity that often characterizes the library-bound scholar—to rush

[1] In *Style*, X, 184.

[2] See pp. 165 and 258.

in where he was utterly incompetent to pronounce judgment. The immediate, practical problems of sociology, on which political opinions depend, were never more than roughly tangential to De Quincey's main preoccupations. Freedom, for instance, which had been for his early contemporaries so burning a concept, really meant very little to him; he had no use for it in his life, which was given to various disciplines and authorities of a private, but sufficiently imperious, kind. Men in the mass were a logical concept to him, not a reality, and as such his judgments of them were consistently and astonishingly crude. Hence his views on the emancipation of slaves ("sentimental folly", "light-minded precipitancy"),[1] on the French, the Freemasons—in fact on everything that was not either British or Christian. "It is not often that one looks with hope and expectation to the capacities of hatred and scorn in one's friends," he wrote to his daughter Margaret, when the Indian Mutiny broke out and his feelings, not unnaturally heated by the dangers which his son Paul Frederick and his son-in-law Colonel Baird-Smith were running, rose high against the Sepoys. But his scorn and hatred were the same, whether the object of them was the Sepoys, the Chinese, or merely the British Radical.

His attitude to war was most inconsistent. In theory he held the Christian-Pacifist view: "The final step for its extinction will be taken by a new and Christian mode of international law."[2] But in practice, this view was always breaking down. Having announced that most dangerous and bolt-shooting doctrine, that "every nation's duty, first, midst, and last, is to itself",[3] he finds himself committed to the belief, expressed in the essay on War, that the latter must always be unavoidable.[4] He was shrewd enough to perceive the economic origins of war,[5] but did not carry the argument a step further, to the international solution which he proposed elsewhere. Just as he was in favour of duelling, from the point of view of honour among individuals, so he was fundamentally in favour of war, as a means of preserving the 'honour' of a nation. But this principle only applied to British honour: it is quite evident that he considered the French and the Chinese, for instance, wholly incapable of entertaining the notion. Again, the mass of stuff

[1] IX, 215.
[2] VIII, 236.
[3] VIII, 380.
[4] VIII, 373 ff.
[5] VIII, 380.

which he wrote on the British difficulties in China [1] is distinguished by an entirely imperialist point of view: it never seems to have occurred to him that our presence in China at all could be questioned (" our national expansion brought us into a painful necessity of connecting ourselves with the conceited and most ignorant inhabitants of China ").[2] This attitude, the complete ignorance which he shows of Chinese history, and the incomprehension of Chinese civilization (" this horrible Chinese degeneration of moral distinctions " [3]—" incurably savage in the moral sense " [4]—" incapable of a true civilization ") make one wish to draw a veil over the whole performance.

The idea and the spectacle of the British Empire were a strong intoxicant to De Quincey, as to the majority of his class, throughout the nineteenth century. So strong was it that his mind, essentially liberal and humane, became blind whenever the idea or the spectacle was in any way threatened. On this subject, as on that of philosophy, he allowed a number of arbitrary full-stops to check the course of his reasoning faculty and thus to deprive his pronouncements of any claim to permanent value.

5. Fantasy

This heading describes three pieces which are among the best and most famous their author ever wrote: the 1854 Postcript to *Murder Considered as One of the Fine Arts,* the *English Mail-Coach* [5] (originally intended to form part of the *Suspiria,* but very carefully revised [6] and republished as a self-subsistent fantasy, in 1854), and the *Spanish Military Nun* (originally published in *Tait's,*[7] but altered and rearranged for the Collected Edition in 1854).

De Quincey's afterthoughts were not usually very happy; but the postcript to the *Murder* articles is by far the best of them, just as it is the most satisfactory portion of the whole piece. The minute

[1] *The Opium Question with China in* 1840 (*Blackwood's,* 1840), and *The Chinese Question in* 1857 (three articles printed in " Titan ", afterwards enlarged and brought out as a pamphlet, and finally published in an abbreviated form in Vol. XIV of the Masson edition).

[2] XIV, 350. [3] XIV, 190. [4] XIV, 193. [5] 1849.

[6] The *Posthumous Works* (I, 323) contain an early draft of the *Dream-Fugue,* which may profitably be compared with the final version, as an example of De Quincey's more careful revision.

[7] 1847.

and poring description of the Williams murders has a grim, macabre quality, which recalls the fearful thinness, the rickety limbs and threadbare clothes, of a drawing by Cruikshank. In this mood, De Quincey triumphantly recaptures the London of his boyhood adventure—the underworld of the early nineteenth century, with its crazy hovels, whose shapes recall the poor wretches who lived in them—all the violent and pathetic chiaroscuro of squalid crime. In the *Posthumous Works* [1] there are some supplementary notes for a third article on the same theme, which shows how persistently De Quincey's imagination returned to the fascinating subject of crime; but the proposal contained in these notes, for a series of statues to be erected to various 'great' murderers, suggests him in his facetious, and therefore less attractive, mood.

The *English Mail-Coach* has already been so extensively quoted in this book,[2] that not much further expatiation on its unique and wonderful qualities is required. Its effectiveness as a virtuoso evocation of speed is sometimes objected to nowadays on the ground that De Quincey's ascription of terror and violence to even the maximum speed of a coach is rendered comic to us by our own experience of racing motors and aeroplanes. This seems to me a foolish objection and one which, moreover, De Quincey himself has been at pains to meet. It is the *sensation* of speed which counts, not the actual miles-per-hour. "The modern modes of travelling . . . boast of more velocity,—not, however, as a consciousness, but as a fact of our lifeless knowledge, resting upon alien evidence. . . . The vital experience of the glad animal sensibilities made doubts impossible on the question of our speed; we heard our speed, we saw it, we felt it as a thrilling; and this speed was . . . incarnated in the fiery eyeballs of the noblest amongst brutes, in his dilated nostrils, spasmodic muscles and thunder-beating hoofs." [3]

Although the second and third sections of the piece are those for which it in the main continues to be read, the introduction, which deals with the 'Glory of Motion' in general, and connects the journey to be described with De Quincey's earlier coaching experiences, does not detract from the effectiveness of the whole. Though rambling and jocular, in its author's high-spirited, reminiscent manner, it is neither arch nor tiresome; and its scherzando

[1] *Posth. Works*, I, 77. [2] See p. 167 ff. [3] XIII, 283–4.

effect is admirably devised as a prelude to the far-flung, rhapsodic style of the succeeding movement.

The *Spanish Military Nun* belongs to the end of De Quincey's fourth opium crisis and is distinguished by that hallucinative intensity of imagination which is noticeable at other such periods in his life. It possesses many of the extraordinary features of the *English Mail-Coach*—the amazing, musical quality, the intensity of appeal, the fantasy, and also an odd kind of humour which is absent from the other piece; but unfortunately, three of the worst faults of De Quincey's writing are also present—prolixity, facetiousness, and inability to leave well alone. The story, which is founded on an article contributed to the *Revue des Deux Mondes* for February 1847, by a certain Alexis de Valon, is amusingly picaresque. The heroine, whose name is Catilina—or Kate, as De Quincey calls her—appears first as the inmate of a convent in San Sebastian. Resolved on escape, she assumes male attire and makes her way to her uncle's house at Vitoria. She manages to get round him, but soon tires of conjugating Latin verbs (his sole amusement) and makes her way to Valladolid, where she becomes an usher. Before long, however, the sea claims her—as it was bound, sooner or later, to claim such a born pirate. Wrecked on the coast of Peru, Kate, still successfully carrying off her travesty, becomes clerk to a draper in Paita, where she is soon imprisoned for killing a man who has insulted her. This is her first victim. A female relation of the murdered man offers to marry her, that she may escape hanging. In order to avoid an embarrassment far worse than death, Kate escapes to sea in an open boat and is eventually taken on to a ship which is bound for Concepcion. Arrived there, she meets her brother, fights in the Chilian army against Indians and is wounded, but manages, even so, to conceal the fact that she is a woman. After a painful incident, in which, by mistake, she kills her brother in a duel, Kate ascends the Andes on horseback, in the company of two deserters.

This passage and that which follows it are the most remarkable of the whole piece; they have the panoramic sweep of the landscape which they describe, and the prose is De Quincey at his symphonic best. One incident, too, is unforgettable in its macabre vividness. Kate remarks, in the distance, a man sitting in the snow, a rifle by his side. She hails him, but he gives no answer. Then: "Coming close behind him, Kate touched his shoulder, and said, 'My friend, are you sleeping?' Yes, he *was* sleeping—sleeping the sleep from which there is no awaking; and, the slight touch of Kate having disturbed the equilibrium of the corpse, down it rolled on the snow: the frozen body rang like a hollow iron cylinder; the face uppermost, and blue with mould, mouth open, teeth ghastly and bleaching in the frost, and a frightful grin upon the lips." [1]

Then begins the gradual descent of the Cordilleras, from the heights of snow down into the sunny warmth of the lower valleys, —a wonderful example of the composer's skill, where the effect of the description is achieved almost purely by the variety and continuity of the impression of *movement*, so that one can almost feel the uneven slope of the ground under the traveller's feet:

Oh! verdure of human fields, cottages of men and women (that now suddenly, in the eyes of Kate, seemed all brothers and sisters), cottages with children around them at play, that are so far below—oh! spring and summer, blossoms and flowers, to which, as to *his* symbols, God has given the gorgeous privilege of rehearsing for ever upon earth his most mysterious perfection—Life, and the resurrections of Life—it is indeed true that poor Kate must never see you more! Mutteringly she put that question to herself. . . . Dimmed and confused had been the accuracy of her sensations for hours; but all at once a strong conviction came over her that more and more was the sense of descent becoming steady and continuous. Turning round to measure backwards with her eye the ground traversed through the last half-hour, she identified by a remarkable point of rock, the spot near which the three corpses were lying. The silence seemed deeper than ever. Neither was there any phantom memorial of life for the eye or for the ear, nor wing of bird, nor echo, nor green leaf, nor creeping thing that moved or stirred, upon the soundless waste. Oh, what a relief to this burden of silence would be a human groan! Here seemed a motive for still darker despair. And yet, at that very moment, a pulse of joy began to thaw the ice at her heart. It struck her, as she reviewed the ground from that point where the corpses lay, that undoubtedly for some time it had been slowly descending. Her senses were much dulled by suffering; but this thought it was, suggested by a sudden apprehension of a continued descending movement, which had caused her to turn round. . . .

[1] XIII, 194.

Frightful was the spasm of joy which whispered that the worst was over. It was as when the shadow of midnight, that murderers had relied on, is passing away from your beleagured shelter, and dawn will soon be manifest. It was as when a flood, that all day long has raved against the walls of your house, ceases (you suddenly think) to rise. . . . Kate faced round in agitation to her proper direction. She saw, what previously, in her stunning confusion, she had not seen, that hardly two stones' throws in advance lay a mass of rock, split as into a gateway. Through that opening it now became certain that the road was lying. Hurrying forward, she passed within these natural gates. Gates of paradise they were. Ah, what a vista did that gateway expose before her dazzled eye! What a revelation of heavenly promise! Full two miles long, stretched a long narrow glen, everywhere descending, and in many parts rapidly. All was now placed beyond a doubt. She *was* descending,—for hours, perhaps, *had* been descending insensibly, —the mighty staircase. Yes, Kate is leaving behind her the kingdom of frost and the victories of death. . . . And very soon, as the crest of her new-born happiness, she distinguished at the other end of that rocky vista a pavilion-shaped mass of dark green foliage —a belt of trees, such as we see in the lovely parks of England, but islanded by a screen of thick bushy undergrowth! Oh! verdure of dark olive foliage, offered suddenly to fainting eyes, as if by some winged patriarchal herald of wrath relenting—solitary Arab's tent, rising with saintly signals of peace in the dreadful desert— must Kate indeed die even yet, whilst she sees but cannot reach you? Outpost on the frontier of man's dominions, standing within life, but looking out upon everlasting death, wilt thou hold up the anguish of thy mocking invitation only to betray? Never, perhaps, in this world was the line so exquisitely grazed that parts salvation and ruin. As the dove to her dovecot from the swooping hawk— as the Christian pinnace to the shelter of Christian batteries from the bloody Mahometan corsair—so flew, so tried to fly, towards the anchoring thickets, that, alas! could not weigh their anchors, and make sail to meet her, the poor exhausted Kate from the vengeance of pursuing frost.

And she reached them; staggering, fainting, reeling, she entered beneath the canopy of umbrageous trees. But, as oftentimes the Hebrew fugitive to a city of refuge, flying for his life before the avenger of blood, was pressed so hotly that, on entering the arch-way of what seemed to *him* the heavenly city gate, as he kneeled in deep thankfulness to kiss its holy merciful shadow, he could not rise again, but sank instantly with infant weakness into sleep—sometimes to wake no more; so sank, so collapsed upon the ground, without power to choose her couch, and with little prospect of ever rising again to her feet, the martial nun.[1]

But of course she does rise again, and is taken in by a Spanish lady, whose daughter loses no time in falling in love with her. It seems, this time, as if Kate will not be able to escape; but, in the inevitable delay before the marriage can take place, she is cheated at dice by a couple of Portuguese, one of whom, with her usual impetuosity, she proceeds to kill. Haled before justice, she is condemned to death, but is reprieved on the gallows. Thence she flies to La Paz, only to get mixed up in an illicit amour which ends in another murder—this time *not* committed by herself. Kate abducts the lady on the back of her horse, and, pursued by the furious husband, they take refuge in a convent in Cuzco. There she is attacked by the husband and kills him, thus accounting for her fourth victim. But in the course of the fight she has been wounded in the breast; this leads to the eventual discovery of her secret and her extradition to Spain, at the order of Philip IV. Arrived there, she is welcomed like the film-heroine she is, after which she proceeds to Rome, where the Pope gives her leave to continue to wear man's apparel. She then sets sail once more for South America, only to disappear again—between the ship and the shore.

As a fiction, the *Spanish Military Nun* is not as successful as the earlier tales of De Quincey—*Klosterheim, Mr. Schnackenberger, The King of Hayti*—because the method in which it is told hovers awkwardly between that of the essay and that of the short story. And, as an extravaganza, it is inferior to the *English Mail-Coach* and some of the *Suspiria*, owing to a similar hesitation, whereby the poet effect becomes diluted. But for all that, amateurs of De Quincey will continue to read it, not only for its high lights (one of which I have quoted) but for its bouquet—the strange pungency which exhales from the grim humour, the gusto, and the elaborate filigree of the writing. Reading this little work, one is tempted to regret that De Quincey did not try his hand at an extended fiction of the picaresque order—a form so exactly suited

[1] XIII, 201–4.

to the rhythm of his mind. It would, no doubt, have been at times as intolerably long-winded as its Spanish prototypes; but its imagination would have been of a more exalted and poetical kind, and the high points, purged of dross by the long digressions which De Quincey would surely have permitted himself elsewhere, might have formed a mountain range of impressive dimensions—an entire 'view', instead of the couple of hillocks which is all that the *Spanish Military Nun* has time to raise.

6. Literary Theory

De Quincey's theories of literary style—of the relation between matter and manner—are chiefly contained in the three very important essays on *Rhetoric, Style,* and *Language.* The first of these belongs to the year 1828, the second to 1840–1, the third probably to the same year. Not only are they in themselves among the best pieces of analytical writing which De Quincey achieved, but they are of great importance in placing his preferences, prejudices, and so on, in the history of style, and in determining his own position as a stylist, which might otherwise remain ambiguous.

In the first essay, De Quincey states the two popular views of rhetoric as (1) a form of intellectual pleasure, (2) fraud. For his own part, he takes the Aristotelian position, but with undue emphasis on the enthymeme as the logical statement of a probability to be made persuasive. Thus: "Rhetoric is the art of aggrandizing and bringing out into strong relief, by means of various and striking thoughts, some aspect of truth which of itself is supported by no spontaneous feelings, and therefore rests upon artificial aids." [1] And: "By Eloquence we understand the overflow of powerful feelings upon occasions fitted to excite them." [2] Then he proceeds to trace the history of rhetoric, according to his own rather peculiar definition, from which he deduces that Rome was the "true Eldorado of Rhetoric" and the Greek fathers "Birmingham rhetoricians". Running his finger down the list of famous figures in this genre, he singles out Donne, Burton, Milton, Taylor, Pitt, Burke, and Canning. But—and this is significant—he will not include Bacon, because the latter's thought reposed upon real, not fanciful analogies.[3] The distinction does not seem particularly real;

[1] X, 92. [2] *Ibid.* [3] X, 109.

analogies should surely be separated into the successful and the unsuccessful, according as they heighten the definition of two things, by pointing their similarity, or fail to do so. But De Quincey's distinction would seem to point to some preoccupation with analogies which are poetic and those which are drawn from abstract processes of thought. And this suggestion receives support from his conclusion, that political rhetoric is now dead, at any rate in our parliaments, owing to the exclusively *terre-à-terre* nature of the subjects discussed (gas bills, and the like)! [1] This rather superficial view comes naturally, however, from a man who was accustomed, by sympathy and upbringing, to associate the poetic with the gorgeous, and to perpetuate this association in his own writings. As a late rhetorician himself, De Quincey may perhaps be excused for failing to perceive the exact nature of what lay so close to his own eyes.

The essay on *Style* brings us nearer the heart of the problem. But it is in still other places that De Quincey gives us a precise description of what he means by the word, rather than a history of its manifestations:

The two capital secrets in the art of prose composition are these: 1st, The philosophy of transition and connection, or the art by which one step in an evolution of thought is made to arise out of another: all fluent and effective composition depends on the connections;—2ndly, The way in which sentences are made to modify each other; for the most powerful effects in written eloquence arise out of this reverberation, as it were, from each other in a rapid succession of sentences; and, because some limitation is necessary to the length and complexity of sentences, in order to make this interdependency felt.[2]

Style is the disentangling of thoughts or ideas reciprocally involved in each other.[3]

Style has two separate functions: first, to brighten the *intelligibility* of a subject which is obscure to the understanding; secondly, to regenerate the normal *power* and impressiveness of a subject which has become dormant to the sensibilities. Darkness gathers upon many a theme, sometimes from previous mistreatment, but oftener from original perplexities investing its very nature. . . . The writer is not summoned to convince, but to persuade. . . .

[1] X, 121. [2] II, 65. [3] *Posth. Works*, I, 225.

Now, these offices of style are really not essentially below the level of those other offices attached to the original discovery of truth . . . Light to *see* the road, power to *advance along* it—such being amongst the promises and proper functions of style, it is a capital error, under the idea of its ministeriality, to undervalue this great organ of the advancing intellect—an organ which is equally important considered as a tool for the culture and *popularization* of truth and also . . . as a mode *per se* of the beautiful and a fountain of intellectual pleasure. The vice of that appreciation which we English apply to style lies in representing it as a mere ornamental accident of written composition. . . . On the contrary, it is a product of art, the rarest, subtlest, and most intellectual; and . . . it is then finest when it is most eminently disinterested—that is, most conspicuously detached from gross palpable uses. Yet, in very many cases, it really *has* the obvious uses of that gross palpable order . . . when it gives light to the understanding or power to the will, removing obscurities from one set of truths, and into another circulating the life-blood of sensibility.[1]

The first and second of these *dicta* describe preoccupations which are common to all writers, of whatever kind; the third, however, applies only—or anyhow more pertinently—to what is nowadays called *emotive* writing, and which De Quincey himself called 'the Literature of Power'. That this kind of writing was his own province, has all along been sufficiently obvious; what now requires insistence is that he considered the fact of paramount importance and that his theory of style was framed round it. Thus we find him, at the outset of his essay, pointing out the fact that the English people seem always to have laid emphasis on *matter* rather than *manner*; and proceeding to destroy this false distinction.

The more closely any exercise of mind is connected with what is internal and individual in the sensibilities,—that is, with what is philosophically termed *subjective*,—precisely in that degree . . . does the style or the embodying of the thoughts cease to be a mere separate ornament, and in fact the more does the manner . . . become confluent with the matter.[2]

The rest of the essay, which is radiant with De Quincey's peculiar brand of cleverness, does however shift the attention from himself to the whole history of the 'Literature of Power.' The main

[1] X, 260 (*Language*). [2] X, 229.

course of his argument starts with the tendency of intellectual genius to crystallize round a nucleus—a theory borrowed from Velleius Paterculus, an author whom De Quincey would seem to have been on the whole mistaken in admiring, but whose views in this case are of interest.[1] The instances given are the two phases of Greek literature, grouped round Pericles and Alexander of Macedon; but De Quincey develops the theory to include a constant oscillation, throughout the ages, between creative periods and those which assimilate and regurgitate what has been amassed (the image may equally be applied to the history of his own intellectual progress). To the first category belong the age of Shakespeare and the turn of the eighteenth century; to the second, the intervening period. The reason for the crystallization of such groups of genius is rather lamely described by De Quincey as "sympathy"; but in the fourth part of the essay it becomes clear that what he means to indicate is the sudden birth of some creative movement in a society. He attributes the rise of Greek literature to the national self-consciousness awoken by the attack from Asia, and likens this process to the creation of the schoolmen by the rise of the Western church. In both cases a "subjective order of intellectual pursuits"[2] engendered the cultivation of style, *i.e.* of a *persuasive* manner of writing (in the schoolmen's case, a kind of algebra).[3] This brings us round again to De Quincey's theory of rhetoric,[4] which we are now in a better position to see as part and parcel of his general theory. In all cases, as will be noticed, the emphasis is still on the 'subjective' trend of the writing involved. The meaning is clear enough, though the epithet is for many reasons an unfortunate one and begs questions of which De Quincey appears to be unaware.

All through these essays, in which the vexed question of style receives a treatment which is now minute, now cavalier, there runs another and not less interesting thread: De Quincey's attitude to the writers of Greece and Rome. His opinions of these, which are often eccentric, but never dull, require sorting; when this has been done, it will be found that, where poetry is concerned, De Quincey—as might be expected—was sound enough. His paper on the *Theory of Greek Tragedy*[5] is extremely stimulating and can be accepted with far fewer reservations than the *Brief Appraisal of*

[1] X, 186 ff. [2] X, 226. [3] X, 231.
[4] See p. 324. [5] 1840.

Greek literature, where his conclusions are largely vitiated by the distortions created by a too narrowly Christian view of the Greek prose-writers and even of some poets (Pindar, Hesiod, Theognis), whose outlook belonged to a different moral world.

Again, in the little essay on *Language*, which contains the very important remarks on style quoted on page 325, De Quincey, while fully acknowledging the *beauty* of Greek verse, yet finds it possible to say that because the Greek was " too intensely a child of the earth " he can have no hold on the " deeper and more abiding nature of man "—which hold is therefore transferred to the Hebrew.

Perhaps De Quincey's position is not so surprising after all. Attempts have been made, from time to time, to provide Christians with excuses for admiring the ideology of the ancient world. But these excuses are more specious than real; for the Greek and Christian views of life form an absolute and fundamental dichotomy; it is the Greek *Anschauung*, not that of Science, which has always been, and still is, the real opponent of Christianity. The two can be bridged after a fashion—the German poet Hölderlin made a magnificent attempt to do so, in his poem *Bread and Wine*; but it is not a bridge that will support the orthodox Christian. For this is the most fundamental of conflicts, under which all others can be subsumed; and the present situation of Europe is alive with signs that, in the next fifty years, it will be fought out again—perhaps for the last time.

As for De Quincey, he cannot be said to have wavered in his allegiance to Christianity; but his writings bear witness to the tension which persisted up to the end and produced some of the wildest paradoxes which even that tortuous brain ever evolved. Like Goethe, Hölderlin and Heine, he had seen the face of Apollo and, try as he might, could not forget it.

. . . . . .

De Quincey's estimates of living writers deserve a moment's attention, because they throw light on the subject of this section. As a literary critic, he was in no sense an epigrammatist; his best effects are achieved in long periods, into which he managed to pack an astonishing number of ideas.[1] Those, therefore, who wish to form a conception of this facet of his genius at its best, cannot do

[1] See, for instance, his summing up of Lamb, V, 216. Also V, 115 (Dr. Parr.)

better than study together the later essays on Pope and Charles Lamb (both written in 1848), in which, besides much that is objectively acute, will be found many an indication of his own stylistic leanings. The comparison of divers literary methods indeed forms the framework of his later criticism; his brilliant intellect never worked better than when it was engaged in comparing the methods of Dr. Johnson and Burke,[1] or drawing a parallel between Greek Tragedy and the drama of Shakespeare.[2]

As a critic of his contemporaries he did not suffer from the bitterness, envy, and romantic hankering after past ages, which vitiates the outlook of so many critics. "I see more to admire," he said in 1848,[3] "more power and vital force of every kind, in my own generation than in any other. And I refuse to be duped by the scenical effects of distance or abstraction. It does not follow that our literature is in a good state. I think it far otherwise; but its faults are not from want of power."

We have already examined in full his opinion of those writers who stood nearest to him—Wordsworth, Coleridge, Hazlitt, Southey. His judgments of figures remoter from himself are more uneven: he hailed Thomas Lovell Beddoes as "a man of real genius",[4] deeply admired Walter Savage Landor (though his essay on that writer[5] is very disappointing), and paid a qualified tribute to Hawthorne and Emerson.[6] But his remarks on Keats [7]*are entirely valueless: "waxwork filigree or gilt gingerbread" [8] does not constitute an interesting criticism of *Endymion*, nor is it even approximately true that Keats "trampled" on the English tongue "as with the hoofs of a buffalo." [9] Here De Quincey is writing from mere ignorant prejudice, and his singling out of *Hyperion* for praise does not redeem the general folly of the article.

The essay on Shelley,[10] on the other hand, is surprisingly shrewd, considering the fundamental lack of sympathy which De Quincey must have felt for that young man's point of view. He does not discuss Shelley's poetry, but implies admiration for it; and, while setting down the 'bloody tyrant' furniture of the poet's mind, and his eccentricities of behaviour, as mere manifestations of

[1] X, 270. [2] X, 347.
[3] *Letter to a Young Man about to take up a Literary Career*: Japp, 269.
[4] IV, 343, Note I. [5] XI, 394 ff. [6] Japp, 308.
[7] XI, 377 ff. [8] XI, 389. [9] XI, 393.
[10] XI, 354 ff.

adolescence (a fact too often passed over by admirers of Shelley), he declares his belief in the poet's sincerity and essential beauty of character.

His judgments of contemporary novelists are not particularly happy. Regarding the novel, as he persisted in doing, exclusively from the 'Gothic' point of view, from which *action* was the main consideration, he could not perceive the value and importance of the 'psychological' trend which the novel was now definitely assuming. Hence his neglect of Jane Austen, and his disparagement of Dickens, whose enormous zest he mistook for vulgarity [1] and "want of fidelity to human nature", and to whom he once referred as "Albert Smith, Dickens, etc.," [2] thus reducing to one level an immortal name and one which has been completely forgotten.[3] Thackeray he likewise dismissed for "caustic cynicism",[4] and when the novelist came to Edinburgh, De Quincey refused to meet him.

The Brontë sisters, who much admired De Quincey, sent him their books; but, though he thought well of their poetry (especially of Emily's), he quite failed to appreciate the qualities of their novels. "I fear this lady or gentleman, which ever the author is, is making a mistake," he said to his daughters. "Young ladies, who are the chief readers of novels, will never stand to be interested in that sort of people: what they like is some heroic person, say a young or successful officer." [5] As far as Charlotte Brontë herself was concerned, he swallowed Mrs. Gaskell whole and was much shocked by the Brussels episode.[6]

7. Conclusion

In the community of the Helpless, De Quincey will always occupy a throne of eminence; yet too much emphasis can easily be laid on this most obvious feature of his character. For his achievement, though little appreciated to-day and perhaps never likely to reach a very wide public, was in fact considerable. His youthful ambition, that "by long and painful labour, combining with such faculties as God had given me, I might become the

[1] See letter to Florence, Japp, p. 264. [2] *Posth. Works*, I, 199.
[3] Albert Smith (1816–60) was a contributor to *Punch*, and a writer of extravaganzas. (*Dic. Nat. Bio.*)
[4] Japp, 301. [5] Japp, 440. [6] Letters, II, 196 and 207.

intellectual benefactor of my species,"[1] was realized in the end. Yet any attempt to fit De Quincey the writer neatly into his period must be doomed to failure. He is every bit as special a case as Carlyle and though he never made as much stir in his lifetime, his best work seems likely to survive that of the Chelsea prophet, which is so largely invalidated for us by the fact that most of the ideas on which it is based have been proved false. Carlyle suffers the fate of all false prophets; but De Quincey built his most considerable works with more durable material—that of poetry—which confers a universality of emotional appeal, so that they glow brighter as the years pass over them.

Growing up into the full flood of the romantic revival, he yet contrived to remain untouched by all save its purely literary ideas. What Professor Crane Brinton has called the "claim of the individual to emancipation from outward restraint by reason of a natural grace inherent in us all"[2] was not a doctrine to which De Quincey at any time subscribed. In this he escaped the early influence of Wordsworth, Coleridge and Southey, by appearing on the scene only when their *Sturm und Drang* period was over. Thus the French Revolution and all that it implied played no part in his life; he remained an individualist pure and simple, to whom the dogmatic views of the romantic polemical writers were entirely foreign. His love of Grasmere, again, was the love of a poet and was quite unconnected with theories about Nature and Art, or any of the other dichotomies so dear to Jacobin writers. His view of the social structure he accepted ready-made and there is no evidence that the 'message' of novels like Bage's *Barham Downs*, or Mrs. Inchbald's *Nature and Art*, which it is probable that he read during the Everton period, made any impression on him—as it had on Coleridge, for instance.[3]

His position, then, reduces itself to that of a scholar and an artist. Of the former calling he was perfectly aware; but how far was he a *conscious* artist? I think the foregoing sections of this chapter should have given the impression that he was one in so far as he regarded style (*i.e.* method of communication) as of vital importance in the conveyance of the kind of matter in which he personally dealt—the literature of Power. But his artistry ends here: he is

[1] See p. 42. [2] *Political Ideas of the English Romantics*, p. 28.
[3] See Crane Brinton, *op. cit.*, p. 40.

hardly interested in Form at all. In this sense he is a slapdash writer, and even his best works are as far removed as possible from the classical ideal.

The reasons for this neglect are implicit in his works: his object in writing was not to give his readers isolated sensations, but to make them aware of implications in life of which they might be unconscious, but which it had been his privilege, through a highly special medium of pain and sorrow, to experience and analyse. Moreover, he was born too early to have been contaminated by the paralysing doctrine of Art-for-art's-sake, which was later responsible for a whole series of works which exist in complete isolation from life and are separated from their audience by a sort of transparent jelly that keeps them rigid and confers on them the terrible aspect of old women whose faces have been 'lifted'. De Quincey knew better than to indulge so insane a divorce:

> That function of literature by which it reacts upon all these great interests (science, ethics, philosophy), so as to diffuse them, to popularize them, to protect them, and to root them, is apt enough to escape the notice of most men, who regard literature as a mere embellishment of life, not as one of its *deep-sunk props.*[1]

> Everyone . . . owes to the impassioned books which he has read many a thousand more of emotions than he can consciously trace back to them. Dim by their origination, these emotions yet arise in him, and mould him through life, like forgotten incidents of his childhood.[2]

> It is clear that the writer exists for the sake of the reader, not the reader for the sake of the writer.[3]

This is explicit enough. And if his anxiety to emphasize the communicative aspect of his work led him to neglect the stricter formal arrangements which might have aided it, he is nevertheless in no doubt as to the sole means by which his effect could be achieved.

> *All* the steps of knowledge . . . carry you further on the same plane, but could never raise you one foot above your ancient level of earth: whereas the very *first* step in power is a flight. . . .[4]

[1] VIII, 142. (My italics.)
[2] XI, 60.
[3] X, 397.
[4] XI, 56.

It is certain that, were it not for the literature of Power, these ideals [justice, hope, etc.] would often remain amongst us as mere arid notional forms; whereas, by the creative forces of man put forth in literature, they . . . germinate into vital activities.[1]

Poetry, or any one of the fine arts . . . can teach only as nature teaches . . . by deep impulse, by *hieroglyphic suggestion.*[2]

But if De Quincey cannot be neatly situated among his contemporaries, some effort must be made to compare the quality of his writing with that of Lamb and Hazlitt, whose work most nearly resembles his in form and aim. Take, for example, the first paragraphs of Lamb's essay on *Imperfect Sympathies.* These might conceivably have been written by Hazlitt, but never by De Quincey. The reasons for this judgment resume the differences between the writers involved: (1) the sentences are all comparatively short; they are flung at the reader in a series of brisk gestures ("Here! catch!"), while De Quincey's enormous sentences weave themselves round the mind of the reader until they seem to assume its very shape; (2) Lamb's punctuation is much simpler than De Quincey's, being practically confined to commas, dashes and full-stops; the colons and semi-colons which play so prominent a part in De Quincey's elaborately symphonic style rarely appear in Lamb—though more often in Hazlitt; (3) the chattiness, which is so original and important a feature in all three writers, is in each case of a different kind. Here we touch what is presumably the root of the problem. Lamb talks to a tableful of people who have just dined well; Hazlitt—in a graver voice, less consistently jocular and with overtones of bitterness, exasperation and ecstatic hatred—to a man who has dined alone, frugally, and has drawn up his arm-chair to the winter fire. But De Quincey's is the voice that whispers to us in the strictness of privacy, as it were our own mind talking to itself, in moments of joy and sorrow and lassitude, at the crises of wonder and in the last depths of terror and remorse—pausing on the staircase of memory to catch some queer reflection of light which lingers in a dark corner, or ascending to the attics of childhood, to tap the springs of secret wisdom which murmur there in the dusty sunbeams, telling of Death and Summer, of things near and far, of old and new beliefs, of the strange humours of

[1] XI, 57.

[2] *Ibid.*, 88. (My italics.)

man and the grace and fidelity of women, the desperate beauty of irrecoverable moments, and the tortuous ways of Truth.

But, much as he loved rhetoric, De Quincey once threw off a chastening remark about it: "Rhetoric, according to its quality, stands in many degrees of relation to the permanencies of truth; and all rhetoric, like all flesh, is partly unreal, and the glory of both is fleeting." [1] Yet this caution did not always prevent the marvellous elaboration of his style from degenerating into mere clumsiness:

Often enough, the seconds hold the fate of their principals entirely in their hands; and instances are not a few, within even my limited knowledge, of cases where murder has been really committed, not by the party who fired the fatal bullet, but by him who (having it in his power to interfere without loss of honour to any party) has cruelly thought fit—(and, in some instances, apparently for no purpose but that of decorating himself with the name of an energetic man, and of producing a public 'sensation', as it is called —a sanguinary affair)—to goad on the tremulous sensibility of a mind distracted between the sons of honour on the one hand, and the agonizing claims of a family on the other, into fatal extremities that might, by a slight concession, have been avoided.[2]

—a kind of slovenly drooling which defeats its own ends. Again, in the following:

His [Herodotus'] transitions are the most fluent whilst they are the most endless, justifying themselves to the understanding as much as they recommend themselves to the spirit of hurrying curiosity; and his narrations or descriptions are the most animated by the generality of their abstractions, whilst they are the most faithfully individual by the felicity of their selection amongst circumstances.[3]

the burden of opaque Latinity makes the reader feel that his tongue has swelled until his mouth will no longer contain it.

It is only just to call attention to these lapses: as great a writer as De Quincey shines the brighter by comparison with the worst that he has done. And, even at his worst, he is hardly ever dull. "In matters of dulness," he said wittily, "a man is easily original"; [4] yet it is one of the few kinds of originality of which he himself can seldom be accused. As I have endeavoured to establish, in the course of this critical retrospect, De Quincey excelled in several

[1] V, 232. [2] III, 190. [3] VI, 107. [4] X, 29.

genres; but his immortality is most securely rooted in those passages where the natural poetry of his mind found expression in the numerous perfection of large periods, grand and fantastic as the crowded tapestries of the seventeenth century:

And yet, compared with the mystery of man himself, these physical worlds of mystery are but as a radix of infinity. Chemistry is in this view, mysterious and Spinosostically sublime—that it is the science of the latent in all things, of all things as lurking in all. Within the lifeless flint, within the silent pyrites, slumbers an agony of potential combustion. Iron is imprisoned in blood. With cold water . . . you may lash a fluid into angry ebullitions of heat; with hot water, as with the rod of Amram's son, you may freeze a fluid down to the temperature of the Sarsar wind. . . .[1]

What a melodious ascent as of a prelude to some impassioned requiem breathing from the pomps of earth, and from the sanctities of the grave! What a *fluctus decumanus* of rhetoric! Time expounded, not by generations or centuries, but by the vast periods of conquests and dynasties; by cycles of Pharoahs and Ptolemies, Antioch and Arsacides! And these vast successions of time distinguished and figured by the uproars which revolve at their inaugurations; by the drums and tramplings rolling overhead upon the chambers of forgotten dead—the trepidations of time and mortality vexing, at secular intervals, the everlasting sabbaths of the grave![2]

That slumber that towered above her brain was like that fluctuating silvery column which stands in scientific tubes, sinking, rising, deepening, lightening, contracting, expanding; or like the mist that sits, through sultry afternoons, upon the river of the American St Peter, sometimes rarefying for minutes into sunny gauze, sometimes condensing for hours into palls of funeral darkness.[3]

It is the child's sense of mystery in common things— the original gift of the poet—which is responsible for De Quincey's most startling and far-flung imagery, as shown in the above three passages, in the intense vision of the *Confessions* and the *Autobiographic Sketches*, in the *Knocking at the Gate* in *Macbeth*, in the *English*

[1] VII, 252.
[2] X, 105 (of a passage in the *Urn-Burial* of Sir Thomas Browne).
[3] XIII, 205. (*The Spanish Military Nun.*)

Mail-Coach, the *Revolt of the Tartars,* the *Last Days of Kant*, the *Reminiscences*. . . .

The most unsophisticated of men, he was the most sophisticated and eclectic of writers. A cunning alchemist, his enormous knowledge and astounding memory enabled him to distil the most complex and musical style ever invented—a style of which, except on rare occasions, he was the complete master.

Professor Saintsbury has opined [1] that De Quincey probably did not care for poetry, apart from what it *said*. This seems to me a wrong view, in consideration of, among other things, the passionate enthusiasm with which, as a young man, he greeted the early poems of Wordsworth and Coleridge—an enthusiasm which a mere interest in the matter of poetry would be insufficient to provoke. And what of the profound influence which the poems of Milton always exercised over him?

Accordingly, spite of the triumphs of Satan—spite of Sin and all-conquering Death, who had left the gates of Hell for their long abode on Earth . . . yet by means of this one sublime artifice, which brings together the Alpha and Omega, the beginning and end of time, the last day of man's innocence and the first of his restoration, it is contrived that a twofold peace—the peace of resignation and the peace of hope—should harmonise the key in which the departing strains of this celestial poem roll off; and its last cadences leave behind an echo, which, with the solemnity of the grave, has also the halcyon peace of the grave, and its austere repose.[2]

I submit that the man who contrived the beautiful cadence in that sentence, must have cared for something in poetry beyond just what it said.

This something was the quality of music, which is also the essential quality of poetry. Having it, De Quincey is assured of immortality; without it, he would not be the writer we know, and, moreover, we should scarcely know him at all. For all literature, if it is to survive, must be informed by the sense of poetry, which consists in seeing all things in their essences, unencumbered by insignificant detail, and uniting them one to another in the proportions of eternity. This is the one absolute standard by

[1] In the essay in *Macmillan's Magazine* for July, 1890. [2] V, 105.

which to judge what De Quincey called the Literature of Power. A writer may possess every other quality under the sun; but if he have not this sense, his work will not live, as *literature*. Those writers whose importance resides solely in new acquisitions and discoveries of knowledge (the "Books of Knowledge")—a Newton, a Mommsen—survive only in the works of those who supersede them. Novelists who are mere entertainers, or whose work misses universal validity, through narrowness of appeal, or which 'dates', through tasteless insistence on topicality and what is merely ephemeral in the social scene; even those—a George Gissing, an H. G. Wells, an Arnold Bennett—who possess every qualification of the novelist save one—the sense of poetry: these are doomed, sooner or later (unless, like Trollope, they happen also to be historians of a period), to oblivion. But De Quincey possessed that sense, and so he is safe, whatever his failings when attention ebbed and spirits fell low and nervousness tugged at his elbow; for in his finest achievements he rose to those heights of impassioned beauty and truth which proclaim the great writer—the poet and the seer.

CHAPTER XII

FINALE—LENTO SOSTENUTO

"TIME, if it does not diminish grief, alters its character. At first we stretch out our hands in very blindness of heart, as if trying to draw back again those whom we have lost. But, after a season, when the impotence of such efforts has become too sensibly felt, finding that they will not come back to us, a strange fascination arises which yearns after some mode of going to *them*. There is a gulf fixed which childhood rarely can pass. But we link our wishes with whatsoever would gently waft us over. We stretch out our hands and say, 'Sister, lend us thy help, and plead for us with God, that we may pass over without much agony.'"[1]

As the Collected Edition proceeded, De Quincey began to feel a great weariness come over him. "I have a few more things still to say. But I am too weary at present (*i.e.* till resting) to say them," he wrote to Hogg, in the autumn of 1859. "It kills me to write notes, after writing all day upon margins."[2] His health had not improved in the last few years; he had had influenza twice, which left its usual trail of minor ills; his eyes had given him increasing trouble; and, during the anxiety of the Indian Mutiny, he had suffered from insomnia and somnambulism.

It is clear that his constitution, which had suffered so much for so long, was at last giving out, under the strain of over-work. Yet in 1857 he pulled himself together to visit his daughter Mrs. Craig, in Ireland. The visit was a success; and when, a short time before, his son Paul Frederick returned from India, De Quincey was filled with delighted pride in the young man's splendid, robust appearance, his chest "like a *chest of drawers*."[3] He was living again in his children and grandchildren, so that the end, when it should soon come, would be as imperceptible as possible.

When his final weakness (it can scarcely be described as illness)

[1] *Posth. Works*, I, 26. [2] Japp, 358. [3] Japp, 415.

came upon him, he was at Lothian Street. For a long time he refused to see a doctor; but at last, on the twenty-second of October, Dr. Warburton Begbie was sent for. He found the old man sitting on a sofa with his head on a cushion, which was placed on a chair in front of him. This curious position, which Dr. Begbie attributed to weakness, may also have been assumed to ease the cramp in the stomach from which De Quincey had always suffered.

In spite of his previous aversion, he did what the doctor told him and became slightly better, though fever and catarrh persisted for a time.

During these last six weeks of his life, he saw no one except his daughter Emily, his landlady Miss Stark, who read aloud to him when he was tired, and three of his friends—J. R. Findlay, Professor Lushington, and Thomas Hill Burton. He displayed much interest in Allibone's new *Dictionary of English Literature*, in which his own work was flatteringly mentioned, and also spoke with pleasure of the appreciation with which the American edition of his works was being received, in that country.

By November he realized that he was dying, but referred to the fact vaguely and without fear. Indeed, it was hardly the approach of death which he was facing. Infinitely slowly and softly, as a convalescent sinks into a chair, so he let himself sink to a standstill at which, free from all thoughts save those of a far but cherished past, he might await the inception of a new health.

The days were dull and foggy in which Emily De Quincey watched over the unbelievable mildness and gradualness of her father's retreat towards death. But in his own brain, the remotest of memories returned once more, with their final benediction. "The bewildering romance, light tarnished with darkness, the semi-fabulous legend, truth celestial mixed with human falsehoods, these fade even of themselves as life advances. The romance has perished that the young man adored; the legend has gone that deluded the boy; but the deep, deep tragedies of infancy, as when the child's hands were unlinked for ever from his mother's neck, or his lips for ever from his mother's kisses, these remain lurking below all, and these lurk to the last."[1] Elizabeth, in whose dead figure, lying on the bed under the long summer sunbeam, he had

[1] XIII, 349.

had his first vision of human reality, and who had recurred in his life in so many guises, rose again at the last to "illuminate the clouds of death".[1]

But it is given to few to die in perfect silence, and De Quincey was not among them. As the end of the month approached, he became frequently delirious, speaking of the footsteps of angels and seeming to live surrounded by children, to whom he spoke and for whose happiness he expressed anxiety.

One night he woke suddenly and, seeing Emily sitting by his bedside, said: "By the way, I wished to tell you what has displeased me much. I am grieved at the coarse manners that some rough fellows displayed."

"Why?" replied Emily. "What have they done?"

"Well, you know, I and the children were invited to the great supper. Do you know what supper I mean?"

"No."

"Well, I was invited to come, and to bring the children to the great supper of Jesus Christ. So, wishing the children to have suitable dresses for such an occasion, I had them all dressed in white. They were dressed from head to foot in white. But some rough men in the streets of Edinburgh, as we passed on our way to the supper, seeing the little things in complete white, laughed and jeered at us, and made the children much ashamed."[2]

In this manner were the early years of his marriage transfigured. Another day, in entire self-possession, he spoke of his father and expressed regret that he had not known him better. But the deepest regrets were still to come. . . .

On December 4th, Miss De Quincey's anxiety increased, and the next day she sent for her sister, Mrs. Craig.[3] Two days later De Quincey was sitting up in his chair, but he was very feeble and would eat nothing. The following day, it was plain that the end was near. He seemed to recognize Mrs. Craig, when she arrived, but addressed her continually as "Mama". In the evening his weakness increased and, as his father had done at a similar moment, he said to Margaret: "Mama, I cannot bear the weight of clothes upon my feet."

[1] I, 43. [2] Japp, 449.

[3] Mrs. Baird-Smith, who was hurrying home from India with her first child, which she wished her father to see, arrived just too late to see him alive.

Mrs. Craig pulled off some of the blankets and asked him if that was better.

"Yes, my love," he answered; "much better; I am better in every way—I feel much better. You know these are the feet that Jesus washed."[1]

Night fell, and with it the sounds of the town died away, so that the loud breathing of the dying man filled the room where the two women watched. Dr. Begbie came before the end, but De Quincey had long ceased to recognize anyone in the world of the living; he was already with the dead, peering at the shade of an old remorse. "My dear, dear mother. Then was I greatly mistaken," he said, faintly but distinctly.

(To what did this refer? To his escape from Manchester, when, on that last evening in his study, he had seemed to hear a voice warning him of the irrevocability of the step he was taking? It is impossible to tell.)

Dawn began to break, and with it the first scattered rumours of the awakening city. Suddenly, on the very edge of death, De Quincey threw up his arms and cried out, in accents of extreme surprise, as at an unexpected meeting: "Sister! Sister! Sister!"

And then, as the noises of Edinburgh increased and grew together into one continuous murmur, the sound of breathing in the room faded away into the gathering light.

Day was come and De Quincey was dead.

[1] Japp, 450.

EDITORIAL FOOTNOTES

page xv Horace Eaton's full-length biography (*Thomas De Quincey*: New York, 1936) appeared the same year as Sackville West's. For other, more recent lives see the Bibliography.

page xvii Probably not much of De Quincey's writings still remain unpublished. For an account of listings of known manuscripts and work published elsewhere than the editions Sackville West mentions, see the chapter on De Quincey in *The English Romantic Poets and Essayists, A Review of Research and Criticism*, ed. C. W. and L. H. Houtchens, rev. ed., 1966, pp. 292, 295–8. Add *New Essays by De Quincey: His Contributions to the* Edinburgh Saturday Post *and the* Edinburgh Evening Post *1827–1828*, ed. Stuart M. Tave (Princeton, 1966).

page 1 Joseph Bain questions De Quincey's claims of noble ancestry ("De Quincey and His Supposed Descent from the Earls of Winchester", *The Genealogist*, July 1890, pp. 17–21).

page 3 *The Torrington Diaries, containing the tours through England and Wales of the Hon. John Byng (later Viscount Torrington) between the years 1781 and 1794*, ed. C. Bruyn Andrews, 4 vols. (London, 1934–8).

page 7 According to a gravestone in St. Anne Churchyard, Manchester, Jane was born Sept. 1786, which would make her about eleven months younger than Thomas, who was born August 15, 1785. He remembered her, however, as "about two years older" (Masson, I, 33).

page 8 Eaton thinks the consensus of Manchester antiquarians favours as De Quincey's birthplace a house at the corner of Cross and John Dalton Streets, which was later known as The Prince's Tavern (p. 9n).

page 26 By references to "Letters" Sackville West means *De Quincey Memorials. Being Letters and other Records here first Published*, ed. Alexander Japp (London, 1891), 2 vols.

page 31 The quoted verses are from "She was a Phantom of Delight", by William Wordsworth, a favourite source of De Quincey's quotations.

page 44 De Quincey's reference to the Whispering Gallery that Sackville West quotes was added in the 1856 revision of *The Confessions* and may be more a device for artistic unity than a real boyish reflection.

page 45 What De Quincey says about the books in his pockets when he ran away from Manchester Grammar School is that one was Canter's " Euripides " and the other " a favourite English poet " (M, III, 299) ; the poet may well have been Wordsworth.

page 46 Sackville West may be right in thinking that De Quincey's story of giving the letter to the woman to return to the Post Office was a fabrication, but De Quincey's account is really more plausible than Sackville West's version indicates : he did not go up to an " entire stranger " and ask her to take the letter ; rather he was frightened by the Bore and ran, causing the woman to do the same, this resulting in conversation and a kind of camaraderie which might justify a sudden confidence, especially when De Quincey wished to return the letter but feared that he would be apprehended in doing so.

page 50 De Quincey explains in detail that the £150 deducted from his estate was the cost of a wild-goose chase after him through the Lake District and nearly to York—more than 600 miles—by his sister Mary, a maid, and a friend of the family in a carriage and four horses (M, III, 319–20).

page 58 Sackville West's confidence in De Quincey's " patent innocence " of sexual experience may be unwarranted : as he notes later (see p. 68), soon after the London episode De Quincey recorded in his Diary (June 4, 1803) visiting a " fat whore " for what was not the first time.

page 59 De Quincey says he " fell backwards on the steps " (M, III, 361), not that he " sank down unconscious "—how could he then have heard Ann's " cry of distress ", or " terror ", as he puts it?

page 65 For both versions of De Quincey's significant first letter to Wordsworth, as well as all of the correspondence between the Opium-Eater and the Wordsworths, see *De Quincey to Wordsworth : A Biography of a Relationship*, ed. John E. Jordan (Berkeley, 1962).

page 76 René Wellek argues that De Quincey did not really understand Kant (" De Quincey's Status in the History of Ideas ", *Philological Quarterly*, XXIII [1944], 248–72).

Page 77 Peter Bayley, Jr. published in 1803 *Poems*, containing "The Fisherman's Wife, Dedicated to all admirers of the familiar style in tale-writing, so popular in 1800", which Wordsworth read as a parody of "The Idiot Boy".

page 84 Wordsworth answered De Quincey's letter of 6 April on 5 May (*The Letters of William and Dorothy Wordsworth, II. The Middle Years, Part I, 1803–1811*, ed. Ernest de Selincourt, rev. Mary Moorman [1969], 26).

page 86 De Quincey later denied that he and Coleridge had ever really been friends (*Posthumous Works*, ed. A. H. Japp, II, 16).

page 87 Coleridge might not "naturally have accompanied" his family to Keswick, because he was—apparently unknown to De Quincey—just separating from his wife.

page 93 Richard Woodhouse says De Quincey told him that he was disgusted because the oral Greek examination was changed to be conducted in English ("Notes on Conversations with Thomas De Quincey", in *De Quincey and His Friends*, ed. James Hogg [London, 1895], p. 99).

page 98 The version of Coleridge's letter to De Quincey published by E. L. Griggs (*Unpublished Letters of S. T. Coleridge*, II, 293–9) differs from that printed by Japp in *De Quincey Memorials* and makes it pretty clear that De Quincey had reminded Coleridge of the £300 debt. De Quincey listed it among his assets when he declared bankruptcy in 1833; with interest it then amounted to a total of £708 15s. (Kenneth Forward, "De Quincey's 'Cessio Bonorum'", *PMLA*, 1939, pp. 511–25).

page 108 Lloyd's novel *Edmund Oliver* appears to draw upon the life of S. T. Coleridge.

page 113 The correspondence on the *Convention of Cintra* episode is not quite so dull as Sackville West found it. At any rate, De Quincey's side is now available in *De Quincey to Wordsworth* and William and Dorothy's in *The Letters of William and Dorothy Wordsworth, II. The Middle Years, Part I.* (See notes to pp. 65 and 84.)

Page 125 Certainly one would expect that Coleridge's habit of writing marginalia would have enriched De Quincey's books, but I have examined all of the copies of volumes written in by Coleridge that I can find without having been able to identify any as having belonged to De Quincey.

page 133 De Quincey's illness following Catherine's death has been diagnosed as polio (Cecelia H. Hendricks, "Thomas De Quincey, Symptomatologist", *PMLA*, 1945, 828–40).

page 140 The "I will be with you . . . D.V." story comes from Francis Jacox's "Recollections" (*De Quincey and His Friends*, p. 224), and is only tentatively assigned to Gillies.

page 146 Dove Cottage did not belong to the Wordsworth, although they rented it from 1799–1808 and as late as 1817 Dorothy referred to it as "our cottage". The Wordsworths took it for De Quincey when he was in London seeing *The Convention of Cintra* through the press, for an initial period of six years, early in 1809, but he continued to rent it until early 1835.

page 148 On March 13, 1802 Dorothy recorded: "Little Peggy Simpson was standing at the door catching the Hail stones in her hand". This section of the Journals has now been published in *Journals of Dorothy Wordsworth*, ed. E. de Selincourt (London, 1952), I, 123, and somewhat more fully in *Journals of Dorothy Wordsworth: The Alfoxden Journals 1798; The Grasmere Journals 1800–1803*, ed. Helen Darbishire (London, 1963), p. 131.

page 163 On April 14, 1818 De Quincey wrote to Wordsworth asking for his assistance in getting the editorship of the projected *Westmorland Gazette*, to be published in Kendal to support the Tory cause. After the first editor proved unsatisfactory De Quincey, probably with the poet's help, was appointed in July 1818 and served until Nov. 1819, when the proprietors respectfully requested his resignation. See *De Quincey to Wordsworth*, pp. 284–90; Charles Pollit, *De Quincey's Editorship of the* Westmorland Gazette (Kendal and London, 1890).

page 166 The honour done by the Committee to De Quincey's paper was apparently to publish it as *Close Comments upon a Struggling Speech* (Kendal, 1818).

page 167 De Quincey hired a sub-editor, a Mr. Kilmer, who resided in Kendal and, unfortunately, received most of the compensation. See p. 176.

page 176 Footnote 3 refers to Mrs. Margaret Oliphant, *Annals of a Publishing House: William Blackwood and Sons* (Edinburgh, 1897–8).

page 178 Correspondence between De Quincey and William Blackwood indicates that De Quincey finished an article on Schiller and a piece on the "English Lakes", the latter of which Blackwood did not like. (See Eaton, pp. 260–8.) The piece on Schiller may be a translation published in *Blackwood's* in 1821 as " The Sport of Fortune ". (I am indebted for this identification to Mr Richard Downing.)

page 196 De Quincey did not reprint the translation of *The Love Charm* in his *Selections*, and H. K. Galinsky has argued persuasively that it was actually by Julius Hare (*Modern Language Notes*, 1937, 389–94).

page 201 In April 1829 De Quincey entered into a very complicated financial deal in which he " bought " the Nab from his father-in-law and raised by a mortgage money they divided. For different interpretations of this event, see M. L. Armitt, *Rydal* (Kendal, 1916), pp. 675–704, and Eaton, pp. 320–22.

page 206 " Mr. Schnackenberger ; or, Two Masters for one Dog " was published in the *London Gazette* for May and June, 1923 as " From the German ". De Quincey did not reprint it in *Selections Grave and Gay*. " The King of Hayti ", also headed " From the German ", was published in the *London Magazine* (Nov. 1823) and in Vol. XII of *Selections* (1859).

page 209 Albert Goldman (*The Mind and the Mint* [Carbondale, Ill., 1965], pp. 68–75) has shown that " The Last Days of Immanuel Kant " is a close adaptation and condensation of E. A. Wasianski, *Immanuel Kant inseinen letzten Lebens jahren* (Koenigisberg, 1804), rather than a " resumé of the chief German authorities ", although De Quincey gives the latter impression.

page 228 MSS in the National Library of Scotland demonstrate that from March 7, 1835 to Nov. 12, 1838 Tait paid De Quincey £179.7.5. They seem to make clear, however, that De Quincey received only £14 a sheet (NSL MS 1670, ff. 16–7).

page 257 Goldman (*The Mind and the Mint*, p. 32) points out that De Quincey's articles on Bentley, which appeared in *Blackwood's Magazine* for Sept. and Oct. 1830, are " slavishly dependent " on James Henry Monk's *The Life of Richard Bentley, D.D.* (London, 1830).

page 258 De Quincey does, however, accept a belief in general, if not regular, progress, on the grounds that the " going to the dogs " idea is shameful to Christianity (*Posthumous Works*, I, 181–4, 242 ; II, 236).

page 262 The question of the sources of *The Revolt of the Tartars* has been discussed more recently, with different conclusions, by Joseph A. Sandhaas, " De Quincey's *Revolt of the Tartars* seen in the light of Chinese, French, German and English Source Materials " (unpublished Ph.D. dissertation, Boston Univ., 1946) and Goldman (*op. cit.*, pp. 114–27).

page 301 The 1821 *Confessions* is now available in Malcolm Elwin's edition (London, 1956), which also prints the 1856 version and the *Suspiria de Profundis.* For an analysis of the difference between the two versions of the *Confessions*, see Ian Jack, "De Quincey Revises His *Confessions*", *PMLA*, 1957, 122–46.

page 329 De Quincey's "remarks on Keats" appeared in a review of Gilfillan's *Gallery of Literary Portraits* published in *Tait's* in 1845–6. When he republished the section on Keats in volume VI of *Selections Grave and Gay* (1857), De Quincey apologized in the Preface for his comments on Keats' diction, calling them "much too harsh, and disproportioned to the offence".

BIBLIOGRAPHY

(This list does not pretend to completeness. Only the more important of the works I have consulted are mentioned.)

BAUDELAIRE, CHARLES. *Les Paradis Artificiels.*

Blackwood's Magazine. 1826–1849.

BRINTON, CRANE. *Political Ideas of the English Romantics.* (Oxford, 1926.)

CARLYLE, THOMAS. *Letters and Reminiscences.* (Longmans Green, 1881.)

COLERIDGE, S. T. *Unpublished Letters.* (Ed. Earl Leslie Griggs. 2 vols. Constable, 1932.)

CRABB ROBINSON, HENRY. *Diaries.* (Macmillan, 1869.)

DE QUINCEY, THOMAS. *Works.* (Masson. 14 volumes. Black, 1890.)

—— *Posthumous Works.* 2 vols. (Heinemann, 1891.)

—— *A Diary of Thomas de Quincey.* Ed. by Horace A. Eaton. (Noel Douglas, 1927.)

DE SELINCOURT, ERNEST. *Dorothy Wordsworth.* (Oxford, 1933.)

FAUSSET, H. I'A. *Coleridge.* (Cape, 1926.)

FINDLAY, J. R. *Personal Recollections of Thomas De Quincey.* (Black, 1886.)

FROUDE, J. A. *Thomas Carlyle.* (Longmans Green, 1882.)

GILLIES, R. P. *Memoirs of a Literary Veteran.* (Bentley, 1851.)

GORDON, Mrs. *Memoir of Christopher North.* (Edinburgh, 1862.)

HARPER, G. M. *Life of William Wordsworth.* (Murray, 1916.)

HAZLITT, WILLIAM. *Works.*

HILL BURTON, JOHN. *The Bookhunter.* (Edinburgh, 1862.)

HOGG, JAMES. *De Quincey and His Friends.* (Sampson Low, 1895.)

HOOD, THOMAS. *Literary Reminiscences.* (London, 1861.)

HOWE, P. P. *Life of Hazlitt.* (Secker, 1928.)

JAPP, ALEXANDER H. *Thomas De Quincey.* 2 vols. (Hogg, 1877. Revised Ed. in 1 vol. 1890.)

—— *De Quincey Memorials.* 2 vols. (Heinemann, 1891.)

KNIGHT, CHARLES. *Passages of a Working Life.* (Bradbury, 1864.)

LAMB, CHARLES. *Essays of Elia.*

—— *Letters.* (Ed. E. V. Lucas. Dent, Methuen, 1935.)

Macmillan's Magazine. 1890.

MASSON, DAVID. *De Quincey.* (Macmillan, 1881.)

MUSSET, A. DE. *L'Anglais, Mangeur d'Opium.* (Paris, 1828.)

PAYN, JAMES. *Some Literary Recollections.* (Murray, 1884.)

POTTER, STEPHEN. *Coleridge and S.T.C.* (Cape, 1935.)

—— *Minnow among Tritons. Mrs. S. T. Coleridge's Letters to Thomas Poole.* (Nonesuch, 1934.)

SPERRY, WILLARD L. *Wordsworth's Anti-Climax.* (Oxford, 1935.)

STEPHEN, LESLIE. *Hours in a Library.* Vol. I. (Murray, 1874.)

SWANN, E. *Christopher North.* (Oliver & Boyd, 1934.)

Tait's Magazine. 1833–1851.

TALFOURD, T. N. *Final Memorials of Charles Lamb.* (London, 1876.)

The London Magazine. 1821–1824.

WILSON, JOHN. *Noctes Ambrosianae.*

SUPPLEMENTARY BIBLIOGRAPHY

ABRAMS, M. H. *The Milk of Paradise: The Effect of Opium Visions on the Works of De Quincey, Crabbe, Francis Thompson and Coleridge.* Cambridge, Mass., 1934.

BISLAND, J. W. " On De Quincey's Theory of Literary Power ", *U. Toronto Quart.*, XXVI (1957), 469–80.

BONNER, W. H. ed. *De Quincey at Work: As seen in One Hundred and Thirty New and Newly Edited Letters.* Buffalo, 1936.

BROWN, C. S., Jr. " The Musical Structure of De Quincey's Dream-fugue ", *Musical Quart.*, XXIV (1938), 341–50.

BURWICK, F. " The Dream-Visions of Jean Paul and Thomas De Quincey ", *Comp. Lit.*, XX (1968), 1–26.

BYRNS, R. H. "De Quincey's Revisions in the Dream-Fugue", *PMLA*, LXXVII (1962), 97–101.

COOPER, L. *Prose-poetry of De Quincey*. Leipzig, 1902.

DUNN, W. A. *De Quincey's Relation to German Literature and Philosophy*. Strassbourg, 1900.

EATON, H. A. *De Quincey: A Biography*. Oxford, 1936.

ELWIN, M. *De Quincey*. London, 1935.

FORWARD, K. "'Libellous Attack' on De Quincey", *PMLA*, LII (1937), 244–60.

—— "De Quincey's 'Cessio Bonorum'", *PMLA*, LIV (1939), 511–25.

GALINSKY, H. K. "Is Thomas De Quincey Author of the Love-Charm?", *Mod. Lang. Notes*, LII (1937), 389–94.

GOLDMAN, A. *The Mine and the Mint: Sources for the Writings of Thomas De Quincey*. Carbondale, 1965.

GOULD, G. M. *Biographic Clinics: The Origin of the Ill Health of De Quincey, Carlyle, Darwin, Huxley and Browning*. Philadelphia, 1903.

GRANT, D. In *Some British Romantics*, ed. J. V. Logan, J. E. Jordan, N. Frye. Columbus, Ohio, 1966.

HAYTER, A. *Opium and the Romantic Imagination*. Berkeley, 1968.

HENDRICKS, C. H. "Thomas De Quincey, Symptomatologist", *PMLA*, LX (1945), 828–40.

JACK, IAN. "De Quincey Revises His Confessions", *PMLA*, LXXII (1957), 122–46.

JORDAN, J. E. "De Quincey's Dramaturgic Criticism", *ELH*, XVIII (1951), 32–49.

—— *Thomas De Quincey, Literary Critic*. Berkeley, 1952.

—— De Quincey on Wordsworth's Theory of Diction", *PMLA*, LXVIII (1953), 764–78.

—— *De Quincey to Wordsworth: A Biography of a Relationship, with the Letters of De Quincey to the Wordsworth Family*. Berkeley, 1962.

—— *De Quincey as Critic*. London, 1973.

KOBAYASHI, S. *Rhythm in the Prose of Thomas De Quincey*. Tokyo, 1956.

LYON, J. S. *Thomas De Quincey*. New York, 1969.

MAYOUX, J.-J. "De Quincey et le sens du temps", *Les lettres nouvelles*. New ser., XXXVI (1960), 39–47.

METCALF, J. C. *De Quincey: A Portrait.* Camb., Mass., 1940.

MICHELSEN, P. *Der Traümer und die Ratio: zu Leben und Werk De Quinceys.* Deutsche Universitats-Zeitung IX, 1954.

—— "Thomas De Quincey und Schiller", *German Life and Letters,* new ser. IX (1956), 91–9.

—— "Thomas De Quincey und Goethe", *Euphorion,* L (1956), 86–102.

—— "Thomas De Quinceys Lessing-Bild", *Monatshefte für Deutschen Unterricht,* L (1958), 97–103.

—— "Thomas De Quincey und die Kantische Philosophie", *Revue de Littérature Comparée,* XXXIII (1959), 356–75.

—— "Thomas De Quincey und Jean Paul", *JEGP,* LXI (1962), 736–55.

—— "Thomas De Quincey als vers-Dichter: Seine Übersetzung der 'Luise' von J. H. Voss", *Archiv,* CCII (1965), 277.

MILLER, J. H. *Disappearance of God.* Camb., Mass., 1963.

MOREAUX, F. *Thomas De Quincey: La Vie—L'Homme—L'Œuvre.* Paris, 1964.

PATTERSON, CHARLES I. "De Quincey's Conception of the Novel", *PMLA,* LXX (1955), 375–89.

POLLITT, C. *De Quincey's Editorship of the Westmorland Gazette, with Selections from his Work on that Journal from July 1818 to November 1819.* London, 1890.

POWELL [DODDS], A. E. *Romantic Theory of Poetry.* London, 1926.

PROCTOR, S. K. *Thomas De Quincey's Theory of Literature.* Ann Arbor, 1943.

ROBINSON, CRABB. *Correspondence with the Wordsworth Circle 1808–66,* ed. E. J. Morley. 2 vols. Oxford, 1927.

—— *Crabb Robinson on Books and their Writers,* ed. E. J. Morley. 3 vols. London, 1938.

SALT, H. S. *De Quincey.* London, 1904.

SCHNEIDER, E. *Coleridge, Opium and Kubla Khan.* Chicago, 1953.

TAVE, S. M., ed. *New Essays by De Quincey: His Contributions to the* Edinburgh Saturday Post *and the* Edinburgh Evening Post *1827–1828.* Princeton, 1966.

WELLEK, R. *Immanuel Kant in England 1798–1838.* Princeton, 1931.

—— "De Quincey's Status in the History of Ideas", *Phil. Quart.,* XXIII (1944), 248–72.

WOLFE, R. H. *Priest and Prophet: Thomas De Quincey and William*

Wordsworth in their Personal and Literary Relationships. Indianna Univ. diss., 1960.

WOODHOUSE, R. "Notes on Conversations with De Quincey" (in Hogg, J., *De Quincey and his Friends* (London, 1895) and *Confessions*, ed. R. Garnett (London, 1885)).

WRIGHT, B. "The Cave of Trophonius: Myth and Reality in De Quincey", *Nineteenth-Century Fiction*, VIII (1954), 290–99.

INDEX

E

F

G

M

N

O